George Wilkes

Shakespeare, from an American Point of View

Including an Inquiry as to his Religious Faith, and his Knowledge of Law....

George Wilkes

Shakespeare, from an American Point of View
Including an Inquiry as to his Religious Faith, and his Knowledge of Law....

ISBN/EAN: 9783337060664

Printed in Europe, USA, Canada, Australia, Japan

Cover: Foto ©Thomas Meinert / pixelio.de

More available books at **www.hansebooks.com**

SHAKESPEARE,

FROM AN AMERICAN POINT OF VIEW;

. INCLUDING

AN INQUIRY AS TO HIS RELIGIOUS FAITH,

AND HIS KNOWLEDGE OF LAW:

WITH

THE BACONIAN THEORY CONSIDERED.

BY

GEORGE WILKES.

NEW YORK:
D. APPLETON AND COMPANY,
549 AND 551 BROADWAY.
1877.

PREFACE.

THE following Essays were originally addressed to a public consisting for the most part of American readers: and it was the intention of the author to publish them first, in a collected form, in the United States. It, however, having become apparent, in the course of his researches, that it would be advisable to consult the British libraries, he concluded to issue the work in London. This was the more desirable, because a judgment rendered from the fountain head of English criticism, on what may be deemed a conspicuously English subject, would be more authoritative and satisfactory than if given from any other source. The author, therefore, takes this opportunity to say that the most rigorous criticism will not be unwelcome; not, indeed, from any vain confidence in his own views, but because they are put forward in good faith, and in order to elicit truth concerning a genius who is the richest inheritance of the intellectual world. Should, indeed, his views be controverted, the author must even in that event be a gainer in common with the other admirers of Shakespeare; for it can never be a true source of mortification to relinquish opinions in favour of those which are shown to be better.

Presenting these pages, therefore, rather as a series of inquiries than as dogmatic doctrine, the author strives to support them by only such an amount of controversy as is legitimately due from one who invites the public to a new discussion.

G. W.

CONTENTS.

———

Part I.

GENERAL CIRCUMSTANCES,

HISTORICAL AND BIOGRAPHICAL.

CHAPTER VIII.

CHAPTER IX.

Part II.

THE TESTIMONY OF THE PLAYS.

CHAPTER X.

CHAPTER XI.

CHAPTER XII.

CHAPTER XIII.

CHAPTER XIV.

CHAPTER XV.

viii Contents.

Part I.

GENERAL CIRCUMSTANCES,

HISTORICAL AND BIOGRAPHICAL.

SHAKESPEARE,

FROM AN AMERICAN POINT OF VIEW.

———•———

CHAPTER I.

THE RESPONSIBILITIES OF GENIUS.

THE question as to the authorship of what are known to the world as Shakespeare's plays, first raised in 1856, and projected in favour of Sir Francis Bacon, did not attract much attention until some time after it was propounded. Indeed, I had not heard that the Shakespearian authorship of these plays ever had been doubted until the year 1867, when in the course of a conversation with General B. F. Butler, he asked me whether I had read "The Philosophy of Shakespeare's Plays Unfolded," by Delia Bacon—remarking, at the same time, he thought her arguments to be of great force, and that he favourably regarded the Baconian theory.

The judgment of so keen a critic for a moment staggered me, but the proposition was so utterly at variance with the settled convictions of my mind, that the influence of his opinion soon yielded to my prepossessions, and I readily attributed the General's Baconian inclination to a professional predilection in favour of one of his own craft. The question, therefore, when it was afterward raised by others, failed to engage my serious attention, until it was again broached to me, in Bacon's favour, by an American cavalry officer, during an afternoon lounge near Richmond, on the Thames, in the latter part of the summer of 1874. Just about that time, there had appeared in the August number of *Fraser's Magazine* an exceedingly ingenious article, written by a young American, under the title of " Who wrote Shakespeare ? " and singularly enough my West Point friend and I accidentally met the author of this very article three nights afterwards, at a dinner party in London, which included a number of English and American literary men.

On the following morning, I sought, at the bookstands, the magazine alluded to, but the edition having been exhausted, I was obliged to have recourse to the politeness of the author, who kindly furnished me with one of six supplementary proofs he had procured to be stricken off for his own use, before the forms had been distributed.

Soon afterward, stimulated doubtless by this publication, the controversy as to the authorship of the Shakespeare plays spread to the United States, and, under the manipulation of the American Press, elicited a flood of multifarious opinion. Amid this ocean of expression, the article in *Fraser* was by far the most notable for plausibility and force; but what surprised me most in running through the views of all these writers was, that not one of them touched a fact which had long puzzled me concerning Shakespeare, and which had led me, several years before, to read his plays with laborious scrutiny, under the idea of writing an essay upon his character and principles, from an American point of view. Though not a blind worshipper of Shakespeare, I had always been among the warmest admirers of his genius, but I never had been able to comprehend why it was, that, unlike all the great geniuses of the world who had come before or after him, and who seem, as such, to have been deputized with the creative faculty of God, he should be the only one so deficient in that beneficent tenderness toward his race, so vacant of those sympathies which usually accompany intellectual power, as never to have been betrayed into one generous aspiration in favour of popular liberty. Nay, worse than this, worse than his servility to royalty and rank, we never find him speaking of the poor with respect, or alluding to the working classes without detestation or contempt. We can understand these tendencies as existing in Lord Bacon, born as he was to privilege, and holding office from a queen; but they seem utterly at variance with the natural instincts of a man who had sprung from the body of the people, and who, through the very pursuits of his father, and likewise from his own beginning, may be regarded as one of the working classes himself.

Bacon, through his aristocratic training, and influenced by the monarchical system under which he served, may barely be forgiven, by even his most extreme defenders, for his barrenness of that beneficence, which genius is delegated, as it were, to bring to us from Heaven; but the son of plain John Shakespeare has no such excuse. Dickens, who wrote mainly for the lowly; Byron, who, though a noble, fought for human liberty; Cervantes, Junius, Eugene Sue, Le Sage, De Foe, Walter Scott, Victor Hugo, Oliver Goldsmith, and Sheherezade—the never-to-be-forgotten Sheherezade, who talked to a Prince for a thousand and one nights in such sentiments as have made the literature of Arabia a hymn—never forgot the hopes and joys and distresses of the poor. Shakespeare alone of these elevated souls prefers to be the parasite of the rich and noble, and seldom, if ever, permits the humble to escape him without a derisive jest or sneer.

William Shakespeare nevertheless possessed a larger share of the divine creative faculty than any other mortal; and let it not be said that too much is claimed for this poetic attribute. If the characters produced by mortal imaginations have not souls for divine judgment, they certainly have forms and shapes for human comprehension and for penal criticism. They are as much of the world as the world is of us. Othello, Manfred, Aladdin, Quasimodo, Fleur de Marie, Gil Blas, Robinson Crusoe, Rasselas, Micawber, Don Quixote, the Vicar of Wakefield, and Ivanhoe, are as actual to our appreciations as the real Mahomet, Cæsar, Zenghis Khan, Napoleon, or Martin Luther; as real, in fact, as are Vesuvius and Ætna to those who have never seen them. And the manner, consequently, in which these fictitious characters are developed to the reader, imposes as great responsibilities upon their authors, in the way of morals, as do the just presentation of the truths of history.

The singular oversight of so salient a point as Shakespeare's aristocratic tendencies, by the Baconians, may perhaps be accounted for by the fact that their theory is still quite new, the ground having first been broken by Delia Bacon, of Boston, as late as 1856, and only languidly followed since by a few American lawyers and aristocratic Englishmen, severally stimulated by pride of profession, or conceit of caste. To the masses of the English people it is really a matter of no great importance whether one Englishman or another was the author of the Shakespearian dramas; for the dust of two centuries has fallen so evenly on both of those who are now under our consideration, that all minor preferences are levelled out. With Americans, however, the question is somewhat different.

The pamphlet of the American lady, who had been inspired to the Baconian theory doubtless by a mere pride of name, began to attract favourable attention from the English aristocracy in 1858, and some of its leaders brought themselves to the opinion, that it would be a good thing for the *prestige* of their order if the world could be made to believe that the great writer, who had dwarfed them all for over two hundred years, was a scion of their caste. It has always been the tendency of patrician politics, when the merit of the lowly-born cannot be underrated, to mask its origin by artfully recruiting it into its own ranks, so that talented poverty may file thereafter down the aisles of the future under the aspect of a lord. This policy has been so conspicuous during the last hundred years, that there can hardly be a doubt that had the author of Othello lived a few generations later he would have figured upon the title-page of his immortal works as Lord Shakespeare, or Sir William at the least. The British nobility would have thus been spared the desire of adopting the American woman's theory in transferring the glory of William Shakespeare to Sir Francis Bacon.

Conspicuous among the noblemen who favoured the Baconian theory in England was (as we are informed by the article in *Fraser*) "Lord Palmerston, who maintained that the plays of Shakespeare were written by Lord Verulam (Sir Francis Bacon), who had passed them off under the name of an actor for fear of compromising his professional prospects and philosophic gravity." On being opposed in this declaration (says the author of the article in *Fraser*) by the positive testimony of Ben Jonson as to Shakespeare's authorship, Palmerston replied, "Oh, those fellows always stand up for one another, or perhaps Jonson" (added his Lordship) "may have been deceived like the rest."

Here was the weighty authority of two prominent statesmen and lawyers, Palmerston and Butler, relatively of England and America, fencing the very threshold of my inquiry; and it consequently behoved me to advance with wary footsteps into the shades of the enigma, and prove, at the very outset, if I desired to controvert them, that the author of the Shakespeare plays could not have been (like Bacon) either a statesman or a lawyer—a proof that must, of necessity, be sought from internal evidence furnished by the plays themselves, since all contemporary testimony had left these points unsettled. The only means remaining, therefore, after the lapse of two hundred years, was to question the *souls* of the departed Titans, as they *still* live and breathe, within their respective imperishable pages.

2

CHAPTER II.

SHAKESPEARE'S EARLY LIFE.

ONE of the objects of this inquiry will be an attempt to establish the degree of difference, if any, in which the Shakespearian volume should be regarded, relatively, in England and America, as a family text-book; and whether, as a household teacher, it should, among Americans, as with Englishmen, divide domestic reverence and authority almost with the Bible. And this inquiry will logically extend itself so as to comprehend the social and religious, as well as the political inculcations of the Shakespearian volume.

And following the inquiry still further, we shall endeavour to ascertain what difference, if any, in "musical car," or sense of music, is exhibited relatively in the Plays and Essays; so as to enable us to determine, with almost absolute certainty, whether one and the same man could have been the author of both. In this latter branch of my inquiry I shall be obliged to depend largely upon the musical experts.

Dealing with almost any other poet than the author of Shakespeare's Plays, it would be a matter of comparative indifference what his ideas were as to the separation of the classes, or upon the science of government; but if we are to install a monitor within our homes as a domestic god, or adopt a writer as a political instructor, it is of some importance that we should know how much credit to concede to such an author's conscience and principles. It will readily be seen, therefore, that Shakespeare is a character of much more consequence to Englishmen, and especially to the ruling classes of Great Britain, than he can ever be to the republican citizens of the United States. With us, he is but the poet, mighty beyond all comparison; but to the ruling classes of Great Britain he is not only the Poet, but the Patron of their order, and also the tireless inculcator of those forms of popular obsequiousness, which long have been the marvel of the civilized world, under the almost purely personal form of English patriotism. The author of the Shakespeare plays has been, in this way, the unseen source, the incessant fountain, the constant domineering influence, which has done more to continue the worship of the English people for royalty and rank, than all other agencies combined. Well may the nobility of England be jealous of his pre-eminence, and defend him as the greatest genius ever given to the world. They have an interest in his popular supremacy, which they cannot afford to surrender, and he has been worth to them, during the last two hundred years, millions of men and billions upon billions of money. He deserves at their hands a monument more lofty than the Pyramids; while it is very questionable, on the other hand, if the English masses owe him anything beyond their involuntary admiration for his mind. It suggests itself to me at this point, therefore, that it would perhaps be a better policy for the British aristocracy, to leave this mighty Voice to continue to speak from among The People, rather than as one of the aristocratic masters of The People.

But we must not be beaten back by the awe of generations. We must demand boldly who and what this mighty genius was, —what were his principles, his character, his faith, his motive in writing as he did, and what manner of man he was in his familiar way of life. And all this is necessary in order, first, to decide the question as between Shakespeare and Bacon, and then to assign to the actual writer of the Shakespeare plays the position, as a poet, moralist, and public teacher, to which he may be entitled among the English-speaking race of both sides of the Atlantic.

The first objection to the authorship of William Shakespeare, which the Baconians raise, is that no man of such humble origin, deficient scholarship, and loose, easy-going way of life as Shakespeare, could have been possessed of such profound knowledge as he exhibited, and be capable of such transcendant imagery as these plays develope, nay, that no common play-writer could have possessed such a familiarity with court etiquette and with the language of nobles, and of kings and queens, as he. But the force of these objections is seriously damaged by the fact that none of the disciples of the Baconian theory who have sprung up since 1856, ever had the advantage of studying the manners or the "set phrase of courts," themselves.   And here I may be allowed to add that it may be considered certain that the writer of the Shakespeare plays himself spoke much better English than any prince or noble of Elizabeth's court.

As to the character and morals of William Shakespeare, he certainly suffers nothing from a comparison with Sir Francis Bacon.   Shakespeare commenced life as a deer-stealer and a drunkard,[1] had a child born to him in less than six months after

---

[1] This latter seems to be a harsh declaration, but I find my authority for it in pages 8 and 9 of the Memoir of Shakespeare by the Rev. William Harkness, M.A., in Cooledge and Brother's New York edition of Scott, Webster, and Geary's London edition of the Works of Shakespeare.   I need not say to Shakespearian scholars that the authority of Mr. Harkness is entitled to the highest respect.

"The gaiety of his (Shakespeare's) disposition," says Mr. Harkness, "naturally inclined him to society; and the thoughtlessness of youth prevented his being sufficiently scrupulous about the conduct and the character of his associates. 'He had, by a misfortune, common enough to young fellows, fallen into ill company,' says Rowe; and the excesses into which they seduced him, were by no means consistent with that seriousness of deportment and behaviour which is expected to accompany the occupation that he had adopted.   The following anecdote of these days of his riot is still current at Stratford, and the neighbouring village of Bidford.   I give it in the words of the author from whom it is taken.   Speaking of Bidford, he says, 'There were anciently two societies of village yeomanry in this place, who frequently met under the appellation of Bidford topers.   It was a custom of these heroes to challenge any of their neighbours, famed for the love of good ale, to a drunken combat; among others, the people of Stratford were called out to a trial of strength, and in the number of their champions, as the traditional story runs, our Shakespeare, who foreswore all thin potations, and addicted himself to ale as lustily as Falstaff to his sack, is said to have entered the lists.   In confirmation of this tradition, we find an epigram written by Sir Aston Cockany, and published in his poems in 1858; it runs thus:—

"'TO MR. CLEMENT FISHER, OF WINCOT.

Shakespeare, your *Wincot* ale hath much renown'd,
That fox'd a beggar so (by chance was found
Sleeping) that there needed not many a word
To make him to believe he was a lord:
But you affirm (and in it seem most eager),
'Twill make a lord as drunk as any beggar.

marriage,[2] and lived in London during all his theatrical career without his wife. He was so mean as to sue one man for a debt of £6, and another for £1 19s. 10d.,[3] when he had an income of

> Bid *Norton* brew such ale as Shakespeare fancies
> Did put Kit Sly into such lordly trances:
> And let us meet there (for a fit of gladness),
> And drink ourselves merry in sober sadness.

"'When the Stratford lads went over to Bidford, they found the topers were gone to Eversham fair, but were told, if they wished to try their strength with the sippers, they were ready for the contest. This being acceded to, our bard and his companions were staggered at the first outset, when they thought it advisable to sound a retreat, while the means of retreat were practicable, and then had scarce marched half a mile before they were all forced to lay down more than their arms, and encamp in a very disorderly and unmilitary form, under no better covering than a large crab-tree, and there they rested till morning.

"'This tree is yet standing by the side of the road. If, as it has been observed by the late Mr. T. Wharton, the meanest hovel to which Shakespeare has an allusion interests curiosity and acquires an importance, surely the tree which has spread its shade over him, and sheltered him from the dews of the night, has a claim to our attention.

"'In the morning, when the company awakened our bard,' the story says, 'they entreated him to return to Bidford and renew the charge, but this he declined, and looking round upon the adjoining villages, exclaimed, "No! I have had enough, I have drunk with

> Piping Pebworth, Dancing Marston,
> Haunted Hillbro', Hungry Grafton,
> Dudging Exhall, Papist Wicksford,
> Beggarly Broom, and Drunken Bidford."

"'Of the truth of this story I have very little doubt. It is certain that the crab-tree is known all round the country by the name of Shakespeare's crab, and that the villages to which the allusion is made all bear the epithets here given them: the people of Pebworth are still famed for their skill on the pipe and tabor: Hillborough is now called Haunted Hillborough, and Grafton is notorious for the poverty of its soil.'"

The above relation, if it be true, presents us with a most unfavourable picture of the manners and morals prevalent among the youth of Warwickshire in the early years of Shakespeare, and it fills us with regret to find our immortal poet, with faculties so exalted, competing the bad pre-eminence in such abominable contests. It is some relief to know that, though he erred in uniting himself with such gross associations, he was the first to retreat from them in disgust.

[2] Knight's "Shakespeare," Appleton and Co.'s American edition, p. 144; R. Grant White, p. 145.

[3] Knight, vol. i. p. 158.

1000*l.* a year, and died, at the age of fifty-two, from the effect of too much drink at dinner.[4]   Sir Francis Bacon, on the other hand, was all his life a clamorous office-seeker, a time-server, and a corrupt judge.   He was condemned to the Tower, when Lord Chancellor, for having sold his judicial opinions for money, and, worse still, confessed the crime in order to mitigate his sentence. On a review of his whole character, Pope, the poet, stingingly characterized him as

"The wisest, brightest, meanest of mankind."

So, between William Shakespeare and Sir Francis Bacon, in a moral point of view, there was no great gulf.   Indeed, if there were any disparagement of degradation, it was against Sir Francis.

Most of the Shakespearian biographers and critics make it a matter of regret that so little being known of the history of the great poet, it is exceedingly difficult to form a true estimate of his personal character; but the difficulty which I find in that respect is, that these biographers and commentators nearly all start from the one point, of endeavouring to conceal, or at least to palliate, those follies and defects which might impair Shakespeare's influence or credit with the people.   They set out, consequently, with the desire to describe Shakespeare as they would like to have him.   His robbing of a gentleman's park, a very high crime at any time in England, is patronized gently as a youthful escapade, and the premature appearance of the first child of his marriage has been justified by the presumed privileges of a Warwickshire betrothal.

There has been some dispute among Shakespeare's biographers about his religious faith, a few having presented evidences tending to show that he was a Roman Catholic; but the great majority, being of Protestant politics, discourage that idea. Bacon we know to have been a Protestant of an extreme type, and from this difference springs an interesting point of our inquiry.   The question presents itself at once as to which religious faith is most manifested in the plays.   If they were the production of a Roman Catholic, Bacon could not have been their author.

[4] Richard Grant White, pp. 46, 55.

What we have first upon our hands, however, is the singular anomaly presented by the spectacle of a genius of the life-giving order, who was born in comparative humbleness, never betraying one emotion for, or exhibiting a single sympathy with the down-trodden classes, whose degradations and miseries must have constantly intruded upon his subtle comprehension. But the mist lifts before the light of facts. We have abundant evidence that Shakespeare was, in his personal way of life, though of a cheerful, amiable disposition, a calculating, money-making, money-saving man, and the conclusion from the circumstances of his business in London and at Stratford must be, that he suppressed his natural sentiments to a convenience of association and a sense of interest. His first patron, when he was a theatrical manager, was the Earl of Southampton, a prodigal young nobleman of enormous wealth, who, together with the Earls of Essex and of Rutland, were constant visitors at his theatre.[*]

So thoroughly had Shakespeare established himself under the patronage of Southampton, that he dedicated to him his "Venus and Adonis," and in the following year also his "Lucrece." By way of showing, moreover, the extent to which the dramatist had advanced himself into his lordship's favour, Richard Grant White states (p. 97), that Shakespeare took this liberty in the matter of "Venus and Adonis" without, "as the dedication shows," asking his lordship's permission; a very unusual responsibility, says the same commentator, to assume with the name of any man, much less a nobleman, unless he had felt himself secure in his lordship's good graces. Southampton was at this time under twenty years of age, and Essex (subsequently the favourite of Queen Elizabeth) was but four years older. In speaking of these young noblemen and their associates, who it may be as well to state were Catholics, Judge Holmes in his essay in favour of the Baconian theory says, that Southampton, Rutland, and the rest of Essex's jovial crew "pass their time in London in merely going to plays every day."

It was about this time, says Rowe, that "my lord Southampton at one time gave Shakespeare 1000*l.* to enable him to go through a purchase he had a mind to." This princely gift is, of course, ascribed to Southampton's estimation of the muse of Shakespeare,

---

[*] The "Authorship of Shakespeare," Nathaniel Holmes, p. 95.

but inasmuch as Southampton never exhibited any appreciation of literature beyond having the run of Shakespeare's theatre, we are justified in attributing the earl's attachment to the manager to considerations which frequently operate with young men of means and fashion down to the present day. It is true that, in Shakespeare's time, there were no actresses attached to theatrical companies, the female parts being performed by boys, but it was the custom of ladies of quality to sit upon the stage during theatrical entertainments, and there are several anecdotes of intrigues having taken place between them and young gallants, under such circumstances.[6] And this theory of personal familiarity between Shakespeare and a coroneted gallant of nineteen is all the more likely, than the one which ascribes Southampton's liberality to his patronage of literature, since that nobleman lived till he was fifty-four without having given any other evidence of a love of letters, or, indeed, without having made any mark beyond getting himself into the Tower for taking part in Essex's foolish Irish-Jesuit expedition, which cost the latter unhappy nobleman his life.

Considerations such as the foregoing would as satisfactorily account for the absence in Shakespeare of liberal sentiments, as the natural tendencies of Bacon's rank would account for the latter's aristocratic coldness of heart.

Let not the rapt worshippers of Avon's bard, whose sacred ecstasy is thus rudely broken in upon, suppose I take pleasure in these hard statistics. Nothing can reduce Shakespeare from the supreme elevation which he holds in the United States as the poet of the English-speaking race; but we in America take no interest in him as a politician, nor yet as a moralist; and, surely it is wiser for us, who are not involved in any tangles of allegiance, to disenchant ourselves of the spells fumed up by loyalty and doctrine, and treat this mighty mortal as a man. Perhaps the most curious and interesting problem which can thus be brought to our comprehension is—what amount of dirt may mix with, and be instrumental in, the production of a flaming gem. And Bacon is as subject to this criticism as Shakespeare.

[6] Queen Elizabeth used sometimes to sit behind the scenes, and on one occasion crossed the stage in view of the audience while Shakespeare himself was performing a character.

CHAPTER III.

LORD BACON.

> "They say, best men are moulded out of faults."
> *Measure for Measure*, Act. V. Scene 1.

THE theory that Lord Verulam (familiarly known as Lord Bacon) was the author of the plays attributed to Shakespeare, first became a matter of general discussion, as I have already stated, in consequence of an article by Delia Bacon, in the January number of *Putnam's Magazine* for 1856, published in America— three hundred and fifteen years after Bacon was born, and two hundred and fifty-nine years after William Shakespeare had been buried. The claim set up for Bacon, therefore, is barely nineteen years old, as against the nearly three hundred years of general acceptance, by history, of Shakespeare's rights. Shortly after the appearance of Miss Bacon's essay in the American magazine, she published it, somewhat enlarged, in pamphlet form, with an introduction by Nathaniel Hawthorne, in which shape it crossed the Atlantic, and had its ideas adopted by an English writer named William H. Smith, who supported and extended her views in an ingenious treatise published by him in London in 1857. Eight years afterwards, the November number of *Fraser's Magazine* for 1865 showed that Lord Palmerston had become a convert to the Baconian theory, and in the following year Nathaniel Holmes, Professor of Law in Harvard University, Cambridge, Mass., issued an elaborate volume of 600 pages supporting Miss Bacon's view. Here we have the whole scope of the Baconian pretension, comprising at the most a period of twenty years, with a meagre following of conspicuous advocates ; while, on the other hand, stand grouped in silent protest a crowd of Baconian biographers, stretching through well-nigh three centuries, who, with the greatest desire to aggrandize the object of their worship, never dropped a hint of the idea that Bacon could possibly have been the author of the plays of Shakespeare. Nay, more, one of the latest, W. Hepworth Dixon, writing as late as 1861,[7] alludes to Shakespeare as a separate person from the subject of his work.

Having thus marshalled the forces of the two parties to the controversy (for the silence of Bacon's biographers practically arrays them on the side of Shakespeare), it now suggests itself that we should inquire briefly into the separate histories of Bacon and Shakespeare, and ascertain what connexion each had with the literature of their age; and what, if any, were their relations to one another. They are consigned to us by the history of the times in which they lived, as *two* characters; one as the unapproachable Master of Philosophy and Law, and the other as the most transcendent genius of Poetry and Imagination.[8]

————

Sir Francis Bacon, Lord Verulam, Viscount St. Albans, and Lord High Chancellor of England, was born Jan. 22, 1560. He matriculated at Trinity College, Cambridge, at the age of thirteen, and soon afterward passed two years in travel on the European continent. In 1584 he first sat in the House of Commons as member for Melcombe, and from this time (though he was by courtesy the Queen's Lord Keeper at the age of ten), may be dated the commencement of his public official career.

In the parliamentary sessions of 1586-7-8 young Bacon played a most influential part. "These three sessions," says Dixon, "had to save the liberties of England and the faith of nearly half of Europe. They crushed the Jesuits and broke and punished the Romanist conspiracies." This fixes Bacon's faith, like that of his mother, the pious Lady Ann (whom he speaks of as "a saint of God"), to be of the Protestant persuasion, though we find a more decisive proof of Bacon's doctrine in the fact,

---

[7] Dixon's "Personal History of Lord Bacon," Boston, 1861.

[8] "Those two incomparable men, the Prince of Poets and the Prince of Philosophers, who made the Elizabethan age a more glorious and important era in the history of the human mind than the age of Pericles, of Augustus, or of Leo."—Lord Macaulay, "Essay on Burleigh and his Times," vol. v. p. 611, ed. Trevelyan.

that he was one of a committee which, in 1587, waited upon Queen Elizabeth to demand the execution of Mary, Queen of Scots. To use the words of Dixon in describing the scene: "The Queen (Elizabeth) holds out. A grand committee, of which Bacon is a member, goes into the presence, and, kneeling together at her feet, demand that the national will shall be done —that the Protestant faith shall be saved."[*]

About the year 1589, we find Bacon, who was then between twenty-nine and thirty years of age, the associate of Essex, who was twenty-three, of Southampton, who was nineteen, Montgomery, Pembroke, Rutland, "and the rest of Essex's jovial crew, which passed their time in going to Shakespeare's theatre every day." At this time Shakespeare himself, though already famous, was but twenty-five. This brings the above nobleman so in communication with Shakespeare, that nothing is more probable than that some of his unplayed manuscripts were read to "Essex, Southampton, and the rest," perhaps in Bacon's presence—a common custom with authorship and patronage in the Elizabethan age.

On the other hand, it is not impossible that Shakespeare, who doubtless was a great reader, touched now and then upon some of Bacon's theories, and thus we may readily account for any supposed plagiarism of one upon the other. I do not wish to be understood, however, as admitting, at this point, that either of these wondrous men was ever indebted to the other for an idea; though the most exacting devotee of Bacon might readily admit the occasional obligation of the latter to the poet, without brushing a single grain of the golden powder from his idol's wing. The likelihood, indeed, is far greater that Bacon insensibly fell into the habit, during the midsummer of Shakespeare's current popularity, of drawing from him as from a common well of language. This has been the custom of the world since he appeared, and even such a man as Bacon could hardly have resisted the temptation.

The spinal column of the Baconian claim is, that Sir Francis Bacon considered the reputation of a playwright to be so derogatory to his social and literary pretensions, as well as to his high political aspirations, that he concealed his taste for dramatic writing under the convenient mask of the good-natured and popular manager of the Blackfriars Theatre ; or, to use the language of the article in *Fraser*, that he (Bacon) " passed the plays off under the name of an actor for fear of compromising his professional prospects and philosophic gravity." But the main difficulty in the way of this theory is, that successful dramatic composition was recognized by very high honours in the times of Elizabeth and James I., Shakespeare himself having reached the high compliment of an introduction to Court for his successes in that way. In addition to this, the dramatists of that day were most of them men of scholarship ; several being of a social position quite worthy of ranking with that of Sir Francis Bacon. For instance, Massinger, " second to none but him who never had an equal," received his education at Oxford, and lived to an old age, " solaced by the applauses of the virtuous." [1] Beaumont and Fletcher (the latter of whom was buried in the same grave with Massinger) were lawyers—in all ages the profession of gentlemen. Marlowe, the tragic poet, matriculated at Cambridge; Shirley studied at Oxford; Ben Jonson " had the singular happiness of receiving his education under the illustrious Camden." His studies were interrupted by his change of circumstances, through his mother's death, but they were finally completed at Cambridge ; Quarles was educated at Cambridge; Lyly went first to Oxford and finished at Cambridge; and grouped with these come Thomas Sackville, subsequently Lord Treasurer, Lord Buckhurst, and we may add, Sir Philip Sidney, the equal of princes, who " wrote one dramatic piece, 'The Lady of the May,' a masque, acted before Elizabeth in the gardens of Wanstead, in Essex." Sidney was Elizabeth's " ambassador to the German powers, but when the fame of his valour and genius became so general that he was put in nomination for the kingdom of Poland, she refused to sanction his advancement lest she should lose the brightest jewel in her court." [2] Surely this illustrious example of honour and advancement might have justified Bacon, after the mighty merits of such productions as "Lear," "Hamlet," and "Othello" had been recognized by the best critics of the time, to accept the credit of their composition to himself—provided always that he was their author. Besides,

---

[1] Knight's octavo, published by Guy and Baine, London, p. 37.

[2] Knight's octavo, p. 43.

Bacon openly wrote dramatic compositions under the form of masques and mysteries; first, for the gentlemen at Gray's Inn during the Christmas Revels of 1587, and subsequently, in 1594, for the entertainment of the court.[3]

Bacon married Alice Barnham at the age of forty-six; at fifty-two he was made Attorney-General, and became Lord Chancellor at the age of fifty-seven. In the fourth year of this great office he was detected in taking bribes for his decisions, and, having confessed his crime in order to propitiate the mercy of his judges, was sent to the Tower on May 3, 1621. After remaining a prisoner for ten months, the fine inflicted on him was remitted and he was released in March, 1622. He never resumed public life, but died three years afterwards in 1625. Bacon was a thorough specimen of the politician of that time, being a persistent applicant for office, and always selfish, sordid, and unfaithful. He was exceedingly greedy of money, and though his revenues most of the time were liberal, he was constantly the victim of the usurers. Some of his biographers describe him as pure in his morals and temperate in his habits, which certainly does not represent the case of William Shakespeare.

Dixon speaks of Bacon as "a man born to high rank who seeks incessantly for place," while according to Pope and Lord Campbell, Cecil and Coke, he is "in turn abject, venal, proud, profuse—ungrateful for the gifts of Essex, mercenary in his love for Alice Barnham, servile to the House of Commons, and corrupt on the judicial bench."[4] The most noteworthy feature of the work of Dixon is, that its author does not make even the slightest allusion to the Bacon-Shakespeare theory, though that theory had then been projected full five years. And, perhaps, at this point, it is worthy of mention that Bacon, on the other hand, never, in all his voluminous writings, made the most distant allusion to Shakespeare.

Such was Bacon, for whom the Baconians claim, that he possessed more of the education, wit, emotional elevation, and moral fitness for the production of such intellectual light as beams through the plays before us, than the man to whom these plays have always been ascribed, and who indisputably wrote "Venus and Adonis."

[3] Holmes, p. 90.
[4] Dixon's "Personal History of Lord Bacon," Boston, 1861, p. 4.

CHAPTER IV.

WILLIAM SHAKESPEARE.

" IT is quite a fallacy," says Halliwell, one of the most pains-
taking and reliable of the biographers of Shakespeare, " to
complain how little we are acquainted with William Shakespeare's career and worldly character. On the contrary, we should
be thankful we know more of him than we do of Spenser, or of
many others, the history of whose lives would be so interesting
and so valuable." [1] " We know more of William Shakespeare
before he was forty years old," says Richard Grant White, taking
up this cue from Halliwell, " than we do of Oliver Cromwell at
the same age ; than the Greeks knew of Æschylus, the father of
their tragedy ; or of Aristophanes, the father of their comedy,
two centuries after they died ; or than the French do of Molière,
not a page of whose manuscripts is known to be in existence."
"The same truth," adds this writer, "is illustrated in the
biography of Washington, whose own nephew, to whom were
open all family papers and records, was unable to discover the
date of his marriage, although his wife, Mrs. Custis, was one of
the richliest dowered widows in all Virginia." [2] The truth is, as
I have said before, there were abundant details of the personal
life of William Shakespeare open to the hands of the early,
and even the later English biographers, if they had only
thought it politic to state frankly and without subterfuge, all
they knew about him. Some of the reasons for their reticence
I have already given. In dealing with Shakespeare's history
for the purposes of this inquiry I shall endeavour to be very
brief.

[1] Halliwell's " Shakespeare," p. 2.
[2] Richard Grant White, p. 182, 4, 5.

William Shakespeare was born at Stratford-upon-Avon, on the 23rd April, 1564. His father, John Shakespeare, was, according to Rowe, a considerable dealer in wool, and had been first alderman and then high bailiff of the body corporate of Stratford. He had also been chamberlain, and possessed lands and tenements which were said to have been the reward of his grandfather's faithful services to King Henry VII. It has also been said that John Shakespeare at one time followed the occupation of a butcher, but this report doubtless grew out of his occasionally adding to his trade in wool, the sale of furs; and, when opportunity invited, according to the custom of country stores, the sale of butcher's meat. At the birth of our poet, who was a first son, John Shakespeare was in a thriving condition, and this prosperity continued for some years afterward. William, as soon as he had arrived at a proper age, was placed at a free grammar school of the town of Stratford, where Latin and other liberal acquirements were taught; but at the age of fourteen he was rather suddenly withdrawn, in consequence of the decline in his father's circumstances, either to assist him in his business, or to lend a hand in gaining his own livelihood. Some of the commentators think, that from school he went into the office of a country attorney, or was placed with the seneschal of some manor court, "where," says one writer, "it is highly probable he picked up those law phrases that so frequently occur in his plays, and which could not have been in common use, unless among professional men.[3] This view, in addition to being in itself very plausible, derives its main support from an attack made upon Shakespeare by one of his London dramatic cotemporaries, Robert Greene, who, jealous of our poet's rapid rise over all his rivals in popular estimation, sneered at him for presuming to be "the only Shake-scene in a countrey."[4] Nash, a parasite of Greene's, and of the same coarse, envious character, next attacks and practically advises our poet to return to his original "trade

[3] Duyckinck's "Life of Shakespeare," in Porter and Coate's edition, Philadelphia, 1874, p. 3.

[4] "Trust them not (*i. e.* the players), for there is an upstart crow, beautified with our feathers, that with his tiger's heart wrapt in a player's hide, supposes he is as well able to bombast out a blank verse as the best of you; and being an absolute Johannes factotum, is, in his own conceit, the only Shak-scene in a countrey."—Greene's "Groat's Worth of Wit."

of *noverint*," [5] which indicates the calling of an attorney's clerk.[6]
The age of fourteen, therefore, which sees Shakespeare retire
from the Stratford school, is the true commencement of his
public life.

It now becomes a matter of great importance to our inquiry
to ascertain with what religious sentiments or leanings William
Shakespeare embarked upon the world; (for, after all, it matters
not how men may drop the observance of religious forms,
as the constant pressure of expanding worldly knowledge chips
that reverence away) the early teachings of a religious mother
always represent a large dormant influence, which awakens at
every opportunity, to give direction to the general flow of
judgment.   And it is entirely well settled that Mary Arden, the
mother of William Shakespeare, daughter and heiress of Robert
Arden, of Wellingcote, styled "a gentleman of worship," was a
Roman Catholic.   We have already seen that the mother of
Francis Bacon was a Protestant.   By following this line of
inquiry, and gauging it carefully, as we go along, by the invariable religious sentiment of the Shakespeare plays, we must
finally reach a point decisive.   For, though Essex and Southampton, Shakespeare's great patrons were Catholics, and though
Shakespeare may be supposed to have been influenced by their
political predilections, from any expression savouring of democracy
in his writings, it is not to be credited for an instant that a man
of such early training could have been domineered by them from
the natural flow of his *religious* sentiments.   On the contrary,
there is much reason to believe that, in this particular, he and
they were in full accord.

Let me add at this point that it is certainly known that Sir
Thomas Lucy, whose deer were stolen by Shakespeare soon after

---

[5] *Noverint universi per presentes* is the Latin for "know all men by these
presents," hence attorneys were often called *noverints* from their frequent
use of that term.   The nickname could apply to no other class.

[6] "It is a common practice now-a-days, among a sort of shiftless companions that run through every art and thrive by none, to leave the trade of
noverint, whereto they were born, and busy themselves with the endeavours
of art, though they could scarcely latinize their neck-verse if they should
have need; yet English Seneca, read by candle-light, yields many good sentences—and if you entreat him fair in a frosty morning, he will afford you
whole Hamlets, I should say, handfuls of tragical speeches."—Nashe's Introduction to "Greene's Menaphon," 1589, and Knight, vol. i. p. 102.

he left school, and under whose persecutions it seems the future poet was finally driven out of Stratford was, of that strict shade of the reformed faith known as Puritan, and as such, was one of a commission appointed by the government to report against heretics and nonconformists.[7] As such commissioner, Sir Thomas Lucy, with the rest of the board, reported against John Shakespeare, the father, and about fourteen other persons, for not having, during several weeks, made their appearance at church. Eight of these derelicts, among whom we again find John Shakespeare, were likewise impugned with the further motive of desiring by such non-attendance to evade the service of process for debt. This latter imputation is rather eagerly adopted by the Protestant biographers of Shakespeare in pre-

---

[7] Harness, in describing the incident between Sir Thomas Lucy and young William Shakespeare, which had such a decisive influence upon the poet's life, says, "One of the favourite amusements of the wild companions with whom Shakespeare in his youthful days allied himself, was the stealing of deer and corries. In these hazardous exploits Shakespeare was not backward in accompanying his comrades. The person in whose neighbourhood, perhaps on whose property, these encroachments were made, was of all others the individual from whose hands they were least likely to escape with impunity in case of detection. Sir Thomas Lucy *was a Puritan;* and the severity of manners which has always characterized this sect, would teach him to extend very little indulgence to the excesses of Shakespeare and his wilful companions. He was, besides, a game preserver: in his place as a member of Parliament he had been an active instrument in the formation of the game laws, and the trespasses of our poet, whether committed on the demesne of himself or others, were as offensive to his predilections as to his principles. Shakespeare and his compeers were discovered, and fell under the rigid lash of Sir Thomas Lucy's authority and resentment. The knight attacked the poet with the penalties of the law, and the poet revenged himself by sticking some satirical verses on the gate of the knight's park. The following are the first and last :—

Verses on Sir Thomas Lucy.

"A parliement member, a justice of peace,
  At home a poore scarecrowe, in London an asse ;
  If Lucy is Lousie, as some volke misscall it,
  Sygee Lousie Lucy whatever befall it.

    ＊   ＊   ＊   ＊   ＊

"If a iuvenile frolick he cannot forgive,
  We'll synge Lousie Lucy as long as we live ;
  And Lucy the Lousie a libel may call it,
  We'll synge Lousie Lucy whatever befall it."

3

ference to the first, because, perhaps, they are thus enabled to escape the inference that the Shakespeare family was of the Roman Catholic faith.

Before proceeding farther as to Shakespeare's religious faith, I will return to the historical narration, in order that the decisive questions of our poet's social, political, and religious sentiments may follow in regular order, and lead up to the door of the text, with as little further interruption as possible. In this, as I have already said, the objects of our inquiry only permit me to be brief.

We have seen that Shakespeare, owing to his father's straitened circumstances, left school at the age of fourteen; but we are justified in the conclusion that he acquired a sufficient knowledge of the classics, during the last two or three years of his studies, to qualify him for all the use which is exhibited of such learning in the plays, and this, from the fact (says Malone) "that other Stratford men, educated at the same school, were familiarly conversant with Latin, and even corresponded in that language." [8] Upon this point Mr. Lofft asserts, in his introduction to the "Aphorisms," that Shakespeare "had what would now be considered a very reasonable proportion of Latin; he was not wholly ignorant of Greek; he had a knowledge of French so as to read it with ease, and, I believe, not less of the Italian. If it had been true that he had *no* Greek, as some contend from Ben Jonson's famous line, that he had 'little Latin and *less* Greek,' it would have been as easy for the verse as for the sentiment to have said '*no* Greek.'" [9] It is hard to defeat this reasoning; Aubrey and Dr. Drake agree with it, and Harness, in subscribing to it, remarks, "That Shakespeare should appear *unlearned* in the judgment of Jonson, who perhaps measured him by the scale of his own enormous erudition, is no imputation upon his classical attainments." I think it may be properly suggested at this point, that nothing is more likely than that Shakespeare keenly pursued his studies after he left school; and if, as there seems to be but little doubt, he went into an attorney's office, he had ample leisure for such application. The experience of every man who has ever had a taste for study will tell him how natural such a course would be; nay, how strange it would have been if

[8] Malone's "Shakespeare," Boswell's Edition, vol. ii. p. 182.
[9] "Aphorisms from Shakespeare." pp. 12, 13, 14.

the eager mind of Shakespeare had not followed it. The extent of proficiency acquired by a mind like his, after such a good start as it had received, cannot be captiously limited. It is fair, therefore, to terminate the analysis of this first period of our poet's life with the conclusion that William Shakespeare, though not so great a scholar as Lord Bacon, possessed all the reading and classical accomplishment requisite to the production of the Shakespeare plays; and though he never became a lawyer in any true sense of that term, he had, in some lesser way, acquired all the "conveyancer's jargon," and phrases of attorneyship which are to be found sprinkled through his dramatic works. The period for this educational improvement, in the semi-solitude of a little country town like Stratford ran, in Shakespeare's case from fourteen till the age of twenty-two, at which latter date he went up to London. I may here be met by the remark, in objection to the probability of Shakespeare's studious habits, that he began by leading a wild, dissipated life, and married at the age of eighteen. But every married man's experience will tell him that the conjugal condition rather promotes serious reflection than otherwise; while Shakespeare's drunken bouts, his matches at intoxication, and his infractions of the game-laws under the form of deer-stealing, may be regarded as the necessary vents and excesses of an intensely active nature, which could not be "cribb'd, cabin'd and confined" of its natural instincts by the sleepy decorum of a place like Stratford.

Yielding to these wilful impulses in yet another way, he made his precocious and imprudent marriage. The object of his choice was Ann Hathaway, the daughter of a substantial yeoman of Shottery, a little village about three miles from Stratford. She was eight years older than Shakespeare, which circumstance doubtless had its effect in producing the long separations that took place between them in the form of extended stays in London during his after-life. This marriage took place in December, 1582, and their first child subsequent to it was Susanna, born May 23, 1583, a period of little more than five months. Shakespeare showed his superior affection for this child, however, by leaving her the bulk of his property. It would seem, therefore, that he could not have doubted her paternity, whatever scandals may have got into circulation on the subject. It does not appear, indeed, that there ever was any positive disagreement between himself and wife; though it is worthy of observation, that in the first copy of his will he made no mention of her name, and only inserted it afterward to the extent of leaving her "his second-best bed." He probably was influenced to the slightness of this bequest, by the fact that she was sufficiently provided for out of his real estate by the usual common-law right of dower.

Nearly all of Shakespeare's biographers show a disposition to shield him and Ann Hathaway from the inferential reproach of the premature *début* of Susanna, by assuming that the period of betrothal in that age, in some portions of England, imparted all the liberties of wedlock. Perhaps we have Shakespeare's own opinion on the subject in the following lines of Claudio's in "Much Ado about Nothing," where he replies to Leonato's reproaches for slandering the honour of his daughter Hero, whom Claudio stood engaged to marry :—

> CLAUDIO. I know what you would say; if *I* have known her,
> You'll say she did embrace *me* as a husband
> And so extenuate the "forehand sin."
>
> *Much Ado, Act IV. Scene* 1.

And, again, in the Duke's advice to Mariana, in "Measure for Measure :"—

> DUKE (*disguised as a priest*). Nor, gentle daughter, fear you not at all.
> He is your husband on a pre-contract:
> To bring you thus together, 'tis no sin,
> Sith that the justice of your title to him
> Doth flourish the deceit.
>
> *Measure for Measure, Act IV. Scene* 1.

On the subject of his wife's superior age, we find Shakespeare again testifying in "Twelfth Night" as follows :—

> DUKE. Let still the woman take
> An elder than herself; so wears she to him,
> So sways she level in her husband's heart.
>
> *Twelfth Night, Act II. Scene* 4.

And still again, in the same piece, to Viola, who is disguised as a young man :—

> DUKE. Then let thy love be younger than thyself,
> Or thy affection cannot hold the bent:
> For women are as roses, whose fair flower,
> Being once displayed, doth fall that very hour.
>
> *Twelfth Night, Act II. Scene* 4.

Further on in the same play, the poet puts his own case with still more distinctness. Olivia, the heroine of the piece, having mistaken Sebastian for Viola, whom she has seen only as a page, and with whom she is madly in love, invites him with expressions of the utmost fondness to her apartments. Sebastian, who has never seen Olivia before, follows her wonderingly, and they pass some hours together. After the interval of a scene with other characters, Sebastian reappears in Olivia's garden, musing and alone, and hardly able to contain himself with his good fortune. After gazing with rapture on a pearl Olivia has given him, he says,—

> I am mad,
> Or else the lady's mad;
> But here my lady comes.

Enter OLIVIA *and a Priest.*

OLIVIA (*to Sebastian*). Blame not this haste of mine; if you mean well,
Now go with me, and with this holy man,
Into the chantry by; there, before him,
And underneath that consecrated roof
Plight me the full assurance of your faith;
That my most jealous and too doubtful soul
May live at peace; he shall conceal it,
Whiles you are willing it shall come to note,
What time we will our celebration keep,
According to my birth. What do you say?
SEBASTIAN. I'll follow this good man, and go with you,
And having sworn truth, ever will be true.
OLIVIA. Then lead the way, good father; and heavens so shine
That they may *fairly* note this act of mine.

> *Act IV. Scene* 3.

There are two further passages in the plays bearing upon this subject of troth-plight and premature birth which may as well be noticed at this point. The first of these we find in "The Winter's Tale."

LEONTES. My wife's a hobby-horse; deserves a name
As rank as any flax-wench, that puts to
Before her troth-plight.

> *Act I. Scene* 2.

The other occurs in "King John," in the scene between the King, Robert, and the Bastard.

ROBERT FAULCONBRIDGE (*alluding to the Bastard*).

> And this my mother's son was none of his;
> And, if he were, he came into the world
> Full fourteen weeks before the course of time.

Act I. Scene 1.

These fourteen weeks, which Sir Robert thus refers to, represent just about the precocity of Susanna Shakespeare, and it will be seen that the poet, in neither case, made the deficiency the subject of a reproach or penalty. Whether this frequent recurrence to an important incident in Shakespeare's life was most natural to Shakespeare or to Bacon, the reader can readily settle for himself. In this connexion our attention becomes directed to the frequency with which the author of the plays indulges in a word which, though common enough in Shakespeare's time, I must be excused for quoting. I allude to the word *cuckold*. It is surprising to note the extent to which he revels in this term. It is profusely sprinkled through all his comedies and his historical plays. His tragedies also plentifully bear the soil of the idea; and, indeed, there are very few of the plays which are free from this strange fantasy. The word, and even its equivalents, seem to operate upon him like a spell. Their merest mention provokes in his mind the most unbounded merriment. Like the introduction of a syringe to a French audience, the fancy never tires. Indeed, it appears to deprive our poet of all self-control, and he rolls before the reader, and hold his sides like one who is on the brink of a fit, from excess of the ludicrous.[1] The question which presents itself in connexion with this observation is, whether such a development of comic ecstasy would be more likely to Sir Francis Bacon, who was not married until he was forty-six, or to William Shakespeare, who, at the age of eighteen, married a matured

---

[1] In looking over the "Dramatic Miscellanies" of Thomas Davies, published in London in 1784, I find the following allusion to Congreve's frequent use of the same word in his plays: "The audience in Congreve's time," says Davies, "were particularly fond of having a city-cuckold dressed up for their entertainment, and Fondle-wife in Congreve's "Old Bachelor" is served up with very poignant sauce, for the several incidents in the scene are very diverting."—Davies' "Miscellanies," vol. iii. p. 316.

Congreve was doubtless governed in this matter by the taste which Shakespeare had so industriously inculcated.

woman, and was rewarded with a child in little more than five months afterwards?

Within eighteen months after the birth of Susanna, Shakespeare's wife bore him twins, a son and a daughter, who were baptized by the names of Hamnet and Judith; "and thus, when little more than twenty, Shakespeare had already a wife and three children dependent on his exertions for support." He remained at home in Stratford until 1586, when, as we have already seen, he went to London to seek new fortunes, in that larger sphere. Whether he had written anything beyond sonnets previous to that time does not appear. It seems that he went at once to the neighbourhood of the theatres, and it is reported that he began by holding gentlemen's horses at the doors. Having probably thus become acquainted with the management, he readily worked his way inside the temple of the drama, and was soon promoted to the position of call-boy on the stage.

CHAPTER V.

SHAKESPEARE'S PERSONAL CHARACTERISTICS.

SHAKESPEARE'S progress from this point appears to have been very rapid. He soon was permitted to play minor parts, and in three or four years acquired an interest in the management of the Globe, and also in the summer theatre, which was known as the playhouse at Blackfriars. At what precise time he began to write his plays is not definitely known, as they all found their way into print without any effort on his part, and the dates of their production was consequently, to a large extent, confounded with the order of their publication ; but, taking Furnival's table for our guide, it may safely be concluded that he began to write them as early as 1588-9. It is a singular fact that he appeared to take no interest in the vast renown they were building up for him ; for it was not until seven years after his death that the first collection of them was printed together, in what has been universally known as "the folio of 1623." Of his poems and sonnets he seemed to be a great deal more considerate, having published most of them over his own name and supervision, and dedicating the "Venus and Adonis," and the "Rape of Lucrece" in 1593 and 1594 respectively to the young Earl of Southampton. In his dedication of the former poem to the Earl, he characterizes it as "the first heir of his invention," but it is known that he wrote plays previous to its appearance, so it is not improbable that the "Venus" had been written much earlier, and had perhaps been begun previous to his leaving Stratford. He followed the profession of an actor for upwards of seventeen years, and the production of his plays, which began probably when he was twenty-four, covered a period of twenty-six years. During this period he produced thirty-seven plays.

"The latter part of his life," says Rowe, "was spent in ease, retirement, and the conversation of his friends," and he died on his birthday, April 23rd, 1616, at the age of 52, in the full maturity of his powers, and leaving a large property behind him. The immediate cause of his death is reported by Ward, the vicar of Stratford, to have been a merry meeting which he had with Drayton and Ben Jonson; at which, says the vicar, "it seems he drank too hard, for Shakespeare died of a fever there contracted." Knight is unwilling to give absolute confidence to this tradition, because the vicar wrote forty years after the event, "but," he remarks, "if it were absolutely true our reverence for Shakespeare would not be diminished by the fact that he accelerated his end in the exercise of hospitality, according to the manner of his age, towards two of the most illustrious of his friends." Knight's objection, that Ward wrote forty years after the event, has but little force when we learn that the good vicar's work, in which the above fact is stated was his diary, published naturally at the close of his career.

In person Shakespeare is represented as having been of full size, comely and prepossessing; of agreeable manners, but not marked either by bearing or in features with that dignity of presence which we naturally associate with our ideas of his genius. He was chiefly remarkable as a good-natured, amiable, easy-going man, with more heart than conscience, of a convivial inclination, with full conversational powers, supported by a readiness of wit which made him a desirable companion for men of any amount of acquirement or rank. "Every contemporary who has spoken of him," says one writer, "has been lavish in the praise of his temper and disposition. 'The *gentle* Shakespeare' seems to have been his distinguishing appellation." "No slight portion of our enthusiasm for his writings," says another, "may be traced to the fair picture which they present of our author's character; we love the tenderness of heart, the candour and openness and singleness of mind, the largeness of sentiment, the liberality of opinion, which the whole tenor of his works prove him to have possessed; his faults seem to have been the transient aberrations of a thoughtless moment, which reflection never failed to correct." All agree that Shakespeare's presence was very attractive, while many incidents are given by his contemporaries to show that with women he was very fascinating. The general disposition evinced by his biographers, most of whom approach him only in awe and almost upon their knees, is to disbelieve the broadest of these anecdotes, as if it were discreditable to his intellect for him to have been so much a man. But the character of Bacon has already revealed to us that morals are not indispensable to intellectual force, and that the divine afflatus of the poet may find its way to the most sublime developments through the muddiest of filters. I am disposed, therefore, to accept most of the stories about Shakespeare's conviviality and gallantry, and think them less to his discredit, even when they stretch to the extremity of deer-stealing, than were the low contrivances by which Bacon sought and retained office, or the sale of his judicial opinions from the bench.

One of these stories about Shakespeare is recorded by Oldys in his MSS., and it is supported by such additional authority that we cannot help giving it full credence. It seems that it was the habit of our poet, in his trips between Stratford and London, to bait his horses at the Crown Inn or Tavern, in Oxford, which was kept by Mr. John Davenant, "a grave, melancholy man," never known to laugh, who was subsequently Mayor of Oxford, and whose son *William* became afterward a poet under the title of Sir *William* Davenant. But Mrs. Davenant, the hostess, was by no means a grave and melancholy woman. On the contrary, tradition says she was "very mettlesome," and withal quite pretty. During the several years through which these London and Stratford trips and Oxford stoppages continued, scandal was very free about the terms existing between the buxom hostess and the London manager. "One day," and we have this story on the authority of Pope, the poet, "an old townsman, observing the boy running homeward, almost out of breath, asked him whither he was posting in that heat and hurry. He answered, to see his *god*-father Shakespeare. 'There's a good boy,' said the other, 'but have a care that you don't take *God's* name in vain.'" This story, Pope told at the Earl of Oxford's table, upon the occasion of some discourse which arose about Shakespeare's monument, then newly erected in Westminster Abbey; and he quoted Mr. Betterton, the player, for his authority."[1] The tale is also mentioned by Anthony Wood;

[1] Reed's "Shakespeare," vol. i. pp. 124, 125.

and certain it is that the traditionary scandal of Oxford
has always spoken of Shakespeare as the father of Davenant; [2]
"but it imputes a crime to our author," says a reverend commentator, "of which we may, without much stretch of charity,
acquit him.   It originated in the wicked vanity of Davenant
himself, who, disdaining his honest, but mean descent from the
vintner, had the shameless impiety to deny his father, and
reproach the memory of his mother by claiming consanguinity
with Shakespeare."

Before leaving the sketch of Shakespeare at this point, I desire to call attention to the fact, as bearing upon the question of
the claims set up for Bacon, that his contemporary, Ben Jonson,
wrote a laudatory sketch of Shakespeare in his introduction to
the plays, and gave the highest stamp of his approbation to the
Bard of Avon's genius by the famous, but generally misquoted line,

"He was not *of* an age, but for all time."

This naturally brings us to the disposal of a common error, on
which the Baconians place very great reliance.   I allude to the
popular tradition that Shakespeare thought with such facility that
he never blotted out a line.   Ben Jonson, in his "Discoveries,"
mentions this preposterous statement as follows: "I remember
the players have often mentioned it, as an honour to Shakespeare, that in writing (whatsoever he penned) he never blotted
out a line.   My answer hath been, 'Would he had blotted out a
thousand!' which they thought a malevolent speech.   I had not
told posterity this, but for their ignorance who chose that circumstance to commend their friend by, wherein he most faulted;
and to justify mine own candour, for I loved the man, and do
honour his memory, on this side idolatry, as much as any.   He
was, indeed, honest, and of an open and free nature, had an excellent fancy, brave notions, and gentle expressions; wherein he
flowed with that felicity that sometimes it was necessary he
should be stopped; *Sufflaminandus erat*, as Augustus said to
Haterius.   His wit was in his own power; would the rule of it
had been so too."

I have said that this report of the players is perfectly pre-

[2] Reed, note ix., pp. 126, 127.

posterous, because nothing is better known to those who are at all familiar with theatrical affairs that actors rarely or ever see an author's manuscript, the necessities of distribution of the text and of study among the various members of a dramatic company, requiring always the assistance of the copyist's art.   But to set this fable at rest, I request attention to the following specimens of Shakespeare's handwriting in the form of signatures on the pages of his will.

These, and two other signatures, one in a book and the other to a mortgage deed, are the only five specimens of Shakespeare's

"hand" extant,[2] and the bare sight of all of them is sufficient to refute the idea that they represent facility; or, that when his penmanship had reached this cramped condition, it could have been made serviceable in the way of copying.   And it must not be supposed that the above signatures were appended to Shakespeare's will during the feebleness of his last moments, for the document to which they are attached bears date 22nd March,

---

[2] The utter extinction of all the Shakespeare manuscripts is attributed to the great fire of London, and two fires which occurred in Stratford.

1616; whereas he did not die until the 23rd of the next month —and then rather unexpectedly, as we have seen. Besides, the two other signatures are precisely similiar.

There is still another proof against the copying theory that logically connects itself with this portion of the case. Among the ear-marks which indicate the plays to be the production of one who had been a professional player, are the constantly recurring evidences in the body of the text of what is known among actors as "stage business." Striking specimens of this professional mystery are to be found in Hamlet's directions to the players, and in Peter Quince's distribution of the copied parts and "properties" to Bottom and his mates, in "Midsummer Night's Dream." But these proofs of the playwright's technical and professional experience abound throughout the Shakespeare plays to such a degree that it has been said by actors that the very language and disposition of the scenes in the Shakespeare pieces make "stage business" of themselves. This kind of expertry could hardly have been acquired by Bacon; neither could it have been imparted by a teacher; nor yet could a copyist of less intellectual capacity than the author have written such matter "in" and made it fit. In fact, this "stage business" in Shakespeare is so blended with, and fashioned to the text, that it could not have been inserted after writing without ruining the structure; nor could it have been removed therefrom without bleeding out a portion of its life.

CHAPTER VI.

THE RELIGION OF THE SHAKESPEARE FAMILY.

WE have now brought our observations down to a point, as between Bacon and Shakespeare, where it becomes in order to follow our inquiry into the religious belief of William Shakespeare; and if it shall appear that our poet was beyond all reasonable doubt a Roman Catholic, we shall be able to account for several things which might otherwise remain disputable. If, finally, we shall show—after tracing all the probabilities of circumstantial proof—that the unvarying sentiment and verbal testimony of the plays indicate the writer to have been of the religion of the Church of Rome; that they show him to be entirely familiar with its dogmas, tenets, practices, and formula; that he rarely if ever alludes to a priest without apparently folding his arms across his breast and reverently bowing his head; and, beyond all, that he not only betrays a profound ignorance of the formula of Protestantism, but never alludes to a Protestant preacher, or a Puritan as he prefers to call him, without derision and contempt; I think it may be considered we have brought the Baconian portion of our inquiry to a close—to a close, through what must then become the general verdict, that the plays ascribed to William Shakespeare could not possibly have been the work of a confirmed and bitter Protestant like Sir Francis Bacon.

—— The ancestors of William Shakespeare, on both sides, seem to have been persons of some note. It is claimed by several writers that the name of Chacksper, or Shackspeare, or Shakespeare, " a martial name however spelt," says Knight, figured among squires at arms as early as the battle of Hastings, won by the " Conqueror " in 1066. The battle of Bosworth Field, however,

in which the Earl of Richmond (afterwards Henry VII.) overthrew Richard III. in 1485, makes the first definite historical
presentation of both the paternal and maternal lines of the
Shakespeare family.   The grant of a coat of arms in 1599 to
Shakespeare's own father, recites of " John Shakespeare, now of
Stratford-on-Avon," that his " antecessor, for his faithful and approved service to the late most prudent prince, King Henry VII.,
of famous memory, was advanced and rewarded with lands and
tenements, given to him in those parts of Warwickshire where
they have continued by some descents in good reputation and
credit."

The mother of Shakespeare was Mary Arden, the youngest of
the seven daughters of Robert Arden, one of whose ancestors
had rendered some public service (probably at Bosworth Field)
for which he was rewarded with the position of Groom of the
Chamber to Henry VII.   " He seems," says Malone, "to have
been a favourite ; for he had a valuable lease granted to him by
the king, of the manor of Yoxsall, in Staffordshire, and was also
made keeper of the royal park of Aldear."   " Mary Arden ! " exclaims Knight in a sort of rhapsody; " the name breathes of
poetry.   It seems the personification of some Dryad, called by
that generic name of Arden—a forest with many towers.   High
as was her descent, wealthy and powerful as were the numerous
branches of her family, Mary Arden, we doubt not, led a life of
usefulness as well as innocence within her native forest hamlet."
Her father died in December, 1556, and his will, which bears
date 24th November of that year, indicates his religious faith by
opening as follows :—

" First, I bequeath my soul to Almighty God, and to our
blessed Lady St. Mary, and to all the holy company of heaven."
Mary had the best position in her father's will, and was made
one of its executors, along with her sister Alice.   Knight, who
will not have Shakespeare to have been a Catholic on any showing, does not think " that the wording of this will is any proof
of Robert Arden's religious opinions; " but Halliwell, who is
equally as stiff as Knight in his Protestantism, says that the
testator " was undoubtedly a Catholic, as appears by his allusion
to our blessed Lady Saint Mary in his will." [1]   And the faith of

---

[1] Halliwell's "Shakespeare," p. 15.

the father thus solemnly expressed, and made the vehicle of his last fond paternal trust, doubtless remained precious to the daughter.

Of the religious faith of John Shakespeare, the father of our poet, who married Mary Arden, Halliwell and the great majority of the biographers express the opinion, or leave it to be inferred, that he was of the reformed religion, and consequently Protestant. They support this view with the fact that John Shakespeare had held municipal offices in Stratford, which required him to swear adhesion to the principles of Protestantism, and to acknowledge the Queen of England instead of the Pope, as the head of the Church. This is a plausible presentation, certainly; but when we reflect upon the bitter religious strifes of that transition period between the Romish and the Reformed Church, and observe to what extent the Catholic clergy excused such political oaths, when they might assist them in picketing out adherents to posts of power, the argument loses a great portion of its force. The domestic history of every civil war will show numerous instances of malcontents and nonconformists getting into office under government by deceptive protestations. The period of the Cavaliers and the Roundheads was full of such cases, and to be more familiar, I may refer to the fact that during the late contest in the United States between the North and South there were swarms of Confederates snugly nooked in the Union Custom-houses; while, on the other hand, many a Northern hypocrite was supporting rebellion in the South with the view of stealing cotton, or of profiting by his perfidy in some other way; all readily swallowing the ironclad oaths of allegiance of either section, without the palliating pressure of either conscience or religion.

But we have what may be regarded as direct proofs on the subject of John Shakespeare's religious faith. One of these proofs is the fact that a Protestant commission, which had been appointed by the Government to inquire into the conformity of the people of Warwickshire to the established religion, " with a special eye to Jesuits, priests, and *recusants*," reported many persons " for not coming monthlie to the churche, according to hir Majestie's lawes." Among these derelicts was John Shakespeare, but the commissioners specially note him, and eight others, as possibly not coming to church for fear of process for debt. One of these commissioners was Sir Thomas Lucy, a Puri-

tan, which latter fact, as well as this report against the poet's
father, may account for the subsequent invasion by Shakespeare
of Sir Thomas Lucy's park, and also for the bitter pasquinade
which the poetic youngster launched against Sir Thomas for his
prosecution of that trespass.

The most direct and absolute proof, however, that John Shakespeare was of the Roman Catholic religion, may be seen in his
formal "Confession of Faith," which was found nearly two
hundred years after his death, and the discovery of which is
described by Dr. Drake as follows :—

"About the year 1770 a master bricklayer of the name of
Mosely, being employed by .Mr. Thomas Hart, the fifth in
descent in a direct line from the poet's sister, Joan Hart, to new
tile a house, in which he (Hart) then lived, and which is supposed
to be that under whose roof the bard was born, found hidden between the rafters and the tiling of the house a manuscript, consisting of six leaves stitched together, in the form of a small
book. This manuscript Mosely, who bore the character of an
honest and industrious man, gave (without asking or receiving
any recompense) to Mr. Peyton, an alderman of Stratford, and
this gentleman very kindly sent it to Mr. Malone, through the
medium of the Rev. Mr. Davenport, vicar of Stratford."[2]
Drake, p. 9 ; Reed, vol. iii. pp. 197, 198.

Chalmers, in his "Apology for the Believers in the Shakespeare Papers," remarks upon this document that, "From the
sentiments and the language, this confession appears to be the
effusion of a Roman Catholic mind, and was probably drawn up
by some Roman Catholic priest. If these premises be granted
it will follow, as a fair deduction, that the family of Shakespeare
were Roman Catholics—a circumstance which is wholly consistent
with what Mr. Malone is now studious to inculcate, viz., that
this confession could not have been the composition of any of our
poet's family. The thoughts, the language, the orthography, all
demonstrate the truth of my conjecture, though Mr. Malone did
not perceive this truth when he first published this paper in 1790.
But it was the performance of a clerk—the undoubted work of
the family priest. The conjecture that Shakespeare's family were

[2] For extracts from this " Confession of Faith," and remarks thereon by
Drake, see Note at the conclusion of this chapter.

Roman Catholics is strengthened by the fact that his father declined to attend the Corporation meetings, and was at last removed from the corporate body."

" But," continues Chalmers, " this reasoning is confirmed by the consideration that the reign of Elizabeth was a period of *apparent* piety, and the reign of James I. an age *of religious speculation.* To own particular modes of faith became extremely fashionable during both those periods. It was probably by this fashion that Lord Bacon, the prince of philosophers, was induced to draw up *his Confession of Faith,* in order to please a monarch who interested himself in religious theories." [3]

" Every logician would infer," still continues Chalmers, " that if it (John Shakespeare's ' Catholic Confession of Faith ') had been the custom of the family, which was followed by the father, it is extremely probable the same custom would be also followed by the son, who at times cannot conceal *his faith,* even in his dramas."

This last surmise of Chalmers suggests the thought that the Great Fire of London, several fires at Stratford, and especially the fire by which the Globe Theatre was destroyed (to which accidents the absence of any scrap of William Shakespeare's handwriting has been attributed), may also be held to account for the non-appearance of any " Confession of Faith " on his part. It appears, by the allusion which Chalmers makes above to Lord Bacon's " Confession of Faith," that such religious documents were common in that age to men of all persuasions. Nevertheless they appear to have had a sort of solemn secrecy attached to them, and from what we gather from Dr. Drake's remark in a subjoined note it is not unlikely that Shakespeare's " Confession of Faith," if he made one, was quietly buried with him. Perhaps this particular fact was reliably known (through the Fulman papers) to the Rev. Richard Davies, who, writing after 1688, flatly says that " Shakespeare died a Papist." [4]

---

[3] "Chalmers's Apology," sect. v., pp. 198—200.

[4] The Rev. William Fulman, who died in 1688, bequeathed his biographical collections to his friend, the Rev. Richard Davies, rector of Sapperton, in Gloucestershire, who made several additions to them. Davies died in 1708, and these manuscripts were presented to the library of Corpus Christi College, Oxford, where they are still preserved. Under the article "Shakespeare" Fulman made very few notes, and those of little importance; but

"But are not the official situations held by Shakespeare's father in the borough conclusive against the opinion which Mr. Chalmers has grounded upon it?" indignantly exclaims a reverend biographer. Knight, in the same tone, says of the "Oath of Supremacy," which Shakespeare's father must have taken in order to hold office, that "to refuse this oath was made punishable with forfeiture and imprisonment, with the pains of *præmunire* and high treason." To such objections I think I have already opposed cogent reasons why the aspiring John Shakespeare should not have refused to take the oath, and these of themselves suggest why he should have so carefully concealed his "Catholic Confession of Faith."

If it is clear that the parents of William Shakespeare were both devout Catholics, it is reasonable to suppose that the poet followed the usual instinct of a child by imbibing the religious sentiment which filled his home, and which was breathed over him into his spiritual lungs, as it were, by his mother while he was lying in his cradle.

The first piece of proof we have upon this subject is very positive in its character. It comes from a clergyman who knew Shakespeare, and upon the examination of whose papers another clergyman, the Rev. Richard Davies, declares that the poet, who was born a Papist, died one. Surely it should require something

---

Davies inserted the curious information so important in the consideration of the deer-stealing story. The following is a complete copy of what the MS. contains respecting Shakespeare, distinguishing the addition made by Davies by italics :—

"William Shakespeare was born at Stratford-upon-Avon, in Warwickshire, about 1563 or '64. Much given to all unluckiness in stealing venison and rabbits, particularly from Sir — Lucy, who had him oft whipt and sometimes imprisoned, and at last made him fly his native country to his great advancement ; but his revenge was so great that he is his Justice Clodpate, and calls him a great man, and that in allusion to his name bore three louses rampant for his arms. From an actor of plays he became a composer. He died April 23, 1616, ætat. 53, probably at Stratford, for there he is buryed, and hath a monument (Dugd., p. 520) on which he lays a heavy curse upon any one who shall remove his bones. He dyed a papist."

This testimony has been doubted, because no such character as Clodpate occurs in any of Shakespeare's plays ; but it was a generic term of the time for a foolish person, and that Davies so used it there can, I think, be little doubt.—Halliwell, p. 123.

more than mere incredulity on the part of Protestant biographers to annihilate this authoritative statement.

The positive declaration of the Rev. Dr. Davies, founded as it was upon documentary and other evidence, furnished to him as a legacy by one who may be regarded almost as cotemporary with the poet, must therefore be taken as proof of that fact, not to be affected by any testimony less absolute in its character, and certainly not removed, unless sapped quite away by a steady and resistless flow of circumstantial evidence, breaking constantly as *our* proofs do, through the current of the poet's life, and continually dropping from him in his writings.

Unfortunately for the Protestant side of the argument, the first thing we fall upon in corroboration of the Rev. Dr. Davies' declaration, is the fact that it was made two years *previous to* the discovery by Mosely of John Shakespeare's "Confession of Faith." The next proof we have of the tendency of circumstances to keep William Shakespeare faithful to the precepts of his infancy is the Puritan persecution, by Sir Thomas Lucy and the other Protestant Commissioners of Stratford, of John Shakespeare, the father, and subsequent punishment by Sir Thomas of William the son. In London the young adventurer was immediately met by the same spirit of sectarian intolerance as had harassed his family in Stratford, and which again challenged him, as it were, upon the very threshold of his new efforts to pluck a living from the world. For we are told by the historians of the Shakespearian period that the contest which the Theatre had to undergo for an existence, about the time Shakespeare went up to London was between the holders of opposite opinions in religion. "The Puritans," says Knight, "made the Theatre the special object of their indignation." So the Protestant crusade, which began against Shakespeare's father, which had been continued against Shakespeare himself, before he arrived at man's estate in Stratford, maintained a ceaseless, unremitting warfare against his chosen avocation in the great metropolis.

Thus, having shown the religious conditions under which the poet's mind was formed, the pressure of circumstances operating upon his filial bent and tending to render inexorable the opinions thus initiated, we come logically to the examination of Shakespeare's personal testimony on the subjects of doctrine and religious faith, as exhibited in the spontaneous utterances of his plays.

I confess that I have, from the first, contemplated the discussion of this portion of my subject with some misgiving, but the manifest reluctance betrayed by most of the Shakespearian commentators to touch the question, and the disposition exhibited to follow in the beaten track, makes me less diffident than at the outset. The readiest instance which comes to me to illustrate this tendency of the reviewers to follow the old finger-posts, is 'the common idea that Shakespeare had such a miraculous poetic intuition that he needed no learning to acquire knowledge, as did other men. One of the familiar proofs which is offered of this wondrous faculty of the Bard of Avon is, the felicity and force with which they say he handles the mariner's art, and especially in the power and truth with which he describes the behaviour of a vessel in a gale.

"The very management of the ship in the 'Tempest,'" says one of these learned commentators, "may have been the fruit either of casual observation or of what men of letters call 'cram,' rapidly assimilated by his genius." And again, this same writer, in expressing his sense of the power of the poet's intuitive comprehension, directs our attention to that fine description in Henry the Eighth of "the outburst of admiration and loyalty of the multitude at sight of Anne Bullen, as if he (Shakespeare) had spent his life on shipboard."

> "Such a noise arose
> As the shrouds make at sea in a stiff tempest;
> As loud, and to as many tunes."

"And yet," concludes this writer, "*of all negative facts in regard to his* (Shakespeare's) *life, none, perhaps, is surer than that he never was at sea.*"[5] Why, who does not know that Shakespeare was an Englishman, and as such may be almost said to have been born at sea? The shores of England lie among roaring waves, and a poet can often find before his eyes as much turbulent, spiteful, howling, and dangerous water by looking from the cliff at Dover, or even from the jetty at Margate, as he would meet with in traversing a thousand miles at sea. Every Londoner who can afford a holiday goes to the seaside in summer, and a man who ventures in a fishing-boat a mile from shore on any portion of the English or Irish coast is as wide at sea—ay, and

---

[5] Richard Grant White's "Shakespeare," p. 259.

sometimes worse at sea than if he were wearily swinging round
Cape Horn. The Earl of Salisbury, who probably had never been
more at sea than Shakespeare, and who, like all Englishmen who
had travelled on the continent only, doubtless got all his knowledge of the ocean from the twenty-one mile trip between Dover
and Calais, in the English Channel, is made to say, in "King
John,"—

> "And like a shifted wind unto a sail,
> It makes the course of thoughts *to fetch about;*
> Startles and frights consideration."

This shows no more than that Shakespeare had at some time
been out on a fishing or boating excursion, or had looked upon
the chafing ocean from the land.

Mr. White, pursuing the same subject of Shakespeare's wonderful intuitiveness, says, "We may be very sure that he made no
special study of natural phenomena; and indeed no condition of
his life seems surer than that it afforded him neither time nor
opportunity for such studies. Yet, in the following lines from
the sixty-fourth sonnet, an important geological fact serves him
for illustration :—

> "When I have seen the hungry ocean gain
> Advantage on the kingdom of the shore,
> And the firm soil win of the watery main,
> Increasing store with loss, and loss with store. * * "

"Where, and how, and why had Shakespeare," exclaims Mr.
White, "observed a great operation of nature like this, which
takes many years to effect changes which are perceptible?" The
answer suggests itself—Why what New York boy, say we, who
has enjoyed holiday afternoons in visits to the beach at Coney
Island; or what Londoner who has made similar trips to portions of the English coast, has not seen the shore, one season
over-reached and devoured by the flood, receive restitution
during the next season by the ocean heaving the plunder
back to some adjacent spot? And pray where did Mr. White
get *his* knowledge of this phenomenon from? Did he get it
from his books? Again Mr. White, while defending Shakespeare with much warmth, from what he terms "the reproach of
Papistry," states that the Bard nowhere shows a leaning towards
any form of church government or towards any theological
tenet or dogma. And this, notwithstanding the poet's constant

allusions to holy friars, to shrift, to purging fires and confession ; is about as sensible as to declare him a moral writer, in face of the abominably foul-tongued characters of Parolles, Falstaff, and Doll Tear-Sheet.[6]

I find but one point made by Mr. White in favour of his declaration that Shakespeare was not a Roman Catholic, which appears at first sight to be well taken. "If Shakespeare became a member of the Church of Rome," says he, "it must have been after he wrote "Romeo and Juliet," in which he speaks of *evening mass;* for the humblest member of that church knows that there is no mass at vespers." A mistake which, I admit, that Bacon with his learning could not possibly have made; though Shakespeare might have done so; as it is doubtful if he ever heard mass performed either at Stratford or in London.

Reserving this point to be treated of in the next chapter, I herewith append the full confession of the "Confession of Faith" of John Shakespeare previously referred to.[7]

[6] In the famous scene between the Ghost and Hamlet there are many strokes of a Roman Catholic pen. "Shakespeare, apparently through *ignorance,*" says Warburton, "makes *Roman Catholics* of these Pagan Danes" (Steevens' Shak., 1793, vol. xv. pp. 72—75). But this is not so much an example of *ignorance* as of *knowledge*, though perhaps not of his prudence, when the poet avows, covertly indeed, his *own opinions*. In "Othello," Shakespeare makes Emilia say, "I should venture *purgatory* for't." The readers of Shakespeare will easily remember other expressions of a similar kind, which plainly proceeded from the overflow of Roman Catholic zeal. He is continually sending his characters to *shrift*, or confession : "Riddling *confession* finds but riddling *shrift ;*" "Bid her devise some means to come to *shrift* this afternoon." On the other hand he is studious to show his contempt for *the Puritans*. In "Twelfth Night" : "Marry, sir, he seems sometimes a kind of Puritan." In "The Winter's Tale" : "But one Puritan among them, and he sings psalms to hornpipers."—Chalmers's "Apology," p. 200.

[7] "JOHN SHAKESPEARE'S CONFESSION OF FAITH :—
Section I.

"'In the name of God, the Father, Sonne, and Holy Ghost, the most holy and blessed Virgin Mary, Mother of God, the holy host of archangels, angels, patriarchs, prophets, evangelists, apostles, saints, martyrs, and all the celestial court and company of heaven : I, John Shakspear, an unworthy member of the holy Catholic religion, being at this, my present writing, in perfect health of body, and sound mind, memory, and understanding, but calling to mind the uncertainty of life and certainty of death, and that I may be possibly cut off in the blossome of my sins, and called to render an account of all my transgressions externally and internally, and that I may be unprepared for the dreadful trial either by sacrement, pennance, fasting, or prayer, or any other purgation whatever, do in the holy presence above specified, of my own free and voluntary accord, make and ordaine this, my last spiritual will, testament, confession, protestation, and confession of faith, hopinge hereby to réceive pardon for all my sinnes and offences, and thereby to be made partaker of life everlasting, through the only merits of Jesus Christ, my saviour and redeemer, who took upon himself the likeness of man, suffered death, and was crucified upon the crosse, for the redemption of sinners.

[*Here follow the remaining sections, down to Section XIII. inclusive.*]
Section XIV., and last.

" ' I, John Shakspeare, having made this present writing of protestation, confession, and charter, in presence of the blessed Virgin Mary, my angell guardian, and all the celestial court, as witnesses hereunto: the which my meaning is, that it be of full value now, presently, and for ever, with the force and vertue of testament, codicil, and donation in course of death : confirming it anew, being in perfect health of soul and body, and signed with mine own hand ; carrying also the same about me, and for the better declararation hereof, my will and intention is that it be finally buried with me after my death.

" ' Pater noster, Ave Maria, Credo.
Jesu, son of David, have mercy on me.   Amen.' "

" If the intention of the testator, as expressed in the close of this will, were carried into effect, then of course the manuscript which Mosely found must necessarily have been a copy of that which was buried in the grave of John Shakespeare.

" Mr. Malone, to whom, in his edition of Shakespeare, printed in 1790, we are indebted for this singular paper, and for the history attached to it observes, that he is unable to ascertain whether it was drawn up by John Shakespeare, the father, or by John, his supposed eldest son : but he says, ' I have taken some pains to ascertain the authenticity of this manuscript, and, after a very careful inquiry, am perfectly satisfied that it is genuine.'   In the ' Inquiry,' however, which was published in 1796, relative to the Ireland papers, he has given us, though without assigning any reasons for his change of opinion, a very different result.   ' In my conjecture,' he remarks, ' concerning the writer of that paper, I certainly was mistaken : for I have since obtained documents that clearly prove it could not have been the composition of any one of our poet's family.'

" This conjecture of Mr. Chalmers appears to us in its leading points very plausible ; for that the father of our poet might be a Roman Catholic, is, if we consider the very unsettled state of his times with regard to religion, not only a possible, but a probable supposition, in which case it would undoubtedly have been the office of the spiritual director of the family to have drawn up such a paper as that which we have been perusing.   It was the fashion also of the period, as Mr. Chalmers has subsequently observed, to draw up confessions of religious faith, a fashion honoured in the observance by the great names of Lord Bacon, Lord Burghley, and Archbishop Parker. That he declined, however, attending the corporation meeting of Stratford from religious motives, and that. his removal from that body was the result of non-attendance from such a cause, cannot readily be admitted; for we have clearly seen that his defection was owing to pecuniary difficulties; nor is it in the least degree probable that, after having honourably filled the highest offices in the corporation without scruple, he should at length, and in a reign too popularly Protestant, incur expulsion from an avowed motive of this kind, especially, as we have reason to suppose, from the mode in which this profession was concealed, that the tenets of the person whose faith it declares were cherished in secret.

"From an accurate inspection of the handwriting of this will, Mr. Malone infers that it cannot be attributed to an earlier period than the year 1600, whence it follows that if dictated by, or drawn up at the desire of, John Shakespeare, his death soon sealed the confession of his faith; for, according to the register, he was buried on September 8, 1601."—Drake, vol. i. pp. 9—14.

CHAPTER VII.

EVENING MASS.

AT the conclusion of the last chapter we found ourselves confronted with the apparent difficulty of Shakespeare's alleged erroneous use of the word *evening* mass, and in pursuing the inquiry upon this point we have White's view supported by similar observations from H. von Friesen in his "Alt-England und William Shakespeare" (1874), pp. 286-7, and also by Staunton, who, says Dowden, "had previously noticed the same difficulty." But the word *mass*, continues Dowden, as used in the passage from "Romeo and Juliet," is explained by Clarke as meaning generally *service, office, prayer.*[1]

I do not find this explanation satisfactory, however; neither can I assign great importance to the opinion of Harness and others, that it was probably a printer's error, or at any rate not an error of Shakespeare's own, since it is well known that he had never superintended the publication of a single copy of his plays, and that some of the first copies "appeared to have been taken by the ear, during representation, without any assistance from the originals belonging to the play-houses." Hence, they conclude, that such a mistake might have easily crept in, through the ignorance of a copyist or printer. "Hundreds of spurious lines," says one of these reasoners, "have thus been insinuated in Shakespeare's text; and it is known that no complete collection of his plays was published until seven years after his death."

This is very plausible, but it must be recollected that "Romeo and Juliet" was published during the poet's lifetime, as early as 1597; and I cannot, therefore, bring myself to believe that Shakespeare could have permitted himself to be indifferent to such an error, had he believed it to have been an error.

[1] Dowden's "Shakespeare's Mind and Art," 1875, p. 39.

The greatest probability is that he had never heard mass otherwise than secretly, and in the evening; except, indeed, during some transient trip to Paris (if he had ever found time during his busy London life to make one); and even then it is doubtful if he would have spent any of his precious holiday hours at church. His general knowledge of the doctrines, dogmas, tenets, rites and formula of the Church of Rome might have been obtained from his mother, or from the carefully-hidden Prayer-book of the family; while his entire comprehension of the ceremony of mass was probably obtained from the hedge priests whom the devoted piety of his mother gave stealthy admission to the Shakespeare homestead, during the Elizabethan period of Catholic persecution. I have found many illustrations from Catholic reviews, and other reliable authorities, of the practices of the hedge priests, as they were called, in times of Catholic persecution, whose business it was to go in the darkness of the evening to the houses of the faithful, to celebrate a nocturnal mass. This was probably the case with Shakespeare's paternal home and family, and " evening mass " was doubtless the only mass our poet ever heard.[2]

In regard to mass in general, authoritative Romish works indicate that the main reason why it is fixed as a morning ceremony, is because owing to the extraordinary sanctity which Catholics attach to the consecrated elements (believing them as they do to be transubstantiated into the real body and blood of Christ), the early Popes deemed it irreverent on the part of the clergy and faithful to partake of them after a meal of a material kind. It would also seem, from the works of the most learned Catholic divines, that mass was said during that period of church history called " History of the Catacombs " at night; and

[2] " In the darkest days of the penal code, when learning was proscribed in Ireland, and when it was treason for the Catholic Celt to teach or be taught, to receive or communicate instruction, the hedge schoolmaster braved the terrors of the law, eluded the vigilance of spies, and kept the lamp of knowledge still burning in darkness, storm, and desolation. If we cherish the memory of the *Soggarth Aroon*, who often at dead of night fled to the mountain cave, the wooded glen, and wild rath to celebrate mass for the faithful and persecuted flock, and, like the Hebrew priests of old, to preserve the sacred fire till the dawn of a happier era, when the sun of freedom would kindle it into a blaze."—" Paper on Bishop England," by Professor Mulrenan; published in New York in the *Manhattan Monthly* for March, 1875.

indeed, in the Apostolic age it was undoubtedly a nocturnal service, since it is in reality only a commemoration of the Last Supper. According to the best authorities, it was Pope St. Telesphorus, A.D. 128, who ordered this service to be said in the morning at tierce, or at nine o'clock. This Pope likewise decreed that on Christmas eve a mass might be celebrated at twelve o'clock at night in honour of the Nativity, and he added to the missal the noble hymn of praise, Gloria in Excelsis. Still, even after the publication of this decree, masses were said, during periods of persecution, in the vaults and chapels of the catacombs quite late at night. Once the church emerged thence into broad day-light, this practice ceased, and the decree of Pope Telesphorus was obeyed to the letter.

During the middle ages even Catholic historians confess that many abuses crept into their Church, and it would seem that there were many gross ones concerning even the solemn rite of mass. The custom of saying mass for the dead was doubtless one of the principal causes of this deplorable state of affairs; for, as is well known, persons of rank and wealth would often leave in their wills large sums of money to the priests, in order to defray the expenses of a number of masses to be said for the repose of their souls, and of those of their relations and friends. To rid themselves of the obligation of celebrating so many masses, the dissolute and conscienceless amongst the clergy would even run one mass into another, or say as many as three and four in a morning, without leave from their ecclesiastical superiors.[3] They likewise invented a service called the *Missa Sicca*, which was generally said for the repose of the dead. It consisted of the recitation of the first part of mass, or *Introit*, and was a "dry mass," since none of the liquids were introduced into it; for, as already stated, the act of consecration did not take place. It was, however, called a mass, and was celebrated most frequently in the afternoon. The Council of Trent abolished it as a gross abuse, since it had occasioned much scandal. It sprang into existence towards the eleventh century, and continued down to the close of the sixteenth. It was an invention doubtless of some unworthy clergymen, in order to free themselves of a portion of the numerous masses they were paid to say for the dead. It

[3] See Appleton's "Encyclopædia," 1875, Father O'Reilly's article on the Mass.

could be said at any time, and as often as they chose, and hence
they could naturally rid themselves of their responsibility at a
very short notice; moreover, as they could only solemnize one
genuine mass a day, without running the risk of being suspended
by their bishops, they could say twenty of these mutilated
services, and count them to their purchasers as regular work.
It is not improbable, besides, that this *Missa Sicca* was known to
the common people before the Reformation as "evening mass."
For in Ivanhoe, Sir Walter Scott says that Rowena arrived late
at the banquet, as she had only just returned from attending
"evening mass" at a neighbouring priory. It seems to me
that Scott, who was exceedingly well versed in all things concerning the history and rites of the Catholic Church, would not
have made this statement unless he had good authority for so
doing.[4] Shakespeare may have heard of the *Missa Sicca* as an
evening service, and thus alluded to it in this play; and it may
as well here be observed that the monastery to which Friar
Laurence belonged was a Franciscan house, which order was,
and is still, remarkable—to use the Catholic phraseology[5]— "for
its devotion to the dead and to the souls in purgatory;" in other
words, for its popularity in praying and saying masses for the
departed. Another explanation of this much disputed phrase,
"evening mass," may also be gathered from the fact that in
Catholic countries, to this day, the fashionable mass is the last;
said often at one, and even at two o'clock in the afternoon.
In the sixteenth century, one or two o'clock in the day was
already a late hour, for people rose at five, breakfasted at six,
dined between ten and eleven, and had supper at seven in the
evening; thus closing the day at an hour when modern "society"
is most occupied. Shakespeare may have considered the last, or
one o'clock mass, "an evening mass;" and this is not so improbable, since the text leads us to understand that Juliet designs to wait upon him in his cell alone, which she could
not have done under the circumstances of the play, as a young

---

[4] On the other hand, by way of showing the habitual licence of poets, we
will direct the attention of the reader to the following lines from the exquisite
poem of "Under the Violets," by Oliver Wendell Holmes:—

> "The crickets, sliding through the grass,
>   Shall pipe for her an evening mass."

[5] "History of the Franciscans." Albany, Baxter and Co.

girl of her age would certainly not have been allowed out alone at midnight.

There is another piece of textual testimony which the Protestant biographers of Shakespeare refer to, in order to resist the theory that he was of the Roman Catholic faith. It is put forward in its most prominent form by Charles Knight, who, combatting the inferences of Chalmers and Drake in favour of Shakespeare's Romanism as evinced in his frequent references to "purgatory," "shrift," "confession," &c., in his dramas, says, "Surely the poet might exhibit this familiarity with the ancient language of all Christendom without thus speaking from the overflow of Roman Catholic zeal." Was it "Roman Catholic zeal" which induced him to write those strong lines in "King John" against the "Italian priest," and against those who

"Purchase corrupted pardon of a man"?

Was it "Roman Catholic zeal" which made him introduce these words into the famous prophecy of the glory and happiness of the reign of Elizabeth :—

"God shall be truly known"?

The first of the quotations by Knight looks very formidable; and when I read the above artificial presentation of it I fancied I had run against an insurmountable obstacle to the theory that Shakespeare was a Roman Catholic. But turning to the fountain of the phrase in the body of the text, I found that the quotation had been warped from its true meaning by the critic, and made, by a few accompanying words, to present a proposition which was not the author's. No one could read Knight's presentation of the quotation, along with his unwarranted words, without supposing it was launched not only against the one person addressed, but against *all* "*those* who purchased ' corrupted' pardon of a man," or without coming to the conclusion that Shakespeare meant to deride and reject the sanctity of that vital principle of the Roman Catholic faith, the rite of confession—and the consequent prerogatives of punishment and absolution ! And I readily admit that no Roman Catholic writer could ever have permitted himself to do this under any pressure of poetical necessity. But William Shakespeare never did it—never in the plays ascribed to him, at least.

The line above quoted by Knight against Shakespeare's Catholicity is addressed by King John to King Philip Augustus of France, and applies to Pandulph, the Legate of the Pope, who had then recently been despatched from Rome to England, to demand of King John the immediate appointment of Stephen Langton, the Pope's nominee, to the archbishopric of Canterbury on pain of excommunication ; and also to interrogate him (King John) why he had thus far been contumacious to the supreme orders of his Holiness in this respect. Pandulph, in pursuance of this insolent commission, finds John in France, at the head of an English army of invasion, confronting a like array of the French legions under the command of Philip. Seizing the opportunity thus afforded him of making his insolence the more conspicuous, Pandulph, in the presence of the two kings, surrounded by their respective nobles, delivers his arrogant message. The English king is naturally roused to anger and resistance by this insult, whereupon Shakespeare, through the mouth of John, treats the prelate in the political attitude he had assumed, and makes John speak with the spirit and dignity which became an English king. The practice of " fitting " his characters, is invariable with our poet, and is also in full accordance with dramatic rules and common sense. It is in agreement, likewise, with the practice of other Roman Catholic writers, as may be seen in the treatment given by Dumas to the Cardinals Mazarin and Richelieu. When the churchman sinks his profession in the character of an ambassador, he is dealt with as a politician ; and when a king (whom, as a king, Shakespeare always worships upon bended knees) abandons himself to crime and despotism, he is always, as in the case of Richard III. and of John also, treated as a tyrant and a murderer. In these crimes the assassin sinks the king ; as the primate, by his ambition, veils the priest. It was the only method by which the poet could protect his faith from the necessities of history, and consequently the epithets he uses through the mouths of his incensed characters, as " false priest " and " meddling priest," are only such as are irresistible to anger under any and all circumstances. Shakespeare was too well versed in human nature not to know that an inflamed mind will always assail its enemy where he is most false, and consequently where he is most weak—always preferring an accusation of hypocrisy to any other. But here I prefer to let the text speak to the reader for itself :—

KING JOHN, Act III. Scene 1.

France—the French King's tent.   Present—King John, King Philip,
Archduke of Austria, Faulconbridge, Lewis, the French Dauphin, Salis-
bury, Arthur, Constance, Blanche, Elinor, and attendants.

Enter PANDULPH.

K. PHI.   Here comes the holy legate of the pope.
PAND.   Hail, you anointed deputies of Heaven!
To thee, king John, my holy errand is,
I Pandulph, of fair Milan cardinal,
And from pope Innocent the legate here,
Do, in his name, religiously demand,
Why thou against the church, our holy mother,
So wilfully dost spurn; and, force perforce,
Keep Stephen Langton, chosen archbishop
Of Canterbury, from that holy see?
This, in our 'foresaid holy father's name,
Pope Innocent, I do demand of thee.

K. JOHN.   What earthly name to interrogatories
Can task the free breath of a sacred king?
Thou canst not, cardinal, devise a name
So slight, unworthy, and ridiculous,
To charge me to an answer, as the pope.
Tell him this tale; and from the mouth of England
Add thus much more,—That no Italian priest
Shall tithe or toll in our dominions;
But as we under heaven are supreme head,
So, under Him, that great supremacy
Where we do reign, we will alone uphold
Without the assistance of a mortal hand;
So tell the pope; all reverence set apart,
To him, and his usurp'd authority.

K. PHI.   Brother of England, you blaspheme in this.
K. JOHN.   Though you, and all the kings of Christendom,
Are led so grossly by this meddling priest,
Dreading the curse that money may buy out;
And by the merit of vile gold, dross, dust,
Purchase corrupted pardon of a man,
Who, in that sale, sells pardon from himself;
Though you, and all the rest, so grossly led,
This juggling witchcraft with revenue cherish;
Yet I, alone, alone do me oppose
Against the Pope, and count his friends my foes.

PAND.   Then by the lawful power that I have,
Thou shalt stand cursed, and excommunicate:
And blessed shall he be that doth revolt
From his allegiance to an heretic:

And meritorious shall that hand be call'd,
Canonized, and worshipp'd as a saint,
That takes away by any secret course
Thy hateful life.

*   *   *   *   *   *

        Philip of France, on peril of a curse,
Let go the hand of that arch-heretic;
And raise the power of France upon his head,
Unless he do submit himself to Rome.

*   *   *   *   *   *

K. Phi. My reverend father, let it not be so:
        Out of your grace, devise, ordain, impose
        Some *gentle* order; and then we shall be bless'd
        To do your pleasure, and continue friends.

Pand. All form is formless, order orderless,
        Save what is opposite to England's love.
        Therefore, to arms, be champion of our church!
        Or let the church, our mother, breathe her curse,
        A mother's curse, on her revolting son.
        France, thou may'st hold a serpent by the tongue,
        A chafed lion by the mortal paw,
        A fasting tiger safer by the tooth,
        Than keep, in peace, that hand which thou dost hold.

*   *   *   *   *   *

Lew. I muse, your majesty doth seem so cold,
        When such profound respects do pull you on.
Pand. I will denounce a curse upon his head.
K. Phi. Thou shalt not need:—England, I'll fall from thee.
K. John. France, thou shalt rue this hour within this hour.

In the light of these quotations it becomes obvious that Knight's presentation of the first italicized line, with its inferential words, had the object of making it appear that Shakespeare was deriding and mocking at the sanctity of the rite of confession; and this plain perversion of the author's meaning was, consequently, not only an abuse of the truth, but an insult, by Mr. Knight, to the understanding of his readers. The whole scene represents no independent sentiment of Shakespeare as a writer, any more than does the language of John, when he orders Hubert to commit murder upon Arthur, represent Shakespeare's sentiments; or than the words of Richard III. represent the poet's principles, when Richard directs the assassination of the Princes in the Tower. But we can perceive by the course of the play of King John, where the poet *does* step in and takes sides; and, when he does make his individual inclinations thus seen, he decides most

5

signally in favour of the Prelate and the Church. He shows that John, on the contrary, with all his resolution and surroundings, cannot withstand its power, but surrenders to it, humbles himself abjectly before the Legate, and is finally consigned to an ignominious death. In the scene immediately following the above, we find King John, while still in the height of his resentment, giving an order to his creature, Faulconbridge, to hasten to England, and ransack and plunder the monasteries :—

KING JOHN (*to the Bastard*),

    Cousin, away to England; haste before;
    And, ere our coming, see thou shake the bags
    Of hoarding abbots; imprisoned angels
    Set at liberty: the fat ribs of peace
    Must by the hungry now be fed upon:
    Use our commission in his *utmost force!*

BASTARD. Bell, book, and candle shall not drive me back,
    When gold and silver becks me 'to come on.

At the opening of Act V. we find that King John, unable to contend any longer, even in his own dominions, against the power of the Pope, makes absolute submission and resigns his crown, in order that he may undergo the utter humiliation of receiving it back from his haughty hands and of holding it subject to his breath :—

Act V.—*A Room in the Palace.*

Enter KING JOHN, PANDULPH *with the crown, and attendants.*

K. JOHN. Thus have I yielded up into you hand
    The circle of my glory.

PAND.   Take again [*Giving* JOHN *the crown.*
    From this my hand, as holding of the pope,
    Your sovereign greatness and authority.

K. JOHN. Now keep your holy word: go meet the French:
    And from his holiness use all your power
    To stop their marches, 'fore we are inflamed.
    Our discontented counties do revolt;
    Our people quarrel with obedience
    Swearing allegiance, and the love of soul,
    To stranger blood, to foreign royalty.
    This inundation of mistemper'd humour
    Rests by you only to be qualified.
    Then pause not; for the present time's so sick,
    That present medicine must be minister'd,
    Or overthrow incurable ensues.

PAND. It was my breath that blew this tempest up,
Upon your stubborn usage of the pope :
But, since you are a gentle convertite,
My tongue shall hush again this storm of war,
And make fair weather in your blustering land.
On this Ascension-day, remember well,
Upon your oath of service to the pope,
Go I to make the French lay down their arms.

Here the Pope's Legate finishes with John. Now let us see what luck the poet assigns to Pandulph, in his assumptions of Papal supremacy over the King of France. Carrying out his contract with King John, Pandulph next appears before the French forces, which, under the charge of Lewis the Dauphin, have invaded England, and are lying in camp near St. Edmunds-Bury :—

Act V. Scene 2.

Present—LEWIS, *the* DAUPHIN, SALISBURY, MELUN, PEMBROKE, BIGOT, *and Soldiers.*

Enter PANDULPH, *attended.*

LEW. And even there, methinks, an angel spake ;
Look, where the holy legate comes apace,
To give us warrant from the hand of heaven ;
And on our actions set the name of right, ·
With holy breath.

PAND.   Hail, noble prince of France ;
The next is this—King John hath reconcil'd
Himself to Rome : his spirit is come in,
That so stood out against the holy church,
The great metropolis and see of Rome ;
Therefore, thy threat'ning colours now wind up,
And tame the savage spirit of wild war ;
That, like a lion foster'd up at hand,
It may lie gently at the foot of peace,
And be no further harmful than in show.

LEW. Your grace shall pardon me, I will not back ;
I am too high-born to be propertied,
To be a secondary at control,
Or useful serving-man, and instrument,
To any sovereign state throughout the world.
Your breath first kindled the dead coal of wars
Between this chastised kingdom and myself,
And brought in matter that should feed this fire ;
And now 'tis far too huge to be blown out
With that same weak wind which enkindled it.

> You taught me how to know the face of right,
> Acquainted me with interest to this land,
> Yea, thrust this enterprise into my heart;
> And come you now to tell me, John hath made
> His peace with Rome?   What is that peace to me?
> I, by the honour of my marriage-bed,
> After young Arthur, claim this land for mine;
> And, now it is half conquer'd, must I back,
> Because that John hath made his peace with Rome?
> Am I Rome's slave?   What penny hath Rome borne,
> What men provided, what munition sent,
> To underprop this action?   is't not I,
> That undergo this charge?   Who else but I,
> And such as to my claim are liable,
> Sweat in this business, and maintain this war?
> Have I not heard these islanders shout out,
> *Vive le roy!* as I have bank'd their towns?
> Have I not here the best cards for the game,
> To win this easy match play'd for a crown?
> And shall I now give o'er the yielded set?
> No, on my soul, it never shall be said.

PAND.   You look but on the outside of this work.
LEW.   Outside, or inside, I will not return
> Till my attempt so much be glorified—
> As to my ample hope was promised
> Before I drew this gallant head of war,
> And cull'd these fiery spirits from the world,
> To outlook conquest, and to win renown
> Even in the jaws of danger and of death.

The Legate then curses the other side, whereupon the fight takes place, and the French, as becomes them, under the effects of Pandulph's new anathema, get the worst of it; but King John is led from the field sick during the middle of the mêlée, and retires to Swinstead Abbey in the neighbourhood. In the following scene his approaching death is thus described, and the lines I have italicized are those which the Protestant biographers stoutly rely upon to show that Shakespeare could not have been a Roman Catholic :—

HUBERT. *The king, I fear, is poisoned by a monk :*
> I left him almost speechless, and broke out
> To acquaint you with this evil, that you might
> The better arm you to the sudden time,
> Than if you had at leisure known of this.
BASTARD. How did he take it?   Who did *taste* to him?

HUBERT. *A monk, I tell you ; a resolved villain,*
Whose bowels suddenly burst out : the king
Yet speaks, and peradventure may recover.

The monk who did this deed had evidently prepared himself to carry out Pandulph's curse of excommunication, and also to revenge John's sacrilegious plunder of the monasteries. In those days of the absence of newspapers, this monk doubtless had not been informed of the very recent pardon of John by Pandulph, and therefore, instead of being regarded as "a resolved villain," as Hubert, King John's minion, naturally terms him, he would be esteemed by the faithful, for this brave devotion of himself, as being worthy rather of "canonization" (which, indeed, was promised by Pandulph) and a high place "among the glorious company of the apostles" than of harsh terms, or any form of condemnation whatsoever. That the monk had long been "resolved" in his purpose of poisoning the King and to that extent was "a resolved villain, is evident from the fact that it must have cost him much time and considerable court influence to become "taster" to his Majesty, as a preliminary to the glorious canonization which he expected, for carrying out the orders of the Legate, at the expense of his own life.

As to Knight's second exception to Shakespeare's Catholicity, I deem it hardly worthy of an argument. The prophecy made in the play of "Henry VIII.," that under the reign of the infant Elizabeth

"God shall be truly known,"

is the expression of Cranmer, a Protestant prelate, and it is put into his mouth by the author during the reign of Protestant James I., through whose graciousness he still got his living as one of "her Majesty's players." Besides, the expression as to the worship of God the Father is as correct, in a Christian sense, in the mouth of a Roman Catholic as in that of a Protestant. Moreover, the speech of Cranmer, containing the above line, is almost universally attributed to Ben Jonson, who wrote it in compliment to King James.

This seems to meet the Protestant arguments based upon the text of "King John." We come next to the evidence offered on the same side from "King Henry VI.," Parts I. and II.

Two of the principal characters in both these plays are

Humphrey Duke of Gloster, brother of the deceased Henry V., and the Duke of Beaufort, who is Bishop of Winchester, and subsequently Cardinal Beaufort. Gloster, who was brother to the deceased Henry V., is Lord Protector of the infant Henry VI., and, being beloved by the people, is popularly known throughout the country by the name of the Good Duke Humphrey. In fact, the original title of the latter of these plays was " The Second Part of King Henry the Sixth, with the Death of the Good Duke Humphrey." The Bishop of Winchester, on the other hand, is shown by all the histories of the time to have been a lewd, unprincipled, treacherous, conspiring, and bloody-minded villain, as bad in every respect as Iago, Angelo, or Edmund. The part which he performs is entirely political, and his principal aim is to supplant the Lord Protector, whom he finally succeeds in having basely murdered. These two characters come in conflict at the very outset of the dramatic history of " Henry VI." The first scene of their contention takes place before the Tower, into which the Lord Protector, though entitled to arbitrary access to all public places in the realm, finds himself and his retainers refused admittance by the servants and followers of the Bishop of Winchester, who are in possession. While Gloster is clamouring at the gates, and threatening, by virtue of his supreme authority, to burst them open, the following scene occurs in Act I. Scene 3 :—

Enter WINCHESTER, *attended by a train of Servants in tawny coats.*

 WIN. How now, ambitious Humphrey ? what means this ?
 GLO. Piel'd priest, dost thou command me to be shut out ?
 WIN. I do, thou most usurping proditor,
  And not protector of the king or realm.
 GLO. Stand back, thou manifest conspirator ;
  Thou, that contriv'dst to murder our dead lord ;
  Thou, that giv'st bawds [6] indulgences to sin :
  I'll canvas thee in thy broad cardinal's hat,
  If thou proceed in this thy insolence.

---

[6] I have changed this word, for the purpose of these pages, out of regard for modern ears. The curious reader may consult the text. The line, and the reproach which it conveys, will be better understood when it is known that " the public stews in Southwark were under the jurisdiction of the Bishop of Winchester. In the office-book of the court all fees were entered that were paid by the keepers of these brothels—the church reaping the advantages of these pests to society."

WIN. Nay, stand thou back, I will not budge a foot:
This be Damascus, be thou cursed Cain,
To slay thy brother Abel, if thou wilt.

GLO. I will not slay thee, but I'll drive thee back:
Thy scarlet robes, as a child's bearing cloth
I'll use, to carry thee out of this place.

WIN. Do what thou dar'st: I beard thee to thy face.

GLO. What? am I dar'd, and bearded to my face?—
Draw, men, for all this privileged place;
Blue coats to tawny coats.   Priest, beware your beard;
        [GLOSTER *and his men attack the Bishop.*
I mean to tug it, and to cuff you soundly:
Under my feet I stamp thy cardinal's hat;
In spite of pope, or dignities of church,
Here by the cheeks I'll drag thee up and down.

WIN. Gloster, thou'lt answer this before the pope.

The two parties are here about falling upon one another when the Mayor of London enters with his officers, and commands the peace, whereupon Gloster, out of respect for the law, at once calls off his men, and says,—

GLO. Cardinal,[7] I'll be no breaker of the law:
But we shall meet, and break our minds at large.

WIN. Gloster, we'll meet; to thy dear cost be sure:
Thy heart-blood I will have, for this day's work.

MAYOR. I'll call for clubs, if you will not away:
This cardinal is more haughty than the devil.

GLO. Mayor, farewell: thou dost but what thou may'st.

WIN. Abominable Gloster! guard thy head;
For I intend to have it, ere long.   [*Exeunt.*

In a subsequent scene Gloster says to Winchester:—

Thou art reverent
Touching thy spiritual function, not thy life.

Thus showing that he is neither a questioner of Winchester's religion, nor a heretic himself.

Again, after Winchester has been created cardinal, he challenges Gloster to a duel, which is finally settled by King Henry. In Act III. Scene 1, Queen Margaret and Suffolk, her paramour, plot with York and Beaufort Gloster's assassination, and thus the Cardinal :—

---

[7] The use of the word Cardinal in this place shows that Shakespeare was not always precise in his expressions. Beaufort at this time was only Bishop of Winchester.

> But I would lay him dead, my lord of Suffolk,
> Ere you can take due orders for a priest:
> Say, you consent, and censure well the deed,
> And I'll provide his executioner.

The assassination is performed in pursuance of this conspiracy, and the following is the scene of the conscience-stricken murderer's death-bed :—

Cardinal Beaufort's Bedchamber.

Enter KING HENRY, SALISBURY, WARWICK, *and others.* *The* CARDINAL *in bed; Attendants with him.*

K. HEN. How fares my lord? speak, Beaufort, to thy sovereign.
CAR. If thou be'st death, I'll give thee England's treasure,
  Enough to purchase such another island,
  So thou wilt let me live, and feel no pain.
K. HEN. Ah, what a sign it is of evil life,
  When death's approach is seen so terrible!
WAR. Beaufort, it is thy sovereign speaks to thee.
CAR. Bring me unto my trial when you will.
  Died he not in his bed? where should he die?
  Can I make men live, whe'r they will or no?—
  O! torture me no more, I will confess.—
  Alive again? then show me where he is:
  I'll give a thousand pound to look upon him.
  He hath no eyes, the dust hath blinded them.—
  Comb down his hair; look! look! it stands upright,
  Like lime-twigs set to catch my winged soul!—
  Give me some drink; and bid the apothecary
  Bring the strong poison that I bought of him.
K. HEN. O thou eternal Mover of the heavens,
  Look with a gentle eye upon this wretch!
  O, beat away the busy meddling fiend,
  That lays strong siege unto this wretch's soul,
  And from his bosom purge this black despair!
WAR. See how the pangs of death do make him grin.
SAL. Disturb him not, let him pass peaceably.
K. HEN. Peace to his soul, if God's good pleasure be!
  Lord cardinal, if thou think'st on heaven's bliss,
  Hold up thy hand, make signal of thy hope.—
  He dies, and makes no sign; O God forgive him!
WAR. So bad a death argues a monstrous life.
K. HEN. Forbear to judge, for we are sinners all.—
  Close up his eyes, and draw the curtains close;
  And let us all to meditation.   [*Exeunt.*

At this point I desire to call attention to the king's use of the word "meditation," which is a form of Catholic worship, or pious practice, prescribed by the Romish Church for certain hours. King Henry, as a Catholic, had doubtless observed this devotion, and, of course, referred to it; but William Shakespeare could hardly have made this doctrinal reference to it unless he had been a Catholic himself.

By the foregoing extracts from the text, it will be seen that the parties were all Catholics together; and the assumption that the author, because he makes one of them berate another, and reproach him with misrepresenting his clerical pretensions, is, therefore, not a Catholic, seems to me to be without much force. Against this theory we find Gloster distinctly recognizing Beaufort's faith, though he reprehends the sinfulness of the man; while King Henry himself, the leading feature of whose character is devoted piety, consigns the accursed Cardinal to hell. Had Shakespeare been writing under the suspicion that the sincerity of his own faith might at some day be questioned for the freedom with which he makes Duke Humphrey curse the Cardinal, he could not have provided a more complete justification of his unswerving Romanism, or devised a more perfect excuse for his maledictions of the Cardinal, than is made by the pious king, when, looking in vain to see the dying wretch hold up his hand for mercy from his God, he sadly exclaims,—

" He dies, and makes no sign."

Henry, in this exclamation, means of course no sign of repentance, without which, according to Catholic doctrine, no sinner can be allowed to enter heaven.

CHAPTER VIII.

SHAKESPEARE'S CONTEMPT FOR PROTESTANTS.

THE determination of the English biographers of William Shakespeare to resist the theory that he was a Papist, is actuated by entirely different motives from those which govern our present inquiry. Their object is to defend to the Protestant persuasion, the prestige of a writer who, in his influence over the minds of the English people, is next in authority to God, and who has devoted the highest efforts of his genius to the constant inculcation of the most submissive loyalty to the aristocratic classes and the Crown.

The question of the religious faith of the author of the Shakespeare plays was of very trivial importance to the governing classes of Great Britain at the time when Shakespeare wrote, and, indeed, for some time afterward. At the date of his career, the country had barely emerged from universal Romanism ; and the old faith received its first wound under Henry VIII., who died only seventeen years before Shakespeare was born. The blow which Henry struck at the Church, moreover, was known to be one of politics rather than of faith. Besides, that faith, still suppressed during the short reign of Edward VI., was revived throughout the land by his daughter, Bloody Mary, in seven years after his decease, (1553), which pious princess enforced its re-establishment, after the earnest manner of her estimable father, by a persuasive multiplicity of burnings and boilings in oil of all stubborn Nonconformists.

Protestantism was again restored by Elizabeth and James, whose reigns covered Shakespeare's period. But no influence which he or any writer for the stage then possessed, was of the least importance to the Government. Churchmen at that time were either politicians or wore coats of mail, and conformity was secured for the established faith by sheriffs' officers or files of troops. These were tendencies which even the Muse of Shakespeare was bound to respect, and, instead of looking through his plays for distinct evidences of adherence to a doctrine which would not only have stripped him of his friends at court, but lost him the favour of both the last-named sovereigns, the wonder should rather be that, under such great temptations to be politic, he never was induced to allude to a Protestant without contempt. Indeed, the only Lutheran he ever permitted to escape from the point of his pen without a stab was Cranmer, who baptized Queen Elizabeth. The evidences of this contempt by Shakespeare for the Protestant persuasion may be found in his portraiture of Sir Hugh Evans, the Welsh parson, in "The Merry Wives of Windsor," described as a vain, profane, pragmatic, obscene creature, who frequents taverns, engages in a duel, and enters readily into a plot to pervert a marriage;[1] also of Nathaniel and of Holofernes,[2] respectively a country curate and a Protestant pedagogue, in "Love's Labours Lost," and likewise of Sir Oliver Martext[3] in "As You Like It." All of these three are mere

[1] See "The Merry Wives of Windsor," Act III. Scene 1.

[2] "Love's Labours Lost," Act IV. Scene 2:—

Scene—Sir NATHANIEL, *the* CURATE, *and* HOLOFERNES.

NATH. Sir, I praise the Lord for you; and so may my parishioners; for their sons are well tutor'd by you, and their daughters profit very greatly under you: you are a good member of the commonwealth.

HOL. *Mehercle*, if their sons be ingenious, they shall want no instruction: if their daughters be capable, I will put it to them: but, *vir sapit, qui pauca loquitur:* a soul feminine saluteth us.

[3] "As You Like it," Act III. Scene 2:—

Scene—TOUCHSTONE, AUDREY, *and* JAQUES.

TOUCH. But be it as it may be, I will marry thee, and to that end, I have been with Sir Oliver Martext, the vicar of the next village; who hath promised to meet me in this place of the forest, and to couple us.

. . . .

Enter SIR OLIVER MARTEXT.

Here comes Sir Oliver:—Sir Oliver Martext, you are well met. Will you despatch us here under this tree, or shall we go with you to your chapel?

SIR OLIV. Is there none here to give the woman?

TOUCH. I will not take her on the gift of any man.

. . . .

JAQ. And will you, being a man of your breeding, be married under a bush, like a beggar? Get you to church, *and have a good priest that can tell you what marriage is: this fellow will but join you together as they*

buffoons, while the " Twelfth Night " is made to contribute its
quota of derisive presentation of Protestant character by an
illusory drunken parson called Sir Topas;[4] though the Roman

join wainscot: then one of you will prove a 'shrunk pannel, and, like green
timber, warp, warp.

TOUCH. I am not in the mind, but I were better to be married of him
than of another ; for he is not like to marry me well ; and not being well
married, it will be a good excuse for me hereafter to leave my wife. [*Aside.*

JAQ. Go thou with me, and let me counsel thee.

TOUCH. Come, sweet Audrey,
We must be married, or we must live in bawdry.
Farewell, good master Oliver !
[*Exeunt* JAQUES, TOUCHSTONE, *and* AUDREY.

SIR OLIV. 'Tis no matter; ne'er a fantastical knave of them all shall flout
me out of my calling. [*Exit.*

4 " Twelfth Night," Act II. Scene 3 :—

Scene—SIR TOBY BELCH, MARIA, *and* SIR ANDREW.

SIR TO. Possess us, possess us ; tell us something of him.

MAR. Marry, sir, sometimes he is a kind of Puritan.

SIR AND. O if I thought that, I'd beat him like a dog.

SIR TO. What, for being a Puritan ? Thy exquisite reason, dear knight?

SIR AND. I have no exquisite reason for't, but I have reason good enough.

MAR. The devil a Puritan that he is, or anything constantly but a time-
pleaser ; an affection'd ass.

Act IV. Scene 2.—SIR TOBY BELCH, MARIA, *and* CLOWN *as* SIR TOPAS,
the Parson.

SIR TOBY. Jove bless thee, master parson.

CLOWN (*to Sir Toby*). *Bonos dies*, Sir Toby ; for, as the old hermit of
Prague, that never saw pen and ink, very wittily said to a niece of King
Gorboduc, *That, that is, is ;* so I, being master parson, am master parson.
For what is that, but that ? and is, but is ?

SIR TO. To him, Sir Topas.

MOCK SIR T. What, hoa, I say—peace in this prison.

SIR TO. The knave counterfeits well : a good knave.

MAL. (*in an inner chamber*). Who calls there?

CLOWN. Sir Topas, the curate, who comes to visit Malvolio, the lunatic.

MAL. Sir Topas, Sir Topas, good Sir Topas, go to my lady.

CLOWN. Out, hyperbolical fiend ! how vexest thou this man ? Talkest
thou nothing but of ladies?

SIR TO. Well said, master parson.

MAL. Sir Topas, never was man thus wronged; good Sir Topas, do not
think I am mad; they have laid me here in hideous darkness.

CLOWN. Fye, thou dishonest Sathan ! I call thee by the most modest

Catholic priest of the same play is most respectfully alluded to. In this reverent tone Shakespeare treats all his Romish clergymen; so if he were really a Protestant, as the English biographers stubbornly insist, it is most extraordinary that, with a Protestant court to write to, and a Protestant people to cater for, his mind was never tempted by the high motive of religion into a single invocation of the faith that filled his soul !

It was not foreseen in Shakespeare's time that his intellectual supremacy over all the intellects of his own nation would acquire for him an amount of moral power which a sagacious government, whether in its legal, religious, or its merely political departments, could not afford to leave unutilized. In degree, as coats of mail were laid aside, the consent of the governed became an increasing element in the control of the State; and then it was found that scholarship and genius were worthy of being officially patted on the back, as, for instance, through the appointment of poets-laureate; or of writers cleverly subsidized in cozy government nooks, with comfortable sinecures. Of all the representatives of the new forces of civilization, Shakespeare, since his hour, has uninterruptedly remained the chief. His progress for a time was tardy, but like the thin column of vapour which slowly curled from the magician's lamp, his genius kept rising and spreading itself before the wondering English people, until it covered the whole heaven of their comprehension,

terms; for I am one of those gentle ones that will use the devil himself with courtesy. Say'st thou that house is dark?

MAL. As hell, Sir Topas.

The Same.—*Scene 3.*
SEBASTIAN, OLIVIA, *and a Priest.*

OLIV. Blame not this haste of mine : If you mean well,
Now go with me, *and with this holy man,*
Into the chantry by : there, before him,
And underneath that consecrated roof,
Plight me the full assurance of your faith ;
That my most jealous and too doubtful soul
May live at peace : he shall conceal it,
Whiles you are willing it shall come to note ;
What time we will our celebration keep
According to my birth.—What do you say?

SEB. *I'll follow this good man,* and go with you ;
And, having sworn truth, ever will be true.
Then lead the way, *good father ;*—And heavens so shine,
That they may fairly note this act of mine ! [*Exeunt.*

and they bowed amazedly before it, utterly enraptured by its glory. Nay, such is the service which, with all his faults, our poet has rendered to mankind, it is not too much to say, that were the two separate questions put, to every man of the English-speaking race who can read and write, as to what was the greatest benefaction God ever made to man? and to whom each of them was indebted for the greatest amount of intellectual pleasure he had enjoyed on earth? the unstudied and immediate answer would be Shakespeare! To the question of who next? the reply of the present generation most likely would be, Dickens— true to his class, true to morality, and the Apostle of the Poor!

It is difficult for Americans who have never been in England to conceive to what an extent religion enters into the machinery of the British government. In fact, the Episcopal Church of England has not only one-third of the actual government in the hands of its representatives in the House of Lords, but it has gradually organized itself into a regular "industry," which covers the land with swarms of its dependents, represents accumulated salaries and annual incomes to the extent of millions upon millions of money, and is, in every respect, as much of an organized business, in the sense of an industry, as the industries of making boots and shoes, of the raising of beeves or of the growing of corn. So potent is this Industry of Religion in the machinery of the British realm, that it claims one day out of every seven, or nearly one-seventh part of the entire year, as a concession to its importance; and this, too, to the subordination of every interest else. It is not to be wondered at, therefore, that this great Episcopal power will permit no traffic but its own, on what it terms the Lord's Day; that it will suffer no doors to be opened in English cities for the transaction of business of any sort, during the hours of service, but church doors, and tolerate no sounds at that time but the sound of church bells. In every other portion of the civilized world (except in the United States, which still retains its tendency for English opinion), and under every form of religion but that of the English Episcopal Church, Sunday is free, and The People enjoy their usual pastimes, even to the extent of going to the races or to the theatres, accompanied often, as I have seen in Rome, France, Italy, Spain, and in other Catholic countries of North and South America, by their religious guides and teachers. The strange feature of this annihilation of the liberty of the Lord's Day is the servile following which the English political Sunday has in the United States; and that, too, under a National Constitution which prohibits all connexion between Church and State, and likewise under State Constitutions every one of which declares that "no laws shall be made affecting religious belief."

This may seem to be a divergence from the purposes of this chapter. But its aim is to exhibit the immense interest which the English Government, and particularly that portion of it confided to the English Church (covering as it does the great domain of English scholarship), has, in concentrating every particle of influence which can contribute toward popular control, within their own hands, for the security of their privileges and the quiet management of the State. This is the reason why the English churchmen and nobility cannot afford to relinquish the tremendous advantages of Shakespeare's inculcations of loyal subserviency upon millions of his worshippers, and why the dignitaries of the Established Church cannot permit that influence to be impaired, by admitting for a moment, that he was a Roman Catholic. This is the key to the denial by the English commentators, that he was an adherent of the latter doctrine, while *my* whole purpose, in tracing the evidences of Shakespeare's attachment to the Catholic faith, is to show that the Shakespeare plays, which so teem with Romish reverence, and which so abound with evidences of the writer's contempt for Protestantism, could not have been the production of the Puritan Lord Bacon. Indeed, to settle this question more certainly, it is only necessary to contrast the decisive illustrations which I have attached to this chapter, in the way of Shakespearian extracts, with the undisputed facts that Bacon wrote metrical versions of the Psalms of David, and dedicated them to his Protestant friend, George Herbert, as "the best judge of divinity and poesy met;"[5] and that he also, while a member of Parliament for Liverpool, wrote a paper on "Church Controversies," to assist a discourse of Secretary Walsingham on the conduct of the Queen's government towards Papists and Dissenters.[6]

Every influence, however, has its period, and Shakespeare's prestige, which was nothing to Government in the arbitrary age

[5] Holmes on "The Authorship of Shakespeare," p. 185.
[6] Holmes, p. 84.

in which he lived, became colossal as his genius developed itself
to the expanding intelligence and growing literary tastes of his
countrymen. Though now threatened with a decline from its
political zenith, his poetic supremacy will not be impaired, even
if its political effectiveness be reduced to a quantity of ordinary
power. Indeed, should it be proven he was a Catholic, it is not
impossible that the nobility of England, which for two hundred
years and more have been claiming for him a divine preeminence
over the poets of all other countries, or that the English Church,
which has been backing these extreme pretensions, may ere
long abandon him to the defences of his own genius, and turn
to other agencies for the protection of their political ascendancy.

It is hardly necessary that I should add anything more, at this
stage of my inquiry, as to the respective religious beliefs of Lord
Bacon and of William Shakespeare; but before taking leave of
Henry VIII., which is an ample field of reference upon this subject, I will direct attention to the fact that the poet makes
Queen Catharine, who is his *beau ideal* of Catholic purity and
elevation, declare that "All hoods make not monks," and
further on, when she addresses the Cardinals Wolsey and Campeius,
he allows her to evince the comprehension that politics soon drives
religion from the soul, by the sarcasm: "If ye be anything but
churchmen's habits." [7] I make this reference because it seems
to me to take the steel out of Knight's point on the passage in
"King John," commencing with

> "The king, I fear, is poisoned by a monk—
>
> . . . .
>
> A monk, I tell you; a resolved villain."

I am reminded by a note from a Protestant friend (and, it
may be as well to state here that I am of the same persuasion),
that I shall probably find some difficulty in accounting for

---

[7] See "Henry VIII." Act III. Scene 1. Also the following remarks by
Dr. Samuel Johnson on the same:—"The play of 'Henry VIII.,'" says
Johnson, "is one of those which still keeps possession of the stage by the
splendour of its pageantry. The coronation scene, about forty years ago,
drew the people together in multitudes for the great part of the winter. Yet
pomp is not the only merit of this play. The meek sorrows and virtuous
distress of Katharine have furnished some scenes which may be justly num-
bered among the greatest efforts of tragedy. But the genius of Shakespeare
comes in and goes out with Katharine. Every other part may be easily conceived and easily written."

Shakespeare's great familiarity with the Bible, inasmuch as Catholics were not allowed to read the sacred volume; but I find no difficulty in this fact at all. John Shakespeare, the poet's father, had been High Bailiff and first Alderman of Stratford, and as such had taken the oath of conformity; so the absence of a Protestant Bible from his house might have led to the loss of his office, and possibly to the arrest of his family. The Bible, no doubt, was always lying conspiciously " around " in the Stratford homestead, and the youthful Shakespeare, with his rage for reading, must have eagerly devoured its splendid imagery—at any rate, whenever he had nothing else at hand. But he was equally, nay, much better informed upon Catholic rites and peculiarities of belief than of Protestantisms, as has been shown by his frequent allusions to their terms and tenets, and especially to *purgatory*—in proof of which I refer to the following exquisite lines in Richard III. :—

QUEEN ELIZABETH.

> Ah, my poor princes ! Ah, my tender babes !
> My unblown flowers, new-appearing sweets !
> *If yet your gentle souls fly in the air,*
> *And be not fix'd in doom perpetual,*
> Hover about me with your airy wings,
> And hear your mother's lamentations.

> "Richard III.," Act IV. Scene 4.

And again by Buckingham in his invocation, on the way to execution, to the souls of those whom Richard (by his own help) had murdered :—

> All that have miscarried
> By underhand, corrupted foul injustice !
> If that your moody discontented souls
> Do through the clouds behold this present hour,
> Even for revenge, mock my destruction !

The most remarkable evidence, to my mind, that Shakespeare could not have been a Protestant, is the restraint which he imposed upon himself during Elizabeth's reign, against writing even a line reflecting upon the manifold atrocities of Bloody Mary, though she at one time even meditated sending his patroness, Elizabeth, to the block. Of the same character are his slavish praises to that unparalleled miscreant, Henry VIII., who stifled Smithfield with the smoke of human sacrifices, for opinion's sake. Nevertheless, Shakespeare has falsely handed

6

down this monster to the English people, gilded by the halo of his genius; nay, has consigned him to their forgiveness, and even to their affections, as Bluff King Hal. There was some reason, perhaps, why the poet should pass him gently by, as the father of Elizabeth (though the play of "Henry VIII." was not written until long after her decease), but I have no doubt that Shakespeare's main reason was because Henry, notwithstanding his persecutions of the Church, died a good Catholic. The same reason may be held to account for the poet's extreme devotion to Queen Catharine, who was conspicious for nothing, except for the profound depth of her Catholic bigotry; which, instead of having been softened by English influences, seems to have deepened from the hour of her leaving Spain.

Before closing this chapter I may add that I find another personal proof of Shakespeare's Romanism in the bitter hatred which he repeatedly exhibits to the Jews. This prejudice does not exist largely among Protestants; at any rate, not among the Protestants of the United States. On the contrary, the Jews mingle here with Christians without any social disadvantage; and, for my own part, I have never heard of any historical, ethnological, or moral reason why they should suffer the least discount in any equitable estimation. They certainly are the purest race known to the world; and this purity could not have been preserved without great traits of character and great sacrifices. They are notoriously brave, for the proofs of their courage are stamped upon every age, from the battle-field to the prize-ring. Their women are proverbially virtuous and beautiful; an intense interior pride keeps them from ever billeting their poor upon the public charities; and the wonder is that, under the prejudice which the society of all Christian countries has unremittingly exercised against them, they remain such useful, inoffensive, law-abiding citizens. The world is not at all indebted to William Shakespeare for what he has done to contribute toward this narrow, grovelling, and contemptible reflection upon the Jews; and, least of all, should he be respected for it in America. Less, than at any time, to-day. Prejudice is the very meanest form of slavery; for it is the slavery of the mind. One black, shrivelling blot, slavery, has recently been exuded from the national conscience. Surely there can be no excuse for allowing even a shadow of this other to remain.

CHAPTER IX.

LEGAL ACQUIREMENTS OF SHAKESPEARE.

HAVING now disposed, in a general way, of the inquiry as to the respective religious beliefs of Sir Francis Bacon and of William Shakespeare, we are now prepared to pass on to the reading of the plays for further evidence in support of the Roman Catholic theory. And also for evidence to test the truth of the declarations in our opening chapter, that the author of the Shakespeare plays was never betrayed into one generous aspiration in favour of popular liberty, and never alluded to the labouring classes without detestation or contempt. Further, that he could not have been a statesman or a lawyer; both of which, beyond all doubt, Lord Bacon was. In dealing with this latter point I am aware that I shall have to undertake the hazard of disagreeing, to some extent, with so powerful an authority as Lord Chief Justice Campbell of England, and also with distinguished lawyers in this country; while, in denying to Shakespeare a single political emotion in favour of liberty for the masses, I am also conscious of the apparent contradiction which presents itself to this assumption, in the one solitary play of " Julius Cæsar," through the character of Brutus. Upon this latter point, however, I shall only stop at this stage of the inquiry to say that Brutus, though a patriot, in the sense of an abounding love of country, was at same time an intense aristocrat, who struck Cæsar purely in defence of an oligarchical form of government and the privileges of his own patrician class, and whose conspiracy never contemplated for a moment the liberation of the People from their fixed condition of bondsmen and of slaves. His invocations to Liberty, therefore, were merely in the interest of the associated nobles, as contrasted with the invidious despotism of a king, and did not comprehend reducing the degrading distance between the Patri-

cians, who were the masters of the State, and the Plebeians, who
were the dirt under their feet.   This was the form of the Roman
Republic in the defence of which Brutus, Cassius, " and the rest,"
struck down the ambitious Cæsar.   They were patriots in their
own estimation, of course, but they were patriots in the same
sense as the Earls of Warwick and of Salisbury were patriots ; and
their love of country was of precisely the same brand as that of
King John and of Henry V.   But of this more in the proper
place.

The assumption that the author of the Shakespeare plays must
have been a lawyer, from the evidences of legal erudition which
are strewed throughout his text, has been a very favourite one with
the majority of the commentators and biographers of William
Shakespeare ; and when the Baconian theory was broached a few
years ago, these evidences were eagerly seized upon by the persons
who claimed the credit of those wonderful productions for the
great Lord Chancellor.   At the outset of this discussion of Shakespeare's legal lore, Bacon was not thought of in connexion with
the puzzle; and the commentators, therefore, were forced, pretty
generally, to come to the conclusion that during the six or seven
years between Shakespeare's leaving school and going up to London he had either been articled to an attorney or been a clerk and
scrivener in some notary's office.   Some critics, whose brows were
more rainbowed than the rest, suggested that any extent of
scholastic accomplishment might fairly be attributed to the vivid,
lambent, quick-breeding conception of such a miracle of genius
as was the poet of our race; but this exceptional theory made
but little headway with more sober reasoners, mainly for
the want of precedents that any man was ever known to have
learned his letters, or attained to the art of making boots or
watches by mere intuition.   The fact is, that the true difficulty
with this portion of the inquiry has been, that too much
erudition and legal comprehension has been attributed to Shakespeare for what his law phrases indicate ; or, in plainer words,
they have been paraded at a great deal more than they are
really worth.

Let me say here for myself, however, that without attributing
too much to the exceptional superiority of Shakespeare's quickness
of conception and intellectual grasp, all the knowledge which he
shows of legal verbiage and of certain general principles of law,

so far as he refers to them in his plays, might, it seems to me,
have been obtained—first, by reading certain elementary works
of law falling in his way; next, by attendance at the courts of
record, held twice a month at Stratford, and courts-leet and
view of frankpledge, held in the same town twice a year. Next,
through his own subsequent experience as an owner of real estate;
which latter position necessarily familiarized him with all the
forms of " purchase," of leases, of mortgages, and sale. Besides,
he might reasonably be credited with much additional law knowledge gained by legal borrowing and lending, and through law-
suits which we know he instituted for the recovery of debt. I
think it would be difficult for Lord Campbell to show that the
law phrases which Shakespeare uses go beyond the wide scope of
this opportunity of acquisition to a bright-minded man; while,
if we are to take into consideration the subsequent advantages
our poet derived in London, from familiar discussion of the great
law cases of the day at " The Maiden "[1] and other popular taverns
he frequented near the Inns of Court, where such men as Ben
Jonson, Beaumont and Fletcher, Seldon, Cotton, Carew, Donne,
Martin, Sir Walter Raleigh, and sometimes even Bacon himself,
found conversational relaxation in absence of newspapers, we
should have to come to the conclusion that Shakespeare must
have been a very dull man if he had not acquired at least as much
legal knowledge as his dramas show.[2]

---

[1] Beaumont, in a friendly letter to Ben Jonson from the country, says,—

> " What things have we seen
> Done at the Mermaid! heard words that have been
> So nimble, and so full of subtle flame,
> As if that every one from whom they came
> Had meant to put his whole wit in a jest."

[2] Lord Campbell says, " At Stratford there was, by royal charter, a
court of record, with jurisdiction over all personal action to the amount
of 30*l*., equal, at the latter end of the reign of Elizabeth, to more than 100*l*.
in the reign of Victoria. This court, the records of which are extant, was
regulated by the course of practice and pleading which prevailed in the
superior courts of law at Westminster, and employed the same barbarous
dialect, composed of Latin, English, and Norman French. It sat every fortnight, and there belonged to it, besides the town clerk, six attorneys, some of
whom must have practised in the Queen's Bench in Chancery, and have had
extensive business in conveyancing. An attorney, steward of the Earl of
Warwick, lord of the manor of Stratford, twice a year held a court-leet and

Chalmers was the first to present the theory that Shakespeare must, for a considerable portion of his unrecorded youthful life, have been an attorney's clerk at Stratford. Malone and others adopted this view from the very necessity of accounting for the oft-recurring law phrases in the Shakespeare text; while Lord Chief Justice Campbell has been carried to such an extent of enthusiasm by these professional terms as to attribute to Shakespeare quite an extensive knowledge of the law. His expression is: " Great as is the knowledge of the law which Shakespeare's writings display, and familiar as he appears to have been with all its forms and proceedings, the whole of this would easily be accounted for, if for some years he had occupied a desk in the office of a country attorney in good business; attending sessions and assizes, keeping leet days and law days, and, perhaps, being sent up to the metropolis in term time to conduct suits before the Lord Chancellor."[3]

My objection to this is, with all due deference to so great a lawyer as a Lord Chief Justice, that the author of the Shakespeare plays did not possess any great knowledge of the law; or, if he did, his dramatic writings do not show it. He exhibits, without doubt, a familiarity in law expressions, and applies them with a precision and a happiness of application in all cases which apparently carries the idea that he may have served in an attorney's office; but not one of them, nor do all of them together, mark anything higher than mere general principles and forms of practice, or such surface clack and knowledge as were within the mental reach of any clever scrivener or conveyancer's clerk. On the contrary, whenever Shakespeare steps beyond the surface comprehension of the solicitor's phraseology, and attempts to deal with the spirit and philosophy of law, he makes a lamentable failure. "The Merchant of Venice," "Comedy of Errors," "Winter's Tale," and "Measure for Measure," contain conspicuous proofs of this deficiency, while the statesmanship of the Duke in the "Two Gentlemen of Verona," who, in his joy at recovering his daughter from a

view of frank-pledge there, to which a jury was summoned, and at which constables were appointed and various presentments were made."—Campbell, p. 22.

[3] "Shakespeare's Legal Attainments," by Lord John Campbell. Appleton's edition, 1869, p. 24.

gang of cut-throats in a forest, endeavours to reform them by appointing them to high posts under Government, is a sort of policy which Lord Bacon was never accused of, while he was a member of the Privy Council.

Lord Campbell's essay on "The Legal Acquirements of Shakespeare" was drawn forth by an inquiry addressed to his Lordship on that subject, by Mr. Payne Collier (one of the most learned and thorough of the Shakespearian commentators), whether his Lordship was of the opinion that Shakespeare " was a clerk in an attorney's office in Stratford, before he joined the players in London "? This led to an answer by his Lordship, under date of September 15, 1858, which shows a discovery of legal phrases and allusions in twenty-three of the thirty-seven Shakespeare plays; and it is this amount of evidence which (though it does not bring the learned replicant to an absolute conclusion) elicits from him the expression which I have already given. His Lordship sets out in his response to Mr. Collier with—" I am obliged to say that, to the question you propound, no positive answer can very safely be given ;" but he adds that, " were an issue tried before me, as Chief Justice, at the Warwick Assizes, whether William Shakespeare was ever clerk in an attorney's office, I should hold that there is evidence to go to the jury in support of the affirmative."

His Lordship, however, does not hesitate to declare, further on, that there is one piece of direct evidence, if not two, that Shakespeare had been so employed in Stratford; and he is brought to this conclusion by libels which Greene and Nash, two jealous play-writing contemporaries, had made upon our poet in the preface to a work of Greene's, edited by Nash, and published in 1589. This preface, which I have already briefly noticed in Chapter IV., characterizes Shakespeare, though his name is not precisely mentioned, as " one of a sort of shifting companions that run through every art and thrive by none, to leave the trade of *noverint* whereto they were born . . . . , and who busy themselves with whole *Hamlets* of tragical speeches, &c." The term *noverint* is recognized by Lord Campbell as indicating the business of an attorney, in Shakespeare's time. Moreover, he believes that the phrase of "whole Hamlets" is a distinct allusion to the great play of our poet, and that the epithet of Shake-scene, applied to him by Greene in a subsequent libel, published in 1592, was an undoubted mimicry of Shakespeare's name.

In view of this direct evidence, supported by the text, and by the general circumstances of the case, Lord Campbell closes his reply to Mr. Collier by saying, "Therefore, my dear Mr. Payne Collier, in support of your opinion that Shakespeare had been bred to the profession of the law in an attorney's office, I think you will be justified in saying that the fact was asserted publicly in Shakespeare's lifetime by two contemporaries of Shakespeare, who were engaged in the same pursuits with himself, who must have known him well, and who were probably acquainted with the whole of his career. I must likewise admit that this assertion is strongly corroborated by internal evidence to be found in Shakespeare's writings. I have once more perused the whole of his dramas, that I might more satisfactorily answer your question, and render you some assistance in finally coming to a right conclusion."

Lord Campbell then goes on to produce his illustrations from the plays and sonnets attributed to Shakespeare, and I cannot help remarking, that it would be well for his Lordship's admirers if he had exhibited as much good sense and judgment in his presentment of these extracts as he did in his decision of Mr. Collier's general question. Two or three examples will give an idea of his Lordship's mode of reasoning, and of the singular earnestness which, tarantula-like, seems to have bitten all the commentators with a sort of mad desire to prove Shakespeare to have been a miracle, in every specialty; and this, too often, without either rhyme or reason.

His Lordship's first illustration of the depth of Shakespeare's legal lore is from the "Merry Wives of Windsor," and is as follows :—

FALSTAFF. Of what quality was your love, then?

FORD. Like a fair house built upon another man's ground; so that *I have lost my edifice by mistaking the place where I erected it.*

Probably not a single well-informed person in England or America, of either sex, does not know as much law as the above indicates—nay, does not even know that a nail driven by a tenant into the wall must remain with the realty—yet our learned Chief Justice thus discourses on it :—

" Now this shows in Shakespeare a knowledge of the law of real property not generally possessed. The unlearned would suppose that if, by mistake, a man builds a fine house on the land of another, when he discovers his error he will be permitted to remove all the materials of the structure, and particularly the marble pillars and carved chimney-pieces with which he has adorned it : but Shakespeare knew better. He was aware that, ' being fixed to the freehold, the absolute property in them belonged to the owner of the soil."

Again, says his Lordship, he remarks as to " Measure for Measure :"—

" In Act I. Scene 2, the old lady who had kept a *lodging-house* of a disreputable character in the suburbs of Vienna, being thrown into despair by the proclamation that all such houses in the suburbs must be plucked down, the Clown thus comforts her :—

> CLOWN. Come; fear not you; *good counsellors lack no clients.*

" This comparison," says Lord Campbell, " is not very flattering to the bar, but it seems to show a familiarity with both professions alluded to."

My observation upon this would be, that the Clown could not have made use of a more trite and ordinary proverb, in application to the subject, even if he had been a more profound person than a clown.

But let us, at the present, go with his Lordship one step further. From " Macbeth" he quotes the lines :—

> " But yet I'll make assurance doubly sure,
> And *take a bond of fate.*"

And this to prove Shakespeare to have been a lawyer! Further on his Lordship takes the following couplet from " Venus and Adonis " to establish the same thing :—

> " But when the heart's *attorney* once is mute,
> The *client* breaks as desperate in the *suit.*"

If this is fair evidence, and fair reasoning upon that evidence, to show Shakespeare to have been a lawyer, then, certainly, Hamlet's direction to the players—

> " To hold as 'twere the mirror up to nature,"

would prove, beyond all doubt, that Shakespeare must have been

a looking-glass maker, or at least a dealer in that trade ; or that
these two lines of Faulconbridge, in " King John," which criticize
the form of attack proposed by the French and Austrian divisions
upon Angiers,—

> " O prudent discipline ! from north to south,
>   Austria and France shoot in each other's mouth,"

would prove Shakespeare to have been a soldier.

Part II

THE TESTIMONY OF THE PLAYS.

CHAPTER X.

" THE TEMPEST."

WE have now arrived at the most important branch of our inquiry; namely, at that by means of which Shakespeare may himself be "interviewed" through the testimony of his text. For this purpose I shall have to make liberal extracts from the plays, as on the faith of my opening declarations I shall not feel at liberty to omit any expression which may seem to bear upon the argument, whether it be for one side or the other, so that the reader may, without regard to my opinion, give judgment for himself. Indeed, if anything deemed pertinent shall chance to be left out, it will be because I have overlooked it; and I will here avail myself of the opportunity to apologize for the extent of the extracts which I have already made from the old biographers as to Shakespeare's personal history. Doubtless, these will be very trite and tiresome to scholars, to whom they are familiar, but I shall be excused when it is recollected that these extracts seemed necessary to substantiate my statements, while, for the convenience of the reader, it is perhaps better they should be in this book, ready to his hand, than be sought after in the public libraries.

For convenience of examination, I shall take the dramas in the order in which they were first published in the original folio of 1623. This publication puts "The Tempest" first; but instead of being one of Shakespeare's earliest plays, it was really one of his latest, for it was not produced, according to Malone, till 1612, only four years previous to our poet's death.

There is not much in "The Tempest" bearing upon the points that I have offered, though it will serve to strengthen my view concerning the aristocratic class of personages chosen invariably by Shakespeare for his favourite characters, and the wide and con-

temptuous distance he always places off between these favourites
of his muse and the "common" people. With this view, I will
give the *dramatis personæ*, along with the first scene, in which
most of the characters are introduced :—

ALONZO, *King of Naples.*
SEBASTIAN, *his brother.*
PROSPERO, *the rightful Duke of Milan.*
ANTONIO, *his brother, the usurping Duke of Milan.*
FERDINAND, *son to the King of Naples.*
GONZALO, *an honest old counsellor of Naples.*
ADRIAN, FRANCISCA, *lords.*
CALIBAN, *a savage and deformed slave.*
TRINCULO, *a jester.*
STEPHANO, *a drunken butler.*
Master of a ship, Boatswain, and Mariners.
MIRANDA, *daughter to Prospero.*
ARIEL, *an airy spirit.*

Act I. Scene 1.

On a Ship at Sea—A Storm, with Thunder and Lightning.
Enter a Shipmaster and a Boatswain.

MAST. Boatswain—

BOATS. Here, master ; what cheer ?

MAST. Good ; speak to the mariners ; fall to't yarely, or we run ourselves
aground ; bestir, bestir.   [*Exit.*

Enter Mariners.

BOATS. Heigh, my hearts ; cheerly, cheerly, my hearts ; yare, yare ; take
in the topsail ; tend to the master's whistle. Blow till thou burst thy
wind, if room enough !

Enter ALONZO, SEBASTIAN, ANTONIO, FERDINAND, GONZALO, *and others.*

ALON. Good boatswain, have care. Where's the master? Play the men.

BOATS. I pray, now, keep below.

ANT. Where is the master, boatswain?

BOATS. Do you not hear him? You mar our labour. Keep your cabins ;
you do assist the storm.

GON. Nay, good, be patient.

BOATS. When the sea is. Hence ! what care these roarers for the name of
king ! To cabin ; silence ; trouble us not.

GON. Good ; yet remember whom thou hast aboard.

BOATS. None that I more love than myself. You are a counsellor ; if you
can command these elements to silence, and work the peace of the present, we
will not hand a rope more ; use your authority. If you cannot, give thanks
you have lived so long, and make yourself ready in your cabin for the mis-
chance of the hour, if it so hap. Cheerily, good hearts.—Out of our way, I
say.   [*Exit.*

Gon. I have great comfort from this fellow; methinks he hath no drowning mark upon him; his complexion is perfect gallows. Stand fast, good fate,
to his hanging! Make the rope of his destiny our cable, for our own doth
little advantage! If he be not born to be hanged, our case is miserable.

[Exeunt.

Re-enter Boatswain.

Boats. Down with the topmast; yare; lower, lower; bring her to try with
main course. [*A cry within.*] A plague upon this howling! they are louder
than the weather, or our office—

Re-enter Sebastian, Antonio, *and* Gonzalo.

Yet again? what do you do here? Shall we give o'er, and drown! Have
you a mind to sink!

*   *   *   *   *   *

Ant. We are merely cheated of our lives by
    This wide-chapped rascal. Would thou mightst lie drowning,
    The washing of ten tides!
Gon. He'll be hanged yet;
    Though every drop of water swear against it,
    And gape at wid'st to glut him.

[*A confused noise within.*] Mercy on us! We split! we split! Farewell
my wife and children! Farewell, brother! We split, we split, we split!

Ant. Let's all sink with the king.   [*Exit.*

After this last touching evidence of loyalty, the storm sub-
sides, and the parties distribute themselves about the island, on
which they have been stranded, and upon which there are but
three other persons—Prospero, Miranda, and Caliban. By the
above it will be perceived that the boatswain, who labours hard
and honestly at his vocation, who speaks nothing but good sense,
and who is doing his utmost to save the ship, is denounced as a
cur and a rogue by the lords, simply because he ventures to
remonstrate hastily with the *gentlemen* of the scene for interfering
with his imperative and vitally important duties. Further on,
Shakespeare, in the character of Prospero, and evidently speaking
in a tone he would have used for himself, directs Ariel to have
the wandering ship's company brought together, in order to behold a *"masque"* of fairies, which he has prepared for the
general entertainment.

    Prospero (*to Ariel*). Go bring the *rabble*,
       O'er whom I give thee power, here to this place!

The rabble meaning, of course, the ship's company, and all of the
dramatis personæ who are not gentlemen.

I think that the unvarying inclination which Shakespeare shows, to speak with contempt of the labouring classes sprang from some notion in the poet's mind that he was a gentleman himself. This idea finds support in the fact that he could trace his name, on one side, to the battle of Hastings, and his ancestors, on both sides, to the battle of Bosworth Field; but more distinctly in the fact of his having laid out a considerable sum of money, after he had become rich by theatrical management, to purchase for his father a coat of arms. This gives a sharp point to the remark of Halliwell upon the death of John Shakespeare, that "it would have pleased us better had we found Shakespeare raising monuments to his parents in the venerable pile which now covers his own remains." The effort to have his father made "a gentleman of worship" supplies the key to the otherwise strange contradiction of his always being so bitterly derisive of "greasy mechanics," "woollen slaves," and peasants," as he terms the masses from whose midst he sprang. New converts, as we know, are usually the most vehement denouncers of rejected associates and principles.

"TWO GENTLEMEN OF VERONA."

It is agreed on all sides that the "Two Gentlemen of Verona" was among the earliest of Shakespeare's dramatic compositions, and some commentators think it was his very first play—"The Comedy of Errors" being, probably, his second. The 'Two Gentlemen" did not reach the dignity of print, however, until the publication of the first general collection, known as the folio of 1623, seven years after Shakespeare's death. The reason why it was not placed first in the catalogue, and the others made to follow, according to the supposed chronological order of their production, was doubtless because it was feared that this plan, by placing the weakest of our poet's productions at the front, would do him injustice with every fresh reader, who, starting with the play as an example, might not be induced to pursue the study further. Therefore, "The Tempest," one of his most highly finished productions, was placed foremost, and the rest followed without order, so far at least as the comedies were concerned, with the view of giving a rapid exhibition of the writer's infinite variety. "But," says Knight, "there must have been years of labour before the genius that produced the 'Two Gentlemen of Verona' could have produced 'The Tempest.'" In fact, it is so far below the mark of the latter magnificently-worked-out conception, that many have seriously doubted the authenticity of the "Two Gentlemen" as a Shakespearian production; while several critics of position, among whom are Hanmer, Theobald, and Upton, denounce the piece as spurious altogether. There can scarcely be a doubt, however (though Shakespeare can easily be convicted of having adopted the story of the piece from others), that the text was all his own. Upon this question Dr. Johnson very pertinently says, at the close of his dictum in favour of its authenticity as a Shakespeare play, "if it be taken from him, to whom shall it be given?" The Doctor, in fixing the literary status of this work, continues :—

"In this play there is a strange mixture of knowledge and ignorance, of care and negligence. . . . . The author conveys his heroes by sea from one inland town to another in the same country; he places the Emperor at Milan, and sends his young men to attend him, but never mentions him more. He makes Proteus, after an interview with Silvia, say he has only seen her picture; and, if we may credit the old copies, he has, by mistaking places, left his scenery inextricable. The reason of all this confusion seems to be that he took his story from a novel, which he sometimes followed and sometimes forsook, sometimes remembered and sometimes forgot." "It has been well remarked that such historical and geographical blunders as these could hardly have been committed by Lord Bacon, even in his earliest youth. In all popular knowledge Shakespeare was a master. He does not err in his illustrations drawn from hunting and hawking and natural phenomena, or in such natural history as is learnt from close observation of the habits of animals. He blunders in things which could only have been derived from book-learning, in which Bacon excelled."[1]

These remarks lead us directly to the further observation, that the production of the "Two Gentlemen," being generally placed at the date of 1591, when Bacon was thirty-one years of age,

---

[1] Wm. H. Smith's "Inquiry," p. 101. London, 1857.

7

could hardly have received these errors at his hands; while the supposition that he could have permitted them to live under his eye, uncorrected, even after the plays had attained the highest fame and the folio had gone through several editions, is not entitled to a moment's entertainment. If the play was thought worthy, by Bacon, of being put surreptitiously into Shakespeare's hands, for transcription and performance, it surely must have been thought deserving, after it had become part of a great fame, of being retouched by a few correctional notes. And these could have been as easily handed to Shakespeare as the original MSS., or have been sent to the publishers of the folio, after Shakespeare's death; for Bacon outlived Shakespeare long enough to know that the poet had already acquired a fame and received an homage from mankind which he, with all of his triumphs in philosophy, could never hope to reach. The idea that Bacon, with his covetous imagination, could have been indifferent to such fame as this, seems to be beyond all the bounds of reason; while the notion that the mind which originally desired the production of the play would not have corrected its errors, after it had detected them, appears to be utterly absurd. In the first place, the experience of Bacon could not have made these errors; but admitting that they had escaped him originally, through the haste of writing, he must have detected them afterward, through the very necessities of his local, legal, and political career. Indeed, if the " Two Gentlemen" is to be received as one of the Shakespeare plays, it seems to me that the whole Baconian theory falls at once. It is simply beyond the reach of belief (if the play were written by Bacon) that he never corrected it; since we know, through Bacon's biographers, that, for greater accuracy, he frequently revised all his works, and transcribed his " Novum Organum" twelve times.

The story of this play is very simple. Valentine and Proteus, who give title to the piece, and who are hardly more than boys, are scions of two wealthy and noble families of Verona. The first act opens with the departure of the former on a travelling tour, by way of increasing his accomplishments, and on taking leave of Proteus (who, being in love, prefers to remain at home) he indulges in some smart reflections on his friend's amorous infatuation. Presently the father of Proteus, having heard that Valentine has gone abroad, declares that his son shall improve himself in like manner; and consequently, at one day's notice, and without giving him more than a bare opportunity to take a hasty leave of his sweetheart Julia, sends him also to the Emperor's court. Before Proteus arrives there, however, Valentine has so well improved his time that he has succeeded in making Silvia, the Duke of Milan's daughter, fall in love with him; the only difficulty, however, being that Silvia stands engaged, by the Duke's special permission, to Sir Thurio, a very wealthy nobleman of his court. By-and-by Proteus appears, and he at once, forgetful of his vows to Julia and his duty to his friend, falls in love with Silvia himself. Nay, worse, though told by Valentine, in the sacred confidence of friendship, that he and Silvia are betrothed, indeed, are on the eve of an elopement for the purpose of marriage, Proteus basely betrays this secret to the Duke, and seeks the ruin of his friend, in the hope of gaining ultimate possession of Silvia himself. The traitor justifies this shocking perfidy to Julia on the one hand, and to Valentine on the other, in a soliloquy, in which occur these abominable lines :—

> Unheedful vows may heedfully be broken;
> And he wants wit that wants resolved will
> To learn his wit to exchange the bad for better.
>
> *Act II. Scene 6.*

The result of this villany by Proteus is the banishment of Valentine, who, falling in with a band of outlaws, is made their captain, while Silvia, rendered desperate by her misfortunes, and spurning the false love of Proteus, escapes from her confinement to a neighbouring forest, under the protection of a gentleman named Sir Eglamour, to whom she appoints a rendezvous—to use her own devout language—

> At friar Patrick's cell,
> Where I intend *holy* confession.

News of her flight, in company with Eglamour, is soon brought to the Duke, and he informs Proteus of it as follows :—

> DUKE. She's fled unto that *peasant* Valentine;
> And Eglamour is in her company.
> 'Tis true; for friar Lawrence met them both,
> As he *in penance* wandered through the forest:

> Him, he knew well, and guess'd that it was she ;
> But, being mask'd, he was not sure of it :
> Besides, she did intend confession
> At Patrick's cell this even ; and there she was not.

Here we find united evidences of that unvarying Catholic reverence which Shakespeare always expresses when speaking of a priest; and likewise of that contempt for humble life which I have pointed out as another of his peculiarities, in the opprobrious use he makes of the word *peasant,* by applying it as an epithet of contempt to the well-born Valentine. Proteus has previously used the same angry epithet to Launce.

But to return to the story. Proteus, having obtained from the Duke, as above described, the direction of Silvia's flight and of his intention to pursue her, takes with him his page, Sebastian, and hastens to the forest, with the view of anticipating the Duke, and of obtaining possession of her for himself, in advance of the Duke's arrival. It appears, however, that, before Proteus gets to the forest with his party, a portion of the outlaws capture Silvia; Sir Eglamour, her escourt, prudently running away. Her deplorable situation then is thus described by Shakespeare :—

Act V. Scene 3.—*The Forest.*
Enter SYLVIA *and Outlaws.*

OUT.   Come, come ;
     Be patient, we must bring you to our captain.
SIL.   A thousand more mischances than this one
     Have learn'd me how to brook this patiently.
2 OUT. Come, bring her away.
1 OUT. Where is the gentleman that was with her?
3 OUT. Being nimble-footed, he hath outrun us,
     But Moyses, and Valerius, follow him.
     Go thou with her to the west end of the wood,
     There is our captain ; we'll follow him that's fled.
     The thicket is beset, he cannot 'scape.
1 OUT. Come, I must bring you to our captain's cave ;
     Fear not : he bears an honourable mind,
     And will not use a woman lawlessly.
SIL.   O Valentine, this I endure for thee.   [*Exeunt.*

The scene then shifts, and shows Valentine, alone, in another part of the forest. He is in a sad mood, and utters a long soliloquy, when, being disturbed by the sound of a noisy conflict

(that turns out to be the rescue of Silvia from the outlaws by
Proteus and his party), he utters these lines :—

> These are my mates, *that make their will their law,*
> Have some unhappy passenger in chase;
> They love me well; *yet I have much to do,*
> *To keep them from uncivil outrages.*
> Withdraw thee, Valentine; who's this comes here?   [*Steps aside.*
>
> *Enter* Proteus, Silvia *and* Julia.

It must now be mentioned that Julia, the betrothed of Proteus,
not having heard from her false lover for a long while, had some
time before left Verona disguised as a page, and had succeeded
in entering the service of Proteus, under the name of Sebastian,
in which character she now accompanies him. With this explanation, and with Valentine listening in the thicket, we will return
to the text.

> Pro. (*to Silvia*). Madam, this service I have done for you
> (Though you respect not aught your servant doth),
> To hazard life, and rescue you from him
> That would have forced your honour and your love.
> Vouchsafe me, for my meed, but one fair look;
> A smaller boon than this I cannot beg,
> And less than this, I am sure, you cannot give.
>
> Val. (*from his concealment*). How like a dream is this I see and hear;
> Love, lend me patience to forbear a while.
>
> Sil. O miserable, unhappy that I am !
>
> Pro. Unhappy were you, madam, ere I came ;
> But, by my coming, I have made you happy.
>
> Sil. By thy approach thou mak'st me most unhappy.
>
> Jul. And me, when he approacheth to your presence.   [*Aside.*
>
> Sil. Had I been seized by a hungry lion,
> I would have been a breakfast to the beast,
> Rather than have false Proteus rescue me.
> *O Heaven be judge, how I love Valentine,*
> *Whose life's as tender to me as my soul ;*
> And full as much (for more there cannot be),
> I do detest false perjured Proteus :
> Therefore, begone; solicit me no more.
>
>   *   *   *   *
>
> Pro. Nay, if the gentle spirit of moving words
> Can no way change you to a milder form,
> I'll woo you like a soldier, at arms' end:
> And love you 'gainst the nature of love,—*force you.*
>
> Sil. O Heaven !
>
> Pro.   *I'll force thee yield to my desire.*

VAL. (*discovering himself*). Ruffian, let go that rude uncivil touch;
    Thou friend of an ill fashion!

PRO.   Valentine;

VAL. Thou common friend, that's without faith or love;
    (For such is a friend now), treacherous man!
    Thou hast beguiled my hopes; nought but mine eye
    Could have persuaded me : Now I dare not say,
    I have one friend alive; thou would'st disprove me.
    Who should be trusted now, when one's right hand
    Is perjured to the bosom? Proteus,
    I am sorry I must never trust thee more,
    But count the world a stranger for thy sake.
    The private wound is deepest. O time, most curst;
    'Mongst all foes, that a friend should be the worst.

PRO. My shame and guilt confound me—
    Forgive me, Valentine; if hearty sorrow
    Be a sufficient ransom for offence,
    I tender it here; I do as truly suffer
    As e'er I did commit.

VAL.   *Then I am paid :*
    And once again I do receive thee honest;
    Who by repentance is not satisfied,
    Is nor of heaven, nor earth; for these are pleased;
    By penitence the Eternal's wrath 's appeased :
    And, that my love may appear plain and free,
    All that was mine in Silvia, I give thee.

JUL. O me unhappy!   [*Faints.*

PRO. Look to the boy.

Julia is then discovered. No wonder that she fainted under the indescribable poltroonery and baseness of Valentine in resigning the devoted and heroic Silvia to the villain Proteus, because the latter, under a sense of policy and fear, expressed sudden contrition for his execrable crimes. Proteus, however, does not think it prudent to accept Silvia under such an offer from the chief of a band of outlaws; so he makes a virtue of necessity by renewing his fealty to Julia in about six lines. Whereupon Valentine, finding that Proteus declines to receive Silvia at his hands, makes the original lovers happy by joining them together.

PRO. O Heaven! were man
    But constant, he were perfect; that one error
    Fills him with faults; makes him run through all sins :
    Inconstancy falls off, ere it begins :
    What is in Silvia's face, but I may spy
    More fresh in Julia's with a constant eye?

Val. Come, come, a hand from either:
    Let me be blest to make this happy close;
    'Twere pity two such friends should be long foes.
Pro. Bear witness, Heaven, I have my wish for ever.
Jul. And I have mine.

Everything being thus amicably settled, it unfortunately happens that those incorrigible fellows, the outlaws, suddenly turn up again in another act of villainy.

        Enter Outlaws, with the Duke *and* Thurio.

Outlaw. A prize, a prize, a prize!
Val.   Forbear, forbear, I say; it is my lord the Duke,
       Your grace is welcome to a man disgraced.

Thurio, hereupon discovering Silvia, at once lays claim to her, but Valentine, who has suddenly recovered *his* affection also, threatens him with instant death if he dare " take but possession of her with a touch," concluding his fiery menace with—

        " I dare thee but to breathe upon my love!"

Thurio, of course, gives Silvia up; upon which the Duke, in disgust with his cowardice, denounces him as base and degenerate, and magnanimously hands Silvia over to Sir Valentine. Then follows the climax, in the following sudden conversions to morality, on the part of the brigands, whose miraculous repentance at once receives a reward which elicits our amazement :—

Val.   I thank your grace : the gift hath made me happy.
      I now beseech you, *for your daughter's sake,*
      To grant one boon that I shall ask of you.
Duke. I grant it for thine own, whate'er it be.
Val.   These banish'd men, that I have kept withal,
      Are men endued with worthy qualities ;
      Forgive them what they have committed here,
      And let them be recall'd from their exile.
      They are reformed, civil, full of good,
      And fit for great employment, worthy lord.
Duke. Thou hast prevail'd ; I pardon them, and thee :
      Dispose of them as thou knowest their deserts.
      Come, let us go : we will conclude all jars
      With triumphs, mirth, and rare solemnity.

Now, as Valentine represents these outlaws (who had given him so much to do to keep them from uncivil outrage) to be men endued with *worthy qualities,* and declares them to be not only "reformed, civil, and good," but "fit for great employment," the *carte blanche* which the Duke gives to him to "dispose of them" as he "know'st their deserts," can hardly mean less than the appointment of them to positions under Government. A fine request, truly, to make *for Silvia's sake*, who had been rudely captured by these thieves; and for a father to make, who had himself just escaped from their attempt to rifle and, perhaps, to murder him. And, in order to make sure that these lawless rascals would have not hesitated, because of any qualms of conscience, to have had recourse to the latter extremity, the reader has only to turn to their own description of themselves at the opening of Act IV., when they chose Valentine to be their captain. But it is no portion of my task to show the contradictions and incongruities of Shakespeare, except where they bear upon the points we have in hand; and I have, therefore, but to say, in excuse for the extent of my extracts from the "Two Gentlemen," that the numerous absurdities they exhibit against our poet, do not seem to be the logical product of the mind of such an exact lawyer, statesman, and philosopher as Bacon.

CHAPTER XI.

"THE MERRY WIVES OF WINDSOR."

THE events of this play are supposed to take place between the First and Second Parts of " Henry IV." Falstaff is still in favour at court, and the compliment of Ford on his *warlike preparations* must, says Mr. Harness, allude to the service he had done at Shrewsbury. Shallow, Bardolph, Pistol, and Nym are the same as in the former plays, though it is evident that Mrs. Quickly, the servant of Doctor Caius, the French physician, is quite a different person from hostess Quickly, of the Boar's Head, in Eastcheap, who subsequently married Ancient Pistol. The tradition respecting the origin of this comedy is that Queen Elizabeth was so well pleased with the admirable character of Falstaff that she ordered Shakespeare to continue it and show him in love. To this we owe " The Merry Wives of Windsor;" and, says Mr. Dennis, who, in 1702, somewhat rearranged the play under the title of " The Comical Gallant," " she was so eager to see it acted that she commanded it to be finished in fourteen days." Tradition further says that she was exceedingly pleased at its representation. All of which, if true, must convince the thoughtful reader who has perused the delectable dialogues between Doll Tearsheet and Sir John and the free language of " The Merry Wives of Windsor," that the charm exercised over her Majesty by such very broad allusions proves her to have been a true daughter of Henry VIII. Let me be excused, therefore, if I quote a supporting picture of her Majesty, by Edward Dowden, LL.D., Professor of English Literature in the University of Dublin, and Vice-President of the new Shakespeare Society, from an admirable volume, entitled " A Critical Study of Shakespeare's Mind and Art," which has just (1875) been issued from the London press :—

"Raleigh rode by the Queen in silver armour; the Jesuit Drexilius estimated the value of the shoes worn by this minion of the English Cleopatra at six thousand six hundred gold pieces."

Now, as Professor Dowden is a devout member of the political Anglican Church, a very learned man withal, and knows exactly what he is writing about, I trust this allusion of his to the possible moral status of the virgin Queen will not be deemed disloyal or irreverent.

"The Merry Wives of Windsor" is deserving of especial notice from the fact that it is the only one of Shakespeare's plays the superior action of which is not devoted to kings and queens and princes and nobles, but which confines itself wholly to the ordinary characters of homely or middle life. It exhibits its relations to our religious theory mainly in the gross ridicule which it lavishes upon the Welsh parson, Sir Hugh Evans, and the fecundity, not to say feculence, of the tavern wit which flows from Falstaff and his mates with a readiness which does not seem peculiarly Baconian.

Sir Hugh, who is hardly a degree above a mere buffoon, declares his sacred calling in the first scene by saying to Shallow, "If Sir John Falstaff have committed disparagements unto you, *I am of the Church*, and will be glad to do my benevolence, to make my atonements and compromises between you." Further on he is made to profanely say, "The tevil and his tam! what phrase is this?" He is next engaged in a duel with the French doctor, in order that he may be made the butt and laughter of the company, and then makes his appearance in a tavern, with the noisy, vulgar host of which he shows himself to be thoroughly check by jowl. Shakespeare never treats a Catholic priest after this irreverent and unseemly fashion.

There is not much more to be said of this play from our point of view, save that Falstaff uses the term of *peasant* in the sense of *cur* against Ford, whose jealousy is filling his purse; or perhaps to notice one further of Lord Chief Justice Campbell's proofs of Shakespeare's legal acquirements, in addition to the one quoted from the same authority in the last chapter.

"In writing the second scene of Act IV. of 'The Merry Wives of Windsor,'" says Lord Campbell, "Shakespeare's head was so full of the recondite terms of law that he makes a lady thus pour them out in a confidential *tête-à-tête* conversation with another lady, while discoursing of the revenge they two should take upon an old gentleman (Falstaff) for having made an unsuccessful attempt upon their virtue :—

"MRS. PAGE. I'll have the cudgel hallowed, and hung o'er the altar; it hath done meritorious service.

"MRS. FORD. What think you? May we, with the *warrant* of womanhood, and the *witness* of a good conscience, pursue him with any further revenge?

"MRS. PAGE. The spirit of wantonness is, sure, scared out of him; if the devil have him not in *fee-simple, with fine and recovery*, he will never, I think, in the way of waste, attempt us again."

"This Merry Wife of Windsor," remarks his lordship, "is supposed to know that the highest estate which the devil could hold in any of his victims was a *fee-simple*, strengthened by *fine and recovery*. Shakespeare himself may probably have become aware of the law upon this subject when it was explained to him in answer to questions he put to the attorney, his master, while engrossing the deeds to be executed upon the purchase of a Warwickshire estate with a doubtful title."[1]

Now, I have no doubt, for my own part, that Shakespeare might have acquired as much legal knowledge as the above indicates, through his own purchases of land. Fine and recovery, as an artifice for perfecting title to land, was like, in policy to the legislative stratagem known to modern times as a "motion to reconsider," accompanied by a supplementary motion to "lay on the table," on the part of a majority who have just carried a bill. The effect of this device is, that the bill is thus made reasonably safe from further peril. Every man of fair experience knows that.

"MEASURE FOR MEASURE."

The date of the production of this fine play is fixed by Mr. F. J. Furnival,[2] in his "Trial Table of the Order of William Shakespeare's Plays," at 1603, when our poet was forty years of age. It was performed, says Gervinius, in 1604, but not pub-

---

[1] Lord Campbell, pp. 40, 41.
[2] Mr. Furnival is the Director of the new Shakespeare Society of London.

lished until 1623. Dr. Johnson speaks of its merits with such indifference that it would almost seem as if he had never read it; while to other equally competent critics it is on a level, so far as the intellectual elevation of its language and imagery are concerned, with the very finest productions of Shakespeare's genius. To my judgment its moral management is faulty, and the great principle of retributive justice is sadly sacrificed to a weak fancy for forgiveness; but nothing can excel the exquisite delicacy, combined with the tremendous illustrative force, of the language allotted to Isabella, who is the main figure in the piece.

The plot was familiar even before Shakespeare's time, but he undoubtedly adopted it from Whetstone's play of "Promos and Cassandra," published in 1578, which had no success, and which was itself translated from an Italian novel by Geraldi Cinthio. The main story is that of a pure sister pleading to a corrupt judge for a condemned brother's life, which sister is allowed to ransom his existence only by a surrender of her chastity to that functionary. The judge, succeeding in his aim, then orders the execution of the brother (Claudio) to take place, for fear he may seek revenge for "so receiving a dishonoured life." This is the original story; but Shakespeare changes it, so that Isabella, the sister, when her honour is at its crisis, sends a female representative, in the undistinguishing darkness of the night, to perform her expected part with Angelo, the judge, and thus herself escapes all taint. To justify her pure mind to the pursuance of this double course, however, Isabella acts under the direction of a holy friar, who provides, as her nocturnal substitute, a maiden under betrothal to Lord Angelo, the judge. The real duke is the disguised friar who counsels Isabella to this act, and who, when he finds that Angelo, his deputy, still orders the sentence of death to be carried out against Claudio, privately interposes his authority with the prison officials, and sends to Angelo the head of a man who had that day died in his cell, as Claudio's head. The severed head deceives Angelo and Isabella both; whereupon the agonized and desperate girl bursts into threats of personal vengeance upon the villainous deputy, and is about starting off to execute them, when the friar, gently checking her rage, informs her that the real duke comes home on the morrow, and advises her to intercept him, along with Mariana, on his public entrance to the city, and then to con-

spicuously lay their wrongs before him, in the very presence of
Lord Angelo.

This advice is followed by Isabella and Mariana, and as the
duke comes into the city, surrounded by his nobles, the young
ladies cast themselves before him, and, denouncing Angelo,
demand justice on him.

DUKE. Relate your wrongs: In what? By whom? Be brief:
    Here is lord Angelo shall give you justice!
    Reveal yourself to him.
ISAB.   O, worthy duke,
    You bid me seek redemption of the devil:
    Hear me yourself; for that which I must speak
    Must either punish me, not being believed,
    Or wring redress from you: hear me, O, hear me, here.
ANG. *My lord, her wits, I fear me, are not firm:*
    She hath been a suitor to me for her brother,
    Cut off by course of justice!
ISAB.   By course of justice!
ANG. And she will speak most bitterly, and strange.
ISAB. Most strange, but yet most truly, will I speak:
    That Angelo's forsworn; is it not strange?
    That Angelo's a murderer; is it not strange?
    That Angelo is an adulterous thief,
    An hypocrite, a virgin-violator;
    Is it not strange, and strange?
DUKE.   Nay, ten times strange.

The duke affects to disbelieve Isabella, and orders her off to
prison. Mariana is then required to tell *her* story. She thereupon recites her betrothal to Angelo, and his abandonment of her
because of the failure of her fortune. Next comes her description
of the midnight consummation of her betrothal by keeping
Isabella's appointment with the deputy in the dark. Finally,
unveiling, Mariana shows her face to Angelo, and claims to be
his wife. The duke hereupon demands of Angelo if he knows
this woman.

ANG. My lord, I must confess, I know this woman;
    And, five years since, there was some speech of marriage
    Betwixt myself and her; which was broke off,
    Partly, for that her promised proportions
    Came short of composition; *but, in chief,*
    For that her reputation was disvalued
    In levity: since which time of five years

> I never spake with her, saw her, nor heard from her,
> Upon my faith and honour.
>
> MARI.   Noble prince,
> As there comes light from heaven, and words from breath,
> As there is sense in truth, and truth in virtue,
> I am affianced this man's wife, as strongly
> As words could make up vows: and, my good lord,
> But Tuesday night last gone, in his garden-house
> He knew me as a wife: As this is true
> Let me in safety raise me from my knees ;
> Or else for ever be confixed here,
> A marble monument !
>
> ANG.   I did but smile till now ;
> Now, good my lord, give me the scope of justice ;
> My patience here is touched : I do perceive,
> These poor informal women are no more
> But instruments of some more mightier member
> That sets them on : Let me have way, my lord,
> To find this practice out.
>
> DUKE.   Ay, with all my heart ;
> And punish them unto your height of pleasure.

The duke now goes out on some pretence, but really to resume
his friar's habit, and to presently return in that disguise.   At the
same time, from the other side of the stage, but still in the custody of officers, again comes Isabella.   Angelo, on the exit of
the duke, had at once resumed all his former arrogance, and as
soon as he sets eyes upon the returning friar, of whom he has
heard so much, and through whose guidance of Isabella and
Mariana he had suffered so much trouble, he assumes a lofty
tone, and orders him to be arrested.   The duke being hustled
by the officers, is then discovered under the friar's cowl, and
being thus recognized, at once assumes his regal dignity, and
waives Angelo from the ducal seat.

> DUKE (*to Angelo*).   Sir, by your leave :
> Hast thou or word, or wit, or impudence,
> That yet can do thee office?   If thou hast,
> Rely upon it till my tale be heard,
> And hold no longer out.
>
> ANG.   O my dread lord,
> I should be guiltier than my guiltiness,
> To think I can be undiscernible,
> When I perceive your grace, like power divine,
> Hath look'd upon my passes ; then, good prince,

No longer session hold upon my shame,
But let my trial be my own confession,
Immediate sentence then, and sequent death,
Is all the grace I beg.

DUKE.   Come hither, Mariana:
Say, wast thou e'er contracted to this woman?

ANG. I was, my lord.

DUKE. Go take her hence, and marry her instantly.—
Do you the office, friar; which consummate, ·
Return him here again:—Go with him, provost.

[*Exeunt* ANGELO, MARIANA, FRIAR PETER, *and Provost.*

DUKE.   Come hither, Isabel:
Your friar is now your prince: As I was then
Advertising, and holy to your business,
Not changing heart with habit, I am still
Attorney'd at your service.

ISAB.   O give me pardon,
That I, your vassal, have employ'd and pain'd
Your unknown sovereignty.

DUKE.   You are pardon'd, Isabel,
And now, dear maid, be you as free to us.
Your brother's death, I know, sits at your heart;
And you may marvel, why I obscured myself,
Labouring to save his life; and would not rather
Make rash remonstrance of my hidden power,
Than let him so be lost: O most kind maid,
It was the swift celerity of his death,
Which I did think with slower foot came on.
That brain'd my purpose: But, peace be with him!
That life is better life past fearing death,
Than that which lives to fear; make it your comfort,
So happy is your brother.

Re-enter ANGELO, MARIANA, FRIAR PETER, *and Provost.*

ISAB.   I do, my lord.

DUKE. For this new-married man, approaching here,
Whose salt imagination yet hath wrong'd
Your well-defended honour, you must pardon
For Mariana's sake; but as he adjudged your brother,
(Being criminal, in double violation
Of sacred chastity and of promise breach,
Thereon dependent, for your brother's life),
The very mercy of the law cries out
Most audible, even from his proper tongue,
An Angelo for Claudio, death for death.
Haste still pays haste, and leisure answers leisure;
Like doth quit like, and *Measure* still for *Measure.*
Then, Angelo, thy fault's thus manifested;

> Which, though thou would'st deny, denies thee vantage ;
> We do condemn thee to the very block
> Where Claudio stoop'd to death, and with like haste ;
> Away with him.

MARI. O, my most gracious lord,
I hope you will not mock me with a husband !

DUKE. It is your husband mock'd you with a husband ;
Consenting to the safeguard of your honour,
I thought your marriage fit ; else imputation
For that he knew you, might reproach your life,
And choke your good to come ; for his possessions,
Although by confiscation they are ours,
We do instate and widow you withal,
To buy you a better husband.

Mariana hereupon sweetly entreats Isabel to help her beg of the duke the life of Angelo ; but the duke checks the movement by the following sublime rebuke :—

DUKE. Against all sense do you importune her.
Should she kneel down in mercy, of this fact,
Her brother's ghost his pavéd bed would break,
And take her hence in horror.

Mariana, nevertheless, perseveres and succeeds in touching the deepest springs of Isabella's saintly nature, who, falling on her knees before the duke, thus addresses him :—

ISAB. Most bounteous sir,
Look, if it please you, on this man condemn'd,
As if my brother lived ; I partly think
A due sincerity govern'd his deeds,
Till he did look on me ; since it is so,
Let him not die : My brother had but justice,
In that he did the thing for which he died ;
For Angelo,
His act did not o'ertake his bad intent ;
And must be buried but as an intent
That perish'd by the way ; thoughts are no subjects,
Intents but merely thoughts.

DUKE. Your suit's unprofitable : stand up, I say—
I have bethought me of another fault :—
Provost, how came it Claudio was beheaded
At an unusual hour ?

In a few minutes afterward Claudio is brought to life, pardoned, and handed over to Isabella, whereupon the all-forgiving

duke thus addresses her, and winds up the situation with one
general joy :—

> DUKE.   And, for your lovely sake,
> Give me your hand, and say you will be mine,
> He is my brother too: But fitter time for that.
> By this, lord Angelo perceives he's safe;
> Methinks, I see a quick'ning in his eye :—
> *Well, Angelo, your evil quits you well :*
> Look that you love your wife; her worth, worth yours.
> I find an apt remission in myself.

It is hardly possible for language to picture a more base, blood-
thirsty, and unpitying miscreant than Angelo.   To the last moment, even in the presence of the duke, he maintains his villany
by misrepresenting Isabella, and by relentlessly defaming the
character of Mariana.   In fact, he does not cease to lie against
them both, until he is actually unmasked beyond all remedy;
and then, like Proteus, he suddenly confesses, and, as every
reader must regret, is as readily forgiven.   In this respect, the
moral of the play is as deplorable as that of the "Two Gentlemen
of Verona," and through its utter defeat of the principle of retributive justice, could hardly have been the inspiration of such a
stern lawyer as Lord Bacon.   With Shakespeare, however, a big-
natured, good-tempered man, with a prodigious and sympathetic
genius, but scarcely any conscience, this pleasant rounding of
the whole story was a natural inclination.   By following this
course, which, it may be remarked, was usual with our poet in
the earlier part of his career (indeed, until he arrived at the
period of his deepest tragedies), he evinced an unruffled serenity
of character.   It may also be observed, that in preferring these
happy terminations, Shakespeare evinces one form of the art of
theatrical management by sending his audiences home pleased,
thus unconsciously testifying to the tender and generous
nature of the people.

But something, at the same time, let me add, is due to the
principle of justice; and there can be no doubt that Coleridge is
right when he says " that sincere repentance on the part of Angelo was impossible," and therefore regrets that the unparelleled
villain was not executed.   But Gervinius finds excuse for the
mercy of the duke in the fact that, " apart from poetry," such a
doom would not have been in strict conformity with either law or

justice. Gervinius' position is, that Angelo's double crime—the intended disgrace of Isabella and the death of Claudio—had not been carried out, and that he had been consequently guilty only in intent. But this argument does not justify his pardon, for Angelo had executed Claudio as far as his bloody and merciless purpose could do so, and had consummated, with Mariana, the very crime for which, under the statutes of Vienna, Claudio had been condemned. Nevertheless, it must be admitted that the penalty for this last particular offence could hardly have been administered by the duke, who, in the habit of a friar, had advised it. Regarding the play as a whole, however, we may safely conclude that it does not inculcate either statesmanship or law; at any rate, not such statesmanship or logical exactitude as might be expected to make their development from the mind of Sir Francis Bacon.

I may here observe, I find but one instance in this play bearing upon Shakespeare's low estimate of the people; and that occurs in the first scene of the first act, when the duke is about going into retirement, or, to speak more strictly, when he is about assuming his incognito, under the name of Friar Lodewick :—

> DUKE.   I love the people,
> But do not love to stage me to their eyes.
> Though it do well, I do not relish well
> Their loud applause and avés vehement.

But this is only a just sneer at popular servility, especially as it must have shown itself to the duke.

SHAKESPEARE'S LAW, I.

Lord Campbell, in his essay examining the legal acquirements of Shakespeare, presents four instances, which he considers rather as affirmative. One of these was treated in Chapter IX., and consisted of the line " good counsellors need no clients "; the other three are as follows :

II.

Says Campbell, "In Act II. Scene 1, the ignorance of special pleading and of the nature of actions at law betrayed by Elbow the constable, when slandered, is ridiculed by the Lord Escalus in a manner which proves that the composer of the dialogue was himself fully initiated in these mysteries :"—

ELBOW. Oh, thou caitiff! Oh, thou varlet! Oh, thou wicked Hannibal! *I* respected with her, before I was married to her?—If ever I was respected with her, or she with me, let not your worship think me the poor duke's officer:—Prove this, thou wicked Hannibal, or I'll have mine action of battery on thee.

ESCAL. If he took you a box o' the ear, you might have your action of slander too.

III.

" The manner in which, in Act III. Scene 2, Escalus designates and talks of Angelo, with whom he was joined in commission as Judge, is," continues Lord Campbell, " so like the manner in which one English judge designates and talks of another, that it countenances the supposition that Shakespeare may often, as an attorney's clerk, have been in the presence of English judges :"—

ESCAL. Provost, *my brother Angelo* will not be altered ; Claudio must die to-morrow. . . . . . If *my brother* wrought by my pity, it should not be so with him. . . . . . I have laboured for the poor gentlemen to the extremest shore of my modesty ; but *my brother justice* have I found so severe, that he hath forced me to tell him that he is indeed JUSTICE.

IV.

" Even when Shakespeare is most solemn and sublime," adds his lordship, "his sentiments and language seem sometimes to take a tinge from his early pursuits, as may be observed from a beautiful passage in this play ; which, lest I should be thought guilty of irreverence, I do not venture to comment upon :"—

ISAB. (*to Angelo.*)   Alas! alas!
Why, all the souls that were, were forfeit once ;
And He that might the 'vantage best have took,
Found out the remedy.   How would *you* be,
If He, which is the top of judgment, should
But judge *you* as *you* are ?   Oh, think on that,
And mercy then will breathe within your lips,
Like man new made !

I do not think that Lord Chief Justice Campbell has done himself much credit, by citing the above four cases in proof of Shakespeare's law learning.[3]

[3] Lord Campbell, pp. 42, 43.

But the great figure in the play—the figure which stands in towering dignity and purity and beauty above all others, and above all other of Shakespeare's women, is Isabella, the nun, or rather, the young novitiate of the convent of St. Clare. It seems to me, that if Shakespeare had any method, beyond the mere usual waywardness of his plots, it was his object in this play to develope, through the characters of Isabella and the Duke, his views of the beautiful philosophy of the Catholic religion. In his portraiture of the villain Angelo, he, on the other hand, paints a perfect picture of Puritan hypocrisy.

> Lord Angelo is *precise*;
> Stands at a guard with envy; scarce confesses
> That his blood flows, or that his appetite
> Is more to bread than stone.

And this oblique sarcasm against the Puritans is again repeated, says Dr. Farmer, in the Constable's account of Master Froth and the Clown: "*Precise* villains they are, that I am sure of; and void of all profanation in the world that good Christians ought to have."

The opening of "Measure for Measure" finds Isabella undergoing her religious probation in that tranquil half-way house upon the road to heaven, the convent of St. Clare. She is conversing sweetly with the nuns upon the sacred mysteries that are just unfolding to her virgin comprehension, when she is suddenly interrupted by a rude clangour at the convent gate. This comes to summon her back to the stirring world in order that she may make solicitation of the newly-appointed savage deputy for her brother's life. She cannot choose but yield to the appeal; but going out, never comes back, having learned "that in the world may be found a discipline more strict, more awful than the discipline of the convent; having also learned that the world has need of her; that her life is still a consecrated life, and that the vital energy of her heart can exert and augment itself as Duchess of Vienna more fully than in conventual seclusion."[4] In speaking of "Measure for Measure," Drake says that "the great charm of the play springs from the lovely example of female excellence exhibited in the person of Isabella. Piety, spotless purity, tenderness combined with firmness, and an eloquence

---

[4] Dowden's "Mind and Art of Shakespeare," pp. 83, 84.

most persuasive, unite to render her singularly interesting and attractive. *C'est un ange de lumiere sous l'humble habit d'une novice.* To save the life of her brother she hastens to quit the peaceful seclusion of her convent, and moves amid the votaries of corruption and hypocrisy, amid the sensual, the vulgar, and the profligate, as a being of a higher order, as a ministering spirit from the throne of grace."

Knight, in alluding to Isabella, says that " the foundation of her character is religion. Out of that sacred source springs her humility—her purity, which cannot understand oblique purposes and suggestions—her courage—her passionate indignation at the selfishness of her brother, who would have sacrificed her to attain his own safety. It is in the conception of such a character that we see the transcendant superiority of Shakespeare over other dramatists. The ' thing enskied and sainted ' was not for any of his greatest contemporaries to conceive and delineate."

And yet, Shakespeare made this female masterpiece—this religious paragon, this beau ideal of his genius—a nun; and while escorting her with solemn dignity throughout her scenes, he commands silence and bent heads for every allusion to the Romish faith. In comment upon this fact, it may be remarked, that if a mere playwright might venture upon such developments of Catholic saintliness in the midst of a Puritan age, Bacon could hardly have lost favour with Elizabeth or James by openly claiming the authorship of the Shakespeare plays himself.

CHAPTER XII.

"COMEDY OF ERRORS."

THE date of this play is put down in Furnival's Table at 1589-91, but it was not published until the appearance of the folio of 1623. It is mentioned in a work by Francis Meares, in 1598, and was performed at Court in December, 1604, before King James.

The story of the piece is taken from the Menæchmi of Plautus, the old Roman dramatist, though it differs from that production to the extent of adding to the two twin Antipholuses of the Roman play, two twin Dromios also.

It has by this time been observed by the reader that Shakespeare exhibits a perfect indifference about the origin of the plots of his plays. He adopts without scruple any fable he can lay his hands upon, and appears to be governed entirely in the composition of his pieces by the aim of making a production which will be amusing to his audiences. In fact, he clearly disdains narrative as the lowest form of composition, and seems always willing to allow any one to help him to his story. It is his task to raise the structure after others have sunk the foundation; to enlarge it by the expanding pressure of his mind, and embroider the surface with his matchless imagery. Even a ballad was quite enough for him to build upon; for there was no end either to the resources of his invention or the productiveness of his fancy. Indeed, every writer of any imagination knows for himself that a tale once begun may be reeled off with undisturbed facility; or, to use Shakespeare's own language in Falstaff, may be continued on "as easy as lying." Witness, in evidence of this, the prolific romance department in the thousand and one of modern weekly newspapers.

The "Comedy of Errors" bears evidence of having been

hastily and carelessly written. It is full of anachronisms and of geographical contradictions; and though laid in the old Roman days it has allusions to America and the Indies; while one of the Dromios calls his female kitchen-friends in the city of Ephesus by the broad English, Irish, and Scotch names of " Maud, Bridget, Marian, Cicely, Gillian, and Jen."

The plot of the play and its staring absurdities make an abso- lute mockery of the fine speculations which the German critics are so fond of indulging in, as to the profound theories which Shakespeare always intended to convey through his plays, for the instruction of mankind. Here we have him presenting two couples of men, who have been living apart from each other in strange countries for nearly thirty years—who, if they do look alike, must necessarily bear themselves differently, talk differently, walk differently, and dress differently—and these, he asks us to believe, succeed in deceiving everybody as to their separate iden- tities and even in baffling the familiar scrutiny of their wives and mistresses! In my opinion, a writer who is thus careless of con- gruities, and who presents his themes without any regard to the possibilities of human belief, is not engaged in the task of giving abstruse lessons in philosophy. The legal lore of the play, more- over, however much it may impress Lord Chief Justice Campbell, seems to me to be actually law run mad. Creditors commence process against debtors before constables, in the street, by word of mouth, and the constable, upon receiving a money fee from the plaintiff, issues process of arrest out of hand, and discharges the debtor with equal readiness upon having the judgment satisfied with cash—thus excusing all function from the court.

Act IV. Scene 1.—*Ephesus.*

ANTIPHOLUS *and* DROMIO, *of Ephesus; a Merchant;* ANGELO, *a Gold-smith; and an Officer.*

MERCH. (*pointing to* ANTIPHOLUS OF E., *whom he charges with owing him the price of a gold chain*).
        Well, officer, arrest him at my suit.

OFF.   I do; and charge you in the duke's name, to obey me.
ANG.   This touches me in reputation:—
        Either consent to pay this sum to me,
        Or I attach you by this officer.
ANT. E. Consent to pay thee that I never had!
        Arrest me, foolish fellow, if thou dar'st.
ANG.   Here is thy fee; arrest him, officer;—

<pre>
            I would not spare my brother in this case,
            If he should scorn me so apparently.
   OFF.   I do arrest you, sir; you hear the suit.
   ANT. E. I do obey they, till I give thee bail :—
            But, sirrah, you shall buy this sport as dear
            As all the metal in your shop will answer.
   ANG.   Sir, sir, I shall have law in Ephesus,
            To your notorious shame, I doubt it not.
</pre>

· Nevertheless, Lord Chief Justice Campbell discovers several evidences in this play of Shakespeare's knowledge of law. He finds, in Act II. Scene 2, another allusion to *"fine and recovery;"* in Act IV. Scene 2, he detects more law in Dromio's description of the above arrest of his master in his use of the phrases of *"before the judgment,"* and *"rested on the case,"* further explaining that he has been arrested on a *bond;* yet, "not on a bond, but on a stronger thing: a chain, a chain!" Now listen to Lord Campbell :—

"Here," says his lordship, "we have a most circumstantial and graphic account of an English arrest on *mesne process* ["before judgment"], in an action *on the case,* for the price of a gold chain by a sheriff's officer or bum-bailiff in his buff costume, and carrying his prisoner to a sponging-house—a spectacle which might often have been seen by an attorney's clerk."

I hope I may be excused for thinking that Lord Campbell does not do himself much credit by this specimen of his critical acumen. He doubtless correctly describes the nature of an arrest on *mesne process,* but there is no evidence that Shakespeare understood all the intricacies of that process, because one of his clowns utters a surface reference to it through the use of a current phrase, any more than there would be in supposing a man to know the geological strata of Mount Caucasus because he mentions it by name. But one thing is certain (however far these technical expressions may be construed to go), that there is not virtue enough in these mere terms of law to overbalance the monstrous absurdity of allowing tipstaves to issue process for debt, and then to hold court for the purpose of taking bail in the streets. I cannot bring myself to believe that Lord Bacon, or any other lawyer, who knew the philosophy of law, would have built any story upon such a ridiculous foundation as this.

And I may add that neither could Bacon, as an experienced traveller and scholar, have made the geographical mistakes with which this and other of the Shakespeare plays abound. Certainly his chronology would not have been so bad as to have alluded to rapiers, striking clocks, and ducats, as having been in use in the early days of Ephesus.

There is but little more for me to notice in this play as bearing upon my objective points, further than that, the epithet of *peasant* is twice opprobriously used in it, as likewise is the term of *slave*, in application to ordinary honest serving-men. I must not omit to observe, however, that the Roman Catholic religion is most gracefully introduced towards the close of the play, in the person of an abbess, who gives sanctuary to one of the heroes of the piece, and refuses to release him at the clamour of his wife, even when threatened with the power of the duke.

ADR. Then let your servants bring my husband forth.

ABB. Neither; he took this place for sanctuary,
And it shall privilege him from your hands,
Till I have brought him to his wits again,
Or lose my labour in assaying it.

ADR. I will attend my husband, be his nurse,
Diet his sickness, for it is my office,
And will have no attorney but myself;
And therefore let me have him home with me.

ABB. Be patient: for I will not let him stir,
Till I have used the approved means I have.
With wholesome syrups, drugs, and holy prayers,
To make of him a formal man again :
It is a branch and parcel of mine oath,
A charitable duty of my order ;
Therefore depart, and leave him here with me.

ADR. I will not hence, and leave my husband here:
And ill it doth beseem your holiness,
To separate the husband and the wife.

ABB. Be quiet, and depart, thou shalt not have him. [*Exit* ABBESS.

By-and-by the duke and his train arrive, whereupon the estimable abbess comes out of the abbey with Antipholus of Ephesus. But Shakespeare continues her as mistress of the situation, and thus winds up the main action of the piece :—

ABBESS. Renowned duke, vouchsafe to take the pains
To go with us into the abbey here,
And hear at large discoursed all our fortunes :
And all that are assembled at this place,
That by this sympathized one day's error
Have suffer'd wrong. go, keep us company,
And we shall make full satisfaction.

" MIDSUMMER NIGHT'S DREAM."

The production of this charming comedy is variously assigned by Drake, Malone, and Schlegel to 1592, 1593, and 1594; but Elze, more accurately, as I think, places it in the spring of 1590, when Shakespeare was twenty-six years of age, affirming that it was written as a masque or revel to be performed at the wedding of the Earl of Essex with Lady Sidney. This was a common custom with the aristocracy of Elizabeth's time, and the following closing lines of Oberon, the fairy king, in compliment to the marriage of Theseus and Hyppolita, would seem to confirm the idea that it was written by our poet to grace some marriage feast :—

> BERON. Now, until the break of day,
> Through this house each fairy stray.
> To the best bride-bed will we,
> Which by us shall blessed be;
> And the issue there create,
> Ever shall be fortunate.
> So shall all the couples three
> Ever true in loving be;
> And the blots of nature's hand
> Shall not in their issue stand;
> Never mole, hare-lip, or scar,
> Nor mark prodigious, such as are
> Despised in nativity,
> Shall upon their children be.—
> With this field dew consecrate,
> Every fairy take his gait;
> And each several chamber bless,
> Through this palace with sweet peace:
> Ever shall in safety rest,
> And the owner of it blest.

The first thing which appears in this play touching the points of our inquiry, is a legal expression that falls from the father of Hermia in the first scene of the first act, when he appeals to the duke to require his daughter to obey his wishes by marrying with Demetrius, or else to grant against her, for the sin of disobedience,—

> " Her death, according to our law,
> *Immediately provided in that case.*"

Both Steevens and Lord Campbell receive this expression as a proof that Shakespeare had served in an attorney's office; and the latter remarks that "there is certainly no nearer approach in heroic measure to the technical language of an indictment."

This legal incident is then immediately followed by the following reverent allusion to the Roman Catholic religion, though the scene of the play is laid in early Greece. The duke, Theseus, thus impresses upon Hermia the necessity of conforming to her father's will :—

> THESEUS. Either to die the death, or to abjure
> For ever the society of men.
> Therefore, fair Hermia, question your desires,
> Know of your youth, examine well your blood,
> Whether, if you yield not to your father's choice,
> *You can enjoy the livery of a nun;*
> *For aye to be in shady cloister mew'd,*
> *To live a barren sister all your life,*
> *Chanting faint hymns to the cold, fruitless moon.*
> *Thrice blessed they, that master so their blood*
> *To undergo such maiden pilgrimage;*
> But earthlier happy is the rose distill'd,
> Than that which, withering on the virgin thorn,
> Grows, lives, and dies in single blessedness.
>
> HER. So will I grow, so live, so die, my lord,
> Ere I will yield my virgin patent up
> Unto his lordship.

One cannot help remarking here that a threatened imprisonment of Hermia for life in a state prison would have been fully adequate to all the necessities of the scene, instead of bringing in a nunnery. So also would a prison have equally served the purposes of the last act of the "Comedy of Errors," in place of the abbey; but Shakespeare evidently wanted to patronize the Catholic religion.

The next evidence we have bearing on our points are the lines at the conclusion of the same act, which show Shakespeare's intimate knowledge of stage business; first, in Snug's inquiry if the lion's part has been written out (i. e. copied) for him; and next, in the arrangements made by Bottom and his mates in the distribution of the written (copied) parts for the actors; likewise in the provision of a "bill of properties" needed for their play before the duke. All of this throws Bacon out of our consideration, so far as this composition is concerned, and at the same time disposes of the fiction of Shakespeare's "fair round hand," which the players reported of his manuscript, and which, according to many of his critics, showed that his mind flowed with such a smooth felicity "that he never blotted out a line." This idea serves the purposes of the Baconians by making it appear that Shakespeare merely copied out the manuscript of Bacon.

The course of our scrutiny now brings us to the first distinct illustrations of Shakespeare's low estimation of the mechanical and labouring classes—the classes which, in the United States, are justly esteemed to be not the least honest, virtuous, and patriotic of the community. This tendency of our poet appears in the underplot of Bottom and the Athenian mechanics who have been selected to perform before the newly-married pair on the classical subject of Pyramus and Thisbe, upon the calculation that their ignorance would certainly burlesque it. We have already had an introduction to these simple-hearted fellows in the second scene of the first act, on the occasion of the distribution of their several dramatic parts; and we now find them, at the opening of the third act, ready for rehearsal, in the wood, near where the fairies are lying around asleep. While the working men are thus engaged, Puck, the fairy messenger and factotum, enters from behind, and in a tone of contempt which must have been graciously appreciated by Essex and the rest of the Elizabethan company, Master Puck thus characterizes the hard-handed men who are doing their best to please their lordly patrons :—

> PUCK. *What hempen homespuns have we swaggering here,*
> So near the cradle of the fairy queen?

Puck, in the next scene, reports to Oberon the laughable metamorphosis he had made of Bottom, and his still more ludicrous exploit of having caused Titania to fall in love with him :—

> PUCK. My mistress with a monster is in love.
> Near to her close and consecrated bower,
> While she was in her dull and sleeping hour,
> *A crew of patches, rude mechanicals,*
> *That work for bread upon Athenian stalls,*
> Were met together to rehearse a play,
> Intended for great Theseus' nuptial day.
> *The shallow'd thick-skin of that barren sort,*

Who Pyramus presented, in their sport
Forsook his scene, and enter'd in a brake:
When I did him at this advantage take,
An ass's nowl I fixed on his head.

Puck continues his report, as to the way he had carried out Oberon's other orders concerning Demetrius and Helena; but he changes his contemptuous tone at once to one of severe respect when he refers to the *ladies and gentlemen* of the story. This treatment of the case by Shakespeare is explainable either through the spontaneous servility he always shows to rank and birth, or, perhaps, to the more excusable object of having to cater to audiences of a people who are born worshippers of wealth and station, and the masses of whom to this day seem to like nothing so much as to look upon a lord.

CHAPTER XIII.

"THE MERCHANT OF VENICE."

THIS remarkable play was produced in 1596, and published, for the first time, in the year 1600. It was regarded as a comedy, and probably was written as such, the character of Shylock being originally consigned to a low comedian. The enjoyment and laughter of its audiences were obtained consequently from the sufferings and discomfiture of the detested Jew. In degree, however, as the prejudice against the Hebrews lifted, "The Merchant of Venice" gradually assumed the title of "a play," and latterly, the rôle of Shylock has been entrusted only to the leading tragedians of the day. There is a world of moral in these simple facts.

The plot, or story, has two leading incidents, both of which Shakespeare, with his contempt for mere narration, has taken bodily from foreign sources. The main action of the play is devoted to the fable of "Antonio the Merchant," borrowing a sum of money from Shylock, the Jew, to help his penniless friend, Bassanio, to inveigle the affections of a lady of exceeding wealth. The Jew, who has been much abused by Antonio for taking usury, proposes to take no interest from the borrower, either in order to recover his good will, or in the event of his failing to pay, to catch him at a deadly disadvantage. Indeed, he asks no security, except such as is to be found in the agreement, but consents to accept, in lieu of the loan, a pound of Antonio's flesh, to be cut by the creditor from off his breast. This foolish fiction, so repugnant to all the philosophy of law, is taken from an Italian novel, published by Giovanni, two hundred years before Shakespeare's time; while the secondary plot, in which the lady courted by Bassanio is subjected to the choice of any lover who is lucky enough to guess one out of three caskets that contains her picture, is, if possible, more trivial still. But this is the kind of thing which Shakespeare would constantly perpetrate in the matter of his plots ; and we are therefore justified in the conclusion, that his first and controlling object was, not to inculcate intricate lessons of philosophy and morals, as many of his biographers assume, but to draw full houses and to please good-natured audiences. Indeed, could Shakespeare be roused from his " paved bed " for a few minutes, to listen to the profound theories ascribed to him by the German commentators upon such plays as " The Merchant of Venice," " Two Gentlemen of Verona," and " The Comedy of Errors," his astonished shade, would, probably, be glad to shrink back into its marble prison, in order to escape the fine but confusing theories about him with which the world has been teased during the last fifty years.

In fact, when I first began the research necessary to this inquiry, I was staggered by the amount of compound insight assumed by the German critics as to Shakespeare's drift and inculcations. So busily had these literary beavers worked at the text of the immortal bard, that they usually allotted to him the credit of six or seven different profundities of purpose in the story of one play, or even in the development of a single character. This complicated cleverness not only amazed but for a time discouraged me, and I almost sank under a sense of hopeless incapacity at being able to understand one-fifth of what they said. Finally, however, I determined to go on, relying for my success upon the resolution with which I had set out—not to make this inquiry an *argument* for one point or another, either of religion, democracy, or law. On the contrary, to keep it as far as I could, rigidly to its true character of an *examination,* in which everything bearing upon the *inquiry,* whether in favour of Bacon or of Shakespeare, should be heard. I believe I have been faithful to this purpose ; but if the facts, thus far, have all borne one way, and, if my intelligence has been obliged to exercise the common privilege of judgment, the cumulation of authority must not be charged to any favouritism on my part.

Now, as to the German exploitation of the compound philosophical inculcations of our. poet, let us look at the simple sketch of the three branches of "The Merchant of Venice" (which, be it remembered, Shakespeare took bodily from other minds), and see what some of these Germans impute to *his* mind in simply reproducing the story in an English form.

First, let us read the following account of the original
sources of Shakespeare's play, as it appears in Rowe's edition of
our poet's dramatic works:—

"The plot of 'The Merchant of Venice' comprises the chief circumstance
of the bond, the auxiliary incident of the caskets, and the sub-story of
Lorenzo and Jessica. The story of the bond is of oriental origin; it first
appeared in Europe, in a work by Giovanni, a Florentine novelist, from which
our dramatist, though indirectly, perhaps, has taken his materials.

"Giannetto obtains permission from his godfather, Ansaldo, to travel to
Alexandria, but changes his mind, in the hopes of gaining a lady of great
wealth and beauty at Belmont, whose hand is proffered to him who can obtain
a premature enjoyment of the connubial rites. Overpowered with sleep,
occasioned by a narcotic given him in his wine, he fails in his enterprise, and
his vessel and cargo, which he had wagered on his success, are forfeited.
Another ship is equipped, which he loses in a second attempt; and a third is
made at the expense of his godfather, who borrows ten thousand ducats from
a Jew, on condition that if they are not returned by a stipulated day, the
lender may cut a pound of flesh from any part of the debtor's body. Giannetto obtains the lady; but lost in delight with his bride, forgets Ansaldo's
bond till the very day it becomes due. He hastens to Venice, but the time
is past, and the usurer refuses ten times the value of his bond. Giannetto's lady arrives at this crisis, and causes it to be announced that she
can resolve difficult questions in law. Consulted in the case of Ansaldo, she
decides that the Jew must have his pound of flesh; but that he shall lose his
head if he cuts more or less, or draws one drop of blood. The Jew relinquishes
his demand, and Ansaldo is released. The bride will not receive money as a
recompense, but desires Giannetto's wedding-ring, which he gives her.
The lady arrives at home before her husband, and immediately asks for her
ring, which he being unable to produce, she upbraids him with having given
it to some mistress. At length, Giannetto's sorrow affects his wife, and
she explains the particulars of her journey and disguise. All this is closely
followed by Shakespeare; but the improbability of a lady's possessing so much
legal acumen is skilfully removed by making her consult an eminent lawyer,
and act under his advice.

"The choosing of the caskets is borrowed from the English Gesta Romanorum, a collection of tales much esteemed by our ancestors. Three vessels
were placed before the king of Apulia's daughter for her choice. The first
was of pure gold, and filled with dead men's bones; on it was this inscription: *Who chooses me shall find what he deserves.* The second was of silver,
and thus inscribed: *Who chooses me shall find what nature covets.* It was
filled with earth. The third vessel was of lead, but filled with precious
stones. It had this inscription: *Who chooses me shall find what God has
placed.* The princess, after praying for assistance, chooses the leaden vessel.
The emperor applauds her wisdom, and she is united to his son."

Here are the two branches of the main story almost completely;

so whatever that *story* inculcates, must be credited to Giovanni, the Florentine originator, and not to Shakespeare. But hear what the German commentators say :—Karl Elze, who is a doctor of philosophy, remarks, " that it might be supposed critics would long since have come to a unanimous and generally recognized æsthetic estimate of such a much-read play as ' The Merchant of Venice,' standing, as it does, on the *répertoire* of almost every stage ; however, the conceptions of the fundamental idea, the opinions concerning the composition and the criticism of the characters, differ here more widely than in the case of most of the other works of our poet." Gervinius finds " a proof of the wealth and many-sidedness of Shakespeare's works to lie in the variety of the points of view from which they may be regarded, as it is not without a certain degree and appearance of correctness that several opinions on one and the same play may be formed." According to Horn, " The Merchant of ·Venice " is based upon a truly grand, profound, extremely delightful, nay, an almost blessed idea, upon a purely Christian, conciliatory love, and upon meditating mercy as opposed to the law, and to what is called right." Surely, this must be very fine, if one could only understand it. Ulrici, in the very best of Latin, finds the ideal of unity in the saying, " *Summum jus, summa injuria ;* " that is to say, the rigour of the law is the very rigour of oppression, and Rötscher so modifies this view, that he considers the inner-most spirit of the play evidently to be " the dialectics of abstract right." He oracularly adds, " By the expression of abstract right, we mean that development by which abstract right by itself, that is, by its own nature, discovers its own worthlessness, consequently destroys itself where it seeks to govern human life, and to assert itself as an absolute power." This logic is so superbly intricate that it seems out of place anywhere but in the mouth of the hair-splitting first grave-digger in Hamlet. Elze thinks, that " the centre of gravity of the play lies in Portia's address to Mercy,"[1] and Gervinius comes again, with the idea that, " in ' The Merchant of Venice,' the poet wished to delineate man's relation to property." He profoundly adds that " to prove a man's relation to property, to money, is to weigh his inner value by a most subtle balance, and to separate that which

[1] " Essays on Shakespeare," by Karl Elze, pp. 67, 68, 69. London, Macmillan and Co., 1874.

clings to unessential and external things from that which, in its inner nature, places itself in relation to a higher destiny." Surely Christy's Minstrels never did anything better than this ! Hebler, objecting to the idea of Gervinius, that " money, the god of the world, is the symbol of appearance and of everything external," admits, nevertheless, that the fundamental idea of the piece " lies in the struggle against appearance and of everything external," but he confesses that it is " by no means only represented symbolically by the caskets, but in a very plastic and classical manner." " According to this conception," says another, " Bassanio's speech, when selecting the casket, contains the key to the poem, and it cannot be denied that it possesses as great a claim to this distinction as Portia's apotheosis to Mercy." Kreysig, lastly, " recognizes the impossibility of comprising the numerous diverse and to some extent opposite elements of the play under one fundamental idea," and concludes by saying, for the benefit of whom it may concern, " that strong feeling, together with clear and sure reasoning, balance each other in the character pervading the whole." All of which profound and eloquent encomiums being due equally to Giovanni and to Shakespeare so far as the story is concerned, and really more to the former than to the latter, bring me to the same state of complication which disturbed the mind of the celebrated negro philosopher when endeavouring to solve the obvious difficulties of the problem of a horse dying on a man's hands.

It seems to me that if Shakespeare had any leading motive in this play, outside of making a success in the way of money, it was to cater to the common hatred of the Jews, which burned so fiercely in the Elizabethan age, and reached its intensest fury among the devotees of the Romish faith. And here let us not overlook the fact that, according to the doctrines of the Catholic Church, " it was a grievous sin to take interest on money : nay, usury was a crime amenable to the ecclesiastical tribunals, and Pope Clement V. declared it heresy to vindicate it. The subsequent Popes, Pius V. and Sextus V. (1585—1590), even Benedict XIV., as late as the middle of the eighteenth century, confirmed this doctrine. The outcast Jew alone was permitted by the law to take interest. And the Protestant Reformers, on this point, adopted the doctrine of the Catholic Church." [2] In

---

[2] Karl Elze's Essay on Shakespeare, p. 86.

the Venetian period of which Shakespeare writes, " the Jews were cooped up in their ghettos, and marked by a conspicuous dress like hangmen and prostitutes. All branches of business were prohibited to them, except those of barter and dealings in money, and this sole source of acquiring the means of existence was branded by the name of usury." Here we have the key to the loathing and contumely put upon Shylock by Antonio, who, in a spirit even meaner than any exhibited by the Hebrew, was guilty of the gross blackguardism of kicking him and of spitting upon his beard ; nay, was shameless enough to boast to his face that he might again, through mere caprice and wantonness, repeat that outrageous conduct. No wonder that Shylock wished to " catch him on the hip." In further proof that Shakespeare meant to cater to the common prejudice of his audiences against the Jews, and doubtless felt it, he permitted Shylock to be represented at his own theatre, with red hair and a long false nose, in order that the audience might not sympathize with his tremendous sufferings, when, after losing his daughter and his fortune, he was ruthlessly required even to abjure his faith.

This portraiture of Shylock continued down to the latter end of the seventeenth century, and reached its climax when Lord Lansdowne, in a version of the play called "The Jew of Venice," introduced a scene of buffoonery for Shylock, at the feast given by Bassanio. In this piece Shylock is represented as the butt of the company, and also as the jester of the table for the amusement of the Christian guests. " This misconception of the character of Shylock," says the writer to the introduction of French's edition of the play, " prevailed until Macklin restored the original text to the stage. This actor's admirable performance of the character, at once so new and striking, drew from Pope the well-known eulogium,—

> ' *This* is the Jew
> That Shakespeare drew.' "

Nevertheless, Shakespeare permitted Shylock to be delineated as a buffoon at his own theatre because, undoubtedly, that form of caricature both pleased and paid. This gives us a singular insight into the worldliness and facility of Shakespeare's money-making nature ; for it is impossible to read his delineation of this tremendous character, and dwell upon the mighty investiture of thought, force, and passion with which he consecrated it to tragic elevation, without conceiving the pain it must have caused him to yield the great portraiture to comic hands—to see his ideal of Judaism, his well-studied representative of an inflexible race, which no wrongs nor contumelies could subvert, speaking in the mirth-provoking tones of a Liston or a Stuart Robson.

It is clear to me that the consideration for the success of the piece which induced Shakespeare, as a manager, to permit Shylock to be burlesqued and perverted to the hands of a low comedian, could not have operated upon the mind of such a man as Bacon. On the contrary, it was purely the consideration of a playwright, and not the intellectual surrender of one who was either wholly a poet or wholly a philosopher. Shakespeare loved money more, apparently, than he loved art; and, in despite of the fine-spun theories of his biographers and the bubbles of the æsthetic Germans, I cannot resist the conviction that he wrote, and especially in this play of "The Merchant of Venice," for pounds instead of principles, and never once bothered his mind about inculcating moral lessons to mankind. I believe, more-over, that he had but a limited ambition for the glory of a poet. Though his brain, when at work, would flame with the genius of a demi-god, his prevailing elements were earthy, and the coarser portion of his nature steered his work. The constant thirst which he had for wealth is exhibited by his early acquisition of houses and lands in London and in Stratford; and the firmness of his grip on his accumulations is manifested by the paltry suits he brought to recover debt—one being for thirty-five shillings and tenpence — after he had come to the enjoyment of an income which would now be equal to twenty thousand dollars a year. Indeed, if he had been governed solely by the elevation of a poet, he could not have submitted his masterly and vigorous ideal of the revengeful Jew to the degrading *rôle* of a jack-pudding; while, if it ever entered into his head to inculcate moral lessons by his plays, he would not have forgiven Proteus and Angelo, or have written that deliberate essay in favour of free love known as "Troilus and Cressida." In fact, Shakespeare had no morals, so to speak; and what he exhibits in that way were just as meagre as any writer would be allowed to have, who was obliged to submit his views to the instinctive goodness of the big-hearted multitude.

Witness this very play. First, we have the blackguard Antonio

"footing" an unoffending man and spitting into his beard because
he differed with him in religious belief, or because he followed a
way of business (within the protection of the law) which he did
not like. And this ruffian is the idol of our poet's admiration.
Next comes Bassanio, an unprincipled, penniless adventurer, a
mere tavern spendthrift and carouser, who borrows money that
he may cheat a wealthy maiden of her dower. And this fine figure
is Shakespeare's second pet! Then follow those poodles and
parasites, Gratiano, Salarino, Salerio, Salanio, and Lorenzo, the
first willing to put up with Portia's waiting-maid, Nerissa, because there is money " all round" in Portia's neighbourhood, and
the latter inducing a little girl to rob her father's house, which
contemptible crime meets with the unlimited approval and active
aid of the whole gang, from Antonio down. If these are Shakespeare's preferred representatives of Christian morals, they appear
in poor contrast to Shylock and Tubal, as revengeful as he makes
the first to be. The moral of the caskets is neither better nor a
whit more wise; for it simply advocates the system of lottery
against that of judgment. Moreover, it cannot be believed
that, among the swarm of suitors who, first and last, had been
at Portia's residence, not one had hit upon the leaden casket
until Bassanio took his turn.³ Neither can any one credit, for

³ PRINCE OF MOROCCO. Why, that's the lady: all the world desires her:
    From the four corners of the earth they come,
    To kiss this shrine, this mortal breathing saint.
    The Hyrcanian deserts, and the vasty wilds
    Of wild Arabia, are as through-fares now,
    For princes to come view fair Portia:
    The wat'ry kingdom, whose ambitious head
    Spits in the face of heaven, is no bar
    To stop the foreign spirits; but they come,
    As o'er a brook, to see fair Portia.
                    Act II. Scene 7.

PORTIA (*to* BASSANIO, *as he is about choosing from the caskets*).
    Before you venture for me. I could teach you,
    How to choose right, but then I am forsworn;
    So will I never be; so may you miss me:
    But if you do, you'll make me wish a sin,
    That I had been forsworn. Beshrew your eyes,
    They have o'erlook'd me, and divided me;
    One half of me is yours, the other half yours,—
    Mine own, I would say; but if mine, then yours,

an instant, the pretence that so keen a girl as Portia would not have jockeyed her foolish father's will by giving her favourite, Bassanio, a wink. Every one, therefore, must agree that the problem of the caskets was worked out in its very weakest way by deciding against the Princes of Morocco and Arragon, who had something to risk, in favour of a beggarly sharper who had nothing to lose; and who was accessory, both before and after the fact, to the robbery of the Jew's house.

This seems to be harsh language, and it doubtless jars with the settled notions of many a worshipper of Shakespeare's heroes; but these are the portraits of our poet's very words. The Antonio party, with the exception possibly of Antonio himself, are profligates and spendthrifts, with, as is evident from Bassanio's pecuniary straits, scarcely a dollar among them. As for Bassanio, he has not only "disabled his estate," by "showing a more swelling port than his faint means would grant continuance," but he is hopelessly in debt on all sides, and most largely to Antonio, for loans obtained to float his pleasures. Nevertheless, he goes to him again, and, like all habitual borrowers, tempts him with the hope of getting his money back, if he will only help him with a little more. His new aim on this occasion is a wealthy lady who has made eyes at him,[4] but whom he does not

> And so all yours: O! these naughty times
> Put bars between the owners and their rights;
> And so, though yours, not yours.
>
> *Act III. Scene 2.*

Bassanio then chooses the leaden casket and wins the lady, whereupon, frankly resigning, she thus describes herself:—

> But the full sum of me
> Is sum of something; which, to term in gross,
> Is an unlesson'd girl, unschool'd, unpractised:
> Happy in this, she is not yet so old
> But she may learn; and happier than this,
> She is not bred so dull but she can learn;
> Happiest of all, is, that her gentle spirit
> Commits itself to yours to be directed,
> As from her lord, her governor, her king.

[4] BASSANIO. In Belmont is a lady richly left,
And she is fair, and fairer than that word,
Of wondrous virtues. *Sometimes, from her eyes
I did receive fair speechless messages.*

pretend to love—his sole object being " to get clear of all the debts he owes" by capturing her fortune ;—and, especially, to square accounts with Antonio. These are the coarse temptations which operate to obtain from Antonio the loan which is the pivot of the piece.

We next have an exhibition of the personal morals of Antonio, who, though he has spit upon Shylock for taking usury, encourages his repetition of that practice by offering to pay him usury himself.

> ANTONIO. Shylock, albeit I neither lend nor borrow,
> By taking nor by giving of excess,
> Yet, to supply the ripe wants of my friend,
> I'll break a custom.

So much for the morals of Antonio and Bassanio. Let us now take the virtuous measure of Lorenzo, Salerio, Gratiano, and Salarino. We find ample opportunity for this process in Scene 6 of Act II., where the two latter are seen lurking about Shylock's house at night, in order to assist Lorenzo in his plot to abduct Jessica, the Jew's daughter; and, as I said before, to rob Shylock's vaults. In connexion with this view let it be borne in mind that Bassanio has aided them in the disgraceful scheme by decoying Shylock to his feast; ay, to the very feast where these shameless rogues are to sit and eat with him after they have rifled him of his jewels and his child.

> Act II. Scene 6.—*Before Shylock's House.*
>
> *Enter* GRATIANO *and* SALARINO, *masqued.*
>
> GRA. This is the pent-house, under which Lorenzo
> Desired us to make stand.

> *   *   *
>
> Nor is the wide world ignorant of her worth,
> For the four winds blow in from every coast
> Renowned suitors; and her sunny locks
> Hang on her temples like a golden fleece;
> Which makes her seat of Belmont Colchos' strand,
> And many Jasons come in quest of her.
> Oh, my Antonio! had I but the means,
> To hold a rival place with one of them,
> I have a mind presages me such thrift,
> That I should, questionless, be fortunate.
>
>   *Act I. Scene* 1.

SALAR. His hour is almost past.

GRA. And it is marvel he outdwells his hour,
For lovers ever run before the clock.

Enter LORENZO.

LOR. Sweet friends, your patience for my long abode :
Not I, but my affairs have made you wait :
When *you* shall please *to play the thieves for wives,*
I'll watch as long as you.

Jessica then appears at a window disguised in boy's clothes
and throws a casket of jewels to Lorenzo, telling him to wait
until she gathers up some more of her father's ducats, when she
will join him at the door. When her flight is discovered, the Jew
rightly suspects that Bassanio, who had decoyed him to his feast,
is a party to the abduction, and follows him to the strand, where
he is embarking for Padua, on his trip to swindle Portia. He
reaches the wharf too late, however, for the adventurer has sailed.
Bassanio next appears in the neighbourhood of Belmont, and,
penniless as he is, approaches it with the flourish of a prince.
He sends a pursuivant before him to announce his coming,
and to lay at Portia's feet " gifts of rich value" out of Antonio's
toughly-borrowed money ; but he fails to acquaint Portia with
his poverty until after he has irrevocably won her in the lottery.
Here are a precious set of scamps, not one of whom has ever done a
worthy act or who owns an honest dollar, to contrast with the
patient and lawful thrift which has made Shylock simply the
Rothschild or the Drexel of his day, in a way of business now
practised by every banking institution in the Christian world.
Finally, that there may be no mistake about the morals
and motives of the Antonio party, the first exclamation which
Gratiano makes to one of the gang arriving at Belmont from
Venice is, while apparently throwing up his hat,—

" We are the Jasons, we have won the fleece ! "

Moreover, the first exercise of liberty by Antonio, on being res-
cued from his penalty, is to decline to pay the principal of the
bond, and to propose, after Shylock has been crushed by the loss
of his only child and the confiscation of his fortune, the inex-
pressibly savage punishment of the abjuration of his faith. The
boundaries of human vengeance had already been reached by the
abduction of his daughter and the judgment of the court; but

the mild-spoken Antonio goes beyond, and pants to kill his Hebrew soul.   Rightly did the Jew exclaim, in view of the specimens which Shakespeare set before him,—

"O Father Abraham, what these Christians are!"

CHAPTER XIV.

"THE MERCHANT OF VENICE" (CONTINUED).

LET us now turn to the main features of the drama—Shylock's bond—which most conspicuously tests Shakespeare's law.

The action of this part of the story begins in the third act, after Bassanio has securely landed Portia from his net, and Gratiano has won the second prize of the expedition, in the possession of Nerissa. Lorenzo has been equally successful with the Jew's daughter, and the whole party are rioting at Belmont over their good fortune, when their hilarity is suddenly dampened by the arrival of a letter from Antonio with the news that all his ships have been wrecked at sea, and that, being unable to meet his bond to Shylock, he will have to undergo its penalty. The messenger, Salerio, who brings these tidings, also informs the startled company that, the day of payment being past, Shylock refuses the satisfaction of the bond, and insists upon the bloody forfeiture.

> SALERIO.   Never did I know
> A creature, that did not bear the shape of man,
> So keen and greedy to confound a man :
> He plies the duke at morning, and at night ;
> And doth impeach the freedom of the state,
> If they deny him justice ; twenty merchants,
> The duke himself, and the magnificoes
> Of greatest port, have all persuaded with him :
> But none can drive him from the envious plea
> Of forfeiture, of justice, and his bond.
>
> JESSICA. When I was with him, I have heard him swear,
> To Tubal and to Chus, his countrymen,
> That he would rather have Antonio's flesh,
> Than twenty times the value of the sum
> That he did owe him ; and I know, my lord,
> If law, authority, and power deny not,
> It will go hard with poor Antonio.

It is at once agreed, at the end of this conference, that Bassanio, Gratiano, and Salerio, shall go immediately to Venice, with a large bag of Portia's money, to meet all exigencies, as well as to pay the bond. In order to draw this money from the lady's coffers, Bassanio here, for the first time, confesses to her that he has no money of his own. At this parting it is mutually agreed by the two newly-married couples that all nuptial joys shall be postponed between them until Antonio is released. Bassanio with his male friends having started upon this business, Portia hits upon the plan of following them with Nerissa, in the disguise of a lawyer attended by his clerk. And, in order to actually play a lawyer's part in the extrication of Antonio, she sends a messenger to a learned old barrister in Padua, named Bellario, who is her cousin, requesting him to send lawyer's robes, and give such directions in the way of legal points as will enable her to defend Antonio in a lawyer-like manner before the court. Having despatched the messenger, she then informs Lorenzo and Jessica, who have already commenced their honeymoon, that she intends to leave them to keep house a few days, while she and her maid Nerissa go to perform a solemn task until her husband's return. And here again Shakespeare brings in the inevitable monastery :—

> PORTIA. Lorenzo, I commit into your hands
> The husbandry and manage of my house,
> Until my lord's return ; for my own part,
> I have toward heaven breath'd a secret vow,
> To live in prayer and contemplation,
> Only attended by Nerissa here,
> Until her husband and my lord's return ;
> There is a monastery two miles off,
> And there we will abide.

Any other place of abode for a week would have suited the purposes of the story quite as well; but Shakespeare must have in his monastery, whenever there is an opportunity to show one off to advantage.

All of this last scene is the very height of absurdity. There might have been some sense in employing Bellario to go to Venice, where the ladies could also have gone in disguise, and have had all the fun they wanted in the way of masking and sideplay while the old doctor was trying the case. But for these two chits, or, as Portia describes herself,—

"An unlesson'd girl, unschool'd, unpractised,"

to go in barrister's garments, and with a handful of mere legal notes to represent the gravity and learning necessary to conduct a capital case, before a court of the highest grade, is an extremity of nonsense which reaches the point of absolute burlesque. We get at the full ludicrousness of this attempt at deception, by the following parting dialogue between Portia and Nerissa, as they set out for Venice on this lunatic enterprise :—

POR.   Come on, Nerissa; I have work in hand,
        That you yet know not of: we'll see our husbands,
        Before they think of us.
NER.   Shall they see us?
POR.   They shall, Nerissa; but in such a habit,
        That they shall think we are accomplished
        With what we lack. I'll hold thee any wager,
        When we are both accouter'd like young men,
        I'll prove the prettier fellow of the two,
        And wear my dagger with the braver grace;
        And speak, between the change of men and boy,
        With a reed voice; and turn two mincing steps
        Into a manly stride; and speak of frays,
        Like a fine bragging youth; and tell quaint lies,
        How honourable ladies sought my love,
        Which I denying, they fell sick and died;
        I could not do withal: then I'll repent,
        And wish, for all that, that I had not kill'd them.
        And twenty of these puny lies I'll tell,
        That men should swear, I have discontinued school
        Above a twelvemonth:—I have within my mind
        A thousand raw tricks of these bragging Jacks,
        Which I will practise.

At the commencement of the fourth act, all the parties, except Lorenzo and Jessica, meet in the great court of Venice, where the Duke, surrounded by his magnificoes, is solemnly presiding. Antonio, Bassanio, Gratiano, Salarino, and Salanio are present at the opening of the proceedings, and presently, upon the order of the Duke, Shylock enters; whereupon the Duke,—

DUKE. Shylock, the world thinks, and I think so, too,
        That thou but lead'st this fashion of thy malice
        To the last hour of act; and then, 'tis thought,
        Thou'lt show thy mercy and remorse, more strange
        Than is thy strange apparent cruelty;

And where thou now exact'st the penalty
(Which is a pound of this poor merchant's flesh),
Thou wilt not only lose the forfeiture,
But, touch'd with human gentleness and love,
Forgive a moiety of the principal;
Glancing an eye of pity on his losses,
That have of late so huddled on his back,
Enough to press a royal merchant down.

*   *   *

We all expect a gentle answer, Jew.

SHY. I have possess'd your grace of what I purpose;
And by our holy Sabbath have I sworn
To have the due and forfeit of my bond:
If you deny it, let the danger light
Upon your charter and your city's freedom.

*   *   *

So can I give no reason, nor I will not,
More than a lodged hate, and a certain loathing,
I bear Antonio, that I follow thus
A losing suit against him. Are you answer'd?

BASS. This is no answer, thou unfeeling man,
To excuse the current of thy cruelty.

SHY. I am not bound to please thee with my answer.

BASS. Do all men kill the things they do not love?

SHY. Hates any man the thing he would not kill?

This latter expression of Shylock's shows express malice, and, along with the testimony which Jessica gave to the company at Belmont, would have justified an arrest of proceedings by the Duke, with an order to take Shylock off to prison.

BASS. For thy three thousand ducats here is six.

SHY. If every ducat in six thousand ducats,
Were in six parts, and every part a ducat,
I would not draw them; I would have my bond.

DUKE. How shalt thou hope for mercy, rendering none?

SHY. What judgment shall I dread, doing no wrong?

DUKE. Upon my power I may dismiss this court,
Unless Bellario, a learned doctor,
Whom I have sent for to determine this,
Come here to-day.

At this point a messenger arrives with a letter from Bellario, representing that, being very sick, he sends in his stead a young and learned doctor named Balthasar. This introduces Portia, who comes dressed as a doctor of laws :—

DUKE.	Give me your hand. Came you from old Bellario?
POR.	I did, my lord.
DUKE.	You are welcome; take your place.
	Are you acquainted with the difference
	That holds this present question in the court?
POR.	I am informed thoroughly of the cause.
	Which is the merchant here, and which the Jew?
DUKE.	Antonio and old Shylock, both stand forth!
POR.	Is your name Shylock?
SHY.	Shylock is my name.
POR.	Of a strange nature is the suit you follow;
	Yet in such a rule, that the Venetian law
	Cannot impugn you, as you do proceed.—
	You stand within his danger, do you not?
	[*To* ANTONIO.
ANT.	Ay, so he says.
POR.	Do you confess the bond?
ANT.	I do.
POR.	Then must the Jew be merciful.
SHY.	On what compulsion must I? Tell me that.
POR.	The quality of mercy is not strain'd:
	It droppeth, as the gentle rain from heaven,
	Upon the place beneath: it is twice bless'd;
	It blesseth him that gives, and him that takes:
	'Tis mightiest in the mightiest; it becomes
	The throned monarch better than his crown;
	His sceptre shows the force of temporal power,
	The attribute to awe and majesty,
	Wherein doth sit the dread and fear of kings:
	But mercy is above this scepter'd sway,
	It is enthroned in the heart of kings.
	It is an attribute to God Himself;
	And earthly power doth then show likest God's
	When mercy seasons justice. Therefore, Jew,
	Though justice be thy plea, consider this—
	That in the course of justice, none of us
	Should see salvation: we do pray for mercy;
	And that same prayer doth teach us all to render
	The deeds of mercy. I have spoke thus much,
	To mitigate the justice of thy plea;
	Which if thou follow, this strict court of Venice
	Must needs give sentence 'gainst the merchant there.
SHY.	My deeds upon my head! I crave the law,
	The penalty and forfeit of my bond.
POR.	Is he not able to discharge the money?
BASS.	Yes, here I tender it for him in the court;
	Yea, thrice the sum; if that will not suffice,

> I will be bound to pay it ten times o'er,
> On forfeit of my hands, my head, my heart:
> If this will not suffice, it must appear
> That malice bears down truth.   And I beseech you
> <div style="text-align:right">[<i>To the Duke.</i></div>
> Wrest once the law to your authority:
> To do a great right do a little wrong;
> And curb this cruel devil of his will.

· Portia, nevertheless, admits that the law must take its course, but perceiving the Jew had made himself ready with his knife, she suddenly interferes :—

> POR.   Tarry a little; there is something else.
> This bond doth give thee here no jot of blood;
> The words expressly are a pound of flesh;
> Take, then, thy bond, take thou thy pound of flesh;
> But in the cutting it, if thou dost shed
> One drop of Christian blood, thy lands and goods
> Are, by the laws of Venice, confiscate
> Unto the state of Venice.

Shylock is then desirous of taking thrice the money; but, Portia objecting, he is willing to accept the principal.   This being objected to also, he curses the debtor and attempts to leave the court.   In this movement, likewise, he is frustrated by the heroine :—

> POR.   Tarry, Jew:
> The law hath yet another hold on you.
> It is enacted in the laws of Venice,
> If it be proved against an alien,
> That by direct or indirect attempts,
> He seek the life of any citizen,
> The party 'gainst the which he doth contrive,
> Shall seize one half his goods; the other half
> Comes to the privy coffer of the state;
> And the offender's life lies in the mercy
> Of the duke only, 'gainst all other voice.
> In which predicament, I say thou stand'st:
> For it appears by manifest proceeding,
> That, indirectly, and directly, too,
> Thou hast contriv'd against the very life
> Of the defendant; and thou hast incurr'd
> The danger formerly by me rehearsed.
> Down, therefore, and beg mercy of the duke!

> DUKE. That thou shalt see the difference of our spirit,
> I pardon thee thy life before thou ask it:
> For half thy wealth, it is Antonio's;
> The other half comes to the general state,
> Which humbleness may drive unto a fine.

Antonio, who has suddenly recovered his spirits at this turn of things, hereupon thriftily suggests that the fine of the Jew's remaining half be turned over to him until Shylock's death, in trust, for Lorenzo and Jessica, thus cleverly making himself the possessor of three-fourths. This modest request shows him to be quite as keen of scent for money as the Jew; but the remainder of the penalty which he proposes exhibits him as infinitely more revengeful and malignant :—

> ANT. So please my lord the duke, and all the court,
> To quit the fine for one-half of his goods,
> I am content, so he will let me have
> The other half in use, to render it,
> Upon his death, unto the gentleman
> That lately stole his daughter:
> Two things provided more,—*That, for this favour,*
> *He presently become a Christian;*
> The other, that he do record a gift,
> Here in the court, of all he dies possess'd,
> Unto his son Lorenzo, and his daughter.
> DUKE. *He shall do this; or else I do recant*
> *The pardon, that I late pronounced here.*
> POR. Art thou contented, Jew, what dost thou say?
> SHY. I am content.
> POR.   Clerk, draw a deed of gift.
> SHY. I pray you give me leave to go from hence:
> I am not well; send the deed after me,
> And I will sign it.
>   *[Exit Shylock.*

This is the last of Shylock, for, utterly broken down by his misfortunes, he disappears to die. But the terrible addition to his sentence, which Antonio devilishly suggests and which the Duke adopts, has been rightly denounced as going beyond all reasonable ideas of human punishment. Looking upon Shylock as one "with whose nature religion is an essential element, and whose Mosaism flows from his very heart," this portion of the sentence put upon him by Antonio, is, to use the words of Elze, " no longer poetic justice or tragical retribution, but mental and moral annihilation, the inevitable consequences of which must lead to physical death." Surely no man who had an enlightened belief in his own religion could have put such a penalty as this upon another.

Now, to take it altogether, here is a fine court, and these are fine proceedings. Can any one believe, for a moment, that Lord Bacon, who was a statesman and a lawyer, or that any other man who was a *lawyer* at all, could have built a story on such a jumble of legal absurdities and impossibilities as are here offered for our entertainment? The supposition that a cultivated State like Venice, in the advanced state of progress represented by the period of this play, or that any organized State one degree removed above barbarism, would permit a citizen to pledge away his life, as an alternative penalty to a money contract, *with no equity of redemption*, is a fiction which no lawyer would tolerate for an instant. A lawyer could not invent it, and would not receive it second-hand for constructive purposes, because he would be at war, at every breath, with his sense of professional congruity. His mind could not work at all on such a plan. Least of all would a proud judge like Bacon, who had sat for years in all the frozen dignity of the Lord Chancellorship of England, have written a scene which yielded all the arbitrary functions of a ducal bench to a beardless, prating boy, or have turned the court-room into a shambles by permitting the creditor to cut his victim up in their presence. He certainly would not have made so high placed a magistrate as the Duke exhibit such imbecile ignorance of the law as Shakespeare imputes to him, nor have conveyed all the functions of authority and judgment upon the young advocate, in the face of the admissions made by other portions of the text that the Duke had ample power not only to adjourn the court, but to remit the death penalty from Shylock. Nay, even to decree confiscation of his goods, and impose every form of judgment, out of hand.

It may be urged, on the other hand, that the laws of Venice were exceptionally rigorous, indeed Draconian; and it has been urged "that the horrible incident of cutting off the flesh found its origin in that atrocious decemviral law of the twelve tables of Rome, which empowered a creditor to mangle the living body of his debtor without fear of punishment." For the honour of the Roman law, however, it is not recorded that this inhuman

10

privilege ever was enforced.   Buddhist legends, and the Guleding law of Norway, show that other countries permitted the creditor to hack off from the debtor, who would not work for him, as much flesh as he liked; but, with all, an equity of redemption was provided for, and the debtor ceased to be a debtor when he could tender the amount of his obligation, with compound interest, or some other penalty of accumulation.   This equity presented itself with peculiar force in Antonio's case, who had not made default through dishonesty, wastefulness, or any form of personal improvidence, but under lightning and storm, and the irresistible visitation of God.

It is surprising that Lord Chief Justice Campbell, in his reply to Mr. Payne Collier's inquiry—whether Shakespeare had ever served in an attorney's office—should not have responded, when treating of the legal evidences in this play, by showing how utterly ignorant Shakespeare was of the *philosophy of law;* but his lordship goes simply over the surface of the play for mere phrases of attorneyship, and satisfies himself with such terms as "single bond," "let good Antonio keep *his day*," and with Shylock's rebuke to the jailor for taking Antonio out of prison for a walk, (which his lordship calls Shylock's threat to prosecute the jailor "with an action for *escape*,") to establish the conclusion that Shakespeare had undoubtedly, at some time, served under an attorney.

I have nothing further to comment upon in connexion with "The Merchant of Venice," as bearing upon our inquiry, except to direct attention to the following allusions, which Shakespeare is so fond of making to the superior human worthiness of princes and kings :—

> Then music is
> Even as the flourish when true subjects bow
> To a new crowned monarch.
>
> > *Act III. Scene 2.*
>
> As, after some oration fairly spoke
> By a beloved prince, there doth appear
> Among the buzzing pleased multitude,
> Where every something, being blent together,
> Turns to a wild joy of nothing, save of joy,
> Express'd, and not express'd.
>
> > *Act III. Scene 2.*

Portia's apotheosis to Mercy contains another striking instance

of this involuntary homage ;—but finally, in the fifth act, she
gives another :—

POR.   How far that little candle throws its beams!
       So shines a good deed in a naughty world.
NER.   When the moon shone we did not see the candle.
POR.   So doth the greater glory dim the less:
       A substitute shines brightly as a king,
       Until a king be by; and then his state
       Empties itself, as doth an inland brook,
       Into the main of waters.

CHAPTER XV.

"MUCH ADO ABOUT NOTHING."

THE plot of this play, according to Pope, was taken by Shakespeare from the fifth book of Orlando Furioso, and was first printed in the year 1600. Steevens thinks that Spenser's Faerie Queene furnished the main incidents and groundwork of the story, while others attribute it to Bandello's 22nd tale, Timbreo of Cardena. Its origin, however, is a matter of no importance to the line of inquiry we are upon, and it has not enough expression bearing upon our points, to claim much attention.

The first thing which strikes us is the dialogue that occurs at the opening of the piece, between Leonato and a messenger, who has just come in with the news of a battle, inasmuch as it shows how Shakespeare constantly ignores all consideration for the welfare of common people from his mind :—

LEONATO. How many *gentlemen* have you in this action?
MESSENGER. But few of *any sort*, and *none of name.*
LEONATO. A victory is twice itself when the achiever brings home full
numbers—

and here Leonato stops, without deigning to inquire how many common soldiers have been killed, wounded, and captured.

The next thing which attracts our attention is the introduction of a friar in the fourth act, who, immediately upon the unjust accusation of Hero, takes up the leading and most estimable action of the piece. He is the first to say to the swooning and barbarously injured maiden, " Have comfort, lady," and to thus beautifully beg of her accusers a fair and patient hearing :—

FRIAR.   Hear me a little ;
        For I have only been silent so long,
        And given way unto this course of fortune,

By noting of the lady; I have mark'd
A thousand blushing apparitions start
Into her face; a thousand innocent shames
In angel whiteness bear away those blushes;
And in her eye there hath appear'd a fire,
To burn the errors that these princes hold
Against her maiden truth :—Call me a fool;
Trust not my reading, nor my observations,
Which with experimental zeal doth warrant
The tenour of my book; trust not my age,
My reverence, calling, nor divinity
If this sweet lady lie not guiltless here
Under some biting error.

LEONATO.　　　　　　　　　Friar, it cannot be;
Thou seest, that all the grace that she hath left,
Is, that she will not add to her damnation
A sin of perjury; she not denies it :
Why seek'st thou then to cover with excuse
That which appears in proper nakedness ?

The benevolent and sagacious friar, nevertheless, persists; and finally, by suggesting the device that the lady shall be reported dead until the slander is cleared up, succeeds in vindicating her fair fame, and in bringing everything to a happy termination. In pursuance of this pious plan of the worthy father, Shakespeare, of course, introduces the convent or monastery, which he ever seems to have on hand, and which, as in the following lines of the friar, he always gives a good account of :—

FRIAR.　　　　　　　You may conceal her
(As best befits her wounded reputation)
In some reclusive and religious life,
Out of all eyes, tongues, minds, and injuries.

Finally the friar is successful, and has the great triumph of being able to exclaim, in the last scene,—

Did I not tell you she was innocent ?

This brings the hymeneal fates of Benedick and Beatrice to a crisis; and, Benedick, having secured the consent of Beatrice, addresses himself to her father for his acquiescence. He thus consigns himself to the hands of the good friar for his mediation :—

BENEDICK. My will is, that your good will
May stand with ours, this day to be conjoin'd
In the estate of honourable marriage;
In which, good friar, I shall desire your *help.*

It will be seen, therefore, that in this play, as in "Measure for Measure," "The Comedy of Errors," and all we have thus far scrutinized, Shakespeare loses no opportunity to exhibit his profound reverence and superior respect for the Roman Catholic faith. His priests and female devotees are filled with all the known virtues, and are always chosen as his favourite instruments for the moral adjustment of his plots.

Before disposing of this piece, I cannot avoid remarking upon the singular and painful inappropriateness of the levity of Claudio in his gibing scene with Benedick, immediately after the degrading and tragic death of his betrothed; nor can I help protesting against the gross obscenity of some of the dialogues in which Beatrice takes a leading part. Though she is represented as a lady of the highest rank and refinement, we are brought irresistibly to the conclusion, that our poet could not have had as good an opportunity of knowing what high-bred ladies were, as had Lord Bacon.

KNOWLEDGE OF LAW.

The evidences which Lord Chief Justice Campbell finds of Shakespeare's knowledge of the *law*, in "Much Ado about Nothing," are hardly worthy of our serious attention. His lordship thinks that the characters of Dogberry and Verges were meant to satirize the ignorance of parish constables, and possibly were aimed as high as at "Chairmen at Quarter Sessions and even Judges of Assize, with whose performances he (Shakespeare) may probably have become acquainted at Warwick and elsewhere." His lordship then delivers himself upon Dogberry's learning as follows :—

"If the different parts of Dogberry's charge are strictly examined, it will be found that the author of it had a very respectable acquaintance with crown law. The problem was to save the constables from all trouble, danger, and responsibility, without any regard to the public safety.

"DOGB. If you meet a thief, you may suspect him by virtue of your office, to be no true man ; and for such kind of men, the less you meddle or make with them, why, the more is for your honesty.

"2 WATCH. If we know him to be a thief, shall we not lay hands on him?

"DOGB. Truly, by your office you may ; but, I think, they that touch pitch will be defiled. The most peaceable way for you, if you do take a thief, is to let him show himself what he is, and steal out of your company.

"Now there can be no doubt," says Campbell, "that Lord Coke himself could not more accurately have defined the power of a peace-officer."

It seems to me that Lord Chief Justice Campbell, who over-looked the gross violations of the philosophy of law exhibited in "The Merchant of Venice" when he was reviewing that play, must have been much below himself, not only at that time, but when he selected the above absurd travestie, or dog-law, as it might be called, as an evidence of Shakespeare's proficiency in law learning.

"AS YOU LIKE IT."

The plot of this play is borrowed, according to Shakespeare's usual custom; but, the characters having passed through the magical alembic of his mind, are distinct and breathing creatures, which are entirely his own. The story is taken from Lynde's "Rosalynd," or "Euphues' Golden Legacy," published in London as late as 1590, and this play appears in 1600. Shakespeare, however, adds three new characters to it—those of Jaques, Audrey, and the Clown, while of the other characters, it may be said, that the passage of them through the hands of our poet, is like the transmutation of base metals into gold.

The first act of "As You Like It" opens by introducing Orlando, the youngest son of Sir Rowland de Bois, deceased, who is living in idle dependence upon his eldest brother Oliver, the heir of the whole of the estate. With Orlando appears an aged servant of Sir Rowland's, who is especially attached to the young man, and who, when the latter is banished, resolves to follow his fortunes into exile, in preference to remaining with the elder brother. This servant's name is Adam, and in the original story by Lynde he is represented to be an Englishman.

The first act contains a scene in which Orlando wrestles with one Monsieur Charles, a professional athlete; and, of course, he overthrows the brawny peasant as (according to all the laws of Shakespearian discrimination) a young nobleman should do. This victory obtains for Orlando the favour of Rosalind, the daughter of the banished duke, but it gets Orlando banished.

Rosalind, thereupon, puts on a disguise and follows him, and Celia (the daughter of the reigning duke), whose heart and Rosalind's have beaten in friendship against each other's ribs since the hour of their mutual truckle-bed, decides promptly to desert her father's court and go along with her.

Faithful Old Adam, of course, accompanies Orlando, and inasmuch as the portrait of this old servitor may be said to be the solitary instance in the whole of Shakespeare's writings, where a poor or an humble person escapes our poet's contempt,[1] I will give it in full.

> ORLANDO. Why, whither, Adam, wouldst thou have me go?
> ADAM.   No matter whither, so you stay not here.
> ORL.   What, wouldst thou have me go and beg my food?
>   Or, with a base and boisterous sword, enforce
>   A thievish living on the common road?
>   This I must do, or know not what to do;
>   Yet this I will not do, do how I can;
>   I rather will subject me to the malice
>   Of a diverted blood, and bloody brother.
> ADAM.   But do not so; I have five hundred crowns,
>   The thrifty hire I saved under your father,
>   Which I did store, to be my foster-nurse,
>   When service should in my old limbs lie lame,
>   And unregarded age in corners thrown;
>   Take that; and He that doth the ravens feed,
>   Yea, providently caters for the sparrow,
>   Be comfort to my age! Here is the gold—
>   All this I give you; let me be your servant;
>   Though I look old, yet I am strong and lusty.
>   For in my youth I never did apply
>   Hot and rebellious liquors in my blood:
>   Nor did not, with unbashful forehead, woo
>   The means of weakness and debility;
>   Therefore, my age is as a lusty winter—
>   Frosty, but kindly. Let me go with you;
>   I'll do the service of a younger man
>   In all your business and necessities.
> ORL.   O, good old man; how well in thee appears
>   The constant service of the antique world,
>   When service sweat for duty, not for meed!
>   Thou art not for the fashion of these times,

---

[1] There is one other *quasi* instance of a servant's faithfulness in "Timon of Athens," but I will deal with that in its due order.

Where none will sweat but for promotion ;
And having that, do choke their service up.
Even with the having : it is not so with thee.
But, poor old man, thou prun'st a rotten tree
That cannot so much as a blossom yield
In lieu of all thy pains and husbandry.
But come thy ways ; we'll go along together,
And ere we have thy youthful wages spent
We'll light upon some settled low content.

ADAM.   Master, go on, and I will follow thee
To the last gasp with truth and loyalty.
From seventeen years, till now, almost fourscore,
Here lived I, but now live here no more.
At seventeen years, many their fortunes seek,
But at fourscore it is too late a week ;
Yet fortune cannot recompense me better
Than to die well, and not my master's debtor.

This is the picture of a poor but grateful and very worthy
man, and from the style in which it is presented, cannot fail to
challenge our admiration. But, there are three motives to be
traced in this instance where Shakespeare has departed from
his contemptuous rule against the poor. First, the servant is an
English servant, which is one inducement for our poet (who
is always intensely English) to represent him favourably ; next,
Adam's fidelity serves the constant Shakespearian purpose of inculcating loyalty and obedience of servants to their masters ; but
Shakespeare's main object doubtless, is, to make Adam operate
as a foil or stimulant to the superior virtues of the noble young
Orlando, who is willing to fight a whole forest full of people to
obtain the old man food. Being exceedingly hungry himself,
however, it is not difficult for us to account for the savage
determination which Orlando exhibits in this enterprise.

It is worthy of observation, however, that Shakespeare, having
found this character of Adam ready made to his hand, could
hardly exclude it from the plot ; and especially deserving of our
notice, that while, in the original story of Lynde, the faithfulness of Adam is rewarded, Shakespeare passes him out of his
hands entirely without recompense. One of the early critics,
noticing this fact, says, " Shakespeare has made an interesting
use of Lynde's story, with the exception of the character of
Adam, whose fidelity is strangely neglected ; whereas in Lynde's
novel he is justly rewarded."

Bearing further upon Shakespeare's estimation of the lower orders, we find the following, Act I. Scene 2 :—

> 1 LORD. Anon a careless herd,
>   Full of the pasture, jumps along by him,
>   And never stays to greet him. "Ay," quoth Jaques,
>   "Sweep on, *you fat and greasy citizens;*
>   'Tis just the fashion; wherefore do you look
>   Upon that poor and broken *bankrupt* there ?"

Among the internal evidences in this play of Shakespeare's religion, the first that comes before us, is the use made by the Duke Frederick of the Catholic word *purgation :* "Thus do all traitors; if their *purgation* did consist in words;" but I admit that this evidence is a slight one. The next, however, which drops from the Duke, senior, in Act II. Scene 7, is a more distinctive Catholic symptom :—

> DUKE S. True is it that we have seen better days;
>   And have with *holy* bell been knoll'd to church.

We know, of course, that Protestant churches, like Catholic ones, summon their devotees together by the tolling of bells; but while the Protestant bells are, in themselves, only an ordinary piece of unrespected church furniture, the church bells of the Catholics are always formally consecrated and blessed. A Protestant would never think of using such a term as "holy bell;" a Catholic could not think of a church bell without applying it.

The next proof we have of Shakespeare's Catholicity in this play, occurs in the third scene of the third act, where Touchstone, the court clown, says to Audrey, the country wench,—

> But be it as it may be, I will marry thee: and to that end, I have been with Sir Oliver Mar-text, the vicar of the next village; who hath promised to meet me in this place of the forest, and to couple us. . . Here comes Sir Oliver—Sir Oliver Mar-text, you are well met: Will you despatch us here under this tree, or shall we go with you to your chapel?
> SIR OLIVER. Is there none here to give the woman?
> TOUCHSTONE. I will not take her on gift of any man.
> SIR OLIVER. Truly, she must be given, or the marriage is not lawful.

At this critical moment, the cynical and philosophic Jaques appears from the covert, and says,—

> Proceed, proceed: I'll give her. . . . Will you be married, motley?
> TOUCHSTONE. As the ox hath his bow, sir, the horse his curb, and the

falcon her bells, so man hath his desires; and, as pigeons bill, so wedlock would be nibbling.

JAQUES. And will you, being a man of your breeding, be married under a bush, like a beggar? Get you to church, *and have a good priest that can tell you what marriage is; this fellow will but join you together as they join wainscot;* then, one of you will prove a shrunk panel, and, like green timber, warp, warp.

TOUCHSTONE. I am not in the mind, but I were better to be married of him than another: for he is not like to marry me well, and not being well married, it will be a good excuse for me hereafter to leave my wife.

JAQUES. Go thou with me, and let me counsel thee.

TOUCHSTONE. Farewell, good master Oliver!

SIR OLIVER. 'Tis no matter; ne'er a fantastical knave of them all shall flout me out of my calling.

It is obvious that this sorry treatment of Sir Oliver by Shakespeare, indicates that Sir Oliver is a Protestant preacher. In the next scene Rosalind says,—

And his kissing is as full of sanctity as the touch of *holy bread.*

What Protestant would ever speak of *holy* bread?

CELIA. He hath bought a pair of cast lips of Diana: a nun of winter's sisterhood kisses not more religiously; the very ice of chastity is in them.

In these extracts we have the contrast clearly marked by Shakespeare's estimation, relatively, between a Protestant vicar and a Catholic priest; and in the latter, with its exquisite definition of conventual purity, we have the spontaneous illustrations of a Catholic soul.

There are but two further observations which I wish to make upon this play. The first is, that Rosalind is more to be condemned for the licentious impropriety of her language than Beatrice in "Much Ado about Nothing;" and, in this respect, is even less of a lady than Beatrice, though Shakespeare tries to make her more of one. My next observation is, that wickedness, as represented in its most execrable form in Orlando's elder brother, is as hastily presented for the forgiveness of the audience, as in the cases of Proteus in the "Two Gentlemen of Verona," and of the fiend Angelo in "Measure for Measure." The moral of the play is, therefore, not only bad, but, what is more to the point, does not indicate that professional sense of the necessities of retribution, which might be expected from any real lawyer's mind. In my opinion, a lawyer like Bacon would never have dreamed of forgiving Oliver, Proteus, or Angelo.

Lord Campbell, nevertheless, finds several evidences of Shakespeare's familiarity with law *practice* or attorneyship in this play, such, for instance, as Rosalind's pert expression, in the first act, of "Be it known unto all men by these presents." His lordship next notices the words *testament* and *bankrupt*, both applied by the poet only to a wounded deer, as indications of Shakespeare's law attainments, and further on reinforces his case, by quoting the casual use of such words as *attorney*, and such phrases as *term and term* as applied to lawyers' habits; even lugging in the following, as applicable to his proof:—

ROSALIND. Well, Time is the old JUSTICE that examines all offenders, and let TIME *try*.

But what Lord Campbell dwells upon, as if conclusive of Shakespeare's possession of very considerable legal attainments, is "that the usurping Duke Frederick, who wishing all the real property of Oliver to be seized, awards a writ of *extent* against him in language which would," says his lordship, "be used by the Lord Chief Baron of the Court of Exchequer :—

"DUKE FRED. Make *an extent upon his house and lands.*

"This," continues his lordship, "is an *extendi facias* applying to house and lands, as a *fieri facias* would apply to goods and chattels, or a *capias ad satisfaciendum* to the person." All of which learned and erudite observation, I beg to remark, goes to show the *extent* to which his lordship had become confused by his unusual literary task, rather than to prove anything else.

CHAPTER XVI.

" THE TAMING OF THE SHREW."

" THE Taming of the Shrew " contributes nothing of importance to our inquiry. It is one of the weakest of our poet's productions, and is founded, says Malone, on an anonymous play of nearly the same title, " The Taming of *a* Shrew," which was probably written about the year 1590, either by George Peele or Robert Greene. Shakespeare produced his play in 1597, and it was first printed in the folio of 1623. The outline of the Induction is supposed to have been taken from " The Sleeper Awakened " of the Arabian Nights. The feature which most strikes us on a general perusal is, that Katharine, the heroine, is not a whit more nice or modest in her language than Beatrice or Rosalind ; and thus contributes to the conviction, that Shakespeare had had but poor opportunities of closely studying true *ladies* and their manners—a study in which Lord Bacon, doubtless, had greatly the advantage of him.

The play contains some evidences of the contempt our poet had for every one of lowly birth or humble calling. In the induction, while a nobleman is amusing himself by misleading the drunken wits of Christopher Sly, a trumpet is heard, and a servant, who is commissioned to ascertain what it means, reports by ushering in a lot of players, whom my lord thus addresses :—

LORD.   Now *fellows* you are welcome.
PLAYERS.   We thank your honour.
LORD.   Do you intend to stay with me to-night?
2 PLAYER. So please your lordship to accept *our duty.*
LORD.   With all my heart.—This fellow I remember,
         Go, sirrah, take them *to the buttery,*
         And give them friendly welcome every one :
         Let them want nothing that my house affords.

In Act IV. Scene 1, Petruchio, angrily addressing Grumio, his servant, exclaims,—

> You *peasant* swain! you whoreson malt-horse drudge!

And in Act V. Scene 2, Katharine folds her arms submissively across her breast and bows as if before anointed royalty :—

> KATHARINE. Such duty as the subject owes the prince,
> Even such, a woman oweth to her husband.

Lord Campbell finds many evidences in " The Taming of the Shrew " of our poet's knowledge of the law. He says that in the " Induction," Shakespeare betrays an intimate knowledge of the matters which may be prosecuted as offences before the *Court Leet,* the lowest court of criminal judicature in England. We quote his lordship :—

" He " (Shakespeare) " puts the following speech into the mouth of a servant, who is trying to persuade Sly he is a great lord, and that he had been in a dream for fifteen years, during which time he had ignorantly imagined himself to be a mere frequenter of alehouses :—

> For though you lay here in this goodly chamber,
> Yet would you say, you were beaten out of door,
> And rail upon the hostess of the house,
> And say you would *present her at the leet,*
> *Because she brought stone jugs, and no seal'd quarts.*

" Now, in the reigns of Elizabeth and James I.," says his lordship, " there was a very wholesome law, that, for the protection of the public against 'false measures,' ale should be sold only in sealed vessels of the standard capacity; and the violation of the law was to be presented at the 'Court Leet,' or 'View of Frankpledge,' held in every hundred, manor, or lordship, before the steward of the leet."

His lordship finds his next illustration in Scene 2 of Act I., where Tranio says,—

> Please ye, we may contrive this afternoon,
> And quaff carouses to our mistress' health;
> And do as *adversaries do in law,*
> *Strive mightily, but eat and drink as friends.*

Really, it would seem as if some of the admiring commentators of Shakespeare labour at times to prove him to have been an idiot. Nothing can be more evident, than that any man of ordinary intelligence must have had the stone-jug law forced upon his observation an hundred times, and particularly in a country town like Stratford; while the fictitious quarrels of paid advocates have been the subject of every yokel's sneer since proceedings at law were first made public. Lord Campbell finally points to Katharine's use of the word *craven*, with the remark that " All lawyers know *craven* to be the word spoken by a champion who acknowledged he was beaten, and declared that he would fight no more, whereupon judgment was immediately given against the side which he supported, and he bore the infamous name of *craven* for the rest of his days."

I doubt if any reader will require a word from me to rebut this sort of argument.

" LOVE'S LABOUR'S LOST."

This play is one of the few that were published during Shakespeare's lifetime, the date of its appearance in print being fixed at 1598. It is one of the weakest of our poet's productions; and, if he had been asked for the plot of it, says Knight, he might have answered, anticipating Canning's knife-grinder, " Story! God bless you! I have none to tell, sir." Dr. Johnson declares it to be filled with passages that are " mean, childish and vulgar, and some which ought not to have been exhibited, as we are told they were, to a maiden queen." " Nevertheless," adds the Doctor, " there are scattered through the whole many sparks of genius : nor is there any play that has more evident marks of the hand of Shakespeare."

The scene is laid in Navarre, but there is no period assigned for the story; which seems to have a roving commission, ranging anywhere through the fifteenth to the seventeenth centuries. The first lines which attract our attention are those by which the Princess of France repels a fulsome compliment paid to her by her Lord Chamberlain, and which contain a contemptuous estimation of persons engaged in trade :—

> PRINCESS. Good Lord Boyet, my beauty, though but mean,
> Needs not the painted flourish of your praise ;

> Beauty is bought by judgment of the eye,
> Not utter'd *by base sale of chapman's tongues.*

The next is a law phrase by one of the Princess's ladies :—

> My lips *are no common, though several* they be.

In Act IV. Scene 2, we have the introduction of Sir Nathaniel, a foolish parson or curate, and of Holofernes, his friend, a Protestant pedant. Sir Nathaniel characterizes himself by saying to Holofernes,—

> SIR NATHANIEL. I praise the Lord for you; and so may my parishioners; for their sons are well tutored by you, and their daughters profit very greatly under you.

Again, the peasants Jaquenetta and Costard call Sir Nathaniel "good master parson." Shakespeare treats both of these characters with contemptuous levity. Finally they are made the derision of the lords and ladies, and the butt of their scurrilous wit in a foolish dramatic personation of the "Nine Worthies," in which the insults of the courtly audience are so mean and merciless, that Holofernes, who is a kindly, worthy man, complains against the outrage with an earnest gentleness which is so absolutely touching, that if the lords and ladies had possessed any sense of shame, the reproach would have covered them with blushes. Being called an ass while reciting his lines to the best of his ability, he thus appeals :—

> This is not generous; not gentle; not humble.

Instead, however, of feeling this rebuke, the scorn of the courtiers rapidly grows coarser. Shakespeare never subjects his monks and priests to this kind of insult. The Princess and her maids of honour, Rosaline, Maria, and Katherine, are all of the Beatrice and Katharina stamp; and their language is frequently of such a licentious character that it could not be transcribed to modern print, outside of the tolerated leaves of Shakespeare. The only shadow of excuse I can find for our poet in this respect, is that Rabelais, whom he quotes in "As You Like It," was then in the height of his obscene popularity, and had, to a certain extent, vilely infected much of the literary mind of Europe. Happily, few but mere scholars reads that singularly objectionable writer now.

The law phrase which I have pointed out above—

> My lips are *no common, though several they be,*

—seems to have escaped the observation of Lord Campbell; but he gives us in recompense the following from the first act :—

" In Act I. Scene 1," says his lordship, " we have an extract from the réport by Don Adriano de Armado, of the infraction he had witnessed of the King's proclamation by Costard with Jaquenetta; and it is drawn up in the true, lawyer-like, tautological dialect,—which is to be paid for, at so much a folio :—

" *Then for the place where ; where, I mean, I did encounter that obscene and most preposterous event, that draweth from my snow-white pen the ebon-coloured ink, which here thou viewest, beholdest, surveyest, or seest. . . . . . Him I (as my ever-esteemed duty pricks me on) have sent to thee, to receive the meed of punishment, by thy sweet grace's officer, Antony Dull; a man of good repute, carriage, bearing, and estimation.*

" The gifted Shakespeare," adds his lordship, " might perhaps have been capable, by intuition, of thus imitating the conveyancer's jargon; but no ordinary man could have hit it off so exactly, without having *engrossed* in an attorney's office."

Finally, our poet, having got through with his gibes and his jeers, his oblique morality, his obscene wit and his merciless roasting of the Protestants, uncovers his reserved monastery, which he always seems to have cosily wrapped in a handkerchief under his arm, and sets it down reverently and complacently before us :—

PRINCESS. Your oath I will not trust; but go with speed
   To some forlorn and naked hermitage,
   Remote from all the pleasures of the world ;
   There stay, until the twelve celestial signs
   Have brought about their annual reckoning :
   If this austere insociable life
   Change not your offer made in heat of blood ;
   If frosts, and fasts, hard lodging, and thin weeds,
   Nip not the gaudy blossoms of your love,
   But that it bear this trial, and last love ; .
   Then, at the expiration of the year,
   Come challenge, challenge me by these deserts,
   And, by this virgin palm, now kissing thine,
   I will be thine; *and, till that instant, shut*
   My woeful self up in a mourning house ;
   Raining the tears of lamentation,
   For the remembrance of my father's death.
   If this thou do deny, let our hands part;
   Neither intitled in the other's heart.

11

This grand coup in favour of a monastery and a convent closes up the play. Be it observed, however, that the introduction of neither is necessary to the year's postponement; the death of the father of the Princess being sufficient, in itself, for that furlough of the action.

CHAPTER XVII.

"ALL'S WELL THAT ENDS WELL."

THE story of this play was taken by Shakespeare from the romantic story in Boccaccio, called "Giletta of Narbon;" though it came immediately to our poet's hand, says Dr. Farmer, from Paynter's "Palace of Pleasure," which was printed in 1575. Shakespeare transposed its scenes into a drama in about 1589, adding the four characters of Parolles, Lafeu, the Countess, and the Clown, which, under his magical touch, have been made, with the exception of Helena, the most interesting characters of the dramatis personæ. The play was published, according to the best accounts, about the year 1598, under the title of "Love's Labour's Won," and was doubtless intended to be an offset or counterpart to "Love's Labour's Lost." It was retouched and reproduced in 1601-2, under the new title of "All's Well that Ends Well," which re-naming was suggested and justified by the words of Helena, towards the close :—

> *All's well that ends well :* still the fine's the crown ;
> Whate'er the course, the end is the renown.

She again uses the same expression in Act V. Scene 1; while the King, in his last speech, closes with "All yet *seems* well." The phrase finally appears in the epilogue, under the form of "All is *well ended*"—though this might have been written in at the time of reproduction, in order to give the change of title a still further warrant.

The story of the piece is very simple. The King, who possesses the highest personal virtues, is ill with an incurable disease, and is fast wearing to the grave, to the unbounded regret of all his subjects. Helena, the heroine, is the beautiful daughter of the deceased Gerard de Narbon, who in his lifetime was the most eminent physician in the kingdom, and had the honour of the King's personal friendship. Helena, herself, though poor, has therefore rank enough to be a gentlewoman, and, as such, is taken under the protection of the Countess of Rousillon, the mother of Bertram, of whom she becomes enamoured. She is prudent enough, however, to conceal her love, in consequence of the difference in degree between herself and that high-born lord. She worships Bertram, therefore, only as the Indian does the sun, without hope of getting possession of him, until she suddenly bethinks her of some secret remedies left by her father, one of which happens fortunately to be a specific for the King's disease. She then conceives the idea of going to the King and agreeing to restore him to health within eight days, at the risk of her own life, provided he will confer upon her the hand of such one of the young feudal lords of his court, who are in ward to him, as she may select. She succeeds in restoring the King to health, and thereupon chooses Bertram. The proud young nobleman resists the match, but being forced to it by the King, he at once absconds to the Italian wars, ordering his new wife back to Rousillon at the hour of his departure, under the falsehood that he will meet her there within two days. Helena obeys him without suspicion; but, upon her arrival at the palace of Rousillon, finds that the Countess, his mother, has received from him the following letter :—

COUNTESS. [*Reads.*] *I have sent you a daughter-in-law: she hath recovered the king, and undone me. I have wedded her, not bedded her; and sworn to make the "not" eternal. You shall hear, I am run away; know it before the report come. If there be breadth enough in the world, I will hold a long distance. My duty to you.*

Helena also finds a letter awaiting herself, which contains the following challenge to her desires :—

HELENA. [*Reads.*] *When thou canst get the ring upon my finger which never shall come off, and show me a child begotten of thy body that I am father to, then call me husband : but in such a then I write a never.*

Helena, whom Dowden characterizes as the very embodiment of *will*, and who he considers would even be enfeebled by the disguise of male attire, does not hesitate to accept the immodest challenge, but starts promptly after Bertram to Italy, leaving behind her a letter to the Countess, which again brings in our poet's pet idea of a convent, and of Catholic discipline :—

I am St. Jaques' pilgrim, thither gone :
Ambitious love hath so in me offended,
That bare-footed plod I the cold ground upon,
With sainted vow my faults to have amended.

    *   *   *

Bless him at home in peace, whilst I from far,
His name with zealous fervour sanctify.

The enterprising lady finds Bertram in Florence, where the Duke has already made him Master of Horse, or commander-in-chief of all the cavalry in the field. He has thus become a hero, but, under the influence of a dissolute favourite, Parolles, he lives, in his hours of relaxation, a most licentious life. Among the exploits of this portion of his career, he attempts the seduction of a young lady of good family, named Diana Capulet, in whose house Helena has taken up her temporary residence, as a pilgrim to Saint Jaques le grand. This illicit suit of Bertram's comes to the ears of Helena, who thereupon, explaining to the Capulet family who she is, succeeds in inducing Diana to make an assignation, by which Bertram may at midnight obtain access to her (Diana's) chamber, in order that, favoured by the dark, she (Helena) may take her place. The following briefly tells this portion of the story :—

DIANA.   Give me that ring.
BER.   I'll lend it thee, my dear, but have no power
     To give it from me.
DIA.   Will you not, my lord?
BER.   It is an honour 'longing to our house,
     Bequeathed down from many ancestors;
     Which were the greatest obloquy i' the world
     In me to lose.
DIA.   Mine honour's such a ring:
     My chastity's the jewel of our house,
     Bequeathed down from many ancestors;
     Which were the greatest obloquy i' the world
     In me to lose: Thus your own proper wisdom
     Brings in the champion honour on my part,
     Against your vain assault.
BER.   Here, take my ring:
     My house, mine honour, yea, my life be thine,
     And I'll be bid by thee.
DIA.   When midnight comes, knock at my chamber window;
     I'll order take, my mother shall not hear.
     Now will I charge you in the band of truth,

When you have conquer'd my yet maiden bed,
Remain there *but an hour, nor speak to me :*
My reasons are most strong; and you shall know them
When back again this ring shall be deliver'd :
And on your finger, in the night, I'll put
Another ring; that, what in time proceeds,
May token to the future our past deeds.
Adieu, till then; then, fail not.

This plot (which is the old artifice practised by Isabella and Mariana upon Angelo in "Measure for Measure") is successful, and Helena's marriage is consummated according to the tenour of the challenge. Moreover, the whole contract is fulfilled by Helena, who not only secures Bertram's monumental ring, but succeeds, when he would have regained it from her in the dark, in replacing it by the royal signet ring which the grateful King had given her. After this singular nuptial rite is consummated, a scene takes place (Act IV. Scene 3), in which two lords, who have just arrived from France to inform Bertram of Helena's death, thus deliver themselves :—

1 LORD. Sir, his wife, some two months since, fled from his house : her pretence is a pilgrimage to Saint Jaques le grand, *which holy undertaking, with most austere sanctimony, she accomplished; and, there residing, the tenderness of her nature became as a prey to her grief; in fine, made a groan of her last breath, and now she sings in heaven.*

2 LORD. How is this justified?

1 LORD. The stronger part of it by her own letters, which makes her story true, even to the point of her death : her death itself, which could not be her office to say is come, was faithfully confirmed by the rector of the place.

2 LORD. Hath the Count all this intelligence?

1 LORD. Ay, and the particular confirmations, point from point, to the full arming of the verity.

2 LORD. I am heartily sorry that he'll be glad of this.

That these gentlemen performed their mission by delivering to Bertram the news of his wife's death, is seen in the following expression of his joy at the sad event and self-gratulation at his supposed success with Diana.

BER. I have to-night despatched sixteen businesses, a month's 'length a-piece, by an abstract of success : I have congied with the duke, done my adieu with his nearest; *buried a wife, mourned for her;* writ to my lady mother, I am returning; entertained my convoy; and, between these main parcels of despatch, effected many nicer deeds; *the last was the greatest, but that I have not ended yet.*

He does not succeed, however, in getting a new interview with Diana, while Helena, having remained long enough in Florence to assure herself that her nuptial interview with Bertram had been fully blessed as she desired, takes Diana and that young lady's mother under her protection, as witnesses of what had been performed, and with them sets out for France by the way of Marseilles. The Italian war being over, Bertram, about the same time, also starts for home, and, taking the direct route, post haste, arrives there first. His calculations are, that the renown he had won in Italy, along with the influence of his mother, now that his wife is dead, may obtain the forgiveness of the King. In this he is correct, but, just as he is about being betrothed by his majesty to a new lady, Diana and her mother, who likewise have arrived, are ushered into the King's presence to stop proceedings. Bertram thereupon does not hesitate to imitate the detestable perfidy of Angelo, in "Measure for Measure," by denouncing Diana as "a common creature of the camp," with whom he "had sometimes laughed;" but at last Helena comes in to clear the whole matter up, just in the nick of time, by an unblushing avowal before the entire court, of the active part which she has borne in this most vulgar performance. Bertram is, of course, immediately forgiven by the King, in order that Helena may be made happy; while Diana Capulet is recompensed for the very questionable help she rendered Helena in the midnight encounter, by having one of the King's young noblemen assigned to her. And thus *all ends well*, save the sorry soiling which these young ladies suffered through their dirty paths.[1]

Nevertheless, such are the caprices of Shakespearian critics and commentators, that Coleridge, one of the ablest of them, regards Helena as "the loveliest of Shakespeare's characters." For my part, I cannot regard her as anything but an amorous Amazon, who, while living beside Bertram at the Castle of Rousillon, had kindled from the mere magnetism of his physical

---

[1] Of the character of Bertram, Doctor Johnson says, "I cannot reconcile my heart to Bertram; a man noble without generosity, and young without truth; who married Helena as a coward and leaves her as a profligate. When she is dead by his unkindness, he sneaks home to a second marriage; is accused by a woman whom he has wronged, defends himself by falsehood, and is dismissed to happiness."

neighbourhood, and pursued till she possessed him. She hits upon the cure of the King merely as a medium of her desires, and so frank is she with her motive, that she admits it to the Countess :—

> My lord your son made me to think of this,
> Else Paris, and the medicine, and the king
> Had from the conversation of my thoughts
> Happily been absent.

Elze, like Coleridge, tells us that Helena is valued "on account of her moral purity, her honesty, her clear understanding, her devotion, and her beauty;" and he calls our attention to the fact that, as soon as the "masculine activity" which was inspired by her object, has been attained, "she relapses into the unselfish humility of a woman," and becomes entirely passive to her lord. Now, it strikes me, that just such a development of tranquillity as hers may be seen in every case, when a desperate energy has been completely satisfied. I may be thought harsh, after all that has been written of the delicate loftiness of Helena's character by so many critics; but I have a purpose that must not be baffled by the halo which surrounds our poet's genius, nor awed by the apparent authority of commentators, who are mere devotees around a shrine. For the correctness of my measurement of the morals of this bold and unscrupulous young woman, I refer the reader especially to the shocking dialogue in which she indulges with that filthy camp-follower, Parolles, in the very first scene where she presents herself before the audience. Though she knows this fellow to be an unprincipled scoundrel and notorious debauchee, she opens an obscene conversation with him in a corner, and encourages it so grossly that every reader of the slightest moral sensibility must shrink at it with irrepressible disgust. It cannot be reprinted even for illustration, and with those who peruse the text, the conclusion is irresistible, that a young woman who could find agreeable pastime in such lascivious allusions, must have pushed after Bertram on pure material impulsion, and contrived his assignation with Diana under the smouldering stimulation of the same coarse fire. It is not too much to say, that it is doubtful if any domicile in England or America could be found, where unfortunate females find a residence, at which such language as Helena uses to Parolles, could be heard at large. Well might Mrs. Jameson, while erroneously subscribing to " the beauty of the character of Helena," denounce the details which surround her " as shocking to our feelings." And well, also, may the wise Gervinius confess, at the end of all his panegyric, that " few readers, and still fewer female readers, will believe in Helena's womanly nature," even after they have read his explanations and have found them indisputable.

The above analysis of the character of Helena brings us again to the comprehension of the difficulty which Shakespeare always experienced when endeavouring to portray *a lady*. As far as we have now followed him, through twelve of his comedies, he has not yet been successful in one delineation. Miranda, who is gentle, pure and beautiful, is a mere filmy and poetic dream. Isabella is a spotless and celestial grandeur; the rest of his girls are a crude, rude, hoyden, and rowdy set, with a bar sinister always running through their composition. Helena is a *woman*, it is true, but a woman of a stripe which the courtly Bacon would hardly have presented to us as a lady. It is the Countess, to whom we are indebted for our extravagant estimation of t purity of Helena's character; but had that kind-hearted and most excellent old lady heard her lewd fencing-match with the profligate Parolles, she would not have expressed such an opinion of her purity again.

Upon the point of the religion of Shakespeare, as exhibited in the text of this play, we have already had two illustrations, one in Helena's letter of departure, and another in the allusion made by two lords, to the *holy* pilgrimage she made to the shrine of St. Jaques le grand. We find still another in their reference to her subsequent and saint-like death. Bertram has also the reverential line,—

> Although before the *solemn* priest I have sworn,

and the widow Capulet says to Helena,—

> Come, pilgrim, I will bring you
> Where you shall host: of enjoined penitents
> There's four or five, to great St. Jaques bound,
> Already at my house.

The clown gives out religious symptoms also. In Act I. Scene 3, he says,—

> If men could be contented to be what they are, there were no fear in mar-

riage: *for young Charbon, the Puritan, and old Poysam, the Papist, how-soe'er their hearts are severed in religion*, their heads are both one. They may jowl horns together, like any deer i' the herd.

Here is a happy equality of derision, which makes the clown distinctly a neutral in doctrine; so that, when he comes to say, afterwards, "Though honesty be no Puritan, yet it will do no hurt; it will wear the surplice of humility over the black gown of a big heart;" and with a still more ribald tongue utters the contrasted scandal of—

As the nun's lip to the friar's mouth.

The manner in which these reflections are balanced, between both sects, make them of no absolute significance. Nothing is more likely, however, than that this last expression is the interpolation of some actor, compiler, or small printer; for, it is thoroughly well-known that introductions of this sort, which were intended to hit simply the humour of the hour, were always numerous in the Shakespeare text, from one source and another. In the face, therefore, of our poet's invariable reverence for the Roman Catholic clergy—for this is the sole instance (save one, in "King John" which I have already discussed) in all of our poet's works where friars are alluded to with levity or reprobation. This motley quip being thus off-setted must, therefore, be taken for what it is worth. Still, I do not believe it to be Shakespeare's line. The number of the *Catholic Progress*, of London, for April, 1875, remarks upon this subject: "If a ribald clown finds a fitness between 'a nun's lip and a friar's mouth,' it is no proof that Shakespeare himself believed it was the ordinary thing for the religious of both sexes to use improper familiarities with each other. Things which suit a certain character he is not particular about saying, even though they do, in some measure, pamper vulgar prejudices against the faith."

As to the legal acquirements of Shakespeare, so far as this play is concerned, Lord Campbell finds a striking proof, in the incident where the King claims to dispose of the hands in marriage, of certain feudal lords, under what is known as the *tenure of chivalry*. This tenure created a wardship of minors, to which class, it appears, Bertram belonged. I do not see, how-ever, why Shakespeare could not have learned as much as this from Holinshed, or from the current dramatic works and histories of his time. In his absorption of mind on the above point, the Lord Chief Justice seems to have quite overlooked a speech which our poet puts into the mouth of Parolles, in Act IV. Scene 3.

PAROLLES. Sir, for a quart d'écu he will sell the *fee simple* of his salvation : the *inheritance* of it, and cut the *entailment* from all *remainders* and a perpetual *succession* of it, *in perpetuity*.

Having, however, escaped his lordship's legal learning on this subject, I have not the slightest intention to inflict the reader with my views upon it.

CHAPTER XVIII.

"TWELFTH NIGHT; OR, WHAT YOU WILL."

THE date of the production of this play is fixed, pretty satisfactorily, at 1601-2, and the origin of the serious portion of the
story is ascribed to a novel, from the Italian, by Bandello. It is
one of Shakespeare's most perfect and charming comedies, and
seems to owe its title to the fact of its having been performed
first, either on Twelfth Night, or during the convivial season of
Shrovetide.   The title seems, however, to have been so small a
consideration of the author, that he practically leaves it to the
reader, or, rather, to his audience, by adding to its first title that
of, "What You Will;" or, as Dowden suggests, "Anything
You Like to Call It." It contributes numerous illustrations to
the inquiry which we have before us, but more especially upon
the point of the probable religion of Shakespeare, than upon any
other. Upon this point its marks are very strong. Hunter,[1]
an able and most reliable authority, is of the opinion that the
main purpose of this play was "to bring into disrepute certain
transactions of a party of *Puritans* of the time, who, in 1599,
made themselves very offensive by some popular delusions, which
had taken a strong hold of the public mind." Hunter, therefore, believes that it was the design of Shakespeare to satirize
that sect in the person of Malvolio, who, says Hunter, is "a person not moved to cheerfulness by any innocent jest, who casts
a malign look upon every person and everything around him,
and who, under a show of humility, hides a proud and tyrannical
heart." "It was intended," he continues, "that Malvolio should
be of a formal, grave, and solemn demeanour, and, as to his
attire, dressed with a Quaker-like plainness, which would heighten

---

[1] "Life, Studies, and Writings of Shakespeare," by Joseph Hunter, a Fellow
of the Society of Antiquaries, and Assistant Keeper of the Public Records.
London, 1845.

the comic effect when he afterward decked himself with all manner
of finery when he sought to please, as he supposed, his mistress."
Finally, says Hunter, " Though in other plays of Shakespeare,
we have indirect and sarcastical remarks on the opinions or
practices by which the Puritan party in the Reformed Church of
England were distinguished, it is in this play that we have his
grand attack upon them. Here, in fact, there is a systematic
design of holding them up to ridicule, and of exposing to public
odium what appeared to him to be the dark features in the
Puritan character. . . . In Malvolio's character Shakespeare's intention was to make the Puritan odious; in the
stratagem of which he is the victim, to make him ridiculous."

We have seen for ourselves that Shakespeare distinctly indulges
this design against the Puritan preacher and pedant in " As You
Like It," while, in direct contrast, he expresses the greatest
respect and reverence for Catholic clergymen and 'the Catholic
faith. The same contrasted expression will be found in the play
before us. The first line we have exhibiting this fact, is an
allusion, by one of the courtiers of the love-sick Duke, to Olivia,
who, still mourning at the end of several years for her only
brother's death, has refused to receive a love-message from his
Grace :—

> VALENTINE. So please my Lord, I might not be admitted,
> But from her handmaid do return this answer :
> The element itself, till seven years' heat,
> Shall not behold her face at ample view ;
> *But, like a cloistress, she will veiled walk :*
> *   *   all this to season,
> A brother's dead love.

Again, in Act II. Scene 3, we have the following :—

SIR TOBY BELCH, MARIA, *and* SIR ANDREW.

SIR TO. Possess us, possess us ; tell us something of him.
MAR. Marry, sir, sometimes he is a kind of Puritan.
SIR AND. O, if I thought that, I'd beat him like a dog.
SIR TO. What, for being a Puritan ? Thy exquisite reason, dear knight ?
SIR AND. I have no exquisite reason for't, but I have reason good
enough.
MAR. The devil a Puritan that he is, or anything constantly but a time-
pleaser ; an affection'd ass.

In Act IV. Scene 2, we have the following :—

Sir Toby Belch, Maria, *and* Clown *as* Sir Topas *the Parson, with*
Malvolio *locked up in an adjoining dark room.*

Sir To. Jove bless thee, master parson.

Clown (*as Sir T.*) *Bonos dies,* Sir Toby; for, as the old hermit of Prague,
that never saw pen and ink, very wittily said to a niece of King Gorboduc,
That, that is, is; so I, being master parson, am master parson. For what is
that, but that? and is, but is?

Sir To. To him, Sir Topas.

Clown (*as Sir T.*) What, ho, I say—peace in this prison!

Sir To. The knave counterfeits well: a good knave.

Mal. (*in an inner chamber*)). Who calls there?

Clown. Sir Topas, the curate, who comes to visit Malvolio, the lunatic.

Mal. Sir Topas, Sir Topas, good Sir Topas, go to my lady.

Clown. Out, hyperbolical fiend! how vexest thou this man! talkest thou
nothing but of ladies?

Sir To. Well said, master parson.

Mal. Sir Topas, never was man thus wronged; good Sir Topas, do not '
think I am mad; they have laid me here in hideous darkness.

Clown. Fye, thou dishonest Sathan! I call thee by the most modest
terms; for I am one of those gentle ones that will use the devil himself with
courtesy. Say'st thou that house is dark?

Mal. As hell, Sir Topas.

Immediately succeeding this, and in the very next scene, in
respectful contrast with the Puritan paces of the mock Sir Topas,
Olivia, accompanied by a priest, enters upon a scene where her
lover, Sebastian, is soliloquising upon some conjugal entertainment she had extended to him the night before:—

Enter Olivia *and a Priest.*

Oli. Blame not this haste of mine: If you mean well,
Now go with me, *and with this holy man,*
Into the chantry by: there, before him,
And underneath that consecrated roof,
Plight me the full assurance of your faith;
That my most jealous and too doubtful soul
May live at peace. He shall conceal it,
Whiles you are willing it shall come to note;
What time we will our celebration keep
According to my birth. What do you say?

Seb. *I'll follow this good man,* and go with you;
And, having sworn truth, ever will be true.

Oli. Then lead the way, *good father;*—And heavens so shine,
That they may fairly note this act of mine!

Sebastian and Olivia are then duly married, as it was time
hey should be; but, being temporarily separated in a succeeding

scene, and Olivia falling in with Viola the sister of Sebastian, while the latter was still in male attire, again mistakes the latter for the brother. Viola, of course, denies the conjugal imputation, whereupon, losing her patience, Olivia sends for the priest who had just married them, with—

> Call forth the holy father.
> *Enter Attendant and Priest.*
>   O, welcome, father!
> Father, I charge thee, by thy reverence,
> Here to unfold (though lately we intended
> To keep in darkness, what occasion now
> Reveals before 'tis ripe) what thou dost know,
> Hath newly past between this youth and me.
> PRIEST. *A contract of eternal bond of love,*
> *Confirm'd by mutual joinder of your hands,*
> *Attested by the holy close of lips,*
> *Strengthen'd by interchangement of your rings ;*
> *And all the ceremony of this compact*
> *Seal'd in my function, by my testimony :*
> Since when, my watch hath told me, toward my grave
> I have travell'd but two hours.

This is an exact and technical description of a Catholic marriage, which ceremony, unlike the Protestant ritual, is regarded as a sacrament by the Romish Church. The same forms are observable in the cases of Benedick and Beatrice, and are also alluded to in Romeo and Juliet. The precision with which the terms of the contract are above recited, indicate pretty clearly that Shakespeare was married under those religious forms himself.

There is one circumstance which I cannot refrain from noticing before disposing of this play, though it is rather out of the line of my inquiry. I allude to the compliment which Shakespeare more than once pays to grey eyes, which, during the whole of the Elizabethan period, were regarded as a distinguishing mark of female beauty ; because, of course, the eyes of Queen Elizabeth were grey. Shakespeare first confers these eyes upon Julia in the "Two Gentlemen of Verona ;" he next gives them to Thisbe, by a hint in " Romeo and Juliet ;" but he lodges them squarely, and with distinct significance upon Olivia, his paragon of beauty. In her own inventory of her charms, as playfully given to Viola, Olivia says,—

"I will give out divers schedules of my beauty. It shall be inventoried; and every particle and utensil labelled to my will—as, item, two lips indifferent red; item, two grey eyes, with lids to them; item, one neck, one chin, and so forth."

The inventory being thus summed up, the following exquisite lines occur :—

VIOLA. 'Tis beauty truly blent, whose red and white
   Nature's own sweet and cunning hand laid on :
   Lady, you are the cruell'st she alive,
   If you will lead these graces to the grave,
   And leave the world no copy.

           Act I. Scene 5.

I have but to add that Lord Chief Justice Campbell finds no evidences of the legal acquirements of Shakespeare in "Twelfth Night, or What You Will."

"THE WINTER'S TALE."

This play is one of the most finished of Shakespeare's pieces. It is pretty well ascertained that it was written as late as 1610, six years before our poet's death, and was played in the following year. It was not published, however, until the folio of 1623, which had so many of his dramas for the first time set " in the custody of type." We have the old story again about the plot, which, it is agreed, on all sides, was taken from the " Pleasant History of Dorastus and Fawina," a novel, published in 1588 by Thomas Green, and subsequently named " Pandosto." Shakespeare has altered the names of the characters ; he has also added the parts of Antigonus, Paulina, and Autolycus, and suppressed some circumstances in the original story. In other respects, he has adhered closely to the novel. The errors of representing Bohemia as a maritime country, with a sea-coast, and Delphos as an island, are not, however, " attributable to Shakespeare," says Harness, " but to the original from which he copied." Such geographical blunders could hardly have proceeded from Lord Bacon, who was not only too learned a scholar, but had been too much of a traveller to be their victim.

The story of " The Winter's Tale " is one of jealousy ; a jealousy deeper, more intense, more unreasoning, more capricious, and, if possible, more baseless than the madness of " Othello ;"

and no one can read the character of Leontes along with that of
Othello, without coming to the conclusion that our poet's own
bosom, under the deceptions of some London traitress, had been
the boiling fountain of the lines—

> That cuckold lives in bliss,
> Who, certain of his fate, loves not his wronger,
> But O, what damned minutes tells he o'er
> Who dotes yet doubts, suspects yet strongly loves!

The first expressions in this play bearing upon our points are
those of Leontes to Camillo, in the second scene of the first act,
where the former, just imbued with suspicions against Hermione,
is beginning to meditate the murder of Polixenes. These lines
themselves may be said to emit a dim religious light:—

> I have trusted thee, Camillo,
> With all the nearest things to my heart, as well
> My chamber councils; *wherein, priest-like, thou*
> *Hast cleansed my bosom;* I from thee departed,
> *Thy penitent reform'd.*

The next instance is an allusion by the clown to the company
which are coming to grace Perdita's rural party. After conning
them over, he says,—

> There is but one Puritan among them, and he sings psalms to hornpipes.

Farther on, Perdita's supposed father, an old shepherd, having
been threatened by Polixenes with death, thus mourns his
fate:—

> But now
> Some hangman must put on my shroud, and lay me
> *Where no priest shovels in dust.*

Our next illustration bears upon Shakespeare's adoration of
princes, and his contrasted estimation of ordinary people:—

> CAMILLO.   To do this deed,
> Promotion follows. If I could find example
> Of thousands that had *struck anointed kings*
> And flourish'd after, I'd not do it: but since
> Nor brass, nor stone, nor parchment, bears not one,
> Let villany itself forswear't.

" Upon this passage," says Hunter, " Sir William Blackstone
founded an argument to prove that 'The Winter's Tale' ' could
not have been written in the reign of Elizabeth, inasmuch as she
was one who had struck, not an anointed king, indeed, but an

12

anointed queen, in the person of the Queen of Scots.' " Let me take this occasion to say that, if this argument of Blackstone's be good to exhibit the repugnance of Elizabeth, how much stronger must the allusion have operated as a repulsion to Bacon (had he been the writer of this play), who wrung from Elizabeth her reluctant consent to Mary's execution.

Farther on, in Act IV., Polixenes having discovered that his son, Prince Florizel, is engaged in marriage to Perdita, the lost daughter of Leontes (yet supposed to be a shepherdess) thus berates him for the baseness of his yearnings :—

> "Mark your divorce, young sir,
> Whom son I dare not call; thou art too base
> To be acknowledged. Thou, a sceptre's heir,
> That thus affect'st a sheep-hook!   *
> *   *   And thou, fresh piece
> Of excellent witchcraft, who, of force, must know
> The royal fool thou cop'st with,
>   *   *   *
> I'll have thy beauty scratch'd with briers, and made
> More homely than thy state.   *   *
>   *   *   If ever, henceforth, thou
> These rural latches to his entrance open,
> Or hoop his body more with thy embraces,
> I will devise a death as cruel for thee
> As thou art tender to 't."

It being discovered soon after, however, that Perdita is a King's daughter, we at once hear of—

"The majesty of the creature, in resemblance of the mother; the affection of nobleness, which nature shows above her breeding; and many other evidences proclaim her, with all certainty, to be the king's daughter."

In contrast to the above strain I pass to the remark of Autolycus, who says to the shepherd and clown, when they are relating their original discovery of the babe Perdita,—

Let me have no lying; it becomes none but *tradesmen.*

I may add, at this point, that our poet makes one of the gentlemen at the court of Polixenes speak of Julio Romano, the celebrated Italian painter, (who was the Raphael of Shakespeare's day,) as a *sculptor*—a mistake which the travelled and scholarly Sir Francis Bacon could hardly have fallen into.

Perdita, every one will be happy to recognize as the purest and

sweetest female character, who, at the same time, partakes of the
gentle, genial qualities of breathing woman, which our poet
has yet drawn. Her language is exquisitely beautiful, and
effuses from her like the breath of an angel, filled at the same
time with the wholesome warmth of a woman. She never ceases
to be a shepherdess, while still a shepherdess; but, though she
seems to be dipped in fresh milk and to smell of the meadow,
the inimitable grace imparted by a perfect nature makes her
move among her companions like a sylvan goddess. So
thoroughly imbued is she with the spirit of modesty that,
though given to the culture of all sorts of flowers, she refuses to
illegitimately graft

> A gentler scion to the wildest stock,

because this process shocks her sense of propriety. Polixenes
reasons to her in favour of grafting contrasted plants as

> An art
> Which does mend nature,—change it rather : but
> The art itself is nature.
>
> PERDITA. So it is.
> POLIXENES. Then make your garden rich in gilliflowers,
> And do not call them bastards.
> PERDITA. I'll not put
> The dibble in earth to set one slip of them :
> No more than, were I painted, I would wish
> This youth should say, 'twere well.

That there is no prudery in this, but only a natural delicacy of
soul, we are warranted in saying, from the involuntary caution
which she gives her foster-brother, the clown, when he announces
that he is about to bring in to her feast, with his pedlar's pack,
that ribald rogue and pickpocket Autolycus, to sell his wares and
at the same time to sing for the party :—

> Forewarn him that he use no scurrilous words in 's tunes.

With this we kiss Perdita, and reluctantly take leave of her;
pausing only upon the previous matter to remark, that the one
person of the *dramatis personæ* of " The Winter's Tale " who, all
the while, meets with the most unvarying prosperity, even in the
perpetration of his crimes, to say nothing of the tranquil enjoyment of their profits, is the pickpocket, liar, and profligate
Autolycus ! Truly, this again revives our suspicions that Shake-

speare, though he possibly had a good heart, was but lightly burdened with moral principle or conscience.

On the subject of the legal acquirements of Shakespeare, as exhibited in "The Winter's Tale," Lord Chief Justice Campbell says,—

"There is an allusion in Act I. Scene 2, to a piece of English law procedure, which, although it might have been enforced till very recently, could hardly be known to any except lawyers, or those who had themselves actually been in prison on a criminal charge,—that, whether guilty or innocent, the prisoner was liable to pay a fee on his liberation. Hermione, trying to persuade Polixenes, King of Bohemia, to prolong his stay at the court of Leontes, in Sicily, says to him,—

> You put me off with limber vows; but I,
> Though you would seek t' unsphere the stars with oaths,
> Should yet say, "Sir, no going."   *   *
> Force me to keep you *as a prisoner*,
> Not like a guest; *so you shall pay your fees*
> *When you depart*, and save your thanks.

But in this I do not agree with his lordship. Hermione, in her use of the word *fees*, doubtless alluded to the habitual *largess* distributed by parting guests, and especially by a king. It is absurd to suppose that she knew anything about *jail fees*. Lord Campbell continues:—

"I remember when the Clerk of Assize and the Clerk of the Peace were entitled to exact their fee from all acquitted prisoners, and were supposed in strictness to have a *lien* on their persons for it. I believe there is now no tribunal in England where the practice remains, excepting the two Houses of Parliament; but the Lord Chancellor and the Speaker of the House of Commons still say to prisoners about to be liberated from the custody of the Black Rod or the Serjeant-at-Arms, 'You are discharged, *paying your fees.*'

"When the trial of Queen Hermione, for high treason, comes off, in Act III. Scene 2, although the indictment is not altogether according to English legal form, and might be held insufficient on a writ of error, we lawyers cannot but wonder at seeing it so near perfection in charging the treason, and alleging the overt act committed by her 'contrary to the faith and allegiance of a true subject.'

" It is likewise remarkable that Cleomenes and Dion, the messengers who brought back the response from the oracle of Delphi, to be given in evidence, are sworn to the genuineness of the document they produce almost in the very words now used by the Lord Chancellor, when an officer presents at the bar of the House of Lords the copy of a record of a court of justice :—

> You here shall swear   *   *
> That you, Cleomenes and Dion, have
> Been both at Delphos; and from thence have brought   ·
> The seal'd-up oracle, by the hand delivered
> Of great Apollo's priest; and that since then
> You have not dared to break the holy seal,
> Nor read the secrets in 't."

To me, these evidences of Shakespeare's legal attainments, though endorsed as such by Lord Campbell, appear to be very light and commonplace, and such only, as any man of extensive reading and authorship could hardly help acquiring, without having even served as a scrivener or clerk in an attorney's office. The paying of jail-fees by a discharged culprit, or the usual verification of a paper, are such obvious details as would have forced themselves upon the observation of any idler in a dull country-town like Stratford, particularly if he were in the habit, either of attending at the courts or visiting the taverns; and it, therefore, was not necessary that Lord Chief Justice Campbell should have gone to the extent of reminding us of Shakespeare's imprisonment for deer-stealing, to account for his familiarity with the practice of prison-fees.   What shall we say, however, of the legal perception and acumen of a great lawyer like Lord Chief Justice Campbell, who will wring a theory of abstruse learning from these surface details, and overlook such an incident as Paulina's rescuing the new-born princess out of prison, against every *principle* of law, on the flimsy pretext that the unborn infant, not having been condemned along with the queen, was not amenable to any process of restraint that could be lodged against it in the jailor's hands.   Let us observe the circumstances.

The Queen, Hermione, under the effects of Leontes' jealousy, had been thrown into prison, precedent to trial, and, being in an advanced state of pregnancy, is delivered of a child. Paulina, a distinguished lady of the court, goes to see her, but is informed by the keeper that he is under express orders that no person whatever shall be allowed to speak to her majesty, except in his presence. Paulina then asks to see Emilia, one of the Queen's waiting-women, who, being brought out, is thus addressed by her :—

>   Dear gentlewoman, how fares our gracious lady?
>
> EMIL.   As well as one so great, and so forlorn,
>   May hold together: on her frights, and griefs
>   (Which never tender lady hath borne greater),
>   She is, something before her time, deliver'd.
>
> PAUL. A boy?
>
> EMIL.   A daughter, and a goodly babe,
>   Lusty, and like to live ; the queen receives
>   Much comfort in 't : says my poor prisoner,
>   I am innocent as you.

Paulina then asks that the infant may be brought to her, but the keeper interposes:—

> KEEP. Madam, if 't please the Queen to send the babe,
>   I know not what I shall incur, to pass it,
>   Having no warrant.
>
> PAUL.   You need not fear it, sir :
>   The child was prisoner to the womb ; and is,
>   By law and process of great nature, thence
>   Free'd and enfranchised : not a party to
>   The anger of the King ; nor guilty of,
>   If any be, the trespass of the Queen.
>
> KEEP. I do believe it.
>
> PAUL.   Do not you fear : upon
>   Mine honour, I will stand 'twixt you and danger.

Here is a fine doctrine, to prevail in an almost absolute monarchy. This most successful of all female lawyers, Paulina, claims that the new-born babe of the imprisoned Queen has such an inherent right to personal liberty that it may demand, through its next friend, that it shall be passed out of prison, not for the purposes of nurture, but purely on its abstract personal right of liberty; and that babe, too, a princess, and subject, consequently, not only to special laws of the realm governing the title to the crown, but also to the peculiar custody and authority of the King, who is, at the same time, its father. And yet Lord Campbell, who occupies his attention with forms of verification and jail-fees, does not perceive this monstrous violation of the spirit, the science, and the philosophy of law, as well as of common sense.

CHAPTER XIX.

THE HISTORICAL PLAYS.

" THE WINTER'S TALE " finishes the *Comedies*, which, as we have seen, are fourteen in number. The next group is denominated *Histories*, of which there are ten. These are succeeded by thirteen *Tragedies*; making a total for the Shakesperian dramas, of thirty-seven.

In taking leave of the comedies, I may remark that, while we find a vast amount of evidence in them, that the writer was deeply imbued with the doctrines and sentiments of the Church of Rome, we find nothing favouring the theory of his Protestantism. Indeed, all of his religious utterances seem to be the spontaneous breathings of a Catholic soul, and our entire scrutiny of this series of the plays has produced but three indifferent expressions to raise even a momentary question to the contrary.

Nor have we found, in going through these fourteen comedies, one generous aspiration in favour of popular liberty, always so hard for genius to repress; or one expression of sympathy with the sufferings of the poor; nay, hardly one worthy sentiment accorded to a character in humble life. And here it may be again observed, that aristocratic tendencies are more especially fostered by the Romish Church than by any other. Finally, we find no support, down to this point, for the theory that Sir Francis Bacon was the author of the Shakespearian plays. On the contrary, it seems impossible that a man of Lord Bacon's gravity and learning could have achieved the facility in vulgar tavern wit, with which these plays abound;—could ever have laved his mind, as it were, in the sorry jests, the puerile equivoques, and the paltry puns (that wretched wit of sound) which form so large a portion of the conversation of Stephano and Trinculo in the play of " The Tempest;" which characterize the colloquy of Speed and Launce in the " Two Gentlemen of

Verona;" of Sir Hugh, of Doctor Caius, and of Falstaff and his vagabond retainers in "The Merry Wives of Windsor." Of Lucio and the Clown in "Measure for Measure;" of the two Dromios in "The Comedy of Errors;" of Dogberry and Verges, and of a deal of the smart repartee between Benedick and Beatrice in "Much ado about Nothing." Of indeed, the greater part of what is said in "Love's Labour's Lost;" of the jargon of Bottom and his mates in "Midsummer Night's Dream;" of much of the clack of the two Gobbos in "The Merchant of Venice;" of the talk of Touchstone, of Rosalind and the exiled courtiers, in "As You Like It;" also of the lewd sparring of Katharine and Petruchio, in "The Taming of the Shrew." And, most notably and deplorably, the obscenity indulged in by Helena and the poltroon Parolles, in "All's Well that Ends Well."

It is much more difficult to believe, therefore, that an austere philosopher, like Bacon, could have familiarized himself with such pitiful stuff as this, than it is to credit William Shakespeare, the play-actor, for his smattering of law, his superficial knowledge of medicine, and his apparent proficiency in the rhetoric of courts. Of course, those who credit Shakespeare for the correctness of his court phraseology could hardly have been at court themselves. And yet, of this class are the critics who pretend to judge familiarly of kings; and who, while thus giving away the argument, stultify themselves still farther, by the assumption, that Shakespeare merely comes up to the level of mere court nothings, even when his superb language is at its best. Equally absurd seems to me to be the theory of that other class of critics, composed mostly of mere scholars, who will not tolerate the idea that any one can have learning, who is not an utter bookworm like themselves. These are the pundits who flatly deny all scholarship, and even all foreign languages, to Shakespeare, simply because they cannot find that he acquired these accomplishments through a regular course at school. These savans, while in one breath they claim Shakespeare to be a miracle of human genius, in the next deny to him the most ordinary gifts of observation and of memory; which faculties, working silently together, always result in that supervening climax of intelligence which the ignorant call *intuition*. This class of critics cannot account for the scraps of Latin, French, Spanish, and Italian which are scattered through the comedies; as if the quick, lambent, and retentive mental faculties of Shakespeare—the outranking poetic genius of the world—are to be measured by the qualities of ordinary men. It is commentators of this class who, weakened by too much attention to details, lose all vigorous range of observation, and consequently become incapable of comprehending such miracles of acquisition, so far as the acquirement of foreign languages is concerned, as are shown by Elihu Burritt and William Shakespeare. The five or six languages, which Shakespeare seems to have partially picked up, during the eight years of comparative idleness he passed at Stratford was, after all, a far inferior exploit to the acquisition of the forty or fifty languages and tongues by Elihu Burritt of America. The signs and features of a foreign language, under the lambent ecstasy of intellects like these, resemble the vivid function of the photographic plate, which in an instant receives and fixes images that are to endure for ever.

Moreover, every one knows, who has ever mastered even the rudiments of a foreign language, that nothing is easier than to scan, offhand, all the leading features of a story from a foreign page, so as to furnish, as did the Italian school of romance to our poet, all the hints, if not all the incidents, necessary for a play. If these incidents were not transcribed exact, so much the more creditable for our author's invention; and if exact sentences from the original were at any time desirable, phrase-books might have been resorted to, as books of attorneys' practice were doubtless pressed into his rapid service for his terms of law. The trouble with the commentators has therefore too often been, that they were either awed from a plain estimation of their idol by too rapt an adoration of him; or, bewildered by their own scholarship, they have undervalued his practical attainments, and erroneously set him down as an unlettered man. And, after all, what are the most of these old scholars and bookworms in the clever world of to-day? Steam, electricity, the revelations by Science of the heavens and the earth, have annihilated whole libraries of philosophic dreams, and placed more true knowledge in the hands of unpretending merchants and mere boys, than dwelt behind the beards of Zoroaster or Confucius, or ever belonged to the old alchemists, who were supposed to have learning and science in valet-like attendance, as familiar spirits. Nay, young men who now get the bulk of their knowledge from the newspapers, can afford almost to smile at the truisms of Lord Bacon, and wonder how he obtained his vast renown by uttering such obvious facts as formed the staple of his essays. But while Bacon has thus receded from the estimation of his period, no one has succeeded in approaching, much less transcending, the conceptions of the mind of William Shakespeare! The one (the Philosopher) laboured through the tedious paths of learning to approximate towards the truth; the Poet caught his conceptions direct from the creative Throne, and transmitted them to mankind through the unerring medium of the soul. Shakespeare is, therefore, always true and fresh and new. Nothing can " stale his infinite variety ;" and as the generations roll before him, each after each, echoes the accord,—

<blockquote>"That he was not of an age, but for all time."</blockquote>

I trust I may not be considered as speaking slightingly of Bacon, in thus contrasting his qualities with those of Shakespeare. Lord Bacon, for his period, was as much the pioneer of thought as Shakespeare was the pioneer of soul; and the misfortune of Bacon, in being subjected to the instructed judgment of the present world is, that he is now obliged to meet with an audience which has, for more than two centuries, been drinking, at third and fourth hands, of the wisdom of which he was the surprising and original fountain. "These two incomparable men," says Lord Macaulay, " the Prince of Poets and the Prince of Philosophers, made the Elizabethan age a more glorious and important era in the history of the human mind than the age of Pericles, of Augustus, or of Leo."[1]

That Shakespeare and Bacon were thus distinct in their separate monarchies of mind, is in no way more evident than by the fact that, though the plays ceased to appear in 1613, three years before Shakespeare's death, the Essays continued until 1625, which was the year before Bacon's death. Indeed, in that latter year, which was the sixty-fifth of Bacon's age, he issued an edition of twenty of them, embracing the subjects of Truth, Revenge, Adversity, of Simulation and Dissimulation, of Envy, of Boldness, of Seditions and Troubles, of Travel, of Delays, of Innovations, of Suspicion, of Plantations, of Prophecies, of Masques and Triumphs, of Fortune, of Usury, of Building, of Gardens, of

---

[1] "Essay on Burleigh and his Times," vol. v. p. 611.

Anger, and of the Vicissitude of Things. These were his pet productions, and that there may be no mistake, as to his own estimation of the superiority of these over any other of his labours, he declares, in the dedication to this edition of 1625, as follows:— "I do now publish my Essays, which, of all my other works, have been most current. For that, as it seems, they come home to men's business and bosoms, I have enlarged them both in number and weight; so that they are indeed a new work."

And be it observed, that this declaration was made by Bacon two years after the collated plays of Shakespeare had been published under the poet's name in the folio of 1623. How is it possible, then, for us to believe, that a man so covetous of literary fame as Bacon, who laboriously prepared his Essays for the press in the sixty-fifth year of his age, and who revised the "Advancement" twelve separate times, never lent a hand to the arrangement of the Shakespearian folio of 1623, if he had really been the author of its plays? Or, stranger still, that, as the author of these plays, he had not discrimination enough to know that they were, beyond all comparison, his greatest works, and had already caught the mind of the world to an extent which promised a fame greater than could be expected for anything he had ever done. Surely no man possessed of the comprehensive intellect and towering genius indicated in the Essays and the Plays combined, could have made the mistake of leaving his reputation with posterity solely to the custody of his subordinate productions.

In passing from the comedies I will take this opportunity to quote the opinion of Dr. Johnson as to our poet's merit in this branch of dramatic composition. "In tragedy," says the Doctor, "he is always struggling after some occasion to be comic, but in comedy he seems to repose, or to luxuriate, as in a mode of thinking congenial to his nature. In his tragic scenes there is always something wanting, but his comedy often surpasses expectation or desire. His comedy pleases by the thoughts and the language, and his tragedy, for the greater part, by incident and action. His tragedy seems to be skill, his comedy to be instinct." Now, while I do not entirely agree with the learned Doctor in all of the above opinion, he must have every careful reader's concurrence largely in the following:—

"Shakespeare, with his excellences, has likewise faults, and faults sufficient to obscure and overwhelm any other merit. I shall show them in the proportion in which they appear to me, without envious malignity or superstitious veneration. . . . . His first defect is that to which may be imputed most of the evil in books or in men. He sacrifices virtue to convenience, and is so much more careful to please than to instruct, that he seems to write without any moral purpose. From his writings, indeed, a system of social duty may be selected, for he that thinks reasonably must think morally; but his precepts and axioms drop casually from him; he makes no just distribution of good or evil, nor is always careful to show in the virtuous a disapprobation of the wicked; he carries his persons indifferently through right or wrong, and at the close dismisses them without further care, and leaves their examples to operate by chance. This fault the barbarity of his age cannot extenuate; for it is always a writer's duty to make the world better, and justice is a virtue independent of time or place. . . . . In his comic scenes he is seldom very successful, when he engages his characters in reciprocation of smartness and contests of sarcasm; their jests are commonly gross, and their pleasantry licentious; neither his gentlemen nor his ladies have much delicacy, nor are sufficiently distinguished from his clowns by any appearance of refined manners. Whether he represented the real conversation of his time is not easy to determine; the reign of Elizabeth is commonly supposed to have been a time of stateliness, formality and reserve; yet, perhaps the relaxations of that severity were not very elegant. There must, however, have been always some modes of gaiety preferable to others, and a writer ought to choose the best. . . . . A quibble is to Shakespeare, what luminous vapours are to the traveller; he follows it at all adventures; it is sure to lead him out of his way, and sure to engulf him in the mire. It has some malignant power over his mind, and its fascinations are irresistible. Whatever be the dignity or profundity of his disquisitions, whether he be enlarging knowledge, or exalting affection, whether he be amusing attention with incidents, or enchanting it in suspense, let but a quibble spring up before him, and he leaves his work unfinished. A quibble is the golden apple for which he will always turn aside from his career, or stoop from his elevation. A quibble, poor and barren as it is, gave him such delight that he was content to purchase it by the sacrifice of reason, propriety, and truth. A quibble

was to him the fatal Cleopatra for which he lost the world, and
was content to lose it."

To these remarks I will only add, that to me, Shakespeare, in
comedy, has frequently seemed to be only Shakespeare in his
cups.   In tragedy, he is a Titan bearing his sublime front above
the clouds ; in comedy, too often an unbuttoned Satyr, grovelling
amid the slops and fragments of the table.   A God, perhaps at
times, but too frequently a God reeling with animal relaxation,
apparently to rest his brain.

" KING JOHN."

This first of the historical plays of Shakespeare was founded on
an anonymous play, called " The Troublesome Reign of King
John, with the Discovery of King Richard Cœur de Lion's base
son ; vulgarly named the Bastard Faulconbridge ; also, the
Death of King John at Swinstead Abbey."   Shakespeare followed
this old tragedy pretty closely, though he was careful to exclude
a scene of the original which irreverently alludes to " the merry
nuns and brothers " when Faulconbridge is practising his extortions on the clergy.   The exclusion of this scene is attributed
by Gervinius, from whom I quote the above expression, to a
very different motive from the one which I fancy is most obvious.
The German commentator, who is evidently a good Protestant,
says, " But Shakespeare did not go so far as to make a farce of
Faulconbridge's extortions from the clergy : the old piece here
offered him *a scene in which merry nuns and brothers burst forth
from the opened coffers of the ' hoarding abbots,'* a scene certainly
very amusing to the fresh Protestant feelings of the time ; but
to our poet's impartial mind the dignity of the clergy, nay, even
the contemplativeness of cloister life, was a matter too sacred
for him to introduce it in a ridiculous form into the seriousness
of history." [3]

From the light heretofore thrown upon the religious faith of
our poet, I read the motive for the exclusion of this Catholic
scandal differently from the learned German Professor.   Shakespeare's motive here seems to be located in the sensitiveness of

---

[3] " Essay on Burleigh and his Times," vol. v. p. 611.

a Catholic for the decorums of his sect—a religious sensitiveness which, be it observed, did not operate to protect the " dignity " of the Protestant clergy, when derision was to be cast upon Sir Hugh, "the jack priest" of the "Merry Wives;" upon Sir Nathaniel, the curate, in "Love's Labour's Lost;" upon Sir Oliver Martext, the Puritan preacher, in "As You Like It;" or upon the illusory Sir Topaz, in "Twelfth Night."

Hunter, like Gervinius, also exhibits the common concern of the English commentators to protect Shakespeare from the suspicion of Roman Catholic convictions. Nevertheless, the evidences of Catholicism in this play insensibly operate upon even Hunter's mind, and develope their force as follows :—

" There is so much in this play which shows that the mind of the poet was intent, when he wrote it, on affairs connected with the Church, that it may be submitted as a probability, not at once to be rejected, that in thus placing Hubert, in imagination, in a scene of horror, to prepare him for conceiving and executing a deed of horror, the poet had in his mind what was alleged to be a practice of the Jesuits of the time. They had their ' Chamber of Meditation,' as they called it, in which they placed men who were ' to undertake some great business of moment, as to kill a king, or the like.' 'It was a melancholy dark chamber,' (says Burton, in his ' Anatomy of Melancholy,') ' where he had no light for many days together, no company, little meat, ghastly pictures of devils all about him, and by this strange usage they made him quite mad, and beside himself.' The word *convertite*," continues Hunter, " which occurs in this play, is an ecclesiastical term, with a peculiar and express meaning, distinct from *convert*. It denotes a person who, having relapsed, has been recovered, and this, it will be perceived, is the sense in which Shakespeare uses it."

It is at this point of our scrutiny of the play of King John that the argument of Knight on the line "Purchase corrupted pardon of a man," forces itself upon our attention ; but inasmuch as that has been pretty thoroughly discussed in the first division of this work, we will refer the reader back to pages 52, 53, 54, 55, 56, and 57 inclusive, as a proper continuation of this chapter. These extracts close our illustrations from " King John " on the subject of religion. We come now to those which exhibit Shakespeare's proclivity to deify and worship kings, and demonstrate his utter want of sympathy with any movement tending to popular liberty. The first and most striking proof this play gives of this latter tendency is, that in the same spirit which directs him to protect the Roman Catholic faith from derision (by leaving out from the old play, which was his model, the scene that scandalized the nuns and monks), he refrains from making the slightest allusion, in *his* version of " King John," to the signing of Magna Charta; an event, unquestionably, the most momentous as well as the most dramatic of his entire reign. In the same spirit and policy, says Gervinius, " he has softened for the better, the traits of the principal political characters, and has much obliterated the bad. His ˙John, his Constance, his Arthur, his Philip Augustus, even his Elinor, are better people than they are found in history. . . . The base previous history of Elinor and Constance is touched upon only in cursory insinuations, or is entirely overlooked. . . . King John himself is kept greatly in the background, and even *his* historical character is softened and refined by Shakespeare."[2]

The following may be classed among our poet's spontaneous laudations of the great.

Act II. Scene 2.

K. PHILIP.   Before we will lay down our just-borne arms,
            We'll put thee down, 'gainst whom these arms we bear,
            Or add a royal number to the dead,
            Gracing the scroll, that tells of this war's loss,
            With slaughter coupled to the name of kings.

BASTARD.   *Ha! majesty, how high thy glory towers,*
            When the rich blood of kings is set on fire.
                *   *   *
            Why stand these royal fronts amazed thus?
                *   *   *
            By heaven, *these scroyles* [scabs or citizens] *of Angiers*
            Flout you, kings!
                *   *   *
            An' if thou hast *the mettle of a king.*

Act III. Scene 1.

CONSTANCE.   Thy word
            Is but the vain breath of a *common man :*
            Believe me, I do not believe thee, *man :*
            I have a *king's* oath to the contrary.

---

[2] Gervinius, pp. 356-7.

PAND. (*speaking to Kings* PHILIP *and* JOHN).
　　Hail, you *anointed deputies of heaven.*

*　　　　　　　*　　　　　　　*

K. JOHN.　What earthly name to interrogatories
　　Can task *the free breath of a sacred king?*

*　　　　　　　*

K. PHILIP.　　　　　Where revenge did paint
　　The fearful difference of incensed kings.

Act IV. Scene 3.

Before the Castle. Present—PEMBROKE, SALISBURY, BIGOT, *and*
　　FAULCONBRIDGE.
　　Enter HUBERT.

HUB.　Lords, I am hot with haste in seeking you.
　　Arthur doth live; the king hath sent for you.
SAL.　O, he is bold, and blushes not at death:—
　　Avaunt, thou hateful villain, get thee gone!
HUB.　I am no villain.
SAL.　Must I rob the law?　　　　　[*Drawing his sword.*
BAST.　Your sword is bright, sir; put it up again.
SAL.　Not till I sheath it in a murderer's skin.
HUB.　Stand back, Lord Salisbury, stand back, I say;
　　By heaven, I think my sword's as sharp as yours:
　　I would not have you, lord, forget yourself,
　　Nor tempt the danger of my true defence;
　　Lest I, by marking of your rage, forget
　　Your worth, your greatness, and nobility.
BIG.　*Out, dunghill! dar'st thou brave a nobleman?*
HUB.　Not for my life: but yet I dare defend
　　My innocent life against an emperor.

Here ends our illustrations from this play except those bearing upon the legal acquirements of Shakespeare; and these again bring us to Lord Chief Justice Campbell.

LEGAL ACQUIREMENTS AS SHOWN IN "KING JOHN."

Lord Campbell, in his review of the play of King John from the above point of view, expresses himself somewhat disappointed that he has not found more, of what he calls *legalisms* in Shakespeare's dramas, founded upon English history. He accounts for this paucity of legal reference, however, by the fact, that "our great dramatist," has in these histories "worked upon the foundations already laid by other men, who had no technical knowledge." "Yet," he continues, "we find in several of the

'Histories' Shakespeare's fondness for law terms; and it is still remarkable, that, whenever he indulges this propensity, he uniformly lays down good law." His lordship gives as a strong illustration of this fact, the decision by King John, between Hubert and Philip Faulconbridge upon the question of bastardy pleaded by the younger brother, against Philip, who, however, like Shakespeare's eldest daughter, Susanna, had made his appearance after the nuptials of parents,

> " Full fourteen weeks before the course of time."

The King legally decides that Philip is legitimate, and is therefore his father's lawful heir, because his

> " Father's wife did *after* wedlock bear him."

So far, however, from receiving this as a substantial evidence of Shakespeare's law learning, it seems to me to evince no more legal knowledge than ought to be expected from any well-educated youth of twenty-one. The next legal illustration which Lord Campbell gives is found within the lines spoken by the Duke of Austria, upon giving his pledge to support the title of Prince Arthur against King John :—

> " Upon thy cheek I lay this zealous kiss,
> *As seal to this indenture of my love.*"

Lord Campbell regards this as a purely legal metaphor, which might come naturally from an attorney's clerk, who had often been an attesting witness to the execution of deeds. I quite agree with his lordship in this view, but the expression might just as naturally have come from any intelligent merchant or poetaster of the time.

His lordship winds up his analysis of "King John" with a reference to some of the king's language, which I have already given, as evidence of the true ancient doctrine of the supremacy of the crown over the pope. Upon this point, his lordship and I do not disagree.

18

CHAPTER XX.

" RICHARD II."

THIS play was written in 1593-4, and first published in 1597. Malone says it was published in quarto no less than five several times during Shakespeare's life. " The first edition appeared in 1597, without the scene of the deposing of King Richard, which was inserted in the edition of 1608," during the reign of King James—the deposition of Richard having been suppressed in an earlier play of " Richard II.," in concession to the suspicion of Elizabeth, that such a scene would familiarize the public with outrages on the royal power, and thus affect her own safety on the throne. Another version has it, that the scene of the deposition was the result of an intrigue of Essex, the favourite of Elizabeth, about the time of his Jesuit plot and disloyal Irish expedition (1598), for which he lost his head.

Gervinius says upon this subject, " When the Earl of Essex, in 1601, wished to excite the London citizens to an insurrection, in order that he might remove his enemies from the person of the queen, he ordered his confidential friend, Sir Gilly Merrick, and others, to act the tragedy of " Richard II." in public streets and houses, previous to the outbreak of the conspiracy, in order to inflame the minds of the people. Elizabeth, hearing of this performance, alluded to it in conversation, calling herself Richard II. There is no doubt that the play employed by these conspirators was the older " Richard II." For Shakespeare's drama, though certainly a revolutionary picture, is of so mild a character, and demands such hearty sympathy for the dethroned king, and most especially in the very scene of the deposition, that it would appear unsuitable for such an object; besides, in the editions before 1601, the whole scene of the deposition of Richard in the fourth act, although it must have been written by the poet at the outset, was not even printed, and certainly, therefore, was not acted in Elizabeth's reign."

For the story, or rather for the facts of this drama, Shakespeare has closely followed the historical chronicle of Holinshed, except, says Rowe, that "he has sought to remedy the defect, which consists in the short period embraced in the action of the drama (the two years between 1398 and 1400), by representing Isabel, Richard's Queen—who was only twelve years of age when he was deposed—with the speech and actions of maturity." "Shakespeare's genius," continues this writer, "has been lavishly poured out upon the character of Richard, but though he could not entirely pass over his bad qualities, they are lightly touched."

It is the historical dramas, and particularly those of "Richard II.," and of the First and Second Parts of "Henry IV.," and of "Henry V.," which Shakespeare makes the especial instruments for his inculcation of subservience to the nobility and king. Though the Houses of York and Lancaster are the contending parties during the entire period covered by these four and the three succeeding plays, he manages to divide his compliments between the nobles of those respective houses, with most obsequious equality, and so keeps on, till the bloody stream of the Roses unites in the person of Henry VII. But while doing this, our poet never evinces the slightest interest in the sufferings of the masses, whose lives are but the fuel of the strife. And, surely, the people endured wrongs enough during the whole of this turbulent period to enlist some slight sympathy from the great genius, before whose piercing and poetic eye the bloody panorama passed in its fresher force. In addition to being torn from their unreaped fields, and cast into the volcano of the civil strife year by year, their moral condition was being constantly aggravated by new oppressions and new shames. Shakespeare is forced to admit this portion of the indictment against King Richard II. in his text; and while he recites, in vivid words, these terrible exactions, our straining thoughts are constantly disappointed of a single note of pity or of protest. His thoughts, his admiration and his impulses, are always with the nobles; his worship ever with the king. The following sketch, by Gervinius, of Richard's wild and profligate expenditure, and of his heartless and unprincipled grinding not only of the masses, but of every man he dared to plunder, presents a forcible picture of the criminal character of his government, and likewise of the deplorably sunken condition of the masses.

"Impoverished by his companions, Richard sees his coffers empty, he has recourse to forced loans, to extortion of taxes, and to fines ; and at last he leases the English kingdom as a tenure to his parasites—no longer a king, only a landlord of England. A traitor to this unsubdued land, he has, by his contracts, resigned the conquests of his father. At length he lays hands on private property, and seizes the possessions of the late old Lancaster and of his banished son, thus depriving himself of the hearts of the people and the nobles. The ruin of the impoverished land, the subversion of right, the danger of property, a revolt in Ireland, the arming of the nobles in self-defence; all these indications allow us to observe, in the first two acts, the growing seed of revolution which the misled king had scattered. The prognostication of the fall of Richard II. is read by the voice of the people in the common signs of all revolutionary periods" (Act II. Scene 4) :—

> Rich men look sad, and ruffians dance and leap,
> The one, in fear to lose what they enjoy,
> The other, to enjoy by rage and war.

"Nevertheless," continues the learned German Professor, "the peculiar right of the king is not esteemed by Shakespeare more sacred than any other. . . . As soon as Richard had touched the inheritance of Lancaster, he had placed in his hands, as it were, the right of retaliation. The indolent York thus speaks to him immediately :—

> Take from time his rights ;
> Let not *to-morrow* then ensue to-day;
> Be not thyself, for how art thou a king,
> But by fair sequence and succession ?

" He tells him that he ' plucks a thousand dangers on his head,' that he loses 'a thousand well-disposed hearts,' and that he ' pricks his tender patience to those thoughts, which honour and allegiance cannot think.' "

That is to say, " the peculiar right of the king, which usually stands over all, is not esteemed more sacred than any other," when it invades the rights of any branch of the royal family, or clashes with those of any of the nobility. But in contrast with the sensitiveness of our poet in regard to the equities of property, we look to him in vain for one word of protest against the inhumanities and oppressions practised upon poverty.

In scanning these spontaneous expressions in our poet's text we get a look, as it were, into his unguarded soul, and we are constantly impressed with the conviction that he wrote as if unconscious he was writing " for all time " and as if labouring only for the hour. His main motive seemed to be to dramatize for the swarm who brought him their sixpences and shillings, and who had a vulgar yearning to look upon a lord and to lave in the sacred atmosphere of even illusory noblemen and kings. He worked for money, for a solid home in Stratford, and for a Shakespearian coat-of-arms. He was a thoroughly pleasant, good-natured man, but apparently without any active generosity, and, I regret to conclude, not burdened heavily with moral principle. In short, an easy-going, kind-hearted, beaming epicure, who had a god in his bosom, without knowing it. When he bent over his desk and set his thoughts flowing downward through his pen, that god, thus summoned, flamed at the electric touch and descended to the earth. The bones of the man William Shakespeare lie as dust within the tomb at Stratford, but the god which inhabited him in life remains with us to-day.

But let us proceed to the illustrations of Shakespeare's catholic and aristocratic tendencies, afforded by this play.

The first note I have marked upon the margin is a religious evidence uttered by the Duke of Norfolk, which occurs in the first scene of the first act, when Norfolk confesses to having meditated the murder of the Duke of Lancaster :—

> NORFOLK. For you, my noble lord of Lancaster,
> The honourable father to my foe,
> Once did I lay in ambush for your life,
> A trespass that doth vex my grieved soul ;
> *But, ere I last received the sacrament,*
> *I did confess it ;* and exactly begg'd
> Your grace's pardon, and, I hope, I had it.

Next comes an illustration of the worship of an "anointed" king, which occurs in the next scene, between John of Gaunt and the Duchess of Gloster :—

> GAUNT. Heaven's is the quarrel : for heaven's substitute,
> *His deputy anointed in his sight,*
> Hath caused his death ; the which, if wrongfully,
> Let heaven avenge ; for I may never lift
> An angry arm against his minister.

In this same colloquy, the Duchess remarks,—

> That which in *mean* men we entitle patience,
> Is pale, cold cowardice in *noble breasts.*

In Scene 4 we have our first glimpse, in this play, of Shakespeare's contempt for the common people, in the following description by King Richard of the obsequious court which his dangerous rival, Bolingbroke, was paying to the populace:—

> K. RICH. He is our cousin, cousin; but 'tis doubt,
> When time shall call him home from banishment,
> Whether our kinsman come to see his friends.
> Ourself, and Bushy, Bagot here, and Green,
> Observ'd his courtship *to the common people :—*
> How he did seem to dive into their hearts,
> With humble and familiar courtesy:
> What reverence he did *throw away on slaves ;*
> *Wooing poor craftsmen with the craft of smiles,*
> *And patient underbearing of his fortune,*
> As 'twere, to banish their affects with him.
> *Off goes his bonnet to an oyster-wench ;*
> *A brace of draymen bid—God speed him well,*
> *And had the tribute of his supple knee,*
> *With—*"*Thanks, my countrymen, my loving friends ;*"
> As were our England in reversion his,
> And he our subjects' next degree in hope.
> GREEN. Well, he's gone; and with him go these thoughts.
> Now for the rebels, which stand out in Ireland ;—
> Expedient manage must be made, my liege;
> Ere further leisure yield them further means,
> For their advantage, and your highness' loss.
> K. RICH. We will ourself in person to this war:
> And, for our coffers—with too great a court,
> And liberal largess—are grown somewhat light,
> We are enforced to farm our royal realm ;
> The revenue whereof shall furnish us
> For our affairs in hand: *If that come short,*
> *Our substitutes at home shall have blank charters ;*
> *Whereto, when they shall know what men are rich,*
> *They shall subscribe them for large sums of gold,*
> And send them after to supply our wants ;
> For we will make for Ireland presently.

In the first scene of the second act, Gaunt, in a patriotic eulogium upon his country, delivers the following :—

> This royal throne of kings, this sceptred isle,
> This earth of majesty, this seat of Mars,

> This other Eden, demi-paradise ;
> This fortress built by Nature for herself,
> Against infection and the hand of war ;
> This happy breed of men, this little world,
> This precious stone set in the silver sea,
> Which serves it in the office of a wall,
> Or as a moat defensive to a house,
> Against the envy of less happier lands ;
> This blessed plot, this earth, this realm, this England,
> *This nurse, this teeming womb of royal kings,*
> *Fear'd by their breed, and famous by their birth,*
> *Renowned for their deeds as far from home,*
> (For Christian service and true chivalry)
> As is the sepulchre in stubborn Jewry
> Of the world's ransom, *blessed Mary's Son ;*
> This land of such dear souls, this dear, dear land,
> Dear for her reputation through the world,
> Is now leased out (I die pronouncing it)
> Like to a tenement or pelting farm.

Then, while rebuking the wasteful King from his dying bed, he goes on—

> Now, He that made me, knows I see thee ill,
> Ill in myself to see, and in thee seeing ill.
> Thy death-bed is no lesser than thy land,
> Wherein thou liest in reputation sick :
> And thou, too careless patient as thou art,
> *Commit'st thy 'nointed body to the cure*
> Of those physicians that first wounded thee.

In Act II. Scene 2, Northumberland appeals to his brother rebels to

> Redeem from broking pawn the blemish'd crown,
> Wipe off the dust that hides our sceptre's gilt,
> *And make high majesty look like itself.*

Of course, I do not insist that these natural expressions about "high majesty," &c., when correctly assigned to the characters, go for much ; but the fact that such reverence and worship are invariable with our author, and that his expressions of contempt for Man, as mere man, are also equally invariable, indicate together, that such expressions are the spontaneous and prevailing sentiments of the writer himself ; and, in that point of view, they go for a great deal.

In the same act and scene the following occurs in a room in the palace,—present : Queen, Bushy, Bagot, Green, and York :—

Enter a Servant.

SERV. My lord, I had forgot to tell your lordship :
  To-day, as I came by, I called there ;
  But I shall grieve you to report the rest.

YORK. *What is it, knave?*

SERV. An hour before I came, the duchess died.

YORK. God for his mercy ! what a tide of woes
  Comes rushing on this woeful land at once !
  I know not what to do :—I would to God
  (So my untruth had not provoked him to it,)
  The king had cut off my head with my brother's.
  What, are there no posts despatch'd for Ireland ?
  How shall we do for money for these wars ?
  Come, sister—cousin, I would say : pray, pardon me.
  Go, fellow (*to the Servant*), get thee home ; provide some carts,
  And bring away the armour that is there.

In Scene 3 of the same act, York rebukes the banished Bolingbroke for invading the kingdom before his sentence is repealed, with

Com'st thou because the *anointed* king is hence ?

That portion of the ceremony of a coronation which consists in "anointing" a newly-crowned monarch with the holy oil had obviously made a deeply religious impression upon Shakespeare's mind, to judge from his frequent reference to it.

In Act III. Scene 2, Richard, just returned from his Irish expedition, learns, as soon as he has landed on the coast of Wales, that the banished Bolingbroke has returned in arms. His weak nature at once sinks under the alarming prospect, and, like all cowards, he seeks comfort in his superstitious hopes :—

Not all the water in the rough rude sea
Can wash the balm from an anointed king :
The breath of worldly men cannot depose
The deputy elected by the Lord :
For every man that Bolingbroke hath press'd,
To lift shrewd steel against our golden crown,
God for his Richard hath in heavenly pay
A glorious angel : then, if angels fight,
Weak men must fall ; for heaven still guards the right.

*   *   *

AUMERLE. Comfort, my liege ; remember who you are.

K. RICH. I had forgot myself : Am I not king ?
  Awake thou sluggard majesty ! thou sleep'st.
  Is not the king's name forty thousand names ?

Arm, arm, my name ! a puny subject strikes
At thy great glory.—Look not to the ground,
Ye favourites of a king ; are we not high ?
High be our thoughts : I know, my uncle York
Hath power enough to serve our turn.   But who
Comes here ?

Again he droops :—

*   *   *

For heaven's sake, let us sit upon the ground,
And tell sad stories of the death of kings :—
How some have been deposed, some slain in war,
Some haunted by the ghosts they have deposed ;
Some poison'd by their wives, some sleeping kill'd ;
All murder'd :—For within the hollow crown,
That rounds the mortal temples of a king
Keeps death his court : and there the antic sits,
Scoffing his state, and grinning at his pomp ;
Allowing him a breath, a little scene
To monarchize, be fear'd, and kill with looks ;
Infusing him with self and vain conceit,—
As if this flesh, which walls about our life,
Were brass impregnable, and, humour'd thus,
Comes at the last, and with a little pin
Bores through his castle wall, and—farewell king !

Act III. Scene 3.

A Plain before Flint Castle, where KING RICHARD *has taken refuge.*
Enter BOLINGBROKE *and forces,* YORK, NORTHUMBERLAND, *and others.*
RICHARD *appears upon the battlements.*

BOLING. See, see, King Richard doth himself appear,
As doth the blushing discontented sun
From out the fiery portal of the east,
When he perceives the envious clouds are bent
To dim his glory, and to stain the track
Of his bright passage to the occident.

YORK. *Yet looks he like a king ; behold, his eye,*
As bright as is the eagle's, lightens forth
Controlling majesty.

K. RICH. We are amazed ; and thus long have we stood
                                        [*To Northumberland.*
To watch the faithful bending of thy knee,
Because we thought ourself thy lawful king :
And if we be, how dare thy joints forget
To pay their awful duty to our presence ?
If we be not, show us the hand of God
That hath dismiss'd us from our stewardship :
For well we know, no hand of blood and bone

Can gripe the sacred handle of our sceptre,
Unless he do profane, steal, or usurp.
And though you think, that all, as you have done,
Have torn their souls, by turning them from us,
And we are barren, and bereft of friends ;—
Yet know,—my master, God omnipotent,
Is mustering in his clouds, on our behalf,
Armies of pestilence ; and they shall strike
Your children yet unborn, and unbegot ;
That lift your vassal hands against my head,
And threat the glory of my precious crown.
Tell Bolingbroke (for yond', methinks, he is,)
That every stride he makes upon my land,
Is dangerous treason : He is come to ope
The purple testament of bleeding war;
But ere the crown he looks for life in peace,
Ten thousand bloody crowns of mothers' sons
Shall ill become the flower of England's face,
Change the complexion of her maid-pale peace
To scarlet indignation, and bedew
His pastures' grass with faithful English blood.

Scene IV.—*A Garden.*

The QUEEN, *who has overheard the Gardener describe the fall of* RICHARD, *comes from her concealment and exclaims,—*

Why dost thou say King Richard is deposed ?
Dar'st thou, *thou little better thing than earth,*
Divine his downfall ? Say, where, when, and how,
Cam'st thou by these ill tidings ? Speak, *thou wretch !*

Act IV. Scene 1.—*Westminster Hall.*

BOLING. In God's name, I'll ascend the regal throne.
BP. OF CAR. Marry, God forbid !—
Worst in this royal presence may I speak,
Yet best beseeming me to speak the truth.
Would God, that any in this noble presence
Were enough noble to be upright judge
Of noble Richard : then true nobless would
Learn him forbearance from so foul a wrong.
What subject can give sentence on his king ?
And who sits here, that is not Richard's subject ?
Thieves are not judged, but they are by to hear,
Although apparent guilt be seen in them :
And shall the figure of God's majesty,
His captain, steward, deputy elect,
Anointed, crowned, planted many years,
Be judged by subject and inferior breath.

     *   *   *.

I speak to subjects, and a subject speaks,
Stirr'd up by heaven thus boldly for his king.

K. RICH.   Gentle Northumberland,
If thy offences were upon record,
Would it not shame thee, in so fair a troop,
To read a lecture of them? If thou would'st,
There should'st thou find one heinous article,—
Containing the deposing of a king.

*

And water cannot wash away your sin.

NORTH.   My lord, despatch; read o'er these articles.

K. RICH.   Mine eyes are full of tears, I cannot see:
And yet salt water blinds them not so much,
But they can see a sort of traitor here.
Nay, if I turn mine eyes upon myself,
I find myself a traitor with the rest:
For I have given here my soul's consent,
To undeck the pompous body of a king;
Make glory base, and sovereignty a slave;
Proud majesty, a subject; state, a peasant.

Act V. Scene 1.

KING RICHARD (*on his way to the Tower*), QUEEN, *and Ladies.*

K. RICH. (*to the Queen*).   Hie thee to France
And cloister thee in some religious house:
Our holy lives must win a new world's crown,
Which our profane hours here have stricken down.

*   *   *

Good sometime queen, prepare thee hence for France:
Think, I am dead; and that even here thou tak'st,
As from my death-bed, my last living leave.
In winter's tedious nights, sit by the fire
With good old folks; and let them tell thee tales
Of woeful ages, long ago betid:
And, ere thou bid good night, to quit their grief,
Tell thou the lamentable fall of me,
And send the hearers weeping to their beds.
For why, the senseless brands will sympathize
The heavy accent of thy moving tongue,
And, in compassion, weep the fire out:
And some will mourn in ashes, some coal-black,
For the deposing of a rightful king.

In Scene 2 of the above act, the pageant of Richard, being led
in triumph at the heels of Bolingbroke, is thus described by the
old York to his Duchess:—

DUCH.   Alas, poor Richard! where rides he the while?

YORK. As in a theatre, the eyes of men,
      After a well-graced actor leaves the stage,
      Are idly bent on him that enters next,
      Thinking his prattle to be tedious :
      Even so, or with much more contempt, men's eyes
      Did scowl on Richard ; no man cried, God save him ;
      No joyful tongue gave him his welcome home :
      But dust was thrown upon his sacred head ;
      Which with such gentle sorrow he shook off,—
      His face still combating with tears and smiles,
      The badges of his grief and patience,—
      That had not God, for some strong purpose, steel'd
      The hearts of men, they must perforce have melted,
      And barbarism itself have pitied him :
      But heaven hath a hand in these events.

In the next scene, which is at Windsor Castle, where Boling-broke at last figures as king, the young Duke of Aumerle rushes into the royal presence, in order to forestall his father, York, in revealing a treason against his majesty. Aumerle, in advance of his father's arrival, confesses his intended crime, declares he has repented of it, and casts himself at the king's feet, imploring pardon.

At this moment, and just as he has received a qualified forgiveness, York comes thundering at the door, and finding it locked—a precaution which Aumerle had taken to prevent interruption while he made his confession to the king—exclaims,—

YORK (*outside*). My liege, beware; look to thyself ;
      Thou hast a traitor in thy presence there.
BOLING. Villain, I'll make thee safe.   [*Drawing*
AUM.   ·   Stay thy revengeful hand,
      Thou hast no cause to fear.
YORK. Open the door, secure, foolhardy king :
      Shall I, for love, speak treason to thy face ?
      Open the door, or I will break it open.
             [*Bolingbroke opens the door.*

Enter YORK.

BOLING. What is the matter, uncle ? Speak ;
      Recover breath ; tell us how near is danger,
      That we may arm us to encounter it.
YORK. Peruse this writing here, and thou shalt know
      The treason that my haste forbids me show.
AUM. Remember, as thou read'st, thy promise past :

I do repent me; read not my name there,
My heart is not confederate with my hand.

YORK. 'Twas, villain, ere thy hand did set it down.—
I tore it from the traitor's bosom, king;
Fear, and not love, begets his penitence;
Forget to pity him, lest thy pity prove
A serpent that will sting thee to the heart.

The Duchess, Aumerle's mother, next arrives, and throwing herself at the King's feet, unites in beseeching his pardon. Old York, however, remains obdurate, and, in reply to Aumerle's ejaculation,—

Unto my mother's prayers, I bend my knee,

replies,—

Against them both my true joints bended be.

The King, nevertheless, forgives Aumerle; whereupon the Duchess, overcome with gratitude for the royal clemency, bursts out with

A god on earth thou art!

This scene distinctly teaches that devotion to a king is a superior obligation to the ties of nature.

Finally, Richard is barbarously murdered by Sir Pierce Exton, by the secret orders of Bolingbroke; who, however, having gained his object in getting Richard out of the way, thus rewards his murderer:—

BOLING. Exton, I thank thee not; for thou hast wrought
A deed of slander, with thy fatal hand,
Upon my head, and all this famous land.

EXTON. From your own mouth, my lord, did I this deed.

BOLING. They love not poison that do poison need,
Nor do I thee; though I did wish him dead,
I hate the murderer, love him murdered.
The guilt of conscience take thou for thy labour,
But neither my good word, nor princely favour:
With Cain go wander through the shade of night,
And never show thy head by day nor light.
Lords, I protest, my soul is full of woe,
That blood should sprinkle me, to make me grow.
Come, mourn with me for what I do lament,
And put on sullen black, incontinent;
I'll make a voyage to the Holy Land,
To wash this blood off from my guilty hand:
March sadly after; grace my mournings here,
In weeping after this untimely bier.

A fine, frank, honest Christian king is this!

The argument of the play of "King Richard II." is, on the one side, that an "anointed" king may devote his life to profligacy, may farm out his revenues to meet his pleasures, seize the lands and incomes of his nobles and bring the State to bankruptcy and ruin, without forfeiting the allegiance of the nobles, the respect of the people, or his right to the throne. On the other side, it is held by Bolingbroke and the nobles who take part with him, that rebellion against the kingly authority is justified *in the aristocracy*, by any attempt on the part of the crown to appropriate or sequester their estates. The whole invasion of Bolingbroke is embarked upon this latter text, and the most notable defect of the presentation is, that the people, all of whom are constantly plundered and outraged, never have their wrongs alluded to as a recognizable element in the picture. Nay, these "*slaves*," these "*craftsmen*," these "*subjects*," these "*common people*," these "*mean men*," these "*little better things than earth*," are only used by Shakespeare to fill up the spaces and make the main scene work. The broadest illustration of this utter contempt for the rights and sufferings of the people may be found, perhaps, in the words of Bolingbroke, when he appears at the head of the revolted nobles and insurgent forces before the King's castle in the third act. On that occasion he directs Northumberland to "go to the rude ribs of that ancient castle" and say, that he, Bolingbroke, has come to England in this warlike form, simply to recover his rights as Duke of Lancaster; and then bids him to give the assurance to Richard, that he

> On both his knees doth kiss King Richard's hand.
> *   *   *
> Even at his feet to lay my arms and power,
> Provided that my banishment repeal'd,
> And lands restored, be freely granted.

Then follows a threat, on the supposition that these conditions be refused, which shows where the people stand and how they are considered, in the mind of an author who makes no declaration in *their* favour:—

> If not, I'll use the advantage of my power,
> *And lay the summer's dust with showers of blood,*
> *Rain'd from the wounds of slaughter'd Englishmen.*

Surely the people, in this connexion, were worth one thought of consideration; and should not have been paraded mechanically before the comprehension, as if they were merely so many horses or oxen incidental to the strife.

A great effort has been made, in connexion with this play, by Nathaniel Holmes, Judge and Professor of Law in Harvard University, Cambridge, U.S.A., the scholarly and ingenious leader of the American Baconians, to prove that Bacon had vaguely acknowledged himself to be the author of " *Richard II.,*" because he had admitted himself to be under the suspicion of the Queen, at the time when " *Richard II.*" was being acted under the express patronage of Essex (1598) with the deposition scene in. The history of the times, however, clearly shows, through the records of the courts in 1600, that the matter which aroused the suspicion of the Queen, on the subject of the presentation to the public mind of the deposition of King Richard, was a pamphlet published by one Dr. Hayward in 1599, in which the story of that political event was insidiously put forward. Bacon was really thought to have secretly favoured the production of Hayward's pamphlet, and so strongly did this suspicion prevail at court, that even Elizabeth once angrily alluded to " something which had grown from him, *though it went about in others' names.*" This enigmatic expression is eagerly seized upon by Judge Holmes as an intimation by the Queen that he, Bacon, had really written the offensive play, though it had been published under Shakespeare's name.

It seems to be absurd that the suspicion of the Queen could have referred to the play, which, as a treatise on the deposition of a king, did not offend her successor James I., and therefore is not likely to have been the offensive matter which " *grew from Bacon,* but went about in other names."

The parallelisms of language between some of the expressions in " *Richard II.*" and in Bacon's " *Essays,*" as presented by Judge Holmes, do not claim that amount of space from us which would be requisite for their presentation. They have failed to impress me in the least, but that no injustice may be done him by this summary disposal of them, I commend his ingenious volume on " The Authorship of Shakespeare " to the reader. It was published by Hurd and Houghton, New York, 1866.

CHAPTER XXI.

"HENRY IV."—PART I.

THERE is but little in this play or in the next (which is the second part or division of the same history), bearing upon the special points of inquiry we are engaged upon. There is enough, however, as well in politics, sentiment, morals, and religion, to make them both important, as supports to our previous analyses, in each of those respects.

The conspicuous figures of Henry IV., in both of its Parts, are Falstaff, Hotspur, and Prince Hal; the former outranking both as a dramatic identity, and tempting my notice in this essay to so great an extent, that I cannot refrain from expressing regret that the peculiar line of our examination does not take Falstaff in. Some future effort, however, of a different character from this may justify me in that pleasure. I will only pause a moment at this point to say, that history had given so bad a character to the Prince of Wales (or " Prince Hal," as the English love to call him), that our poet, in order to elevate him to the plane which would be requisite for the heroic action of his subsequent character as Henry V., ingeniously introduced the portraitures of Falstaff and his low companions as a foil; and also to show how instinctively a royal nature would rise above casual degradation, as soon as touched by a noble and ambitious impulse. Having once created Falstaff, however, the boundless wit of Shakespeare, which, after all, was larger than his worship, made the fat knight a greater stage character than either Harry Percy or the Prince of Wales.

The main theme of the First Part of " Henry IV." is merely a continuation of the political history which is begun in " Richard II." The strife is kept up between the nobles and the crown, and the subject of contention is that of their respective dignities and powers. The people, however, are never brought forward

except in the form of soldiers, and then only as pawns or
"creatures" to fill the game.

The following are the extracts which strike me in the text :—

Act IV. Scene 3.

BLUNT. So long as out of limit and true rule
You stand against *anointed* majesty.

Act V. Scene 2.

HOTSPUR. Arm, arm, with speed! and fellows, *soldiers*, friends,
Better consider what you have to do.

This is the first instance in which I find the common people
addressed even in the name of *soldiers*, without some fling of
undervaluation.

Again Hotspur :—

And if we live, we live to tread on kings;
If die, brave death, when princes die with us.

Scene 4.
(*In the midst of battle.*)

PRINCE JOHN (*Prince Henry's brother*).
We breathe too long—come, cousin Westmoreland,
Our duty this way lies; for God's sake, come.
[*Exit, to re-enter the fight, as becomes a Prince.*

Prince Henry then, finding his father and Douglas engaged
at swords' point, calls the King off, and, after a brief combat
with Douglas, makes the latter fly. Prince Henry next fights
with and kills Hotspur.

Act V. Scene 5.

KING HENRY (*to Worcester*).
Three knights upon our part slain to-day,
A noble earl, and many a *creature* else,
Had been alive this hour
If like a Christian, thou hadst truly borne
Betwixt our armies true intelligence.

THE LEGAL POINTS.

The first *legalism* found by Lord Chief Justice Campbell in
this play is, that "the partition of England and Wales, between
Mortimer, Glendower, and Hotspur" is conducted by Shakespeare in as attorney-like fashion as if it had been the partition
of a manor between joint tenants, tenants in common, or co-
partners.

14

MORTIM. England, from Trent and Severn hitherto,
By south and east is to my part assigned :
And westward, Wales, beyond the Severn shore:
And all the fertile land within that bound,
To Owen Glendower :
And, dear Coz, to you,
The remnant northward, lying off from Trent;
And our indentures tripartite are drawn,
Which being sealed interchangeably—

"It may well be imagined," continues his lordship, "that in composing this speech Shakespeare was recollecting how he had seen a deed of partition tripartite drawn and executed in his master's office at Stratford.

"Afterwards, in the same scene, he makes the unlearned Hotspur ask impatiently :—

"Are *the indentures drawn ?* shall we be gone ?

"Shakespeare may have been taught that 'livery of seisin' was not necessary to a deed of partition, or he would probably have directed this ceremony to complete the title.

"So fond is he of law terms, that afterwards, when Henry IV. is made to lecture the Prince of Wales on his irregularities, and to liken him to Richard II., who, by such improper conduct, lost the crown, he uses the forced and harsh figure, that Richard

" *Enfeoffed himself* to popularity (Act III. Scene 2).

"I copy Malone's note of explanation on this line: 'Gave myself up absolutely to popularity. A feoffment was the ancient mode of conveyance, by which all lands in England were granted in fee-simple for several ages, till the conveyance of lease and release was invented by Sergeant Moor about the year 1830. Every deed of feoffment was accompanied with livery of seisin, that is, with the delivery of corporal possession of the land or tenement granted in fee.' "

The two other lines which Lord Campbell finds to support this view in this play is the line last quoted,—

Enfeoffed himself to popularity,

And the further lines, in the fourth act,—

He came but to be Duke of Lancaster,
To *sue his livery,* and beg his peace.

" HENRY IV."—PART II.

The Second Part of " Henry IV.," followed immediately on
the heels of the First. It was probably written in 1597, as it is
mentioned in Meares' " Wit's Treasury " in 1598, and contains
an allusion to a political event which took place in 1596. It is
but a continuation of the First Part, and carries through it the
same tone, and, with the exception of the brilliant Hotspur and
one or two indifferent figures, the same characters. It supplies
us therefore with no new argument or theme, but I find it chiefly
remarkable for its presentation, without the slightest condemnation by our poet, of one of the most monstrous and frightful
pieces of treachery by the party he favours, which the history of
civilization gives any record of. The murder of the sons of
Amurath the Third, by their brother Mahomet, that took place
in Turkey in February, 1596, and which is the political event
above alluded to, does not begin to equal it in atrocity and
horror. And yet Shakespeare never droops his eye with condemnation of it; nor can I find that this conduct on the part of
our poet arouses the reprobation of any of the commentators.

The shameful deed I speak of occurs in the first scene of the
fourth act. The rebels who, in the First Part, had been led by
Hotspur, Glendower, and Mortimer, were beaten at Shrewsbury,
with the loss of Percy—

> Whose spirit lent a fire
> Even to the dullest *peasant* in his camp—

have again made head under the Archbishop of York, the Duke
of Northumberland, and Lords Hastings and Mowbray, supported
by Glendower, with an army in Wales.

The main body of these rebels, which the forces of the King
under Prince John of Lancaster are hurrying to cope with, lie
in Yorkshire, and are under the command of the Archbishop.
While they stand arrayed, expecting the attack of the royal
army, the Earl of Westmoreland comes as an ambassador from
the royal commander, and thus opens his negotiations :—

> Act IV. Scene 1.
>
> WEST. Health and fair greeting from our general,
>   The Prince, Lord John, and Duke of Lancaster.
> ARCH. Say on, my lord of Westmoreland, in peace ;
>   What doth concern your coming ?

WEST.   Then, my lord,
Unto your grace do I in chief address
The substance of my speech. If, that rebellion
Came like itself, in base and abject routs, '
Led on by bloody youth, guarded with rage,
And countenanced by boys, and beggary ;
I say, if damn'd commotion so appear'd,
In his true, native, and most proper shape,
You, reverend father, and these noble lords,
Had not been here to dress the ugly form
Of base and bloody insurrection
With your fair honours. You, lord archbishop,—
Whose see is by a civil peace maintain'd ;
Whose beard the silver hand of peace hath touch'd ;
Whose learning and good letters peace hath tutor'd ;
Whose white investments figure innocence,
The dove and very blessed spirit of peace,—
Wherefore do you so ill translate yourself,
Out of the speech of peace, that bears such grace,
Into the harsh and boist'rous tongue of war ?
Turning your books to graves, your ink to blood,
Your pens to lances ; and your tongue divine
To a loud trumpet, and a point of war ?

ARCH. Wherefore do I this ?—so the question stands.
Briefly to this end :

The Archbishop then details the rebels' grievances.

Westmoreland replies, and tenders liberal terms if they will lay down their arms. He adds,—

This offer comes from mercy, not from fear :
For lo ! within a ken, our army lies :
Upon mine honour, all too confident
To give admittance to a thought of fear.
Our battle is more full of names than yours,
Our men more perfect in the use of arms,
Our armour all as strong, our cause the best ;
Then reason wills, our hearts should be as good :—
Say you not then, our offer is compell'd.

MOWB. Well, by *my* will, we shall admit no parley.

WEST. That argues but the shame of your offence :
A rotten case abides no handling.

HAST. Hath the prince John a full commission,
In very ample virtue of his father,
To hear, and absolutely to determine
Of what conditions we shall stand upon ?

WEST. *That is intended in the general's name :*
I muse, you make so slight a question.

ARCH.   Then take, my lord of Westmoreland, this,
        For this contains our general grievances:—
        Each several article herein redress'd ;
        All members of our cause, both here and hence,
        That are insinew'd to this action,
        Acquitted by a true substantial form ;
        And present execution of our wills
        To us, and to our purposes, consign'd :
        We come within our awful banks again,
        And knit our powers to the arm of peace.
WEST.   This will I show the general.   Please you, lords,
        In sight of both our battles we may meet :
        And either end in peace, which heaven so frame !
        Or to the place of difference call the swords
        Which must decide it.
ARCH.   My lord, we will do so.   *[Exit* WEST.
MOWB.   There is a thing within my bosom tells me,
        That no conditions of our peace can stand.
HAST.   Fear you not that : if we can make our peace
        Upon such large terms and so absolute,
        As our conditions shall consist upon,
        Our peace shall stand as firm as rocky mountains.

          *   *   *

HAST.   Besides the king hath wasted all his rods
        On late offenders, that he now doth lack
        The very instruments of chastisement :
        So that his power, like to a fangless lion,
        May offer, but not hold.

The scene then changes, so as to bring the hostile commanders
confronted with each other.

Scene 2.—*Another part of the Forest.*

Enter from one side, MOWBRAY, *the* ARCHBISHOP, HASTINGS, *and others ;
from the other side,* PRINCE JOHN *of* LANCASTER, WESTMORELAND,
Officers, and Attendants.

P. JOHN.   You are well encounter'd here, my cousin Mowbray :
          Good day to you, gentle lord archbishop,
          And so to you, Lord Hastings,—and to all,
          My lord of York, it better shew'd with you,
          When that your flock, assembled by the bell,
          Encircled you, to hear with reverence
          Your exposition on the holy text ;
          Than now to see you here an iron man,
          Cheering a rout of rebels with your drum,
          Turning the word to sword, and life to death.
          That man, that sits within a monarch's heart,

And ripens in the sunshine of his favour,
Would he abuse the countenance of the king?
Alack! what mischiefs might be set abroach,
In shadow of such greatness. With you, lord bishop,
It is even so. Who hath not heard it spoken,
How deep you were within the books of God?
To us, the speaker in his parliament;
To us, the imagined voice of God himself;
The very opener and intelligencer,
Between the grace, the sanctities of heaven,
And our dull workings: O, who shall believe,
But you misuse the reverence of your place;
Employ the countenance and grace of heaven,
As a false favourite doth his prince's name,
In deeds dishonourable?
* * *

ARCH.   Good, my lord of Lancaster,
* * *

         I sent your grace
The parcels and particulars of our grief;
The which hath been with scorn shoved from the court,
Whereon this Hydra son of war is born:
Whose dangerous eyes may well be charm'd asleep,
With grant of our most just and right desires;
And true obedience of this madness cured,
Stoop tamely to the foot of majesty.

MOWB. If not, we ready are to try our fortunes
To the last man.

HAST.   And though we here fall down,
We have supplies to second our attempt;
If they miscarry, theirs shall second them;
And so success of mischief shall be born,
And heir from heir shall hold this quarrel up,
Whiles England shall have generation.

P. JOHN. You are too shallow, Hastings, much too shallow,
To sound the bottom of the after-times.

WEST. Pleaseth your grace, to answer them directly,
How far forth you do like their articles.

P. JOHN. *I like them all, and do allow them well:*
And swear, here, by the honour of my blood,
My father's purposes have been mistook;
And some about him have too lavishly
Wrested his meaning and authority.
My lord, these griefs shall be with speed redress'd;
Upon my soul, they shall. If this may please you,
Discharge your powers unto their several counties,
As we will ours; and here, between the armies,

> *Let's drink together friendly, and embrace,*
> *That all their eyes may bear those tokens home*
> *Of our restored love and amity.*

ARCH. I take your princely word for these redresses.

P. JOHN. I give it you, and will maintain my word:
And thereupon I drink unto your grace.

HAST. Go, captain (*to an officer*), and deliver to the army
This news of peace; let them have pay, and part.
I know, it will please them; hie thee, captain. [*Exit Officer.*

ARCH. To you, my noble Lord of Westmoreland. [*Drinks.*

WEST. *I pledge your grace:* [*drinks*] and, *if you knew what pains*
I have bestow'd to breed this present peace,
You would drink freely; but my love to you
Shall show itself more openly hereafter.

ARCH. I do not doubt you.

WEST.   I am glad of it—
Health to my lord, and gentle cousin, Mowbray. [*Drinks.*

MOWB. You wish me health in very happy season;
For I am, on the sudden, something ill. [*Shouts within.*

P. JOHN. The word of peace is render'd. Hark, how they shout!

MOWB. This had been cheerful, after victory.

ARCH. A peace is of the nature of a conquest,
For then both parties nobly are subdued,
And neither party loser.

P. JOHN.   Go, my lord,
And let our army be discharged too. [*Exit* WESTMORELAND.
And good, my lord (*to the Archbishop*), so please you, let your
trains
March by us, that we may peruse the men
We should have coped withal.

ARCH.   Go, good Lord Hastings;
And, ere they be dismiss'd, let them march by.
                                        [*Exit* HASTINGS.

P. JOHN. I trust, lords, we shall lie to-night together.

Re-enter WESTMORELAND.

Now, cousin, wherefore stands our army still?

WEST. The leaders having charge from you to stand,
Will not go off until they hear you speak.

P. JOHN. They know their duties.

Re-enter HASTINGS.

HAST. My lord, our army is dispersed already.
Like youthful steers unyoked, they take their courses
East, west, north, south; or, like a school broke up,
Each hurries towards his home and sporting-place.

WEST. *Good tidings, my Lord Hastings; for the which*
I do arrest thee, traitor, of high treason:—

> *And you, Lord Archbishop,—and you, Lord Mowbray;*
> *Of capital treason I attach you both.*

MOWB. *Is this proceeding just and honourable?*
WEST. *Is your assembly so?*
ARCH. *Will you thus break your faith?*
P. JOHN.   *I pawn'd thee none.*

> *I promised you redress of these same grievances,*
> *Whereof you did complain; which, by mine honour,*
> *I will perform with a most Christian care.*
> *But, for you, rebels, look to taste the due*
> *Meet for rebellion, and such acts as yours.*
> *Most shallowly did you these arms commence,*
> *Fondly brought here, and foolishly sent hence.—*
> *Strike up our drums! pursue the scatter'd stray;*
> *Heaven, and not we, hath safely fought to-day.—*
> *Some guard these traitors to the block of death:*
> *Treason's true bed, and yielder up of breath.*

Upon the conclusion of this treachery, the scene passes off without a word of censure from our poet, to a merry interlude between Falstaff and Sir John Coleville, a gentleman whom the fortunes of war has thrown into the fat knight's hands. While this burlesque is going on, Prince John, Westmoreland, and others, yet dripping and steaming with their most heinous and unspeakable atrocity, come in. After enjoying the fun, Westmoreland, who had temporarily gone out to order the royal forces to desist from further butchery, re-enters, and Prince John addresses him:—

P. JOHN. *Now, have you left pursuit?*
WEST. Retreat is made, *and execution stay'd.*
P. JOHN. Send Coleville, with his confederates,
    To York to present execution:—
    Blunt, lead him hence; and see you guard him sure.
                    [*Exeunt some with* COLEVILLE.
    And now despatch we toward the court, my lords.

The good King, who is always wishing to make a pious pilgrimage to the Holy Land, but who bargained with Sir Pierce Exton to assassinate King Richard, and then refused to pay him for the deed, receives this glorious news with uncriticizing joy, and is ready to go to Jerusalem again.

I think the above recapitulation fully justifies the remark which I have previously made, that while Shakespeare has infinite genius, he seems too often to be devoid of moral principle and conscience.

There are but few other lines which demand our attention in this play. The first that fits our theme occurs in the induction, where Rumour says,—

> My office is
> To noise abroad,—that Harry Monmouth fell
> Under the wrath of noble Hotspur's sword ;
> And that the king before the Douglas' rage
> Stoop'd his *anointed* head as low as death.
> This have I rumour'd through the *peasant* towns.

Next we have, in Act I. Scene 3, the Archbishop of York, thus delivering his opinion of the people :—

> An habitation giddy and unsure
> Hath he, that buildeth on *the vulgar heart.*
> O thou fond *many !* with that loud applause
> Didst thou beat heaven with blessing Bolingbroke,
> Before he was what thou would'st have him be ?
> And being now trimm'd in thine own desires,
> *Thou, beastly feeder,* art so full of him,
> That thou provok'st thyself to cast him up.
> *So, so, thou common dog, didst thou disgorge .*
> *Thy glutton bosom of the royal Richard ;*
> *And now thou would'st eat thy dead vomit up,*
> *And howl'st to find it ?* What trust is in these times !
> They that, when Richard lived, would have him die
> Are now become enamour'd on his grave :
> Thou, that threw'st dust upon his goodly head,
> When through proud London he came sighing on
> After the admired heels of Bolingbroke,
> Cry'st now, O earth, yield us that king again,
> And take thou this ! O thoughts of men accurst !
> Past, and to come, seems best ; things present, worst.

In Act II. Scene 4, we have the following fling at a Protestant clergyman, through the mouth of the not very reputable Dame Quickly, hostess of the Boar's Head tavern :—

HOSTESS. Tilly-fally, Sir John, never tell me ; your ancient swaggerer comes not in my doors. I was before Master Tisick, the deputy, the other day ; and, as he said to me,—it was no longer ago than Wednesday last,— Neighbour Quickly, says he ;—*Master Dumb, our minister, was by then ;* Neighbour Quickly, says he, receive those that are civil ; for, saith he, you are in an ill name.

I have but few observations to make upon these earlier illustrations, but I cannot resist the remark that the theory of the

Baconians, that the Lord Chancellor was ashamed to acknowledge himself as the author of the Shakespeare plays, has a sort of support in the gross immorality and vile language of many portions of this one. For, surely, any well-bred gentleman might well be ashamed of the rank brothel wit and the revolting fecundity of obscene slang which characterize the earlier scenes of this play, in which Doll Tear-Sheet figures with Falstaff and Dame Quickly. Actors delivering such language and figuring through such scenes, may be said to have naturally earned the epithets of " harlotry players " and of " vagabonds." In this connexion, I will avail myself of the opportunity, before passing from the Falstaffian plays, of calling a moment's attention to the puzzling character of Nym. No commentator seems to have been able to grasp, or to comprehend this piece of vague caprice, and, for my own part, I am forced to the conclusion that he must have represented the local caricature of some well-known person—some amorous London alderman, perhaps—who had been caught in some queer scrape and possibly extricated himself with the exclamation of " that's the humour of it ;" the repetition of which comical expression would always be good, with a local audience, for a laugh. Without some such surmise as this, Nym must pass with most persons as a puzzle, or, at best, an idiot.

I have only to add, in passing from this play, that the legalisms exhibited on Shakespeare's behalf in the course of it by Lord Chief Justice Campbell, do not call for any special attention.

CHAPTER XXII.

" HENRY V."

THE date of the production of this play is fixed at 1599 or 1600. It is the opinion of some that Shakespeare approached the subject of Henry V. reluctantly, in consequence of its paucity of domestic incident, and that he finally undertook it only because he felt obliged to keep "the promise made at the close of the Second Part of ' King Henry IV.,' to the effect that he would introduce the wars of King Henry the Fifth upon the stage, and make the audience merry with fair Catherine of France."[1] "The date of the authorship of the play is shown decisively," says Hunter, " to have been in 1599, by the poet's allusion, in the chorus to the fifth act, to the Earl of Essex's campaign in Ireland, and his hoped-for return, which took place in September of that year :—

> As, by a lower but by loving likelihood,
> Were now the general of our gracious empress
> (As, in good time, he may), from Ireland coming,
> Bringing rebellion broached on his sword,
> How many would the peaceful city quit,
> To welcome him ?

" There can be no doubt," remarks Kenny, " that these lines refer to the expedition of the Earl of Essex to Ireland," adding that it was very likely " Shakespeare was the more disposed to indulge in this kindly allusion, from the fact that his own special patron, the Earl of Southampton, served in the expedition as Master of the Horse."[2] It is worthy of observation here, that

---

[1] "Studies and Writings of Shakespeare," by Joseph Hunter, vol. ii. p. 58. London, 1845.

[2] "Life and Genius of Shakespeare," by Thomas Kenny, p. 241. London, 1864.

Hunter, in his notice of " Henry V.," remarks, that " the name of Fluellin, given to the Welsh soldier in this play, was probably taken from the name of William Fluellin, who was buried at Stratford, July 9, 1595 ;" a fact which works to the support of the Stratford authorship of the Shakespearian plays. Schlegel, in speaking of King Henry V., says, it is doubtful if Shakespeare ever would have written the play of " Henry V." " had not the stage previously possessed it in the old play of 'The Famous Victories,' because Henry IV. would have been perfect as a dramatic whole, without the addition of ' Henry V. ; ' but," adds he, " having brought the history of Henry of Monmouth up to the period of his father's death, the demands of an audience which had been accustomed to hail the madcap Prince of Wales as the conqueror of Agincourt, compelled him to continue the story." Knight does not think Shakespeare would have chosen the subject of Henry V. for a drama, " for," says he, " as skilfully as he has managed it, and magnificent as the whole drama is as a great national song of triumph, there can be no doubt that Shakespeare felt that in this play he was dealing with a theme too narrow for his peculiar powers . . . the subject being altogether one of *lyric* grandeur. . . . And yet, how exquisitely has Shakespeare thrown his dramatic power into this undramatic subject. The character of the King is one of the most finished portraits that has proceeded from his master hand. . . . It was for him to embody in the person of Henry V. the principle of national heroism ; it was for him to call forth the spirit of patriotic reminiscence."

Upon this feature of the character of Shakespeare, Gervinius is not so enthusiastic as the English commentator. *He* thinks Shakespeare would have done better if he had not fallen too easily into the weakness of the age for boasting :—

" It seems to me," he says, " more than probable that a jealous patriotic feeling actuated our poet in the entire representation of his Prince Henry ; the intention, namely, of exhibiting by the side of his brilliant contemporary, Henry IV. of France, a Henry upon the English throne equal to him in greatness and originality. *The greatness of his hero, however, would appear still more estimable if his enemies were depicted as less inestimable.* It alone belonged to the ancients to honour even their enemies. Homer exhibits no depreciation of the Trojans, and Æschylus no trace of contempt of the Persians, even when he delineates their impiety and rebukes it. In this there lies a large-hearted equality of estimation, and a nobleness of mind, far surpassing in practical morality, many subtle Christian theories of brotherly love. That Shakespeare distorts the French antagonists, and could not even get rid of his Virgil-taught hatred against the Greeks, is one of the few traits which we would rather not see in his works; it is a national narrow-mindedness with which the *Briton* gained ground over the *man.* The nations of antiquity, who bore a far stronger stamp of nationality than any modern people, were strangers to this intolerant national pride."

Kenny, in treating upon the view which Shakespeare's portrait of Henry V. gives us of the poet's own character, says,—

" We do not know any other work of his in which his national or personal predilections have made themselves so distinctly visible. . . . . A large portion of the story has to be told, or merely indicated, by the choruses, in which the poet himself has to appear and to confess the inability of his art to reproduce the march and shock of armies, and, above all, the great scene on the field of Agincourt.

"Some of the modern continental critics," continues this shrewd observer, " think they can see that not only was Henry V. Shakespeare's favourite hero, but that this is the character, in all the poet's dramas, which he himself most nearly resembled. Many people will, perhaps, hardly be able to refrain from a smile on hearing of this conjecture. We certainly cannot see the slightest ground for its adoption. The whole history of Shakespeare's life, and the whole cast of Shakespeare's genius, are opposed to this extravagant supposition. We have no doubt that the poet readily sympathized with the frank and gallant bearing of the king. But we find no indication in all that we know of his temperament, or of the impression which he produced upon his contemporaries, of that firm, rigid, self-concentrated personality which distinguishes the born masters of mankind.

" Henry V. was necessarily peremptory, designing, unwavering, energetic, and self-willed; *Shakespeare was flexible, changeful, meditative, sceptical, and self-distrustful.* This was clearly the temperament of the author of the sonnets; it was too, we believe, not less clearly the character of the wonderful observer and delineator of all the phases of both tragic and comic passion:

and it was, perhaps, in no small degree, through the very variety of his emotional and imaginative sensibility, *and the very absence of that completeness and steadfastness of nature which his injudicious admirers now claim for him,* that he was enabled to become the great dramatic poet of the world."

I quote this latter paragraph with satisfaction, because it agrees in its conception of Shakespeare's personal character with that which was expressed by me, in Chapter XXI., before I had met with these remarks of Mr. Kenny.

Let me say here, that I give all of the foregoing observations to such large extent, because they indicate, to my comprehension, the vagrant and adaptable imagination of the playright, rather than the philosophical and scholarly responsibility of Bacon.

The first thing which attracts attention in the text of "Henry V.," as bearing upon the points of our inquiry, are the four opening lines in the chorus :—

> O for a muse of fire, that would ascend
> The brightest heaven of invention !
> A kingdom for a stage, *princes to act,*
> *And monarchs to behold the swelling scene !*

The next occurs in the first scene of the first act, and exhibits our poet's predisposition to express himself reverently when referring to the Catholic religion :—

> For all the temporal lands, which men *devout*
> By testament have given to the church.

Again :—

> The king is full of grace and fair regard,
> And a true lover of the *holy* church.

The above two words, " devout " and " holy," could have been easily supplied by other equally descriptive terms; but inasmuch as Shakespeare always selects religious adjectives after this solemn and reverential fashion, they seem to be spontaneous evidences of settled Romanism. I think it is fair to conclude that no rigid Protestant, like Bacon, would invariably refer to the Catholic Church in this worshipful and bending way.

In Scene 2 of the same act we have an intricate and learned exposition of the Salique law of France. It is given as a part of an abstruse legal digest of title for Henry as the lawful King of France, and is so technical that it is impossible to resist the conclusion that Shakespeare must have ordered the statement from some lawyer for his purposes; and it is not impossible he begged it from Lord Bacon. It is a little singular that Lord Chief Justice Campbell should have utterly passed by this most conspicuous of all the evidences of law learning which the plays contain. Lord Campbell must have recognized this as an outside law exploit on the part of our poet, and probably thought it prudent to take no notice of it, inasmuch as it might impair his own previous arguments. It may be remarked, on the other side, that Shakespeare took it almost bodily from Holinshed, the historian; but that argument none the less affects the position of Lord Campbell, for if Shakespeare could utilize as much law learning as this, from the pages of the old chronicler, the field for his smaller scraps of legal phrase was obviously easier to work.

The main action of "Henry V." consists in the invasion of France with thirty thousand men, twenty-four thousand of whom were foot soldiers, and six thousand horse. The embarkation of these forces was made from Southampton, in fifteen hundred ships, on the 11th of August, 1415, and the whole were landed on the coast of France on the second day afterward. The first exploit of this army was to lay siege to Harfleur, for, in those days of pikes and cross-bows, prudent commanders never ventured to advance into an enemy's country with walled towns behind them. The place surrendered on the 22nd of September, after a siege of thirty-six days, when Henry, finding that two-thirds of his force had perished by battle and by the ravages of a frightful dysentery, determined to fall back on Calais, and abandon his expedition. For the performance of this movement the English chroniclers say that the army remaining to him did not amount to more than eight thousand fighting men in all.[a] Before leaving Harfleur, however, we find King Henry thus invoking the devoted remnant of his troops to the assault :—

> K. HEN. Once more unto the breach, dear friends, once more;
> Or close the wall up with our English dead!
> *   *   *
> Now set the teeth, and stretch the nostril wide,
> Hold hard the breath, and bend up every spirit

---

[a] Knight, vol. iii., p. 574, Appleton's New York edition.

> To his full height!—On, on, you *noblest* English,
> Whose blood is fet from fathers of war proof?
> Fathers, that, like so many Alexanders,
> Have, in these parts, from morn till even fought,
> And sheath'd their swords for lack of argument.
> Dishonour not your mothers; now attest,
> That those, whom you call'd fathers, did beget you;
> Be copy now *to men of grosser blood,*
> And teach *them* how to war!—*And you, good yeomen,*
> Whose limbs were made in England, show us here,
> *The mettle of your pasture;* let us swear
> That you are *worth your breeding:* which I doubt not;
> *For there is none of you so mean and base,*
> That hath not noble lustre in your eyes.
> I see you stand like *greyhounds* in the slips,
> *Straining upon the start. The game's afoot;*
> Follow *your spirit:* and, upon this charge,
> Cry—God for Harry! England! and Saint George!

There can scarcely be a wider distinction drawn between the merits of two classes of men than is here given for the nobles against the rank and file; and we can see how Shakespeare holds *mere soldiers* in his estimation, by the following reference to them, immediately afterward, when Henry sent his last summons to the Governor of Harfleur, to surrender:—

K. HEN. If I begin the battery once again,
> I will not leave the half-achieved Harfleur,
> Till in her ashes she lie buried.
> The gates of mercy shall be all shut up;
> *And the flesh'd soldier,—rough and hard of heart,—*
> *In liberty of bloody hand, shall range*
> *With conscience wide as hell; mowing like grass*
> *Your fresh fair virgins and your flowering infants.*
> What is it then to me, if impious war,—
> Array'd in flames, like to the prince of fiends,—
> Do, with his smirch'd complexion, all fell feats
> Enlink'd to waste and desolation?
> What is't to me, when you yourselves are cause,
> If your pure maidens fall into the hand
> Of hot and forcing violation?
> What rein can hold licentious wickedness,
> When down the hill he holds his fierce career?
> *We may as bootless spend our vain command*
> *Upon the enraged soldiers in their spoil,*
> *As send precepts to the Leviathan*
> *To come ashore.* Therefore, you men of Harfleur,

Take pity of your town, and of your people,
Whiles yet my soldiers are in my command ;
Whiles yet the cool and temperate wind of grace
O'erblows the filthy and contagious clouds
Of deadly murder, spoil, and villany.
If not, why, in a moment, look to see
The blind and bloody soldier with foul hand
Defile the locks of your shrill-shrieking daughters ;
Your fathers taken by the silver beards,
And their most reverend heads dash'd to the walls,
Your naked infants spitted upon pikes ;
Whiles the mad mothers with their howls confused
Do break the clouds, as did the wives of Jewry
At Herod's bloody-hunting slaughtermen.

At this terrific threat the town surrenders.

In a few days after the surrender, the king is about to take his
greatly-diminished force, now reduced to certainly less than 9000
men, to Calais ; but, on the point of this retreat, he is intercepted
by the arrival of Montjoy, a herald, who brings from the French
king a peremptory summons to surrender. Henry, after listening
with patience, thus replies :—

K. HEN. Thou dost thy office fairly. Turn thee back,
And tell thy king—I do not seek him now ;
But could be willing to march on to Calais
Without impeachment ; for, to say the sooth,
(Though 'tis no wisdom to confess so much
Unto an enemy of craft and vantage),
My people are with sickness much enfeebled ;
My numbers lessen'd ; and those few I have,
Almost no better than so many French ;
Who, when they were in health, I tell thee, herald,
I thought, upon one pair of English legs
Did march three Frenchmen.

*　　　　*　　　　*

The sum of all our answer is but this :
We would not seek a battle, as we are ;
Nor as we are, we say, we will not shun it ;
So tell your master.

In Act IV. Scene 1, we have Pistol interrogating King Henry,
while the latter is walking about the camp in disguise, during
the night before the battle of Agincourt :—

PISTOL. Discuss unto me ; art thou officer ?
Or art thou *base, common, and popular ?*
KING. I am a gentleman of a company.
15

After a while the king is left alone, when, surveying in his mind the dangers of the morrow, the labours and responsibilities, the suffering and the wakefulness which he is obliged to undergo, he indulges in the following fit of the blues :—

> And what have kings, that privates have not too,
> Save ceremony, save general ceremony?
> And what art thou, thou idol ceremony?
> What kind of god art thou, that suffer'st more
> Of mortal griefs, than do thy worshippers?
> What are thy rents? what are thy comings-in?
> O ceremony, show me but thy worth!
> What is the soul of adoration?
> Art thou aught else but place, degree, and form,
> Creating awe and fear in other men?
> Wherein thou art less happy being fear'd
> Than they in fearing.
> What drink'st thou oft, instead of homage sweet,
> But poison'd flattery? O, be sick, great greatness,
> And bid thy ceremony give thee cure!
> Think'st thou, the fiery fever will go out
> With titles blown from adulation?
> Will it give place to flexure and low bending?
> Canst thou, when thou command'st the beggar's knee,
> Command the health of it? No, thou proud dream,
> That play'st so subtly with a king's repose;
> I am a king that find thee; and I know,
> 'Tis not the balm, the sceptre, and the ball,
> The sword, the mace, the crown imperial,
> The inter-tissued robe of gold and pearl,
> The farced title running 'fore the king,
> The throne he sits on, nor the tide of pomp
> That beats upon the high shore of this world,
> No, not all these, thrice-gorgeous ceremony,
> Not all these, laid in bed majestical,
> Can sleep so soundly *as the wretched slave ;*
> Who, with a body fill'd, and vacant mind,
> Gets him to rest, cramm'd with distressful bread;
> Never sees horrid night, the child of hell;
> But, like a lackey, from the rise to set,
> Sweats in the eye of Phœbus, and all night
> Sleeps in Elysium ; next day, after dawn,
> Doth rise, *and help Hyperion to his horse ;*
> And follows so the ever-running year
> With profitable labour, to his grave:
> And, but for ceremony, *such a wretch,*
> *Winding up days with toil, and nights with sleep,*

> Had the fore-hand and vantage of a king.
> *The slave,* a member of the country's peace,
> Enjoys it; but in gross brain little wots
> What watch the king keeps to maintain the peace,
> Whose hours *the peasant* best advantages.

This gloomy dissertation upon the animal advantages of being a vacant-minded, wretched slave, who, crammed with food, sleeps sound and rises in the morning only too happy to help his lordship to his horse, is naturally followed by a religious fit, in which his majesty continues :—

> O God of battles ! steel my soldiers' hearts !
> Possess them not with fear; take from them now
> The sense of reckoning, if the opposed numbers
> Pluck their hearts from them !—Not to-day, O Lord,
> O not to-day, think not upon the fault
> My father made in compassing the crown !
> *I Richard's body have interr'd new;*
> *And on it have bestow'd more contrite tears,*
> *Than from it issued forced drops of blood.*
> *Five hundred poor I have in yearly pay,*
> *Who twice a day their wither'd hands hold up*
> *Towards heaven, to pardon blood; and I have built*
> *Two chantries, where the sad and solemn priests*
> *Sing still for Richard's soul. More will I do :*
> Though all that I can do, is nothing worth ;
> Since that my penitence comes after all,
> ˙Imploring pardon.

And we shall presently see that, under our poet's patronage, this pious penitence pays a rich percentage. But here let me pause a moment to remark, that it seems impossible the adorable picture presented in the reverential lines—

> Two chantries, where *the sad and solemn priests*
> *Sing still for Richard's soul*—

could have spontaneously formed itself in the mind of any Protestant writer of the Elizabethan period of religious prejudice and persecution.

But the battle of Agincourt is approaching, and Shakespeare thus presents the contrasted condition and numbers of the combatants.

We take the statement as the poet gives it first from the French camp :—

Act IV. Scene 2.—*The French Camp.*
Present—The DAUPHIN, ORLEANS, RAMBURES, *and others.*
Enter CONSTABLE.

CON. To horse, you gallant princes! straight to horse!
Do but behold yon poor and starved band,
And your fair show shall suck away their souls,
Leaving them but the shades and husks of men.
There is not work enough for all our hands;
Scarce blood enough in all their sickly veins,
To give each naked curtle-ax a stain,
That our French gallants shall to-day draw out,
And sheath for lack of sport; let us but blow on them,
The vapour of our valour will o'erturn them.
'Tis positive 'gainst all exceptions, lords,
That our superfluous lackeys and our peasants,—
Who, in unnecessary action, swarm
About our squares of battle,—were enough
To purge this field of such a hilding foe:
Though we, upon this mountain's basis by,
Took stand for idle speculation:
But that our honours must not.   What's to say?
A very little little let us do,
And all is done.   Then, let the trumpets sound
The tucket sonnance, and the note to mount:
For our approach shall so much dare the field,
That England shall couch down in fear and yield.

Enter GRANDPRE.

GRAND. Why do you stay so long, my lords of France,
Yon island carrions, desperate of their bones,
Ill-favouredly become the morning field:
Their ragged curtains poorly are let loose,
And our air shakes them passing scornfully.
Big Mars seems bankrupt in their beggar'd host,
And faintly through a rusty beaver peeps,
Their horsemen sit like fixed candlesticks,
With torch staves in their hands: and their poor jades
Lob down their heads, dropping the hides and hips;
The gum down-roping from their pale dead eyes;
And in their pale dull mouths the gimmal bit
Lies foul with chewed grass, still and motionless;
And their executors, the knavish crows,
Fly o'er them all, impatient for their hour.

The scene now shifts to the English camp.

Act IV. Scene 3.
Enter the English Army, GLOSTER, BEDFORD, EXETER, SALISBURY, *and*
WESTMORELAND.

GLOSTER. Where is the king?

BEDFORD. The king himself is rode to view their battle.

WESTMORELAND. Of fighting men they have *full three score thousand.*

EXETER. *There's five to one ;* besides, they are all fresh.

SALISBURY. God's arm strike with us! 'tis a fearful odds.

This brings us to the battle. The conflict is in favour of King Henry from the first, but it rages with such violence, and the English are so wearied, even by the weight of their success, that in the midst of it Henry issues the order that every soldier kill his prisoners.

> KING. The French have reinforced their scatter'd men :
> Then every soldier kill his prisoners ;
> Give the word through !

One of the English historians, Sir H. Nicolas, thus alludes to the battle :—

" The immense number of the French proved their ruin. . . . The battle lasted three hours. The English stood on heaps of corpses which exceeded a man's height. The French, indeed, fell almost passive in their lines. . . . The total loss of the French was about 10,000 slain on the field ; that of the English *appears* to have been *about twelve hundred.* . . . The English king conducted himself with his accustomed dignity to his many illustrious prisoners. The victorious army marched to Calais in fine order, and embarked for England (on the 17th of November) without any attempt to follow up their victory."

The following is Shakespeare's account of the result :—

Act IV. Scene 8.

Enter an English Herald.

K. HEN. Now, Herald; are the dead number'd?

HER. Here is the number of the slaughter'd French.

[*Delivers a paper.*

K. HEN. What prisoners *of good sort* are taken, uncle?

EXETER. Charles duke of Orleans, nephew to the king ;
John duke of Bourbon, and the lord Bouciqualt :
Of other lords, and barons, knights, and 'squires,
Full fifteen hundred, *besides common men.*

K. HEN. This note doth tell me of ten thousand French,
That in the field lie slain : of princes, in this number,
And nobles bearing banners, there lie dead
One hundred and twenty-six : added to these,
Of knights, esquires, and gallant gentlemen,

Eight thousand and four hundred; of the which,
Five hundred were but yesterday dubb'd knights:
So that, in these ten thousand they have lost,
There are but sixteen hundred mercenaries;
The rest are—princes, barons, lords, knights, 'squires,
And gentlemen of blood and quality.

*   *   *

Here was a royal fellowship of death!—
Where is the number of our English dead?
                                        [*Herald presents another paper.*
Edward the duke of York, the earl of Suffolk,
Sir Richard Ketly, Davy Gam, esquire:
None else of name; and of all other men,
But five and twenty. O God, thy arm was here,
And not to us, but to thy arm alone,
Ascribe we all!—When, without stratagem,
But in plain shock, and even play of battle,
Was ever known so great and little loss,
On one part and on the other?—Take it, God,
For it is only thine!

EXETER.   'Tis wonderful!

K. HEN. Come, go we in procession to the village:
And be it death proclaimed through our host,
To boast of this, or take that praise from God,
Which is his only.

*   *   *

K. HEN. *Do we all holy rites;*
Let there be sung Non Nobis, and Te Deum.
The dead with charity enclosed in clay,
We'll then to Calais; and to England then,
Where ne'er from France arrived more happy men.

Here we have, according to Shakespeare, the loss of only *twenty-nine men* to the English, nobles and all, during three hours' hard fighting, against the slaughter of *ten thousand French!* A result manufactured for the play-house by a playwright who was catering to audiences, as the playwrights of to-day cater for the uproarious swarms of the Surrey Theatre in London, the Porte St. Martin in Paris, or the Bowery Theatre in New York; catering, however, only for their shouts and shillings—which Shakespeare knew how to do—and not for their sensible and historical appreciation, as would have been the aim of a rigid philosopher like Bacon.

One incident occurred at the end of the battle, in Scene 7, which, though we have passed it in the course of our narrative,

must not be overlooked. The French herald enters and asks of
Henry the usual privilege to go over the field and sort out the
dead. The following is his language :—

MONTJOY.   Great king,
          I come to thee for charitable licence,
          That we may wander o'er this bloody field,
          To book our dead, and then to bury them ;
          To sort our nobles from our common men ;
          For many of our princes (woe the while !)
          Lie drown'd and soak'd in mercenary blood ;
          (So do our vulgar drench their peasant limbs
          In blood of princes).

It seems to me that had the author of these lines possessed but
one grain of true consideration for his kind, he might have constructed the above abominable paragraph somewhat after the
following fashion :—

          That we may wander o'er the bloody field,
          To gather up our dear heroic dead,
          Who, whether nobly or obscurely born,
          Have, by thus dying in their country's cause,
          Earn'd equal knighthood at the court of Heaven.

CHAPTER XXIII.

"KING HENRY VI."—PART I.

THIS play, and its two succeeding branches, known as Parts II. and III., though later in their chronology than "King John" and those plays which follow in order up to " Henry V.," were undoubtedly written in advance of all the English historical series ; and, while the authorship by Shakespeare of the First Part, or the fact of his having had any hand in it whatever, has been very seriously disputed, I shall accept its authenticity for the purposes of this inquiry, without entering into the discussion. The play comes to us in the regular and authorized edition of Shakespeare's dramatic works, and this is sufficient warrant for us to proceed as if the origin of its text never had been questioned. Indeed, so much has been written in the dispute, and there is still so much left to dispute about, that, by touching it at all, I fear I should only add to the confusion of the reader. All the commentators agree, however, that if Shakespeare was the author of the First Part of " Henry VI.," it must have been among the earliest efforts of his genius. The other English historical dramas ascribed to him, and running up to " Henry V.," were all finished subsequently to 1593. " Henry VI.," Part I., was certainly written previous to 1592, while Hunter and some others credit its production to as early a period as 1587.

The character of King Henry VI. is that of a weak, variable, puling saint, who, had he been a man, might have saved to England the conquests of his father, and prevented the House of Lancaster from falling before the bolder sword of York. With this mere glimpse at the defective character of such a singular production of a warrior sire, I will proceed to the illustrations from the First Part, which support especial portions of our theme.

It will be recollected that in the course of the examination which arose in the earlier portion of this work, on the subject of

the religious faith of our poet, liberal illustrations were given
from the text of several of the plays.   Among these were
extracts of considerable length from the play before us, all going
to show the spontaneity of Shakespeare's catholic sentiments and
predilections.   To avoid repetition, therefore, I will now simply
refer the reader back to pages 58, 59, 60 and 61, as portions of
this chapter.

As we follow the pomp and pageantry of these dramatic
histories, awed or intoxicated by the swelling imagery which
invites our homage to the kings and nobles who are the darlings
of our poet's soul, we naturally look now and then for courage
or worthiness in some humbler characters, upon whom our poet
might condescend to bestow a portion of his beneficient consideration.   But we constantly look in vain; for William Shakespeare
takes not the slightest respectful interest in anything below
the status of a knight.   On the contrary, he usually prefers to
elevate his aristocratic pets by the mean process of degrading
every character not possessed of rank.

The initial illustration which the First Part of " Henry VI."
gives us of this deplorable tendency, occurs in the speech of Joan
of Arc, when she describes the humbleness of her birth to the
Dauphin of France :—

PUCELLE. Dauphin, *I am by birth a shepherd's daughter,*
        My wit[1] untrain'd in any kind of art,
        Heaven, and our Lady gracious, hath it pleased
        To shine on *my contemptible estate :*
        Lo, whilst I waited on my tender lambs,
        And to sun's parching heat display'd my cheeks,
        God's mother deigned to appear to me :
        And, in a vision full of majesty,
        Will'd me to leave *my base vocation.*

Act I. Scene 2.

We find this disdain for inferior birth still more extravagantly
expressed in Scene 4 of the same act, where Talbot, the leader of
the English forces in France, declares that, on one occasion, when
he was held a prisoner, he preferred the alternative of death, to
the insult of being exchanged for a French prisoner of inferior
condition.

---

[1] The word " wit " in our poet's time, usually meant intellect or intelligence, and not wit as we use the word now.

> TALBOT. The Duke of Bedford had a prisoner,
> Called—the brave Lord Ponton de Santrailles;
> For him I was exchanged and ransomed.
> *But with a baser man of arms by far,*
> *Once, in contempt, they would have barter'd me;*
> *Which I, disdaining, scorn'd; and craved death*
> *Rather than I would be so piled esteem'd.*
> In fine, redeem'd I was as I desired.

The next instance occurs during the course of the quarrel between Somerset and Plantagenet, in the memorable scene in the
Temple Garden, where the plucking of the white and red roses
signalizes the initiative of the long strife, between the houses of
York and Lancaster. Somerset, in this scene, taunts Plantagenet
with the attainder of his father, Richard, Earl of Cambridge,
who was executed at Southampton for treason in the previous
reign of Henry V. Somerset, in his tirade, thus describes the
effect of such a ban :—

> SOMERSET. Was not thy father, Richard, Earl of Cambridge,
> For treason executed in our late king's days?
> And, by his treason, stand'st not thou attainted,
> *Corrupted*, and exempt *from ancient gentry?*
> His trespass yet *lives guilty in thy blood;*
> And, till thou be restored, thou art a *yeoman.*

Again, Talbot, in the next act, taunts the French, who are on
the walls of Rouen.

> TALBOT. Base muleteers of France!
> Like *peasant* footboys do they keep the walls,
> And dare not take up arms like *gentlemen.*

In the First Scene of Act IV., Talbot and Gloster thus denounce a certain Sir John Fastolfe (not our old friend Falstaff,
of the Boar's Head Tavern) with treachery to the English forces
in the field :—

> TALBOT (*to Fastolfe*).   And
> I vow'd, base knight, when I did meet thee next, '
> To tear the garter from thy craven's leg. [*Plucking it off.*
> (Which I have done), because unworthily
> Thou wast installed in that high degree.—
> Pardon me, princely Henry, and the rest:
> This dastard, at the battle of Paray,
> When but in all I was six thousand strong,
> And that the French *were almost ten to one,*—

Before we met, or that a stroke was given,
Like to a trusty squire, did run away:
In which assault we lost twelve hundred men,
Myself, and divers gentlemen beside,
Were there surprised and taken prisoners.
Then judge, great lords, if I have done amiss;
Or, whether that such cowards ought to wear
This ornament of knighthood, yea or no?

GLO. To say the truth, this act was infamous,
And ill-beseeming any common man;
Much more a knight, a captain, and a leader.

TAL. When first this order was ordained, my lords,
Knights of the garter were of noble birth;
Valiant, and virtuous, full of haughty courage,
Such as were grown to credit by the wars;
Not fearing death, nor shrinking for distress,
But always resolute in most extremes.
He, then, that is not furnish'd in this sort,
Doth but usurp the sacred name of knight,
Profaning this most honourable order;
And should (if I were worthy to be judge,)
Be quite degraded, *like a hedge-born swain*
That doth presume to boast of gentle blood.

K. HEN. Stain to thy countrymen! thou hear'st thy doom.
Be packing therefore, thou that wast a knight;
Henceforth we banish thee on pain of death.

Finally, in order to put the climax of reprobation upon low birth and its assumed degraded instincts, Shakespeare makes the inspired maid, Joan of Arc, deny her own father in most opprobrious terms, her chief accusation being against the meanness of his birth. The following is a full description of this extraordinary scene :—

Act V. Scene 4.—*Camp of the Duke of York, in Anjou.*

Enter YORK, WARWICK, *and others.*

YORK. Bring forth that sorceress, condemn'd to burn.

Enter LA PUCELLE, *guarded, and a Shepherd.*

SHEP. Ah, Joan! this kills thy father's heart outright!
Have I sought every country far and near,
And, now it is my chance to find thee out,
Must I behold thy timeless, cruel death?
Ah, Joan, sweet daughter Joan, I'll die with thee!

PUC. *Decrepit miser!*[2] *base, ignoble wretch!*

---

[2] "Miser" means, in this connexion, miserable person.—*Duychinck.*

> *I am descended of a gentler blood;*
> *Thou art no father, nor no friend, of mine.*

SHEP. Out, out!—My lords, an please you, 'tis not so;
I did beget her, all the parish knows:
Her mother liveth yet, can testify
She was the first fruit of my bachelorship.

WAR. Graceless! wilt thou deny thy parentage?

YORK. This argues what her kind of life hath been;
Wicked and vile; and so her death concludes.

SHEP. Fye, Joan! that thou wilt be so obstacle!
God knows, thou art a collop of my flesh:
And for thy sake have I shed many a tear:
Deny me not, I pr'y thee, gentle Joan.

PUC. *Peasant, avaunt! You have suborn'd this man*
Of purpose to obscure my noble birth.

SHEP. 'Tis true, I gave a noble to the priest,
The morn that I was wedded to her mother.
Kneel down and take my blessing, good my girl.
Wilt thou not stoop? Now cursed be the times
Of thy nativity! I would, the milk
Thy mother gave thee, when thou suck'dst her breast,
Had been a little ratsbane for thy sake!
Or else, when thou didst keep my lambs a field,
I wish some ravenous wolf had eaten thee;
Dost thou deny thy father, *cursed drab?*
O, burn her, burn her; hanging is too good. [*Exit.*

YORK. Take her away; for she hath lived too long
To fill the world with vicious qualities.

PUC. First, let me tell you whom you have condemn'd;
Not me begotten of a shepherd swain,
But issued from the progeny of kings;
Virtuous, and holy; chosen from above,
By inspiration of celestial grace.

    *   *   *

YORK. Ay, ay;—away with her to execution.
And hark ye, sirs; because she is a maid,
Spare for no faggots, let there be enough;
Place barrels of pitch upon the fatal stake,
That so her torture may be shortened.

PUC. Will nothing turn your unrelenting hearts?
Then, Joan, discover thine infirmity;
That warranteth by law to be thy privilege.
I am with child, ye bloody homicides;
Murder not then the fruit within my womb,
Although ye hale me to a violent death.

YORK. Now, heaven forfend! the holy maid with child?

WAR. The greatest miracle that e'er ye wrought:

Is all your strict preciseness come to this?

YORK. She and the Dauphin have been juggling:
I did imagine what would be her refuge.

WAR. Well, go to; we will have no bastards live;
Especially, since Charles must father it.

PUC. You are deceived; my child is none of his:
It was Alençon that enjoy'd my love.

YORK. Alençon! that notorious Machiavel!
It dies, an if it had a thousand lives.

PUC. O, give me leave, I have deluded you;
'Twas neither Charles, nor yet the duke I named,
But Reignier, king of Naples, that prevail'd.

WAR. A married man! that's most intolerable.

YORK. Why, here's a girl! I think, she knows not well,
There were so many, whom she may accuse.

WAR. It's sign, she hath been liberal and free.

YORK. And yet, forsooth, she is a virgin pure.—
Strumpet, thy words condemn thy brat, and thee:
Use no entreaty, for it is in vain.

PUC. Then lead me hence;—with whom I leave my curse:
May never glorious sun reflex his beams
Upon the country where you make abode!
But darkness and the gloomy shade of death
Environ you: till mischief, and despair,
Drive you to break your necks, or hang yourselves!
[*Exit, guarded.*

YORK. Break thou in pieces, and consume to ashes,
Thou foul accursed minister of hell!

In Scene 5 of Act V. we have the following expression by Suffolk, in reply to an objection raised by some of Henry's nobles, that the proposed dower of Margaret is insufficient for the consort of a king :—

SUFFOLK. So, worthless *peasants* bargain for their wives,
As market-men for oxen, sheep, or horse.
Marriage is a matter of more worth,
Than to be dealt in by attorneyship.

King Henry, after hearing this speech, orders Suffolk to go and entreat—

That Lady Margaret do vouchsafe to come
To cross the seas to England, and be crown'd
King Henry's faithful and *anointed* queen;
For your expenses and sufficient charge
Among the people gather up a tenth.

Lords, lords, lords; nothing but princes and lords, and The

People never alluded to except as *worthless peasants*, or to be scorned as *scabs* and *hedge-born swains*. Surely the privileged classes of Great Britain cannot defend the supremacy of Shakespeare's intellect too stubbornly. As I have said before, they have an interest in keeping up a prestige for the Bard of Avon which is to them beyond all price!—Though it suggests itself, in this connexion, that those classes exhibit an impolitic greediness when they try to prove, under the leadership of such social autocrats as Palmerston, that the author of these plays was a noble like themselves. The services rendered to their order by the transcendant muse of Shakespeare, would be of tenfold value as coming from a commoner, than through the medium of rank. But errors of this stamp are always made in unjust causes. The bards who string their lyres for liberty receive only the frowns of Corinthian society; and no room is allowed for the unrespected ashes, even of the derogate liberty-loving noble, Byron, in Westminster Abbey.

CHAPTER XXIV.

"KING HENRY VI."—PART II.

WHATEVER the blind idolators of Shakespeare may offer in excuse for his abject servility to the privileged classes, and for his aggressive contempt for humble birth and laborious avocation; whatever extenuation may be made in the name of patriotism for his monstrous perversions of the truth of history,—as in his account of the battle of Agincourt, and for usually making the English whip their enemies at the disadvantage of at least ten to one,—no palliation can be set up for him in regard to the monstrous and inexcusable falsehoods which disgrace the pages of the above-entitled play as to the rebellion of Jack Cade, and about the character of that brave and devoted leader. The "love of country" which is pleaded in excuse for the English poet's exaggerations against the French, while it may be pardoned by some very loyal persons, is a far less worthy motive to any well-regulated mind, than the love of humanity and truth. The first may be characterized as a mere geographical affection, carefully inculcated by monarchs for their own purposes, and extending no further than the boundaries of their dominions; while the latter are sentiments implanted by the Creator, as broad as His own mercy, as active as His own beneficence, and comprehending, through the impulses of every good heart, the welfare and happiness of the whole human race. There can be no excuse for such an entire absence of philanthropy in any man, as to justify his discharging the poor and humble so utterly from his consideration, as Shakespeare did; or to induce him to find his ideals of patriotism and worthiness only amid the throngs of their oppressors. Such a writer is a mere pander to the crimes of tyrants, and he gives evidence, whatever may be his intellectual eminence, that he has been perverted, by accidental circumstances, from the purpose he was commissioned to perform.

Gratitude to earthly patrons, such as William Shakespeare's to Southampton and to Essex, or the weak yearning of the Stratford adventurer to invest his easily-earned money in a coat-of-arms and become a gentleman, can never palliate the monstrous misrepresentations by which the poet has deceived his humble countrymen, from an honest admiration of the patriotism of Jack Cade.

THE REBELLION OF WAT TYLER.

To properly measure this perversion of his powers by Shakespeare, we must look at the social condition of England in the time *of* which he wrote. The rebellion of Jack Cade, against the oppressions of the nobles and the crown, took place in 1450, one hundred and four years before our poet was born. Only one popular uprising had previously taken place in England, and that was known as " the rebellion of Wat Tyler," which occurred in 1381, just seventy-nine years previous to the rebellion of Jack Cade. As the movement of Tyler was the first general rising of the Commons, and marks the dawn of popular liberty in England, we cannot do better than to give a sketch of the social state of affairs, which provoked it, from the most trustworthy chroniclers of the time. The principal of these chroniclers are Hall and Holinshed, by whose pages Shakespeare was mainly guided in his dramatic histories. Mackintosh, who wrote at a subsequent period and under better lights, is more liberal and reliable than either of the other two. In speaking of the oppressions of Wat Tyler's time, Mackintosh says,—

" It is an error to trace to the charters, which the barons extorted from their monarchs, the liberties of England; the triumphs of the nobles were theirs alone, and enured almost exclusively to their own advantage. The mass of the people were villeins or serfs, and they were left, by those boasted charters, in their chains. The condition of the bondmen differed in degrees of degradation and cruelty (for the mere slaves—servi—were known by the names of theow, esne, and thrall, and distinguished from the villeins), but, even where most favourable, it was a dark and inhuman oppression. The villeins were incapable of property, destitute of legal redress, and bound to services ignoble in their nature and indeterminate in their degree; they were sold separately from the land, could not marry without consent, and were, in nowise, elevated above the beasts of burthen with which they drudged in their unrequited and hopeless labour. At length, their sufferings drove them into resistance; and that resistance, provoked and sanctified by unmeasured wrongs, has been, by almost every successive historian made the subject of misrepresentation and obloquy."

Holinshed ascribes the insurrection of Wat Tyler to "the lewd demeanour of some indiscrete officers," but thus indignantly condemns the "disloyal" movement :—

"The commons of the realme sore repining, not onely for the pole grotes that were demanded of them, by reason of the grant made in parlement, but also for that they were sore oppressed (as *they* tooke the matter) by their landlords, that demanded of them their ancient customes and services, set on by some develish instinct and persuasion of their owne beastlie intentions, as men not content with the state whereunto they were called, rose in diverse parts of this realme, and assembled togither in companies, purposing to inforce the prince to make them free and to release them of all servitude, whereby they stood as bondmen to their lords and superiours."

Judge Conrad, of Philadelphia, in an able essay prefixed to his tragedy of "Jack Cade," in writing of these times from an American stand-point, describes as follows the outrage to which Holinshed alludes :—

"The overcharged feelings of the people were at length, by an outrage calculated in the highest degree to excite the passions of the multitude, let loose, and swept the land like a torrent. One of the insolent and rapacious officers for the collection of an oppressive poll-tax entered, during the absence of its proprietor, the cottage of a tiler—a man who seems to have been worthily esteemed by the populace. This tax was leviable upon females only when over fifteen years of age; and the licentious officer, alleging that the beautiful daughter of the tiler was beyond that age, 'therewith,' (we quote again from Hollinshed), 'began to misuse the maid, and search further than honestie would have permitted. The mother straightwaie made an outcrie, so that hir husband being in the towne at worke, and hearing of this adoo at his house, came running home with his lathing staffe in his hand, and began to question with the officer, asking him who

16

made him so bold to keepe such a rule in his house; the officer, being somewhat presumptuous, and high-minded, would forthwith have flown upon the tiler; but the tiler, avoiding the officer's blow, caught him such a rap on the pate, that his braines flue out, and so presentlie he died. Great noise rose about this matter in the streets, and the poor folks being glad, everie man arraied himself to support John Tiler, and thus the commons drew togither and went to Maidestone, and from thence to Blackheath, where their numbers so increased, that they were reckoned to be thirtie thousand. And the said John Tiler tooke vpon him to be their cheefe captaine, etc.'

"It would be difficult to imagine holier motives to justify resistance to oppression than those unwittingly and unwillingly disclosed by the chroniclers, who represent the commons as the guiltiest malefactors. Their wrongs and sufferings were as dark and deadly as any which ever crushed a people. They had no hope of redress from courts or codes; their only reliance was in their own union or hardihood; and the invocation to resistance proclaimed in the outrage upon the helplessness of the Tiler's daughter was as sacred and moving as that by which Brutus or Virginius aroused Rome. Nor does the purity and elevation of the cause suffer reproach from the conduct of its champions. Wat Tyler soon found himself at the head of one hundred thousand men, 'the villeins and poor men' of Kent, Norfolk, Suffolk, Essex, Sussex, and other Eastern counties. Illiterate, unused to freedom, infuriated by wrongs and desperate from misery, it might be supposed that so vast and disorganized a multitude would have rushed into boundless excesses. So far from it, it seems that, from the first, they not only disclaimed treasonable designs, but administered to all an oath that 'they should be faithful to King Richard and the Commons.' They soon obtained possession of London, and the Chancellor and the Primate suffered the death they merited, 'as evil counsellors of the crown and cruel oppressors of the people!'

"The conduct of this vast multitude, provoked by a thousand wrongs, and with the power to secure an ample vengeance, and glut to the uttermost their rapacity on the spoil of their unsparing oppressors, presents a singular contrast with the dishonourable perfidy and sanguinary cruelty exhibited by their lords. Mackintosh, the only historian who does them even stinted justice, says,

'At this moment of victory, the demands of the serfs were moderate, and, except in one instance, just. They required the abolition of bondage, the liberty of buying and selling in fairs and markets, a general pardon, and the reduction of the rent of land to an equal rate. The last of these conditions was indeed unjust and absurd; but the first of them, though incapable of being carried into immediate execution without probably producing much misery to themselves, was yet of such indisputable justice on general grounds, as to make it most excusable in the sufferers to accept nothing less from their oppressors.' But this usually accurate historian fails to inform us that the court, after a mature consideration of the demands of the commons, regularly and formally conceded all that was required. Doubts being entertained, as the result proved not without reason, of the sincerity of the king and court, charters were demanded and granted, securing the abolition of bondage, the redress of grievances, and a full pardon to all engaged in the insurrection. The annals of royalty, clouded as they are with every crime of which human nature is capable, present few instances of such deliberate and atrocious perfidy, or craft so cowardly and base, consummated by cruelty so guilty and unsparing.

"'The commons having received this charter departed home.' The Essex men first left London, and those from other counties shortly followed. The leader of the Kentishmen, the unfortunate Wat Tylér, distrusted the fair dealing of the court, and in an interview with the king at Smithfield, met a melancholy realization of his fears. Mackintosh, in relating the facts, remarks, 'It must not be forgotten that the partisans of Tyler had no historians.' But a careful review of the servile chroniclers of the court will satisfy the reader that Tyler was, in the presence of the king, and under his guaranty of safety, basely assassinated.

"This murder was but the first of thousands. The finale may be readily imagined. The solemn and sacred pardon of the king (Richard II.) was disregarded; the charter, with its sanction of covenants and oaths, was revoked. After the dispersion of the commons, 'the men of Essex,' says Holinshed, 'sent to the king to know of him if his pleasure was, that they should enjoy their promised liberties.' The king, 'in a great chafe,' answered that 'bondmen they were and bondmen they should be, and that in more vile manner than before.' An army was sent against them, and all who did not escape into the woods were slain. Mackintosh admits that 'the revolt was extinguished with the cruelty and bloodshed by which the masters of slaves seem generally anxious to prove that they are not of a race superior in any noble quality to the meanest of their bondmen. More than fifteen hundred perished by the hands of the hangman.' But Henry Kniston states that 'Then the king, of his accustomed clemencie, being pricked with pitie, would not that the wretches should die, but spared them, being a rash and foolish multitude, and commanded them everie man to get him home to his owne house; howbeit manie of them at the king's going awaie suffered death. In this miserable taking were reckoned to the number of twentie thousand.'"

I will adopt Judge Conrad's description of the events of Cade's uprising, preferring his narrative to any recital of my own; first, because a comparison of his with the histories of the period shows it to be entirely trustworthy; and next, because it is not susceptible of improvement at my hands.

THE REBELLION OF CADE.

"The period between this rebellion and the uprising of Cade, in 1450," says Judge Conrad, "had reduced England to the same condition as under the reign of Richard II. Villeinage, with all its sufferings and debasement, continued, and the commons were ground to the dust by the exactions of the court, and the unbridled oppression of the barons. Thus, with disgrace abroad and agony at home, the contrast with the glory of the recent reign was insupportable; and the popular discontent was manifested in risings, which, after the manner of the time, took the name of ' Blue Beard.' So intense was the excitement against Say and Suffolk, that the latter, notwithstanding the efforts of the Queen to screen ' her darling,' met the fate which he so justly merited. Shortly after this execution, a body of the peasantry of Kent met in arms, at Blackheath, under a leader whose brief and eventful career has been made the subject of unmeasured misrepresentation.

"Stowe alone represents his name to have really been Cade, while in a contemporary record he is called Mr. John Aylmere, Physician (Ellis' Letters, I., second series, 112). This account seems to be fully entitled to credit; it accords with the language and deportment of the chief of the commons, and we doubt not that such were his name and profession. It was, however, usual in such commotions to give to prominent actors, probably for purposes of concealment and security, fictitious and popular names. Thus we have seen that Wat Tyler assumed the name of Jack Straw. All the popular leaders appear thus to have borne names for the war. But Aylmere was not only called Jack Cade, for Polychronicon says he was ' of some named John Mendall.' The chronicles furnish no proof that he ever acknowledged the name of Cade. In his communications with the government he used merely the title of ' Captain of the Commons.' Mackintosh characterizes him as ' a leader of disputed descent, who had been transmitted to posterity with the nickname of John Cade. On him they bestowed the honourable name of John Mortimer, with manifest allusion to the claims of the house of Mortimer to the succession, which were, however, now indisputably vested in Richard, Duke of York.' It seems that the friends of the Duke of York favoured the insurrection, a fact of itself sufficient to attach dignity and importance to the movement. Hall and Holinshed agree in this statement. They describe him as ' a certeine young man of a goodlie stature and right pregnaunt of wit, who was intised to take upon him the name of John Mortimer, coosine to the Duke of York, and not for a small policie, but thinking by that surname that those which favoured the house of the Earle of Marche would be assistant to him. And so indeed it came to passe.' If Aylmere permitted this title to be given him, he certainly did not use it in his addresses to the King and Parliament, nor in his letters which have been preserved. It is also certain that the name of Mortimer could not, in any event, have promoted any personal design; and that he never claimed power, rank, or reward for himself, his simple title being The Captain, and his sole efforts confined to the amelioration of the condition of the people. So far from seeking revolution, he most emphatically proclaimed his loyalty, and all his acts were in the name of the king. The title of Mortimer may have been given him as a demonstration of respect, for Fabyan says that ' the multitude named him Mortimer, and this kept the people wondrously togither.'

" The leader who assumed the bold attitude of calm resistance must have been, if a physician at that period, superior to most of his opponents in the limited learning of the age. His letters, his addresses to the King and Parliament, his interview with the commissioners of the court, and the general tenor of his proceedings, prove the possession of an intellect of no ordinary cultivation and force; and his military skill and success indicate experience and sagacity as a soldier. His first measure, after assuming a position on Blackheath, was to proclaim distinctly the object of 'the assembly of the commons.' We learn from Hall and Holinshed that—

"He maintained also a correspondence with London, and his letters of safeguard to citizens passing to and from the camp and city, are formally and well drawn, and prove that even then he received supplies of money and arms from the capital. While thus organizing and disciplining his host, with a calmness and deliberation which manifests anything but the madness ascribed to him, 'he devised,' says Fabyan, 'a bill of petitions to the king and his council, and showed therein what injuries and oppressions the poor commons suffered by such as were about the king.' This proceeding is thus characterized by Holinshed: 'And to the intent the cause of this glorious captain's coming thither, might be shadowed vnder a cloke of good meaning (though his intent nothing so) he sent vnto the king an humble supplication, affirming that his coming was not against his grace, but against such of his councellors as were louers of themselues and oppressors of the poor commonaltie: flatterers of the king and enemies of his honour; suckers of his purse, and robbers of his subjects; parciall to their friends, and extreame to their enimies; through bribes corrupted, and for indifferencie dooing nothing.' The Parliament was then in session; and this bill of complaint, together with the requests of the commons, was sent to that body as well as to the King. The 'Complaint of the Commons of Kent, and the causes of their assemblie on the Blackheathe,' comprises fifteen items, set forth with great clearness and force, and manifesting as high an order of learning and ability as any state paper of the times. This Bill of Complaints, as given by Holinshed, affords conclusive evidence that Aylmere, instead of being the ignorant, ferocious, and vulgar ruffian generally supposed, was a patriot eminently enlightened and discreet.

"The requests of this Bill of Complaints were disallowed by the council, whom they accused, and some days after the king

marched against the force under Aylmere; but that leader seems
to have been averse to the commencement of actual hostilities,
especially against the king in person; and he retired before him,
taking post at Seven Oak, when the king returned to London.
The withdrawal of Aylmere is considered, by the chroniclers,
who can imagine no good of the people's chief, a mere feint to
entice the royal army into a more unfavourable position. The
queen, 'that bare rule,' shortly after sent Sir Humphrey Stafford
with an army, to disperse the rebels. The captain still desired
to avoid the effusion of blood; and we are told by Fabyan that,
'when Sir Humphrey, with his company, drew near to Seven
Oak, he was warned of the captain.' But this generous caution
and unusual moderation, doubtless ascribed to pusillanimity, did
not avail; and Aylmere met the inevitable issue with the skill
and courage of a tried soldier, and defeated them with great loss.

" After this important victory, the leader of the Commons, says
Mackintosh, 'assumed the attire, ornaments and style of a
knight; and, under the title of captain, he professed to preserve
the country by enforcing the rigid observance of discipline among
his followers.' Having refreshed his people, he resumed his
position on Blackheath, 'where he strongly encamped himself,
diverse idle and vagrant persons,' says Holinshead, 'out of Sussex,
Surrie, and other places, still increasing his number.' The king
and his council were now fully aroused to a sense of their danger;
and they determined to have recourse to the policy of negotiation,
promises and perfidy, found so effective in the previous insurrection. They accordingly sent to the leader, whose humble
'requests' they had received with such disdain, the Archbishop
of Canterbury and the Duke of Buckingham, to treat of an
accommodation. The report of this interview, derived as it is
from writers prompt to blacken Aylmere, and reluctant to admit
the slightest point in his favour, establishes, beyond doubt, the
elevation of his character and deportment. Fabyan says that the
royal commissioners 'had with him long communication, and
found him right discrete in his answers. Howbeit, they could
not cause him to lay down his people, and submit him (uncondi-
tionally) to the king's grace.' Holinshed's account after Hall, is
more full and expressive. 'These lords found him sober in talke,
wise in reasoning, arrogant in hart, and stiffe in opinion; as
who that by no means would grant to dissolve his armie, except

the king in person would come to him, and assent to the things he would require.' The captain, it seems, remembered the ill faith practiced towards Wat Tyler, and was unwilling to place it in the power of the court to re-enact that tragedy. Subsequent events proved how just were his suspicions.

"The king was alarmed by the firm attitude of Aylmere, and still more by the disaffection evident among his own followers. . . . . The captain, notwithstanding his recent victory, his great force, and the natural impatience of his host, had forborne to advance against the king; but his retreat rendered some decisive action now necessary. Nothing was to be expected from the court. Time was pressing; for delay multiplied his dangers, and increased the difficulty of holding together and restraining so vast and undisciplined a multitude. His only course was to take possession of the capital, and redress, through such legal authorities as he found in existence, or upon the warrant of the nation's expressed will, the grievances under which the realm was groaning. This step was, however, attended with great difficulty and peril, arising from his own aversion to the assumption of permanent authority, and the absence of the Duke of York, who might then have taken upon him, as he did afterwards, the supreme control of affairs; and from the character of his force and the absence of regular resources for its maintenance. To prevent the excesses so much to be apprehended, he rigidly enforced the laws; or, as Fabyan has it, 'to the end to blind the more people, and to bring him in fame that he kept good justice, he beheaded there a petty captain of his named Parrys, for so much as he had offended against such ordinance as he had established in his host. And hearing that the king and his lords had thus departed, drew him near unto the city, so that upon the first day of July he entered the burgh of Southwark.' Anxious to proceed with the strictest regard to the peace and the privileges of the city, Aylmere, next day, caused the authorities of London to be convened. 'The Mayor called the Common Council at the Guildhall, for to purvey the understanding of these rebels, and other matters, in which assembly were divers opinions, so that some thought good that the said rebels should be received into the city, and some otherwise.'—(Fabyan.) He was, however, admitted. This submission to authority by a rebel at the

head of a victorious army, is, the age and circumstances considered, a remarkable feature of the insurrection. 'The same
afternoon, about five of the clock, the captain with his people
entered by the Bridge : and when he came upon the draw-bridge,
he hew the ropes that drew the bridge in sunder with his sword,
and so passed into the city, and made in sundry places thereof
proclamations in the king's name, that no man, upon pain of
death, should rob or take anything per force without paying
therefor. By reason whereof he won many hearts of the
commons of the city; but,' continues the charitable Fabyan, 'all
was done to beguile the people.' . . . . Thus it seems that he
acted in full concert with the authorities; that he did everything
in his power to prevent and punish disorder ; and that so anxious
was he to avoid popular tumult, that he withdrew his force from
the city, and did not permit his people to enter it, 'except at
lawful times.' The history of the times exhibits no instance of
such consideration for the welfare of the people, on the part of
monarchs or their barons, as is here manifested by 'the villainous
rebel.'

"It was necessary that Lord Say should be brought to trial.
As he was in the custody of Lord Scales, this must have taken
place with the sanction and actual aid of the court. 'On the
third day of July,' says Fabyan, ' the said captain entered again
the city, and caused the Lord Say to be fetched from the Tower
and led into Guildhall, where he was arraigned before the mayor
and other of the king's justices.' Of his guilt there seems to
have been neither doubt nor denial. Holinshed tells us that
'being before the king's justices put to answer, he desired to be
tried by his peeres, for the longer delaie of his life. The capteine
perceiving his dilatorie plea, by force tooke him from the officers,
and brought him to the standard in Cheape ; ' where he suffered
military execution, a result which, in the excited state of public
sentiment, probably could not have been averted, and which the
heavy catalogue of his crimes, and the certainty that the queen,
had time been afforded, would have shielded him, perhaps
justified. William Croumer, his brother-in-law and instrument,
and one of those charged before Parliament, suffered at the same
time. These executions are bitterly denounced by the chroniclers ;
but, according to their own accounts, Aylmere punished more of
his own men for violations of the law, than he did of those whose

crimes and cruelty had provoked the insurrection; and it may
be doubted whether history affords an instance of greater moderation and lenity, under circumstances so peculiar, than were
exhibited by him, with the oppressors of his country in his
power, and a maddened people calling for justice.

" The leader of the Commons continued, from a regard for the
public safety, to occupy his position in Southwark until the
sixth of July. During this period it is alleged that, in two
instances, he made requisitions upon wealthy citizens of London;
and, indeed, it was only by such means that so large a host
could have been sustained. This appears to have alarmed the
mayor and aldermen; and it is also probable that the utmost
vigilance and rigour did not wholly repress occasional outrages
of a character to excite the fears of the more wealthy citizens.
The aid of Lord Scallys and Sir Matthew Gough, ' then having
the Tower in guiding,' was, under these apprehensions, solicited
to prevent the re-entrance of Aylmere into London. This
induced a collision, ' and a battle or bloody scuffle was continued
during the night on London Bridge, in which success seemed to
incline to the insurgents.'—(Mackintosh.) In the morning a
truce for certain hours was effected, during which a negotiation
took place between the Archbishop of Canterbury, representing
the king, and the captain of the Commons. On the part of the
former, everything would naturally be promised, for it was
designed that no promise should be observed; and a covenant
for all that was demanded was as readily violated as one for a
part. The leader of the Commons must have been conscious
that his force could only be maintained by a forcible and
necessarily unpopular levy of contributions; and that even if
maintained, their impatience of discipline and anxiety to return
to their homes rendered them unfit for the protracted struggle
that seemed impending. To continue in the field threatened the
worst horrors of civil war, a war in which he could have but
little hope of long restraining his followers. Every consideration
of humanity and patriotism seemed therefore to dictate an
acceptance of the proffered concessions of the court. The compact
was therefore concluded; and the Commons thus won a seeming
triumph. What was covenanted on the part of the court does
not appear; for the chroniclers are silent on that head, and the
people ' had no historians.' Fabyan, however, informs us that

'the Archbishop of Canterbury, then Chancellor of England, sent a general pardon to the captain for himself, and another for his people; by reason whereof he and his company departed the same night out of Southwark, and so returned every man to his home.'

"The sequel is briefly told; it is the old tale of perfidy and blood. The pardon was immediately revoked. 'Proclamations were made in divers places of Kent, of Southsex, and Sowthery, that who might take the aforesaid Jack Cade, either alive or dead, should have a thousand marks for his travayle.' He was pursued and slain; 'and so being dead was brought into Southwark. And upon the morrow the dead corpse was drawn through the high streets of the city, unto Newgate, and there headed and quartered, whose head was then sent to London Bridge, and his four quarters were sent to four sundry towns of Kent.'— (Fabyan.)"

Nothing can gainsay these historical facts; and to adopt the expression of Judge Conrad, it would be difficult to conceive a leader of nobler or purer purposes than Cade, or "to imagine holier motives to justify resistance to oppression," than those above set forth. And yet we behold how our poet, who is still worshipped as a god by the English-speaking race and who almost divides the authority of the Bible in every American as well as English household, deliberately inverts every fact, in the interest of falsehood, selfishness and tyranny.

CHAPTER XXV.

" KING HENRY VI."—PART II. (CONTINUED).

REBELLION OF CADE.

THE foregoing historical facts, when read in contrast with our poet's wanton perversion of them in the above entitled play, bring his character for truth and fair dealing to a crisis. However much we may have been disposed to humour other portions of his text, and to tread fastidiously when charging him with want of sympathy for the poorer classes, it is obvious that there can be no two opinions about his treatment of Cade; and we resign ourselves, without further struggle, to the feeling of pain and disappointment which must afflict every admirer of Shakespeare's genius, at his deficiency of better nature.

Unfortunately, there is no way of conceiving an excuse which can be creditable to our poet for his misrepresentation of the Kentish patriot. There was no uncertainty about the sources of his information. He had the truth laid before him by the same chroniclers whom he had taken as his guides in his previous dramatic histories; but here, when these accepted servants of his muse present him with a glorious character in a man of humble birth, he wilfully falsifies every material fact concerning him, and consigns the popular cause he represents, to ridicule not only, but even to execration. The daring young leader, who is described by Hall and Holinshed as " a certain young man of goodlie stature, and right pregnaunt of wit " (intellect), he deliberately represents as a mean, vulgar clown; and, in the very face of the proofs that Cade maintained a correspondence with the king's representatives at London, and that " his letters of safeguard to citizens passing to and fro from the camp and city were formally and well drawn," our poet chooses to make him figure as an utterly illiterate brute, who condemns persons to death merely for knowing how to read and write.

What makes this more singular is, that the natural instinct of a poet should have led Shakespeare to the cause of the Liberator and the People. The theme was magnificent. The situation was new to letters and the stage. The temptations to dramatic effect were almost irresistible; and how all these inducements to the truth could have been resisted, with the example of even the old court chroniclers to invite the poet towards liberality, is a matter purely for amazement.

It could hardly have been possible that such extreme syco-phancy was gratifying to a nobleman of such intellectual breadth as Essex, nor yet to his other patron the young Earl of Southampton; for they were knights, and the generous spirit of chivalry had already for generations been emulating Christianity, in inculcating admiration and respect for courage and high purpose, even in an enemy. We are thrown back upon our conjectures, therefore, hopeless of a reason, except between toadyism and venality, and even between these we are unable to conceive a motive adequate to the perversion. The incident, consequently, leaves us as much puzzled as we were by our poet's complacent patronage of the unparalleled perfidy of Prince John of Lancaster, and we therefore, remain still unsettled as to the problem concerning his conscience and his heart.

We may now proceed to the examination of the text of the Second Part of "King Henry VI.," giving the illustrations which bear upon the popular branch of our inquiry as they come in order. The first of these occurs in the third scene of Act I., where York denounces an armourer's apprentice :—

> YORK. Base, dunghill villain, *and mechanical,*
> I'll have thy head for this thy traitor's speech.—
> I do beseech your royal majesty,
> Let him have all the rigour of the law.

The next presents a singular instance of the extent of Shakespeare's familiarity with the intricacies of the Roman Catholic faith. The court is assembled in the palace at St. Alban's; and King Henry, hearing a tumult outside, is informed that the townsmen are coming in procession to present to his majesty a blind man, who had been miraculously restored to sight, upon which the king remarks :—

> Great is his comfort in this earthly vale,
> Although *by sight his sin be multiplied.*

" That is to say," remarks Dowden, in his admirable essay on Shakespeare's mind and art, "if we had the good fortune to be deprived of all of our senses and appetites, we should have a fair chance of being quite spotless; yet, let us thank God for His mysterious goodness to this man!" Dowden's translation of this couplet is, no doubt, correct, for in turning over the leaves of " The Imitation of Christ," by Thomas à Kempis, a standard book of Catholic worship, I find, what appears to me to be the fountain of this theory, in the following paragraphs :—

" For every inclination which appears good is not presently to be followed, nor every contrary affection at first sight to be rejected.

" Even in good desires and inclinations it is expedient sometime to use some restraint, lest by too much eagerness thou incur distraction of mind; lest thou create scandal to others by not keeping within discipline, or even lest, by the opposition which thou mayst meet with from others, thou be suddenly disturbed and fall." [1]

The next instance applies to Shakespeare's aristocratic leanings :—

> YORK. *Let pale-faced fear keep with the mean-born man,*
> And find no harbour in *a royal heart.*
> *   *   *
> And for the minister of my intent,
> I have seduced a headstrong Kentishman,
> John Cade of Ashford.
> To make commotion, as full well he can,
> Under the title of John Mortimer.
> In Ireland have I seen this stubborn Cade
> Oppose himself against a troop of kernes;
> And fought so long till that his thighs with darts
> Were almost like a sharp-quill'd porcupine :
> And, in the end being rescued, I have seen
> Him caper upright, like a wild Morisco ;
> Shaking the bloody darts, as he his bells.
> Full often, like a shag-hair'd crafty kerne,
> Hath he conversed with the enemy,
> And undiscover'd come to me again,
> And given me notice of their villainies.
> This devil here shall be my substitute ;

---

[1] Thomas à Kempis' " Imitation of Christ," p. 206, Edition of Benziger Brothers, New York, 1873.

For that John Mortimer, which now is dead,
In face, in gait, in speech, he doth resemble :
By this I shall perceive the commons' mind,
How they affect the house and claim of York.
Say, he be taken, rack'd, and tortured,
I know, no pain they can inflict upon him
Will make him say I moved him to those arms.
Say, that he thrive, as 't is great like he will,
Why, then from Ireland come I with strength,
And reap the harvest which that rascal sow'd ;
For, Humphrey being dead, as he shall be,
And Henry put apart, then next for me.

Act III. Scene 1.

The rumour of the above adoption of Cade by the Duke of York was doubtless greedily accepted by Shakespeare from the chroniclers, with the view of degrading Cade's purposes in the rising just then about to follow.

The following occurs in a quarrel, during the next scene, between Suffolk and Warwick :—

SUF   Blunt-witted lord, ignoble in demeanour !
If ever lady wrong'd her lord so much,
Thy mother took into her blameful bed
Some stern untutor'd churl, and noble stock
Was graft with crab-tree slip ; whose fruit thou art,
And never of the Nevil's noble race.

    *   *   *

'Tis like, *the commons, rude unpolish'd hinds,*
Could send such message to their sovereign :
But you, my lord, were glad to be employ'd,
To show how quaint an orator you are :
But all the honour Salisbury hath won,
Is—that he was the lord ambassador,
Sent from a sort of tinkers to the king.

Suffolk being taken prisoner by the captain of a boat, is threatened with immediate death, without hope of ransom, and thus attempts to overawe his captor :—

SUF.   *Obscure and lowly swain, King Henry's blood,*
The honourable blood of Lancaster,
Must not be shed by such a jaded groom.
Hast thou not kiss'd my hand, and held my stirrup ?
Bare-headed plodded by my foot-cloth mule,
And thought thee happy when I shook my head ?
How often hast thou waited at my cup,

Fed from my trencher, kneel'd down at the board,
When I have feasted with Queen Margaret?
Remember it, and let it make thee crest-fall'n;
Ay, and allay this thy abortive pride:
How in our voiding lobby hast thou stood,
And duly waited for my coming forth?

     ✳   ✳   ✳

O that I were a god, to shoot forth thunder
Upon these paltry, servile, abject drudges!
Small things make base men proud: this villain here,
Being captain of a pinnace, threatens more
Than Bargulus, the strong, Illyrian pirate.
Drones suck not eagles' blood, but rob beehives.
It is impossible, that I should die
By such a lowly vassal as thyself.
Thy words move rage, and not remorse in me:
I go of message from the queen to France;
I charge thee, waft me safely cross the channel.

     ✳   ✳   ✳

True nobility is exempt from fear:
More can I bear than you dare execute!

Nevertheless, the captain of the pinnace lays Suffolk's head on the gunwale of his boat and strikes it off.

Act IV. Scene 2.—*Blackheath.*

Drum. *Enter* CADE, DICK *the Butcher,* SMITH *the Weaver, and others in great number.*

CADE. We, John Cade, so termed of our supposed father,—

DICK. Or rather, of stealing a cade of herrings.   [*Aside.*

CADE. ——for our enemies shall fall before us, inspired with the spirit of putting down kings and princes,—Command silence.

DICK. Silence!

CADE. My father was a Mortimer,—

DICK. He was an honest man, and a good bricklayer.   [*Aside.*

CADE. My mother a Plantagenet,—

DICK. I knew her well, she was a midwife.   [*Aside.*

CADE. My wife descended of the Lacies,—

DICK. She was, indeed, a pedlar's daughter, and sold many laces. [*Aside.*

SMITH. But, now of late, not able to travel with her furred pack, she washes bucks here at home.   [*Aside.*

CADE. Therefore am I of an honourable house.

DICK. Ay, by my faith, the field is honourable; and there was he born, under a hedge; for his father had never a house, but the cage.   [*Aside.*

CADE. Valiant I am.

SMITH. 'A must needs; for beggary is valiant.   [*Aside.*

CADE. I am able to endure much.

DICK. No question of that; for I have seen him whipped three market days together.   [*Aside.*

CADE. I fear neither sword nor fire.

SMITH. He need not fear the sword, for his coat is of proof.   [*Aside.*

DICK. But, methinks, he should stand in fear of fire, being burnt i' the hand for stealing of sheep.   · [*Aside.*

CADE. Be brave, then; for your captain is brave, and vows reformation. There shall be, in England, seven half-penny loaves sold for a penny : the three-hooped pot shall have ten hoops; and I will make it felony, to drink small beer: all the realm shall be in common, and in Cheapside shall my palfrey go to grass. And, when I am king, (as king I will be)—

ALL. God save your majesty !

CADE. I thank you, good people :—there shall be no money ; all shall eat and drink on my score; and I will apparel them all in one livery, that they may agree like brothers, and worship me their lord.

DICK. The first thing we do, let's kill all the lawyers.

CADE. Nay, that I mean to do. Is not this a lamentable thing that of the skin of an innocent lamb should be made parchment ? that parchment, being scribbled o'er should undo a man ? Some say, the bee stings: but I say, 'tis the bee's wax, for I did but seal once to a thing, and I was never mine own man since. How now ! who's there ?

Enter some, bringing in the Clerk of Chatham.

SMITH. The clerk of Chatham : he can write, and read, and cast accompt.

CADE. O, monstrous !

SMITH. We took him setting of boys' copies.

CADE. Here's a villain !

SMITH. H' as a book in his pocket, with red letters in 't.

CADE. Nay, then he is a conjuror.

DICK. Nay, he can make obligations and write court-hand.

CADE. I am sorry for 't : the man is a proper man, on mine honour; unless I find him guilty, he shall not die,—Come hither, sirrah, I must examine thee : what is thy name?

CLERK. Emmanuel.

DICK. They use to write it on the top of letters.—'T will go hard with you.

CADE. Let me alone.—Dost thou use to write thy name, or hast thou a mark to thyself, like an honest, plain-dealing man ?

CLERK. Sir, I thank God I have been so well brought up that I can write my name.

ALL. He hath confessed : away with him ! he's a villain and a traitor.

CADE. Away with him, I say ! hang him with his pen and ink-horn about his neck.   [*Exeunt some with the Clerk.*

Enter MICHAEL.

MICH. Where's our general ?

CADE. Here I am, thou particular fellow.

MICH. Fly, fly, fly ! Sir Humphrey Stafford and his brother are hard by, with the king's forces.

17

CADE. Stand! villain, stand! or I'll fell thee down. He shall be encountered with a man as good as himself: he is but a knight is 'a?

MICH. No.

CADE. To equal him, I will make myself a knight presently. [*Kneels.*] Rise up Sir John Mortimer. [*Rises.*] Now have at him.

Enter Sir HUMPHREY STAFFORD, *and* WILLIAM *his Brother, with Drum and Forces.*

STAF.　　*Rebellious hinds, the filth and scum of Kent,*
　　　　　Mark'd for the gallows, lay your weapons down :
　　　　　Home to your cottage, *forsake this groom.*
　　　　　The king is merciful, if you revolt.

W. STAFF. But angry, wrathful, and inclined to blood,
　　　　　If you go forward : therefore, yield or die.

CADE.　　As for these silken-coated slaves, I pass not;
　　　　　It is to you, good people, that I speak,
　　　　　O'er whom in time to come I hope to reign;
　　　　　For I am rightful heir unto the crown.

STAF.　　Villain! thy father was a plasterer;
　　　　　And thou thyself a shearman, art thou not?

CADE.　　And Adam was a gardener.

W. STAFF. And what of that?

CADE.　　Marry, this :—Edmund Mortimer, earl of March,
　　　　　Married the duke of Clarence's daughter, did he not?

STAF.　　Ay, sir.

CADE.　　By her he had two children at one birth.

W. STAFF. That's false.

CADE.　　Ay, there's the question; but, I say, 'tis true.
　　　　　The elder of them, being put to nurse,
　　　　　Was by a beggar-woman stol'n away;
　　　　　And, ignorant of his birth and parentage,
　　　　　Became a bricklayer when he came to age.
　　　　　His son am I: deny it, if you can.

DICK.　　Nay, 'tis too true; therefore, he shall be king.

SMITH. Sir, he made a chimney in my father's house, and the bricks are alive at this day to testify it; therefore, deny it not.

STAF.　　And will you credit *this base drudge's* words,
　　　　　That speaks he knows not what?

ALL. Ay, marry, will we; therefore, get ye gone.

W. STAFF. Jack Cade, the Duke of York hath taught you this.

CADE. He lies, for I invented it myself. [*Aside.*]—Go to, sirrah; tell the king from me, that for his father's sake, Henry the Fifth, in whose time boys went to span-counter for French crowns, I am content he shall reign; but I'll be protector over him.

DICK. And, furthermore, we'll have the Lord Say's head for selling the dukedom of Maine.

CADE. And good reason; for thereby is England maimed, and fain to go with a staff, but that my puissance holds it up. Fellow kings, I tell you that

that Lord Say hath gelded the commonwealth, and made it an eunuch; and more than that, he can speak French, and therefore he is a traitor.

STAF. O gross and miserable ignorance!

CADE. Nay, answer, if you can; the Frenchmen are our enemies; go to, then, I ask but this; can he that speaks with the tongue of an enemy be a good counsellor, or no?

ALL. No, no; and therefore we'll have his head.

W. STAFF. Well, seeing gentle words will not prevail,
Assail them with the army of the king.

STAF. Herald, away; and, throughout every town,
Proclaim them traitors that are up with Cade,
That those which fly before the battle ends,
May, even in their wives' and children's sight,
Be hang'd up for example at their doors,—
All you, that be the king's friends, follow me.
[*Exeunt the two* STAFFORDS *and Forces.*

CADE. And you, that love the commons, follow me.—
Now show yourselves men; *'tis for liberty.*
We will not leave one lord, one gentleman;
Spare none but such as go in clouted shoon,
For they are thrifty, honest men, and such
As would (but that they dare not) take our parts.

DICK. They are all in order, and march toward us.

CADE. But then are we in order, when we are most out of order. Come; march forward. [*Exeunt.*

The above is the first use I find of the word "liberty" by Shakespeare in the form of an appeal for human rights; but, inasmuch as he puts the exclamation in the mouth of a man who executes people for reading and writing, the mention is obviously intended to degrade the word, and to represent only general licentiousness and licence.

Scene 3.—*Another part of Blackheath.*
Alarums. The two Parties enter, and fight, and both the STAFFORDS *are slain.*

CADE. Where's Dick, the butcher of Ashford?

DICK. Here, sir.

CADE. They fell before thee like sheep and oxen, and thou behavedst thyself as if thou hadst been in thine own slaughter-house: therefore, thus will I reward thee,—The Lent shall be as long again as it is; and thou shalt have a licence to kill for a hundred years, lacking one.

DICK. I desire no more.

CADE. And, to speak the truth, thou deservest no less. This monument of the victory will I bear: [*Putting on* STAFFORD'S *armour*], and the bodies shall be dragged at my horses' heels, till I do come to London, where we will have the mayor's sword borne before us.

DICK. If we mean to thrive and do good, break open the jails, and let out the prisoners.

CADE. Fear not that, I warrant thee. Come; let's march towards London. [*Exeunt.*

Scene 4.—*London.—A Room in the Palace.*
Enter a Messenger.

K. HEN. How now! what news? why com'st thou in such haste?

MESS. The rebels are in Southwark; Fly, my lord?
Jack Cade proclaims himself lord Mortimer,
Descended from the duke of Clarence house;
And calls your grace usurper, openly,
And vows to crown himself in Westminster.
His army is a ragged multitude
Of hinds and peasants, rude and merciless:
Sir Humphrey Stafford and his brother's death
Hath given them heart and courage to proceed;
All scholars, lawyers, courtiers, gentlemen
They call—false caterpillars, and intend their death.
Enter another Messenger.

2 MESS. Jack Cade hath gotten London-bridge; the citizens
Fly and forsake their houses;
The rascal people, thirsting after prey,
Join with the traitor; and they jointly swear,
To spoil the city, and your royal court.

*   *   *

Scene 6.—*The Same.—Cannon-street.*

Enter JACK CADE, *and his Followers. He strikes his staff on London-stone.*

CADE. Now is Mortimer lord of this city. And here, sitting upon London-stone, I charge and command, that, of the city's cost, the —— conduit run nothing but claret wine this first year of our reign. And now, henceforward, it shall be treason for any that calls me other than—lord Mortimer.
Enter a Soldier, running.

SOLD. Jack Cade! Jack Cade!

CADE. Knock him down there. [*They kill him.*

SMITH. If this fellow be wise, he'll never call you Jack Cade more; I think, he hath a very fair warning.

DICK. My lord, there's an army gathered together in Smithfield.

CADE. Come then, let's go fight with them: But, first, go and set London Bridge on fire; and, if you can, burn down the Tower too. Come, let's away. [*Exeunt.*

Scene 7.—*The Same.—Smithfield.*

Alarum. Enter, on one side, CADE *and his Company; on the other, Citizens, and the King's Forces, headed by* MATTHEW GOUGH. *They fight: the Citizens are routed, and* MATTHEW GOUGH *is slain.*

CADE. So, sirs:—Now, go some and pull down the Savoy; others to'the inns of court; down with them all.

DICK. I have a suit unto your lordship.

CADE. Be it a lordship, thou shalt have it for that word.

DICK. Only, that the laws of England may come out of your mouth.

JOHN. Mass, 'twill be sore law then; for he was thrust in the mouth with a spear, and 'tis not whole yet. [*Aside.*

SMITH. Nay, John, it will be stinking law; for his breath stinks with eating toasted cheese. [*Aside.*

CADE. I have thought upon it, it shall be so. Away, burn all the records of the realm; my mouth shall be the parliament of England.

JOHN. Then we are like to have biting statutes, unless his teeth be pulled out. [*Aside.*

CADE. And henceforward all things shall be in common.

Enter a Messenger.

MESS. My lord, a prize, a prize! here's the lord Say, which sold the towns in France, he that made us pay one-and-twenty fifteens, and one shilling to the pound, the last subsidy.

Enter GEORGE BEVIS, with the Lord SAY.

CADE. Well, he shall be beheaded for it ten times.—Ah, thou say, thou serge, nay, thou buckram lord! now art thou within point blank of our jurisdiction regal. *What canst thou answer to my majesty, for giving up of Normandy unto Monsieur Basimecu, the dauphin of France? Be it known unto thee by these presents, even the presence of Lord Mortimer, that I am the besom that must sweep the court clean of such filth as thou art. Thou hast most traitorously corrupted the youth of the realm in erecting a grammar-school: and whereas, before, our forefathers had no other books but the score and the tally, thou hast caused printing to be used; and, contrary to the king, his crown, and dignity, thou has built a paper-mill. It will be proved to thy face, that thou hast men about thee, that usually talk of a noun, and a verb, and such abominable words as no Christian ear can endure to hear. Thou hast appointed justices of peace to call poor men before them about matters they were not able to answer: moreover, thou hast put them in prison; and because they could not read, thou hast hanged them; when, indeed, only for that cause they have been most worthy to live. Thou dost ride in a foot-cloth, dost thou not.

SAY. What of that?

CADE. Marry, thou oughtest not to let thy horse wear a cloak, when honester men than thou go in their hose and doublets.

DICK. And work in their shirt too; as myself, for example, that am a butcher.

SAY. You men of Kent,—

DICK. What say you of Kent?

SAY. Nothing but this: 'tis *bona terra, mala gens.*

CADE. Away with him! away with him! he speaks Latin.

SAY. Hear me but speak, and bear me where you will.

* * *

         Unless you be possess'd with devilish spirits,
         You cannot but forbear to murder me.

> This tongue hath parley'd unto foreign kings
> For your behoof.—

CADE. Tut! when struck'st thou one blow in the field?

SAY. Great men have reaching hands: oft have I struck
Those that I never saw, and struck them dead.

GEO. O, monstrous coward! what, to come behind folks?

SAY. These cheeks are pale for watching for your good.

CADE. Give him a box o' the ear, and that will make them red again.

SAY. Long sitting, to determine poor men's causes,
Hath made me full of sickness and diseases.

CADE. Ye shall have a hempen caudle, then, and the help of hatchet.

DICK. Why dost thou quiver, man?

SAY. The palsy, and not fear, provoketh me.

CADE. Nay, he nods at us; as who should say, I'll be even with you. I'll see if his head stand steadier on a pole, or no. Take him away and behead him.

SAY. Tell me, wherein have I offended most?

> *   *   *

> Whom have I injured, that ye seek my death?
> These hands are free from guiltless blood-shedding,
> This breast from harbouring foul deceitful thoughts.
> O! let me live..

CADE. I feel remorse in myself with his words; but I'll bridle it; he shall die, 'an it be but for pleading so well for his life.—Away with him! he has a familiar under his tongue; he speaks not o' God's name. Go, take him away, I say, and strike off his head presently; and then break into his son-in-law's house, sir James Cromer, and strike off his head, and bring them both upon two poles hither.

ALL. It shall be done.

SAY. Ah, countrymen! if when you make your prayers,
God shall be so obdurate as yourselves,
How would it fare with your departed souls?
And therefore yet relent and save my life.

CADE. Away with him, and do as I command ye. [*Exeunt some with Lord* SAY.] The proudest peer in this realm shall not wear a head on his shoulders, unless he pay me tribute: there shall not a maid be married, but she shall pay to me her maidenhead, ere they have it. *Men shall hold of me in capite:* and we charge and command that their wives be as free as heart can wish, or tongue can tell.

Let me here remark that I can see no reason why Shakespeare should be denied the learned languages, since Jack Cade can quote Latin.

DICK. My lord, when shall we go to Cheapside, and take up commodities upon our bills?

CADE. Marry, presently.

ALL. O, brave!

Re-enter Rebels with the heads of Lord SAY *and his son-in-law.*

CADE. But is not this braver?—Let them kiss one another, for they loved well when they were alive. [*Jowl them together.*] Now part them again, lest they consult about the giving up of some more towns in France. Soldiers, defer the spoil of the city until night; for, with these borne before us, instead of maces, will we ride through the streets: and at every corner have them kiss.—Away! [*Exeunt.*

Scene 8.—*Southwark.*

Alarum. Enter CADE, *and all his Rabblement.*

CADE. Up Fish-street! down Saint Magnus' corner! kill and knock down! throw them into Thames!—[*A Parley sounded, then a Retreat.*] What noise is this I hear? Dare any be so bold to sound retreat or parley, when I command them kill?

Enter BUCKINGHAM, *and Old* CLIFFORD, *with Forces.*

BUCK. Ay, here they be that dare, and will disturb thee:
Know, Cade, we come ambassadors from the king
Unto the commons whom thou hast misled:
And here pronounce free pardon to them all,
That will forsake thee, and go home in peace.

CLIF. What say ye, countrymen? will ye repent
And yield to mercy, whilst 'tis offer'd you,
Or let a rebel lead you to your deaths?
Who loves the king, and will embrace his pardon,
Fling up his cap, and say—God save his majesty!
Who hateth him, and honours not his father,
Henry the Fifth, that made all France to quake,
Shake he his weapon at us, and pass by.

ALL. God save the king! God save the king!

CADE. What, Buckingham, and Clifford, are ye so brave?—And you base peasants, do ye believe him? will you needs be hanged with your pardons about your necks? Hath my sword therefore broke through London Gates, that you should leave me at the White Hart in Southwark? I thought, ye would never have given out these arms, till you had recovered your ancient freedom: but you are all recreants, and dastards; and delight to live in slavery to the nobility. Let them break your backs with burdens, take your houses over your heads, ravish your wives and daughters before your faces: For me,—I will make shift for one; and so—God's curse light upon you all.

ALL. We'll follow Cade, we'll follow Cade.

CLIF. Is Cade the son of Henry the Fifth,
That thus you do exclaim—you'll go with him?
Will he conduct you through the heart of France,
And make the meanest of you earls and dukes?
Alas, he hath no home, no place to fly to;
Nor knows he how to live, but by the spoil,
Unless by robbing of your friends, and us.
Wer't not a shame, that whilst you live at jar,

The fearful French, whom you late vanquished,
Should make a start o'er seas, and vanquish you?
Methinks already, in this civil broil,
I see them lording it in London streets,
Crying—*Villageois*! unto all they meet.
Better, ten thousand base-born Cades miscarry,
Than you should stoop unto a Frenchman's mercy.
To France, to France, and get what you have lost;
Spare England, for it is your native coast:
Henry hath money, you are strong and manly;
God on our side, doubt not of victory.

ALL. A Clifford! a Clifford! we'll follow the king, and Clifford.

CADE. Was ever feather so lightly blown to and fro, as this multitude? the name of Henry the Fifth hales them to an hundred mischiefs, and makes them leave me desolate. I see them lay their heads together, to surprise me: my sword make way for me, for here is no staying. In despite of the devils and hell, have through the very midst of you! and heavens and honour be witness, that no want of resolution in me, but only my followers' base and ignominious treasons, makes me betake to my heels. [*Exit.*

BUCK. What, is he fled? go, some, and follow him;
And he, that brings his head unto the king
Shall have a thousand crowns for his reward.
[*Exeunt some of them.*
Follow me, soldiers; we'll devise a mean;
To reconcile you all unto the king. [*Exeunt.*

Scene 10.—*Kent. Iden's Garden*
Enter CADE.

CADE. Fy on ambition! fy on myself; that have a sword, and yet am ready to famish! These five days have I hid me in these woods; and durst not peep out, for all the country is lay'd for me; but now am I so hungry, that if I might have a lease of my life for a thousand years, I could stay no longer. Wherefore, on a brick wall have I climbed into this garden; to see if I can eat grass, or pick a sallet another while, which is not amiss to cool a man's stomach this hot weather. And, I think, this word sallet was born to do me good: for, many a time, but for a sallet, my brain-pan had been cleft with a brown bill; and, many a time, when I have been dry, and bravely marching, it hath serv'd me instead of a quart pot to drink in; And now the one word sallet must serve me to feed on.

Enter IDEN, *with Servants.*

IDEN. Lord, who would live turmoiled in the court,
And may enjoy such quiet walks as these?
This small inheritance, my father left me,
Contenteth me, and is worth a monarchy.
I seek not to wax great by others' waning;
Or gather wealth, I care not with what envy;
Sufficeth, that I have maintains my state,
And sends the poor well pleased from my gate.

CADE. Here's the lord of the soil come to seize me for a stray, for entering his fee-simple without leave. Ah, villain, thou wilt betray me, and get a thousand crowns of the king for carrying my head to him : but I'll make thee eat iron like an ostrich, and swallow my sword like a great pin, ere thou and I part.

IDEN. Why, rude companion, whatsoe'er thou be,
I know thee not ; Why then should I betray thee ?
Is't not enough to break into my garden,
And, like a thief, to come to rob my grounds,
Climbing my walls in spite of me the owner,
But thou wilt brave me with these saucy terms ?

CADE. Brave thee ? ay, by the best blood that ever was broached, and beard thee too. Look on me well : I have eat no meat these five days : yet, come thou and thy five men, and if I do not leave you all as dead as a door nail, I pray God, I may never eat grass more.

IDEN. Nay, it shall ne'er be said while England stands,
That Alexander Iden, an esquire of Kent,
Took odds to combat a poor famish'd man.
Oppose thy stedfast gazing eyes to mine,
See if thou canst outface me with thy looks.
Set limb to limb, and thou art far the lesser ;
Thy hand is but a finger to my fist ;
Thy leg a stick, compared with this truncheon ;
My foot shall fight with all the strength thou hast ;
And if my arm be heaved in the air,
Thy grave is digg'd already in the earth.
As for more words, whose greatness answers words,
Let this my sword report what speech forbears.

CADE. By my valour, the most complete champion that ever I heard. Steel, if thou turn the edge, or cut not out the burley-boned clown in chines of beef ere thou sleep in thy sheath, I beseech God on my knees, thou mayest be turned to hobnails. [*They fight.* CADE *falls.*] O, I am slain ! famine, and no other, hath slain me ; let ten thousand devils come against me, and give me but the ten meals I have lost, and I'd defy them all. Wither, garden, and be henceforth a burying-place to all that do dwell in this house, because the unconquered soul of Cade is fled.

IDEN. Is't Cade that I have slain, *that monstrous traitor ?*
Sword, I will hallow thee for this thy deed,
And hang thee o'er my tomb, when I am dead :
Ne'er shall this blood be wiped from thy point,
But thou shalt wear it as a herald's coat,
To emblaze the honour that thy master got.

CADE. Iden, farewell ; and be proud of thy victory. Tell Kent from me, she hath lost her best man, and exhort all the world to be cowards ; for I, that never feared any, am vanquished by famine, not by valour.   [*Dies.*

IDEN. How much thou wrong'st me, heaven be my judge.
. *Die, damned wretch, the curse of him that bare thee !*

> And as I thrust thy body with my sword,
> So wish I, I might thrust thy soul to hell.
> *Hence will I drag thee headlong by the heels,*
> *Unto a dunghill, which shall be thy grave,*
> *And there cut off thy most ungracious head;*
> Which I will bear in triumph to the king,
> Leaving thy trunk for crows to feed upon.
>
> [*Exit, dragging out the Body.*

This closes the cruel caricature and defamation of a leader of the stamp of William Tell, Rienzi, or Marco Bozzaris, and who, but for Shakespeare, would have been the theme of many a lofty lyre; perhaps the subject for ages, of the prayer and song of the nation whose good fortune it had been to profit by his sacrifices. Truly English worship of social superiority is almost inexplicable when contrasted with the decorous subjection to lawful authority to be found in other lands; but with such examples as this play before us, we know where to trace the infatuation to its source; and it is melancholy to reflect, that a transcendent genius, who could have done so much to lift popular thought, should always have endeavoured to degrade it. Shakespeare might have condemned Cade and his cause in reasonable terms, and been to some extent forgiven, but the spontaneous and malignant execration which he lavishes upon the dead patriot, in the interest of the nobles, is simply intolerable. Indeed, it would be a positive relief to us, to be able to attribute the political tendencies of Shakespeare's text to Sir Francis Bacon, who was educated to despise the People. The charm which attends our poet's genius still prevails, but the spell has lost a great portion of its force, and can no longer prevent the condemnation of the poet's principles by the English-speaking and liberty-loving people of America. And, as much may be said for the rugged intelligence and resolute progress of the present liberty-loving English masses.

CHAPTER XXVI.

" KING HENRY VI. *"*—PART III.

THE Third Part of " Henry VI." affords us fewer illustrations than any of the previous plays. The first incident which strikes our attention appears in the second scene of Act 1, and bears upon the question of Shakespeare's legal acquirements; inasmuch as it exhibits a very correct idea, as far as it goes, of the legal crime of " perjury," as distinguished from mere false swearing.

EDWARD. But for a kingdom, any oath may be broken.
RICHARD. An oath is of no moment, being not took
Before a true and lawful magistrate
That hath authority over him that swears.

The above legal illustration seems to have escaped the observation of Lord Campbell.

YORK.   Five men to twenty ! though the odds be great
I doubt not, uncle, of our victory.
Many a battle have I won in France;
When as the enemy hath been ten to one.   Act I. Scene 2.

CLIF.   *The common people swarm like summer flies,*
And whither fly the gnats but to the sun.   Act II. Scene 6.

Enter KING HENRY *(disguised as a churchman) with a prayer-book.*

K. HEN.   From Scotland am I stol'n, even of pure love,
To greet mine own land with my wishful sight.
No, Harry, Harry, 'tis no land of thine ;
Thy place is fill'd, thy sceptre wrung from thee,
Thy balm wash'd off, wherewith thou wast anointed :
No bending knee will call thee Cæsar now,
No humble suitors press to speak for right,
No, not a man comes for redress from thee ;
For how can I help them, and not myself.

＊   ＊   ＊

K. HEN.   I was *anointed* king at nine months old.

＊   ＊   ＊

Why, am I dead ? do I not breathe a man ?
Ah, simple men, you know not what you swear.

Look, as I blow this feather from my face,
And as the air blows it to me again,
Obeying with my wind when I do blow,
And yielding to another when it blows,
Commanded always by the greater gust;
Such is the lightness of *you common men.*   *Act III. Scene* 1.

Q. MAR.   While proud ambitious Edward, duke of York,
Usurps the regal title and the seat
Of England's true *anointed* lawful king.   *Act III. Scene* 3.

Act IV. Scene 6.—*Room in the Tower.*
KING HENRY *to young* RICHMOND—
K. HEN.   Come hither, England's hope: If secret powers
                           [*Lays his hand on his head.*
Suggest but truth to my divining thoughts,
This pretty lad will prove our country's bliss.
His looks are full of peaceful majesty;
His head by nature framed to wear a crown,
His hand to wield a sceptre; and himself
Likely, in time, to bless a regal throne.
Make much of him, my lords; for this is he
Must help you more than you are hurt by me.

K. EDW.   Now march we hence; discharge *the common sort*
With pay and thanks.   *Act V. Scene* 5.

Throughout this play, crime is heaped on crime by the nobles of all parties, with just the same want of scruple that the politicians in America show against one another by false votes; but Shakespeare presides over the shocking turpitude of his period with seldom a word of censure, and rarely the atonement of a moral, as if murder, perjury, and perfidy of every stamp, were the unquestioned rights of noble birth. It may be said he does the world service, by showing these nobles in their true colours; but it must be observed that one who is commissioned with the capacity to write history, should boldly approve good deeds and condemn bad ones, in order to be worthy of his task. Shakespeare, on the contrary, deals with the villanies of kings and nobles as if they were among the ordinary privileges of the ruling classes, and as if crime were the inheritance of the poor. Even Clarence, who was one of the murderers of Prince Edward, at Tewkesbury, is made to enlist our sympathy, by dying almost like a martyr and a saint.

THE LEGAL ACQUIREMENTS OF SHAKESPEARE AS SHOWN IN THE HISTORIES OF THE HENRIES.

AT the close of my review of " Henry IV.," Part II., I briefly stated, that " the legalisms exhibited in Shakespeare's behalf, in the course of it, by Lord Chief Justice Campbell, did not call for any attention at my hands." Upon further reflection, however, it seems to me that, inasmuch as I have heretofore printed, almost in extenso, all of Lord Campbell's illustrations on this subject, I may as well perfect that portion of my task, by giving, even to the end, the substance of everything his lordship has to say in that regard. For, after all, the question of the respective legal acquirements of Bacon and of Shakespeare, runs a line through the very centre of the main inquiry, the course of which is almost as decisive in demonstrating the debated point of author-ship, as the question of the respective religious creeds of the two persons named.

In dealing with the Second Part of " Henry IV.," Lord Camp-bell says, " Arguments have been drawn from this drama *against* Shakespeare's supposed great legal acquirements. It has been objected to the very amusing interview, in Act I. Scene 2, between Falstaff and the Lord Chief Justice, that if Shakespeare had been much of a lawyer, he would have known that this great magistrate could not examine offenders in the manner supposed, and could only take notice of offences when they were regularly prosecuted before him in the Court of King's Bench, or at the assizes. But, although such is the practice in our days, so recently as the beginning of the eighteenth century, that illustrious Judge, Lord Chief Justice Holt, acted as a police magistrate, quelling riots, taking depositions against parties accused, and, where a primâ facie case was made out against them, committing them for trial. Lord Chief Justice Coke actually assisted in taking the Earl and Countess of Somerset into custody when charged with the murder of Sir Thomas Overbury, and examined not less than three hundred witnesses against them."

With all due respect to Lord Campbell, I cannot but consider that he has made a disingenuous use of these two illustrations. The first alludes to a case of *quasi* rebellion, which required the personal energy of the highest magistrate in the kingdom to suppress; and the second was a crime perpetrated by parties so closely related to the crown, that it partook largely of the character of a state affair. Both Lords Chief Justices Holt and Coke, moreover, decorously exercised their jurisdiction in these cases at chambers. I repeat, therefore, that it is at least disingenuous on the part of Lord Chief Justice Campbell, to quote these instances as fair offsets to the unseemly tavern and chance street interviews of Chief Justice Gascoigne with Falstaff, as given in the First Part of " Henry IV." Lord Campbell has one or two other observations on phrases in the text of " Henry IV.," Part II., evincing legal comprehension on the part of Shakespeare, but, as his lordship puts them very lightly, and does not press them, they hardly require any notice at my hands.

Lord Campbell finds no evidence of Shakespeare's legal acquirements in " Henry V." worthy of his notice; or in " Henry VI.," Part I.; so he passes on to " Henry VI.," Part II. where he opens his proofs of our poet's legal proficiency, by burlesque speeches unworthily put into the mouth of Jack Cade and his associates. His lordship, however, might have found in the First Part (Act II. Scene 5) a similar proof of profound legal erudition as that passed over by him in " Henry V." (where the Archbishop of Canterbury demonstrates the origin and character of the Salique law of France) and might also have found a very lawyer-like genealogical recital (by York), in Act II. Scene 2, of the Second Part of " King Henry VI." Now, the fact that of these three purely legal performances (showing, as they do, not merely the proficiency of an attorney's clerk, but the learning of a thoroughly accomplished barrister) are studiously overlooked by Lord Chief Justice Campbell, in his evidences of " Shakespeare's Legal Acquirements," while relying for his proofs to that effect upon the poet's mere mention of such words as " seal," " indenture," " enfeoffment," etc., warrant us in the conclusion that his lordship had discovered that these digests of title and genealogical exploits proved too much for the rest of his argument. His lordship, however, overlooking this suggestive example (suggestive, in short, that Shakespeare ordered his law, when he required any, from other and more competent hands), finds a world of point in the comic extravagances which our poet has put into the speeches of Jack Cade and his band. " In these speeches," says Lord Campbell, " we find a familiarity with the law and its proceedings, which strongly indicates that the author must have had some professional practice or education as a lawyer." The example which his lordship gives to support this opinion is to be found in the second scene of Act IV. and, in order to show how small a stock of logic will serve, at times, even for a Lord Chief Justice, I here give Lord Campbell's quotation and remarks :—

DICK. The first thing we do, *let's kill all the lawyers.*
CADE. Nay, that I mean to do. Is not this a lamentable thing, that the skin of an innocent lamb should be made parchment?—that parchment, being scribbled o'er, should undo a man? Some say the bee stings; but I say 'tis the bee's wax, for I did but seal once to a thing, and I was never mine own man since.

"The Clerk of Chatham is then brought in, who could ' make obligations and write court hand,' and who, instead of ' making his mark like an honest, plain-dealing man,' had been ' so well brought up that he could write his name.' Therefore he was sentenced to be hanged with his pen and ink-horn about his neck.

"Surely" (says Lord Campbell) "Shakespeare must have been employed to write *deeds* on *parchment* in *court hand*, and to apply the *wax* to them in the form of *seals :* one does not understand how he should, on any other theory of his bringing up, have been acquainted with these details.

"Again" (says his lordship) "the indictment on which Lord Say was arraigned, in Act IV. Scene 7, seems drawn by no inexperienced hand :—

"'Thou hast most traitorously corrupted the youth of the realm in erecting a grammar-school : and whereas, before, our forefathers had no other books but the score and the tally, thou hast caused printing to be used; and *contrary to the king, his crown and dignity*, thou hast built a paper-mill. It will be proved to thy face that thou hast men about thee that usually talk of a noun and a verb, and *such abominable words as no Christian ear can endure to hear.* Thou hast appointed justices of peace, to call poor men before them about matters they were not able to answer. Moreover thou hast put them in prison ; and because they could not read, thou hast hanged them, when indeed only for that cause they have been most worthy to live.'

"How acquired I know not, but it is quite certain " (declares

Lord Campbell) "that the drawer of this indictment must have had some acquaintance with 'The Crown Circuit Companion,' and must have had a full and accurate knowledge of that rather obscure and intricate subject—'Felony and Benefit of Clergy.'

"Cade's proclamation, which follows, deals with still more recondite heads of jurisprudence. Announcing his policy when he should mount the throne, he says, 'The proudest peer in the realm shall not wear a head on his shoulders unless he pay me tribute : there shall not a maid be married but she shall . . . Men shall hold of me *in capite ;* and we charge and command that their wives be as *free as heart can wish, or tongue can tell.'*

"He thus declares a great forthcoming change in the tenure of land and in the liability of taxation : he is to have a pole-tax like that which had raised the rebellion ; but, instead of coming down to the daughters of blacksmiths who had reached the age of fifteen, it was to be confined to the nobility. Then he is to legislate on the *mercheta mulierum.*

* * * * * * *

"He proceeds to announce his intention to abolish tenure in *free socage,* and that all men should hold of him, *in capite,* concluding with a licentious jest that, although his subjects should no longer hold in *free socage,* 'their wives should be as free as heart can wish, or tongue can tell.' Strange to say " (continues his lordship) "this phrase, or one almost identically the same, 'as free as tongue can speak, or heart can think,' is feudal, and was known to the ancient law of England."

Now, in relation to this latter instance as presented by his lordship, the suggestion which irresistibly presents itself is, that Shakespeare, if he really had been bred to the law, would have presented the legal phrase above correctly. Bacon certainly would have done so ; unless we are to believe it was purposely perverted for a comic object.

"RICHARD III."

The date of the production of this stirring drama is set down by Furnival as in 1594, and its publication in 1597. The authorities used in its construction were "The History of Richard III.," by Sir Thomas More, and its continuation by

Holinshed. The character of Richard is the most bustling and vigorous of any in the Shakespearian dramas; and so masterly is the sketch of the hero, that, notwithstanding his enormous crimes, he ingratiates himself with every audience by his prodigious intellect and marvellous courage. In evidence of the natural obstacles which stood in the way of his violent acquisition of the throne, I quote the following portrait of him by Sir Thomas More, in the work referred to :—

" Richard, the third son (of Richard, duke of York), was, in wit and courage, equal with either of them—his brothers Edward the Fourth, and George, duke of Clarence. In body and prowess he was far under them both; little of stature, ill-featured of limbs, crook-backed, his left shoulder much higher than his right, hard-favoured of visage, and such as is in states called warlie, in other men otherwise ; he was malicious, wrathful, envious, and from afore his birth ever froward. It is for truth reported, that the duchess, his mother, had so much ado in her travail. . . . None evil captain was he in the way of war, as to which his disposition was more metely than for peace. Sundry victories had he, and sometime overthrows, but never in default as for his own person of hardiness or politic order. . . . He was close and secret, a deep dissembler, lowly of countenance, arrogant of heart, outwardly companionable where he inwardly hated, not letting to kiss whom he thought to kill : dispiteous and cruel, not for evil will alway, but often for ambition, and either for the surety or increase of his estate. Friend and foe was much what indifferent ; where his advantage grew, he spared no man's death, whose life withstood his purpose."

Shakespeare has followed the chronicle with great minuteness, which shows how faithfully he can adhere to the truth when so disposed. On the night before the battle of Bosworth Field, says the old historian :—

" The fame went that he had a dreadful and terrible dream ; for it seemed to him, being asleep, that he did see divers images like terrible devils, which pulled and haled him, not suffering him to take any quiet or rest. The which strange vision not so suddenly strake his heart with a sudden fear, but it stuffed his head and troubled his mind with many busy and dreadful imaginations. . . . And less that it might be suspected that he was abashed for fear of his enemies, and for that cause looked so

18

piteously, he recited and declared to his familiar friends in the morning, his wonderful vision and fearful dream. . . . . When the loss of the battle was imminent and apparent, they brought to him a swift and a light horse, to convey him away; but disdaining flight, and inflamed with ire, and vexed with outrageous malice, he put his spurs to his horse, and rode out of the side of the range of his battle, leaving the vanguard fighting, and, like a hungry lion, ran with spear in rest towards him. The earl of Richmond perceived well the king coming furiously toward him, and because the whole hope of his wealth and purpose was to be determined by battle, he gladly proffered to encounter with him, body to body, and man to man. King Richard set on so sharply at the first brunt, that he overthrew the earl's standard, and slew Sir William Brandon, his standard-bearer; and matched hand to hand with Sir John Cheinie, a man of great force and strength, which would have resisted him, but the said John was by him manfully overthrown. And so, he making open passage by dint of sword as he went forward, the earl of Richmond withstood his violence, and kept him at the sword's point, without advantage, longer than his companions either thought or judged, which being almost in despair of victory, were suddenly re-comforted by Sir William Stanley, which came to succours with three thousand tall men, at which very instant King Richard's men were driven back, and fled, and he himself, manfully fighting in the middle of his enemies, was slain, and brought to his death as he worthily had deserved."

Dowden, in treating of the character of this drama, says, " The demoniac intensity which distinguishes the play proceeds from the character of Richard, as from its source and centre. . . . Richard rathers occupies the imagination by audacity and force than insinuates himself through some subtle solvent, some magic and mystery of art. His character does not grow upon us; from the first it is complete. . . . Coleridge has said of Richard, that pride of intellect is his characteristic. This is true; but his dominant characteristic is not intellectual—it is rather a demoniac energy of will. The same cause which produces tempest and shipwreck produces Richard; he is a fierce elemental power raging through the world."[1]

[1] Dowden's " Shakespeare's Mind and Art," p. 182.

As it is no part of my task to proceed any farther upon this line of observation, I will therefore direct myself, at once, to such portions of the text as illustrate those tendencies of the poet's mind which we have made the subject of our particular analysis.

At the opening of the second act, while Edward is still king, though grievously sick, Lord Stanley comes hastily before him, and implores pardon for one of his servants, who had slain "a riotous nobleman." Edward, however, is suffering under remorse for having ordered Clarence's death, and rebukes the impetuous suitor by reminding him that no one attempted to intercept his purpose when he had hastily sentenced his poor brother :—

> Have I a tongue to doom my brother's death?
> And shall that tongue give pardon *to a slave?*
> *   *   Not a man of you
> Had so much grace to put it in my mind.
> *But, when your carters, or your waiting vassals,*
> Have done a drunken slaughter and defaced
> The precious image of our dear Redeemer.
> You straight are on your knees for pardon, pardon!

In Act III. Scene 2 we find the following Catholic symptoms in our poet :—

Buck. What, talking with a priest, lord chamberlain?
   Your friends at Pomfret, they do need the priest;
   Your honour hath no *shriving* work in hand.

Hastings. Good faith, and when *I met this holy man,*
   The men you talk of came into my mind.

Buck. Now, *by the holy Mother of our Lord!*—
    *   *   *
   Enter, from the castle, Catesby.
   Now, Catesby! what says your lord to my request?

Cate. He doth entreat your grace, my noble lord,
   To visit him to-morrow, or next day:
   He is within, *with two right reverend fathers,*
   Divinely bent to meditation:
   And in no worldly suit would he be moved,
   To draw him from his *holy exercise.*

            Act III. Scene 7.

The following thus describes the ruthless murder of the two young princes in the Tower :—

Tyrrel. Dighton and Forrest, whom I did suborn

> To do this piece of ruthless butchery,
> Albeit they were flesh'd villains, bloody dogs,
> Melting with tenderness and mild compassion,
> Wept like two children, in their death's sad story.
> O thus, quoth Dighton, lay the gentle babes,—
> Thus, thus, quoth Forrest, girdling one another
> Within their alabaster innocent arms:
> Their lips were four red roses on a stalk,
> Which, in their summer beauty, kiss'd each other.
> *A book of prayers on their pillow lay :*
> Which once, quoth Forrest, almost changed my mind.

This assassination being brought to the knowledge of Queen Elizabeth, the mother of these murdered innocents, she exclaims,—

> Ah, my poor princes! ah, my tender babes!
> My unblown flowers, new-appearing sweets!
> *If yet your gentle souls fly in the air,*
> *And be not fix'd in doom perpetual,*
> *Hover about me with your airy wings,*
> *And hear your mother's lamentation !*
>
> Q. MAR.   *Hover about her ;* say, that right for right
> Hath dimm'd your infant morn to aged night.

This instance, which was given in an earlier chapter, shows Shakespeare's recognition of the doctrine of purgatory.

Again, this Catholic doctrine is expressed by Buckingham (when on the way to execution) in remorseful invocation to the souls of those whom he had helped Richard murder :—

> Hastings and Edward's children, Rivers, Grey,
> Holy king Henry, and thy fair son Edward,
> Vaughan, and all that have miscarried
> By underhand corrupted foul injustice:
> *If that your moody discontented souls*
> *Do through the clouds behold this present hour,*
> *Even for revenge mock my destruction !*
>
>   *   *   *
>
> Come, lead me, officers, to the block of shame;
> Wrong hath but wrong, and blame the due of blame.

> Act IV. Scene 4.
>
> K. RICH.   A flourish, trumpets!—strike alarum, drums!
> Let not the heavens hear these tell-tale women
> Rail on *the Lord's anointed !* Strike, I say !
>
>   *   *   *
>
> Act V. Scene 2.
> *Enter RICHMOND and Forces.*
>
> RICH.   Then in God's name march :

True hope is swift, and flies with swallow's wings,
Kings it makes gods, and meaner creatures kings !

Tent Scene.—*Richard's Dream.*
The Ghost of KING HENRY THE SIXTH *rises.*

GHOST.   When I was mortal, *my anointed body*
By thee was punched full of deadly holes.

Scene III.—*Bosworth Field.*

K. RICH.   Why, our battalia trebles that account :
Besides, *the king's name is a tower of strength,*
Which they upon the adverse faction want.

*   *   *

These famish'd *beggars,* weary of their lives ;
Who, but for dreaming on this fond exploit,
For want of means, poor rats, had hang'd themselves.

*   *   *

Remember whom you are to cope withal ;
A sort of vagabonds, rascals and runaways,
A scum of Bretagnes, *and base lackey peasants.*

I return now to the first act, Scene 2, for a final illustration from this play. The Lady Anne, attended by mourners and a guard, is accompanying the body of King Henry VI. to Chertsey monastery, for interment :—

Enter GLOSTER.

GLO.   Stay you, that bear the corse, and set it down.
ANNE.   What black magician conjures up this fiend,
To stop devoted charitable deeds ?
GLO.   Villains, set down the corse ; or, by Saint Paul,
I'll make a corse of him that disobeys.
1 GENT.   My lord, stand back, and let the coffin pass.
                        [He lowers his spear at GLOSTER's *breast.*
GLO.   Unmanner'd dog ! stand thou when I command :
Advance thy halberd higher than my breast,
Or, by Saint Paul, I'll strike thee to my foot,
And spurn upon thee, *beggar,* for thy boldness.

Such is the worship paid to wealth in England, down even to the present day, that the most current expression of contempt is to brand a man with the epithet of *beggar !* as used in the sense of poverty,—" *Get out, you beggar !* "

The stock-in-trade of this play consists of murders, conspiracies and perjuries, and amid this sickening sea of crime the female characters figure to such singular disadvantage, as to give another to the many proofs that Shakespeare did not have a very high estimate of women.

The play which follows " Richard III." and closes the Shakespearian dramatic histories, is that of " Henry VIII.," which leaves the reign of Richmond, or Henry VII., unrepresented in the series. The Baconians seek to make a great point of this hiatus, by producing the fact that Bacon wrote a special prose history of the reign of Henry VII., over his own signature, and that, having thus met all the historical necessities of the subject in prose, his tired muse did not feel called upon to repeat the task, under the disadvantages of dramatic poetry. It strikes me, however, that it is much more reasonable to attribute Shakespeare's neglect of Henry VII. for the purposes of a play to the utter absence of any dramatic incident in a reign which was devoted only to mere social progress and "the establishment of law and order."

CHAPTER XXVII.

"KING HENRY VIII."

THE greatest of all the controversies which have raged among the commentators, both German and English, upon the life, genius, and writings of William Shakespeare, is that concerning the date of our poet's production of the play of "Henry VIII." And the object of the dispute is by no means unworthy of the consequence which has been given to it, for its date defines, to a great extent, the motives which induced Shakespeare to prostitute his pen to the laudation of a monster, whose very name it is the common duty of mankind to execrate. Moreover, the play, as it stands, bears sharply upon the question of Shakespeare's religious faith, and, particularly in that expression in Cranmer's christening speech (upon which Knight so much relies), when the Archbishop predicts that during the reign of Elizabeth— which was a Protestant reign—

God shall be truly known.

Be it observed at this point, however, that the whole of this speech of Cranmer's is generally regarded as spurious by the English commentators, and is attributed by most of them to Ben Jonson, who is supposed to have written it in, subsequent to its production, as a compliment to King James, who ascended the throne at the death of Elizabeth, in March, 1603.[1] Among

---

[1] Doctor Reichensperger, clerical member of the German Parliament, has recently issued a work, in which he says that "Cranmer's prediction of the glories of Elizabeth's reign, at the end of 'King Henry VIII.' is an inter-polation of the low court parasite, Ben Jonson."

The April number of the *Catholic Progress*, published in London, con-tains a paper by "J. B. M.," which says, in referring to "Henry VIII.," "Clap-trap passages about the 'virgin queen,' for instance, may possibly not be Shakespeare's own writing. If they are, they are of course drawbacks.

those who deny the authenticity of Cranmer's speech, and who believe that the play was written by Shakespeare as early as 1602, are Doctor Johnson, Theobald, Steevens, Malone, Collier, and Halliwell, with only Knight and Hunter, among the English critics, to the contrary. "All of the German commentators, however," says Elze, "with the exception of Schlegel and Kreyssig, are in favour of the year 1612." Speddon says, that Shakespeare planned "Henry VIII.," "but wrote less than half of it (1116 lines), Fletcher writing the rest (1761 lines)." [2]

The argument for the production of "Henry VIII." in 1612, has its main support in two private letters (written, one on June 30, and the other on July 6, 1613, by a Mr. Thomas Lorkin and Sir Henry Wotton respectively), describing the burning of the Globe Theatre, of London, on the 29th June previous. During the performance of "King Henry VIII.," says Lorkin, the house was set on fire by the discharge of chambers (small cannon) on the entrance of the king to Wolsey's palace—the wadding of the said chambers having lodged in the thatch of the roof. Sir Henry Wotton's letter, in alluding to the same incident, speaks of the piece which was being performed at the time of the fire as a *new* play, called "All is True, representing some principal pieces of the reign of Henry the Eighth." Now, it is very easy to conceive that Sir Henry Wotton might have thought the piece a *new* one without being correct; or that he may never before have been at a theatre, and consequently knew but little of such matters; but it is not easy to conceive that Shakespeare should have so closely interwoven his pæan to the infant Elizabeth with the panegyric on King James, when it was generally known (and by no one better than by Shakespeare) that James had by no means a good opinion of his predecessor.[3]

This, to my mind, indicates the Cranmer christening speech

No real Catholic would flatter a monster whose savage cruelties were endeavouring to eradicate from her subjects the Catholic faith." To this, I may add, that Henry burnt Protestants as well as Catholics when he took the notion.—G. W.

[2] Gervinius, p. xx of "Introduction."

[3] It is worthy of notice that among the many tributes to the virtues of Queen Elizabeth which immediately followed her death, none came from Shakespeare. This neglect appeared so singular, that Chettle publicly rebuked him for it in the lines,—

to be an interpolation on the text of Shakespeare, and also
favours the idea that Shakespeare wrote the play in 1602, to
please the Queen, and to soften the character of Henry VIII.,
because he was her father.

With these preliminary observations I will pass to the illustrations of the play. The first that arrests our attention is the
one in which Buckingham (after having been condemned in a
most unfair trial by notoriously prejudiced judges and by
testimony so obviously false that it attracted the attention of
Queen Katharine and elicited her womanly protest) is made by
Shakespeare to acquit and bless the royal brute who would
neither hearken to justice nor to her :—

Act II. Scene 1.

For further life in this world I ne'er hope,
Nor will I sue, *although the king have mercies*
More than I dare make faults.

*   *   *

Commend me to his grace ;
And if he speak of Buckingham, pray tell him,
You met him half in heaven ; *my vows and prayers*
Yet are the king's ; and till my soul forsake,
Shall cry for blessings on him ; may he live
Longer than I have time to tell his years !
Ever beloved and loving, may his rule be !
And, when old Time shall lead him to his end,
GOODNESS AND HE FILL UP ONE MONUMENT !

*   *   *

I had my trial.
And, must needs say, a noble one ; [4] which makes me
A little happier than my wretched father :
Yet thus far we are one in fortunes.—Both

Nor doth the silver-tongued Melicert
Drop from his honied muse one sable tear,
To mourn her death that graced his desert,
And to his laies open'd her royal eare.
Shepherd, remember our Elizabeth,
And sing *her* rape done by that Tarquin, Death.

"Mourning Garment," p. 160. Z. Holmes, p. 41.

[4] The character of the witnesses in this "noble trial" was thus prefigured
by the conscientious Queen Katharine to the conscienceless and bloody boar,
King Henry :—

Act I. Scene 2.

Q. KATH. I am sorry that the Duke of Buckingham
Is run in your displeasure.

Fell by our servants, by those men we loved most ;
A most unnatural and faithless service !

At this point one of the Duke of Buckingham's retainers, a surveyor, testifies against him, but with such evident prejudice and malice that the Queen again interposes :—

Enter a Surveyor.

Q. KATH.　　　　　　　If I know you well,
You were the Duke's surveyor, and lost your office
On the complaint o' the tenants.　Take good heed
You charge not in your spleen, a noble person,
And spoil your nobler soul !　I say, take heed !

Act II. Scene 2.

SUFFOLK. How is the King employ'd ?
CHAM.　　　　　　　　　I left him private,
Full of sad thoughts and troubles.
NORFOLK.　　　　　　　　　What's the cause ?
CHAM.　It seems the marriage with his brother's wife
Has crept not near his conscience.
SUFFOLK.　　　　　　　　No, his conscience
Has crept too near another lady.
NORFOLK.　　　　　　　　　'Tis so :
This is the cardinal's doing, the king-cardinal :
That blind priest, like the eldest son of fortune,
Turns what he lists.　The king will know him one day.

NORFOLK *opens a folding-door. The* KING *is discovered sitting, and reading pensively.*

SUFFOLK. How sad he looks ! sure he is much afflicted.
K. HEN. Who is there ? ha ?
NORFOLK.　　　　　　'Pray God, he be not angry.
K. HEN. Who's there, I say ?　How dare you thrust yourselves
Into *my private meditations ?*
Who am I ? ha !
NORFOLK. *A gracious king, that pardons all offences
Malice ne'er meant :* our breach of duty, this way
Is business of estate ; in which, we come
To know your royal pleasure.
K. HEN.　　　　　　　　You are too bold,
Go to ; I'll make ye know your times of business :
Is this an hour for temporal affairs ? ha ?—

K. HEN.　　　　　　　　It grieves many.
　　　　　　•　　　　•　　　　•
WOLSEY.　　　　　　　To your high person
His will is most malignant.
Q. KATH.　　　　　　My learned Lord Cardinal,
Deliver all with charity.

Act II. Scene 2.

CARDINAL CAMPEIUS (*to* KING HENRY).

Your grace must needs deserve all strangers' loves,
You are so noble.

Act II. Scene 3.—*An Antechamber in the Queen's Apartments.*

Present—ANNE BULLEN, *Lady in Waiting, and an old Lady of the Court.*

Enter LORD CHAMBERLAIN.

LORD C. (*observing* ANNE BULLEN, *the mother of the future infant* ELIZABETH, *and speaking aside*).

I have perused her well;
Beauty and honour in her are so mingled,
That they have caught the king; and who knows yet
But from this lady may proceed a gem
To lighten all this isle!

Act II. Scene 4.—*The Trial of Queen Katharine.*

Q. KATH. (*to* WOLSEY).   Again
I do refuse you for my judge; and here,
Before you all, appeal unto the pope,
To bring my whole cause 'fore his holiness,
And to be judged by him.
                    [*She curtsies to the* KING, *and offers to depart.*

CAM.   The queen is obstinate,
Stubborn to justice, apt to accuse it, and
Disdainful to be try'd by it; 'tis not well.
She's going away.

K. HEN.   Call her again.

CRIER.   Katharine, Queen of England, come into the court.

GRIF.   Madame, you are call'd back.

Q. KATH.   What need you note it? pray you, keep your way:
When you are call'd, return.—Now the Lord help!
They vex me past my patience!—pray you, pass on:
I will not tarry: no, nor ever more,
Upon this business, my appearance make
In any of their courts.
                    [*Exeunt* QUEEN, GRIFFITH, *and Attendants.*

K. HEN.   Go thy ways, Kate:
The man i' the world who shall report he has
A better wife, let him in naught be trusted,
For speaking false in that thou art, alone
(If thy rare qualities, sweet gentleness,
Thy meekness saint-like, wife-like government,
Obeying in commanding—and thy parts
Sovereign and pious else, could speak thee out),
The queen of earthly queens: she is noble born:
And like her true nobility, she has
Carried herself toward me.

Act III. Scene 1 presents two remarkable expressions from the devoutly Catholic Queen Katharine, which dispose, entirely, by a parity of reasoning, of all of Knight's Protestant presumptions on the lines in " King John :"—

> The king has been *poisoned by a monk,*
> *A most resolved villain.*

The Queen and her women are at needlework, when a messenger enters and informs her that Cardinals Wolsey and Campeius desire an audience :—

> Q. KATH. Pray their graces
> To come near. What can be their business
> With me, a poor, weak woman, fallen from favour?
> I do not like their coming. Now, I think on it,
> They should be good men : their affairs as righteous :
> *But all hoods make not monks.*

And, again, in the interview which follows, she says to Wolsey :—

> Q. KATH. Ye turn me into nothing : *Woe upon ye,*
> *And all such false professors !* Would ye have me
> (If you have any justice, any pity ;
> *If ye be anything but churchmen's habits*)
> Put my sick cause into his hands that hate me ?

In the next scene Wolsey thus reflects upon the threatening complications which the advent of the beautiful Anne Bullen makes for him, in his profligate master's mind :—

> WOLSEY. Anne Bullen ! No ; I'll no Anne Bullens for him.
> There is more in it than fair visage. Bullen !
> No, we'll no Bullens.
>   *   *   *
> The late queen's gentlewoman : a knight's daughter,
> To be her mistress' mistress ! the queen's queen !
> This candle burns not clear ; 'tis I must snuff it ;
> Then, out it goes. What though I know her virtuous,
> And well deserving ? *yet I know her for*
> *A spleeny Lutheran ; and not wholesome to*
> *Our cause,* that she should lie i' the bosom of
> Our hard-ruled king. *Again, there is sprung up*
> *An heretic, an arch one, Cranmer ;* one
> Hath crawl'd into the favour of the king,
> And is his oracle.

The close of this scene describes Wolsey's fall :—

WOLSEY. I know myself now: and I feel within me
    A peace above all earthly dignities,
    A still and quiet conscience. *The king has cured me,*
    I humbly thank his grace; and from these shoulders,
    These ruin'd pillars, out of pity, taken
    A load would sink a navy, too much honour;
    O, 'tis a burden, Cromwell, 'tis a burden,
    Too heavy for a man that hopes for heaven.

CROM. I am glad, your grace has made that right use of it.

WOL. I hope, I have: I am able now, methinks
    (Out of a fortitude of soul I feel),
    To endure more miseries, and greater far,
    Than my weak-hearted enemies dare offer.
    What news abroad?

CROM.   The heaviest and the worst
    Is your displeasure with the king.

WOL.   God bless him!

*   *   *

    Go, get thee from me, Cromwell;
    I am a poor fallen man, unworthy now
    To be thy lord and master: *Seek the king;*
    That sun, I pray, may never set! I have told him
    What, and how true thou art: he will advance thee;
    Some little memory of me will stir him,
    (*I know his noble nature.*)

Act IV. Scene 2.
The Scene of QUEEN KATHARINE'S *death.*

Q. KATH. In which I have commended to his goodness
    The model of our chaste loves, *his young daughter :* [1]—
    The dews of heaven fall thick in blessings on her!
    Beseeching him to give her virtuous breeding;
    She is young, and of a noble modest nature,
    I hope, she will deserve well; and a little
    To love her for her mother's sake, that loved him,
    Heaven knows how dearly.

*   *   *

    When I am dead, good wench,
    Let me be used with honour; strew me over
    With maiden flowers, that all the world may know
    I was a chaste wife to my grave; embalm me,
    Then lay me forth: although unqueen'd, yet like
    A queen, and daughter of a king, inter me!

Act V. Scene 4.
CRANMER'S *christening speech for the infant* ELIZABETH.

GART.   Heaven,

---

[1] Mary I., sometimes called "Bloody Mary."

> From thy endless goodness, send prosperous life,
> Long, and ever happy, to the high and mighty
> Princess of England, Elizabeth !
>   *Flourish.   Enter King and train.*

CRAN.   And to your royal grace, and the good queen,   [*Kneeling.*
> My noble partners, and myself, thus pray :—
> All comfort, joy, in this most gracious lady,
> Heaven ever laid up to make parents happy,
> May hourly fall upon ye !

K. HEN.   Thank you, good lord archbishop.
> What is her name ?

CRAN.   Elizabeth.

K. HEN.   Stand up, lord.   [*Cranmer rises.*
> With this kiss take my blessing : God protect thee !
> Into whose hand I give thy life.   [*Kissing the child.*
>   CRAN.   Amen !

K. HEN. My noble gossips, ye have been too prodigal.
> I thank ye heartily : so shall this lady,
> When she has so much English.

CRAN.   Let me speak, sir,
> For Heaven now bids me; and the words I utter
> Let none think flattery, for they'll find them truth.
> This royal infant,—Heaven still move about her !—
> Though in her cradle, yet now promises
> Upon this land a thousand thousand blessings,
> Which time shall bring to ripeness.   She shall be
> (But few now living can behold that goodness)
> A pattern to all princes living with her,
> And all that shall succeed : Sheba was never
> More covetous of wisdom, and fair virtue,
> Than this pure soul shall be : all princely graces,
> That mould up such a mighty piece as this is,
> With all the virtues that attend the good,
> Shall still be doubled on her : truth shall nurse her ;
> Holy and heavenly thoughts still counsel her :
> She shall be loved and fear'd : her own shall bless her :
> Her foes shake like a field of beaten corn,
> And hang their heads with sorrow : good grows with her.
> In her days every man shall eat in safety
> Under his own vine what he plants, and sing
> The merry songs of peace to all his neighbours.
> *God shall be truly known ;* and those about her
> From her shall read the perfect ways of honour,
> And by those claim their greatness, not by blood.
> Nor shall this peace sleep with her : but as when
> The bird of wonder dies, the maiden phœnix,
> Her ashes now create another heir,

As great in admiration as herself;
So shall she leave her blessedness to one [King James]
(When Heaven shall call her from this cloud of darkness)
Who, from the sacred ashes of her honour,
Shall, star-like, rise, as great in fame as she was,
And so stand fix'd.   Peace, plenty, love, truth, terror,
That were the servants to this chosen infant,
Shall then be his, and like a vine grow to him:
Wherever the bright sun of Heaven shall shine,
His honour and the greatness of his name
Shall be, and make new nations: he shall flourish,
And, like a mountain cedar, reach his branches
To all the plains about him.   Our children's children
Shall see this, and bless Heaven.

K. HEN.   Thou speakest wonders.
CRAN.   She shall be, to the happiness of England,
An aged princess: many days shall see her,
And yet no day without a deed to crown it.
Would I had known no more! but she must die:
She must; the saints must have her: yet a virgin,
A most unspotted lily shall she pass
To the ground, and all the world shall mourn her.

K. HEN.   O, lord archbishop!
Thou hast made me now a man: never, before
This happy child, did I get anything.
This oracle of comfort has so pleased me,
That when I am in heaven I shall desire
To see what this child does, and praise my Maker.
I thank ye all.   To you, my good lord mayor,
And you, good brethren, I am much beholding:
I have received much honour by your presence,
And ye shall find me thankful.   Lead the way, lords:
Ye must all see the queen, and she must thank ye;
She will be sick else.   This day, no man think
He has business at his house, for all shall stay:
This little one shall make it holiday.   [*Exeunt.*

It is painful to witness such a perversity of genius, to the
injury of truth and morals, as is here exhibited against Shakespeare, in the almost lovable portraiture which he has attempted
to foist upon his countrymen as "Bluff King Hal." Neither the
history of England, nor that of any other country, furnishes for
the loathing of mankind a more cruel and unbounded tyrant
than this same Henry VIII.—this very proper father of Elizabeth,
who, in many of its worst points, emulated her sire's career.
The leading characteristics of this monster in human form are a

constant bloodthirstiness and unbridled sensuality. The life of no man who offended him, or thwarted his smallest purposes, stood for a moment in his way, and the chastity of every woman was at the mercy of his mere caprice. He indulged his rage for murder by indiscriminate burnings of both Catholics and Protestants; while his sensuality is conspicuously shown by his possession of six wives, two of whom he disposed of on the block. Nevertheless, he affected conscientiousness as to the validity of the marriage he had contracted with Katharine of Arragon, because she had been his brother's widow! But he betrayed the false motive which pushed forward that divorce by marrying Anne Boleyn, with whose sister, Mary Boleyn, he had long lived in adultery. Indeed, the only reason why he gave Queen Katharine even the show of a trial, was because she was the daughter of an emperor, and he wished to avoid a war with Spain. In the sense of congruity, it is surely eminently proper that this monster, for whom Shakespeare fondly bespeaks a monument where he might " lie embalmed with goodness for all time," should have reintroduced the obsolete method of punishing religious offenders by boiling them in oil. In one batch this bluff King Hal sent fourteen Anabaptists to be burnt in Smithfield; he afterwards hanged six monks at Tyburn, and executed his more distinguished victims, like the venerable Bishop Fisher and Sir Thomas More, by the axe on Tower Hill.

Elizabeth imitated the bloodthirstiness of Henry, and showed it in the beheading of Mary Queen of Scots at the instance of Sir Francis Bacon; she also closely followed Henry's conjugal policy by condemning her discarded favourite, Essex, to execution. She was too old, probably (though of that we are not certain), to care to supply his place on the following day—according to the example of her illustrious father in his marriage with Jane Seymour, which took place the very morning after the beautiful Anne Boleyn had been beheaded by his orders.

It is noticeable in this play, that Shakespeare speaks tenderly, and with prophetic kindness, of the infant princess, who afterwards became " Bloody Mary ;" and also noticeable that Queen Katharine, whose leading characteristic is Catholic bigotry, receives more reverential homage from his pen than any other female in his works. Perhaps it was Henry's own unswerving devotion to the Catholic faith, in which he devoutly died (despite his battle with the Pope and plunder of the monasteries), which secured for him the unfaltering devotion of our poet. Indeed, it is not unlikely that the Bard of Avon, whose predilections for royalty we have so often noticed, might have derived much of his admiration for the character of Henry VIII. as a ruler, from knowing that he subverted all the guarantees of the constitution, practically abolished the parliaments by suspending them for seven or eight years at a time, and established arbitrary government by "running" the State, solely according to his own despotic will.

We may find a further reason for Shakespeare's tenderness towards Henry VIII., notwithstanding that despot's suppression and plunder of the monasteries, in the fact that he distributed a large portion of the spoils of those institutions, in the way of lands, among his favourite nobles. Probably broad acres of them were inherited by Shakespeare's especial patrons, Essex and Southampton. This fact could hardly have influenced the mind of Bacon, had he been the author of the Shakespeare plays; nor would the Protestant Lord Chancellor have passed so tenderly and so respectfully over the characters of Bloody Mary and the bigot Katharine of Arragon, had his been the pen which traced the drama. He certainly would not have pardoned Henry the burning of the fourteen Anabaptists, and the boiling of many full-fledged Protestants in oil. The most that the minister, who persuaded Elizabeth to execute the Catholic Mary Queen of Scotts, could have done in this connexion, would have been to have preserved a decorous silence upon these points, in deference to his royal mistress. He certainly would not have alluded to the wild boar, her father, whose tusks were always dripping with the blood of martyred innocents, in the beautiful invocation,—

> Ever beloved and loving may his rule be;
> And when old Time shall lead him to his end,
> Goodness and he fill up one monument.

19

CHAPTER XXVIII.

THE TRAGEDIES.—"TROILUS AND CRESSIDA."

THE chief interest of "Troilus and Cressida," as far as our inquiry is concerned, turns, like the play of "King Henry VIII.," mainly on the date of its production by the author.

And this, because the disciples of the theory that Sir Francis Bacon was the author of the Shakespearian dramas find, in the play before us (which they say was produced in 1609), an erroneous quotation from Aristotle, which had previously appeared, in an incorrect form, in Bacon's "Advancement of Learning," printed in 1605.

The phrase alluded to occurs in Act II. Scene 2, where Hector replies to the objections urged by Paris and Troilus against returning the captive Helen to the Greeks :—

> HECTOR.   Paris and Troilus, you have both said well;
> And on the cause and question now in hand
> Have glozed, but superficially; *not much*
> *Unlike young men, whom Aristotle thought*
> *Unfit to hear* MORAL *philosophy.*

"In the 'Advancement of Learning,'" says Judge Holmes (the great chief of the Baconian theorists), "Bacon quotes Aristotle as saying *that young men are no fit auditors of* MORAL *philosophy*," because "they are not settled from the boiling heat of their affections, nor attempered with time and experience."

Now, inasmuch as Aristotle, in the expression thus attributed to him, speaks of *political* philosophy instead of *moral* philosophy, and as this error is repeated in the Shakespearian play, published four years afterwards, Judge Holmes thinks the circumstance indicates that Lord Bacon wrote both that work and the play. He admits "that an older play of this name ('Troilus and Cressida'), perhaps an earlier sketch of this very one, had been entered upon the 'Stationers' Register' in 1602-3, but never printed;" [1] and then volunteers the remark that " there is much reason to believe that it (the earlier sketch) was by another author altogether." We cannot but regret that the judge, having gone to this extremity, did not give us a reason for his opinion.

I do not accept Judge Holmes' dates, nor do I agree with his deductions. The weight of authority among the commentators is, that the earlier piece of 1602-3 was Shakespeare's own ; and that the edition of 1609 was a revised and perfected version of the same; or, to use the phrase of that day, a copy that had been " toucht up." Nevertheless the judgment of the two Shakespearian societies of Germany and England are widely at variance upon this point of date; though it must be remarked that their disagreement does not comprehend the discussion of the Baconian theory.

The " Trial Table" of Mr. Furnival (as to the date of the plays), published under the auspices of the New Shakespeare Society of London, sets the supposed date of the production by Shakespeare of "Troilus and Cressida," at 1606-7, and places the year of its publication at 1609. On the other hand, Professor Hertzberg, a man of great erudition, writing under the auspices of the GERMAN Shakespeare Society, puts the date of its production down at 1603. Hunter again decides for 1609; but the Rev. Wm. Harness [2] declares for 1602-3. Knight does

---

[1] "The Authorship of Shakespeare," by Nathaniel Holmes, Judge, and Professor of Law in Harvard University, pp. 48, 49, 50.

[2] The following is the statement of Harness, at the introduction of this play :—

" This play was entered at Stationers' Hall, Feb., 1602-3, under the title of ' The Booke of Troilus and Cressida,' and was therefore probably written in 1602. It was not printed till 1609, when it was preceded by an advertisement of the editor, stating that ' it had never been *staled* with the *stage*, never clapper-clawed with the palms of the vulgar.' Yet, as the tragedy was entered in 1602-3, as acted by my Lord Chamberlain's men, we must suppose that the editor's words do not mean that it had never been presented at all, but only at court, and not on the public stage.

" There was a play upon this subject, written by Decker and Chettle, in 1599; the original story of ' Troilus and Cressida' was the work of Lollius, a historiographer of Urbino, in Italy. It was, according to Dryden, written in Latin verse, and translated by Chaucer. Shakespeare received the greater

not positively fix upon any date; but I may remark, that had he and his contemporaries foreseen the question of Baconism which has been raised upon the above erroneous duplication, much more attention would probably have been devoted to the date of publication. It must be admitted, however, that very plausible evidence in favour of 1609 is to be found in the printer's preface of the edition of that date.

This printer's or editor's preface is headed or addressed as follows :—

"A NEVER WRITER TO AN EVER READER.
"NEWES.

"Eternall reader, you have heere a new play never stal'd with the stage, never clapper-clawed with the palmes of the vulger, and yet passing full of the palme comicall; for it is a birth of a braine, that never undertook anything comicall vainely; and were but the vaine name of comedies changde for the titles of commodoties, or of playes for pleas, you should see all those grand censors, that now stile them such vanities, flock to them for the main grace of their gravities; especially, this author's comedies that are so fram'd to the life, that they serve for the most common commentaries of all the actions of our lives, showing such a dexteritie, and power of witte, that the most dis-pleased with playes are pleased with his comedies. So much and such savor'd salt of witte is in his comedies, that they seem to be borne in that sea that brought forth Venus. Amongst all there is none more witty than this; and had I time I would comment upon it, though I know it needs not (for so much as will make you think your testern well bestow'd), but for so much worth, as even poore I know to be stuft in it—certainly, there can be no doubt of that, your worship. It deserves such a labour, as well as the best comedy in Terence or Plautus; and, believe this, when hee is gone, and his comedies out of sale, you will scramble for them, and set up a new inquisition. Take this for a warning, and at the perill of your pleasures losse and judg-ments, refuse not, nor like this the lesse for not sullied with the smoaky breath of the multitude; but thanke fortune for the 'scape it hath made amongst you. Since, by the grand possessors'

part of his materials from the 'Troy Booke' of Lydgate, and the romance of 'The Three Destructions of Troy.'"

wills, I believe, you should have pray'd for them, rather than been pray'd. And so I leave all such to be pray'd for (for the states of their wits' healths) that will not praise it.— *Vale!*"

The extremity to which the Baconians are driven for their arguments is strikingly manifest in the assumption, by Judge Holmes, that the above preface was written by the author of the play, inasmuch as " the printer," says the Judge, " would expect the author himself to furnish the preface, as well then as now." Consequently, either Bacon or Shakespeare is supposed to have correctly described himself in the caption or head-line of the address, as—

" A never writer to an ever reader."

Unfortunately for the theory of this assumed confession, Shakespeare has been mentioned, by his contemporary, Meares, as the reputed author of several plays, previous to 1598, two of them bearing his name as author, while in 1593-4, four years earlier, he had dedicated his undisputed " Venus and Adonis," and his " Rape of Lucrece," to the Earl of Southampton, over his own signature. These latter, and the Sonnets which accompany them, are indisputably Shakespeare's productions, and are filled with proofs, not only in the marks of his genius, but in numerous forms of expression, that their author was entirely capable of the production of the dramas which followed under the same name ; nay, that the same mind must have produced them both. If, therefore, William Shakespeare did not write the Shakespearian dramas, the questions arise, who wrote Venus and Adonis, Lucrece, and the Sonnets ? And let me ask who claims the latter for Sir Francis Bacon ?

Besides, it is illogical to attempt to fix the date of the production of " Troilus and Cressida " as subsequent to the production of Bacon's " Advancement " (in 1605), simply because the printer's preface to the edition of 1609 speaks of it as a *new* play, which had never been " sullied with the smoky breath of the multitude." For it is admitted that it had not been played previous to 1609, and that then, having been first performed at court " before the King's Majesty," by the Lord Chamberlain's players, on the occasion of some royal revels, it passed into the printer's hands, on its transition to the general public. Moreover, everything in the preface indicates that the author of the play could not have been the writer of that bombastic effusion. Such self-laudation would have been repulsive; and Shakespeare's well-known modesty about his writings, or, at least, his notorious indifference to their renown, except in the way of dramatic exhibition, is utterly at variance with any such charge against him, and certainly, also, as against Bacon. The whole tenor of the preface indicates rather that Shakespeare, who had written the play in 1602-3, had, after it had been held in reserve for six years, touched it up for the use of the court revels of 1609, and then had sold the copyright to some publisher, that *he* might produce it as a new play, with such introductory remarks as he pleased. Whether the misquoted phrase from Aristotle was in the original sketch of 1602-3, and was copied therefrom into the "Advancement" by Bacon, who had probably heard it read (along with the Lords Essex and Southampton, as was customary between patrons and authors in those days), or whether Shakespeare had interpolated the phrase from the "Advancement" into his perfect play of 1609, is not material to the point of authorship. The instances in literature of such plagiarisms are innumerable, and as the whole world has been trespassing upon the mind of Shakespeare as a general literary common for over two hundred years, the presumption that Bacon copied, from memory, the Aristotlean expression, with its error, from Shakespeare, instead of Shakespeare from Bacon, has far the greatest share of probability. First, because it was an erroneous translation, which Bacon would not have made had he translated the phrase for himself; and, second, because Shakespeare, in his first sketch of 1602-3, undoubtedly changed the Aristotlean term of "*political* philosophy" to that of "*moral* philosophy," in order to adapt the rebuke of Hector to Paris and Troilus—both of whom were notoriously immoral young gallants. I think that in this we have the secret of the paraphrase; and I believe that, while the change of the word *political* for *moral* was intentional with Shakespeare, the plagiarism resulted from Bacon's taking it on trust, in using it. In this connexion it should be mentioned that Bacon expresses the same opinions, somewhat more fully, in the "De Augmentis" (published in 1623), that "young men are less fit auditors of policy than of morals, until they have been thoroughly seasoned in religion and the doctrine of morals." [3]

It must be borne in mind, moreover, that at the time Bacon published the "Advancement" (1605), where this erroneous quotation first appeared under *his* auspices, William Shakespeare was the reigning literary reputation, both as a dramatist and poet; and we may somewhat measure the extent of the fame which our poet acquired in his own day and generation by the fact that, though he died in 1616, there were six reprints of his works, in quarto form, between that date and the appearance of the folio edition of 1623. Yet, though Bacon lived to see the great renown of Shakespeare, and to make a most careful revise of his own works in 1625, these Baconian claimants would have us believe, in one breath, that he was utterly indifferent to the revision of these wondrous dramas, and in the next, that he was secretly so thirsty for their just appreciation, as to have written a printer's preface to one of them, in 1609, claiming it to be the equal of "the best comedy in Terence or Plautus." Again, though these mighty dramatic creations never received any correcting touch from Bacon's hand, one of his own acknowledged works was revised by him twelve times. Another point made by the Baconians is, that the name of William Shakespeare is never once mentioned in all of Bacon's voluminous productions, nor is Bacon's name alluded to by Shakespeare; and yet Shakespeare was the man who notoriously, even to the perceptions of that age, divided with the great philosopher the renown of the realm of thought. The Baconians declare this silence as to Shakespeare to be a part of the philosopher's theory of concealment; but would it not be more natural to regard it as an evidence of literary jealousy? Shakespeare divided the applause of the world with one who had expected to bear the palm alone; Judge Holmes, Delia Bacon, and their followers, try to mend the matter by rolling both these human wonders into one.

The original source of the story of "Troilus and Cressida" was, according to Dryden, one Lollius, a Lombard, who wrote it in Latin verse, from which it was translated by Chaucer, and put into English lines, in the form of a poem of five long

---

[3] Holmes' "Authorship of Shakespeare," p. 49.

cantos. It must be noticed, too, that there were also three English ballads during the sixteenth century which, according to Halliwell, treated of the same subject; and, likewise, a piece of the same title which was written by Chettle and Decker, about 1599. The common originator of all these English productions, however, was the poet Chaucer, "who," remarks Knight, "was the one who would have the greatest charm for Shakespeare . . . . though the whole story, under the treatment of Shakespeare, becomes thoroughly original."

Coleridge thinks that it was the object of Shakespeare, in this grand Homeric poem, "to translate the poetic heroes of Paganism into the not less rude, but more intellectually vigorous, and more featurely warriors of Christian chivalry, and to substantiate the distinct and graceful profiles or outlines of the Homeric epic, into the flesh and blood of the romantic drama." In the estimation of that very scholarly and competent American critic, Gulian C. Verplanck, the beauties of this play "are of the highest order. It contains passages fraught with moral truth and polical wisdom—high truths, in large and philosophical discourse, such as remind us of the loftiest disquisitions of Hooker, or Jeremy Taylor, on the foundations of social law. . . . . The piece abounds, too, in passages of the most profound and persuasive practical ethics, and grave advice for the government of life."

"The feeling which the study of Shakespeare's 'Troilus and Cressida' calls forth," says Knight, "is that of almost prostration before the marvellous intellect which has produced it. . . . . But the play cannot be understood upon a mere superficial reading; it is full of the most subtle art. We may set aside particular passages, and admire their surpassing eloquence—their profound wisdom; but it is long before the play, as a whole, obtains its proper mastery over the understanding."

All of the above eulogiums, upon the merits of the better parts of this most wonderful drama, must be heartily admitted; nevertheless, the main and most conspicuous aspect of the piece is that of an essay inculcating female licentiousness and prostitution. The knights of Troy, with the heroic Hector at their head, wield their swords to protect the abandoned Helen in her adulterous joys; and an uncle and a father scheme to lead the beautiful but sensuous Cressida to a harlot's bed. All that is abandoned and debased in woman is made to figure agreeably in these two alluring wantons; while the language of the latter is deliberately framed to stir the coarser appetites of the general audience. Well may it be assumed that Bacon would naturally have been ashamed to acknowledge his patronage of such a theme as this; and, for the matter of that, William Shakespeare also! Nevertheless, the play, in despite of the lowness of its leading motive, is certainly one of the greatest of our bard's productions.

One thing is certain, the broad text and lascivious pictures of this play, and those also of "Timon of Athens," which follows it, could not have flamed from the cold-brained philosopher whose biographers delight to report as one whose "habits were regular, frugal, and temperate, and whose life was pure." [4]

Certainly, no "frugal, temperate philosopher of sober habits and pure life" could have acquired that quickness of the amorous sense which enabled Shakespeare, through the language of Ulysses, to picture, as it were, that dancing white heat which constantly played about Cressida's dimpled limbs—that satin sheen of procreative mystery; that torrid atmosphere of quivering noon; that lambent loveliness which, in the interest of nature, bathes even ugliness with a lurid charm.

> ULYSSES.   Fye, fye upon her!
> There's language in her eye, her cheek, her lip,
> Nay, her foot speaks; her wanton spirits look out
> At every joint and motion of her body.
> O, these encounterers, so glib of tongue,
> That give a coasting welcome ere it comes,
> And wide unclasp the tables of their thoughts
> To every ticklish reader! Set them down
> For sluttish spoils of opportunity,
> And daughters of the game.

This was not the voice of the philosophic sage issuing from "the tranquil retreats at Gorhambury," breathing from "the

---

[4] See, in Act IV. Scene 1 of "Hamlet," the three last lines of the king's third speech.

classic groves of Twickenham Park," or "the musty cloisters of
Gray's Inn;" but the luxurious soul of the handsome London
manager, whose amorous wrongs at the hands of some London
Cressida were echoed by Leontes in " Winter's Tale," and re-echoed
in the agonized wail :

> But, O, what damned minutes tells he o'er,
> Who dotes, yet doubts; suspects, yet strongly loves !

SHAKESPEARE'S LEGAL ACQUIREMENTS.

The search made by Lord Chief Justice Campbell, through
the text of "Troilus and Cressida," for evidences of the legal
acquirements of Shakespeare is not very largely rewarded, and I
do not think that the manner in which his lordship presents
them adds much to the argument to which they are devoted.
With the view, however, of being thoroughly just to the learned
Judge, I herewith transcribe the entire of his remarks upon this
production :—

"*Troilus and Cressida.*—In this play the author shows his
insatiable desire to illustrate his descriptions of *kissing*, by his
recollection of the forms used in executing deeds.   When Pandarus (Act III. Scene 2) has brought Troilus and Cressida
together in the orchard to gratify their wanton inclinations, he
advises Troilus to give Cressida '*a kiss in fee-farm,*' which
Malone explains to be 'a kiss of a duration that has no bounds,
a fee-farm being a grant of lands in fee, that is, for ever, reserving a rent certain.'

"The advice of Pandarus to the lovers being taken, he
exclaims,—

What! billing again ?   Here's—*In witness the parties interchangeably*—

the exact form of the *testatum* clause in an indenture—'In witness
whereof, the parties interchangeably have hereto set their hands
and seals.'

"To avoid a return to this figure of speech, I may here

mention other instances in which Shakespeare introduces it.   In
" Measure for Measure," Act IV. Scene 1 :—

> But my kisses bring again
> *Seals* of love, but *seal'd* in vain ;

and in his poem of ' Venus and Adonis :'—

> Pure lips, *sweet seals* in my soft lips imprinted,
> What bargains may I make, still to be *sealing ?*"

May I hope that the friends of his lordship will excuse me if I
say that these instances are illustrations only of an acute critical
faculty having been unduly taxed ?

CHAPTER XXIX.

"TIMON OF ATHENS."

THIS play was supposed to have been produced by Shakespeare in 1607-8, but not published until after his death, and then first in the folio of 1623. The story is taken mainly from North's "Plutarch," and partly from Lucian. There was, however, an English manuscript play before it, written by some unknown author, which, inasmuch as it contained the character of a faithful steward, and a mock banqueting-scene like that introduced in our poet's version of "Timon," has naturally received a portion of the credit of its origination. The faithful steward, it may readily be supposed from what we have seen of Shakespeare's tendencies, would not have appeared in "Timon," had not some one else produced him to his hand, as in the case of Adam in "As You Like It;" and it is noticeable, moreover, that in this case our poet exhibits a disposition to reward the steward Flavius for his honesty, according to the original, which was more than he did for poor old Adam. The play is a satire upon the gratitude of the world, in which it seems to me that Timon is too readily transformed into a misanthrope, because a few flatterers, whom he had feasted in his wealthy days, refused to lend him money when he failed.

The first evidence we have of the faithfulness of Flavius is in Act II. Scene 2, where we find the steward deploring, with many moans, the descent of Timon into bankruptcy. Nevertheless, he bewails his master's prodigality with such a natural consideration for the continuance of his own profitable post, that he makes no great impression for virtuous disinterestedness.

> FLAVIUS. Heavens! have I said, the bounty of this lord!
> How many prodigal bits have *slaves and peasants,*
> This night englutted!

In the same, and in the following act, the household servants
of Timon (chorussed by the servants of the faithless friends) pity
his fallen fortunes with a cynical tone and motive ; and, at the
same time, avail themselves of the opportunity to scandalize their
several employers, to an extent quite in accord with Shakespeare's
usual representation of merit in the mean.

At the opening of the fourth act the bankrupt and disgusted
Timon appears, self-exiled, without the walls of Athens, on his
way to the woods, as a recluse :—

> TIM. Let me look back upon thee, O thou wall,
> That girdlest in those wolves ! Dive in the earth,
> And fence not Athens ! Matrons turn incontinent ;
> Obedience fail in children ! slaves, and fools,
> Pluck the grave wrinkled senate from the bench,
> And minister in their steads ! to general filths
> Convert o' the instant, green virginity !
> Do't in your parents' eyes ! bankrupts, hold fast ;
> Rather than render back, out with your knives,
> And cut your trusters' throats ! Bound servants, steal !
> Large-handed robbers your grave masters are,
> And pill by law ! Maid, to thy master's bed ;
> Thy mistress is o' the brothel ! · Son of sixteen,
> Pluck the lined crutch from the old limping sire,
> With it beat out his brains !

Presently, when driven by hunger to dig for roots, he discovers
gold in large quantity at the base of a tree :—

> What is here ?
> Gold ? yellow, glittering, precious gold ? No, gods,
> I am no idle votarist. Roots, you clear heavens !
> Thus much of this, will make black white ; foul, fair ;
> Wrong, right ; base, noble ; old, young ; coward, valiant.
> Ha, you gods ! why this ? What this, you gods ? Why this
> Will lug your priests and servants from your sides ;
> Pluck stout men's pillows from below their heads :
> This yellow slave
> Will knit and break religions ; bless the accursed ;
> Make the hoar leprosy adored ; place thieves,
> And give them title, knee, and approbation,
> With senators on the bench : this is it,
> That makes the wappen'd widow wed again ;
> She, whom the spital-house, and ulcerous sores
> Would cast the gorge at, this embalms and spices
> To the April day again. Come, damned earth,

> Thou common whore of mankind, that put'st odds
> Among the rout of nations, I will make thee
> Do thy right nature.—[*March afar off.*]—Ha! a drum? Thou'rt
>   quick,
> But yet I'll bury thee: Thou'lt go, strong thief,
> When gouty keepers of thee cannot stand.

The news of Timon's possession of gold is carried back to Athens by the army, and soon his old flatterers flock out to the wood to pay fresh court to him. Among the rest comes Flavius, the steward. He alone receives kind treatment from the misanthrope, along with gold, and Timon recognizes his honesty as follows:—

> TIM. Had I a steward so true, so just, and now
>   So comfortable? It almost turns
>   My dangerous nature wild. Let me behold
>   Thy face.—Surely, this man was born of woman.—
>   Forgive my general and exceptless rashness,
>   Perpetual-sober gods! I do proclaim
>   One honest man,—mistake me not,—but one;
>   No more, I pray,—and he is a steward.—
>   How fain would I have hated all mankind,
>   And thou redeem'st thyself: But all, save thee,
>   I fell with curses.
>   Methinks, thou art more honest now, than wise;
>   For, by oppressing and betraying me,
>   Thou might'st have sooner got another service:
>   For many so arrive at second masters,
>   Upon their first lord's neck. But tell me true,
>   (For I must ever doubt, though ne'er so sure),
>   Is not thy kindness subtle, covetous,
>   If not a usuring kindness; and as rich men deal gifts,
>   Expecting in return twenty for one?
> FLAV. No, my most worthy master, in whose breast
>   Doubt and suspect, alas, are placed too late;
>   You should have fear'd false times, when you did feast.
>   Suspect still comes where an estate is least.
>   That which I show, heaven knows, is merely love.
>   *   *   *
> TIM. Look thee, 'tis so! Thou singly honest man,
>   Here, take:—the gods out of my misery
>   Have sent thee treasure. Go, live rich, and happy
>   But thus condition'd: Thou shalt build from men;
>   Hate all, curse all: Show charity to none;
>   But let the famish'd flesh slide from the bone,
>   Ere thou relieve the beggar: Give to dogs

What thou deny'st to men; let prisons swallow them,
Debts wither them: Be men like blasted woods,
And may diseases lick up their false bloods!
And so, farewell, and thrive.

FLAV.   O, let me stay,
And comfort you, my master.

TIM.   If thou hat'st
Curses, stay not; fly whilst thou art blest and free:
Ne'er see thou man, and let me ne'er see thee.

Act IV. Scene 3.

I make this quotation at such length because this is the second instance, only, out of twenty-nine plays, in which a man of less rank than a noble, or a knight, is spoken of with approbation and respect. The first instance, as I have already stated, is that of old Adam, in "As You Like It." It is worthy of observation, however, that one of the characters, at the opening of the next act, reports that Timon had given to his steward "a mighty sum." And here it should be remarked, moreover, that the stewards of great lords and millionaires, like Timon, were often of exceedingly good families, as we see by the steward of Goneril in "King Lear," who is almost a cabinet minister.

This play furnishes us with but one other illustration bearing on our special points of view; and that springs from the rude construction of Timon's epitaph at the close. Those who favour the theory that Sir Francis Bacon was the author of the Shakespearian dramas, denounce the epitaph on our poet's tomb, for the meanness of its style, and boldly assert that it came from Shakespeare when he was drawing near his end, with no one of talent near at hand to help construct it. In order to measure the worth of this opinion, I will here quote the epitaph from Timon, and compare it with the other :—

Here lies a wretched corse, of wretched soul bereft,
Seek not my name. A plague consume you wicked caitiffs left!
Here lie I, Timon, who, alive, all living men did hate,
Pass by and curse thy fill; but pass, and stay not here thy gait.

The following is the epitaph in the Stratford church, and it will be perceived that, so far as style is concerned, one doggerel has but little the advantage of the other :—

Good friend, for Jesus' sake forbear,
To dig the dust enclosed here,
Blest be the man that spares these stones,
And curst be he that moves my bones.

CHAPTER XXX.

" CORIOLANUS."

" IN the arrangement of the plays of Shakespeare in a serial
form, it would seem," says Hunter, " that ' Coriolanus ' should
follow ' Julius Cæsar ' and ' Antony and Cleopatra,' since it was
probably written after them." But he also gives it as his opinion
that, inasmuch as " Coriolanus " belongs to a period of Roman
history antecedent to that of the Cæsars, this play should precede
the other two dramas in the collected editions of the dramatist's
works. The Roman plays are remarkably destitute of notes of
time, internal or external. They were probably produced in
1607, 1608, or 1609.

" ' Coriolanus ' itself was neither entered at Stationers' Hall
nor printed till 1623." " The leading idea of the play and pivot
upon which all the action turns," says Knight, " is the contest
for power in Rome between the patricians and plebeians ;" and
I will add that, in agreement with all Shakespeare's instincts,
tendencies, and previous exhibitions of aristocratic inclination,
he again, in this play, constantly sides with arbitrary and
despotic power against the liberties of the people.

" The whole dramatic moral of ' Coriolanus,' " says Hazlitt, " is
that those who have little shall have less, and that those who
have much shall take all that others have left. The people
are poor, therefore they ought to be starved. They work
hard, therefore they ought to be treated like beasts of burden.
They are ignorant, therefore they ought not to be allowed to
feel that they want food, or clothing, or rest, or that they are
enslaved, oppressed, and miserable." [1]

" We see Coriolanus," says Gervinius, " as the chief representative of the aristocracy, in strong opposition to The

---

[1] Hazlitt's " Characters of Shakespeare's Plays," p. 74, edition 1818.

People and the Tribunes, hence we naturally take up the view expressed by Hazlitt, that Shakespeare had a leaning to the arbitrary side of the question, to the aristocratical principle, inasmuch as he does not dwell on the truths he tells of the nobles in the same proportion as he does on those he tells of The People." [2]

" In this struggle," says the astute German, " the hero finds himself placed in a situation where he has to choose between his patriotism and his private feelings of hatred. . . . Coriolanus renounced a hatred of the enemy of his people, to the ruin of his country, being politically and morally hardened in selfishness." Pursuing his analysis of the character of Coriolanus, the German critic further on exclaims,—

" What induced Shakespeare to endow the hero of this play with this superhuman, demi-godlike greatness? History imposed upon the poet a catastrophe of the rarest kind. Coriolanus, after his banishment, fights against his country, for which, before, he would have striven in the hardest battles without requiring any reward; he enters into a league with his bitterest enemy from a cold, unfeeling thirst for vengeance; then, at the certain peril of his life, he suddenly abandons this revenge at the entreaty of his mother. These contradictions, Shakespeare thought, could only be imputed to a man who, from nature and education, had carried his virtues and his faults to extremes which rendered natural the change of his different qualities into their opposites. This is managed with an art and a delicacy that can scarcely be suspected in the apparently coarse strokes of this delineation. First, his unmeasured thirst for glory, which, in an heroic age, can only seek its satisfaction in the praise bestowed on the highest valour."

" The subject of ' Coriolanus,' " says Dowden, " is the ruin of a noble life through the sin of pride." Further on he remarks, " It cannot be denied that when The People are seen in masses in Shakespeare's plays, they are nearly always shown as factious, fickle, and irrational. . . . Shakespeare studied and represented in his art the world which lay before him. If he prophesied the future, it was not in the ordinary manner of prophets, but only by completely embodying the present, in which the future was contained."

[2] Gervinus, p. 748.

20

This is very subtle and ingenious; but it has no force in face of the monstrous manner in which Shakespeare falsified the character of Jack Cade, and that, too, directly against the authority of Hall and Hollinshed, the two contemporaneous court historians of the period, who in other matters he always trusted.

"The author of 'Coriolanus,'" says Mr. Walter Bagehot,[3] "never believed in a mob, and did something towards preventing anybody else from doing so. But this political idea was not exactly the strongest in Shakespeare's mind. . . . . He had two others stronger, or as strong. First, the feeling of loyalty towards the ancient polity of his country, not because it was good, but because it existed. . . . . The second peculiar tenet of his political creed is a disbelief in the middle classes. We fear he had no opinion of traders. . . . . You will generally find that when a citizen is mentioned, he is made to do or to say something absurd."

With these views from the foreign critics, I desire, on my own part, to direct the attention of the reader, before proceeding to let Shakespeare speak for himself through extracts from this play, to the fact that he will find that its main purpose is to deride the principle of popular suffrage; nay, to deny and scoff at popular rights of all sorts, and especially to make the working classes look mean, meritless, and cowardly. Coriolanus, the haughty patrician, on the other hand, though he is a cruel, conceited, overbearing brute, with no more policy or manners than are necessary to a brawny gladiator, is so handled by our poet as to irresistibly win the sympathies of every audience. The most singular, nay, surprising proof of this power of enchantment on the part of Shakespeare, is elicited from American audiences, who, in the face of their democratic principles, uproariously applaud the patrician despot at every insult he puts upon the masses, and hurrah at every mock he makes at their competency to exercise the suffrage. This, while it says a great deal for the power of Shakespeare, reflects very little credit upon the discrimination of the American people; except, indeed, their admiration for his genius is to be set above their respect for republican principles.

---

[3] "Estimates of some Englishmen and Scotchmen," by Walter Bagehot, pp. 257—260.

I will now proceed to allow Shakespeare to speak for himself, with the simple further explanation that a great extent of text is necessary, because, as I said before, the whole of this play is an essay against human rights and popular liberty :—

Act I. Scene 1.—*Rome. A Street.*

Enter a company of mutinous Citizens, with staves, clubs, and other weapons.

1 CIT. Before we proceed any further, hear me speak.

CIT. Speak, speak.   [*Several speaking at once.*

1 CIT. You are all resolved rather to die, than to famish.

CIT. Resolved, resolved.

1 CIT. First, you know, Caius Marcius [Coriolanus] is chief enemy to the people.

CIT. We know't, we know't.

1 CIT. Let us kill him, and we'll have corn at our own price. Is't a verdict?

CIT. No more talking on't : let it be done: away, away.

2 CIT. One word, good citizens.

1 CIT. We are accounted poor citizens; the patricians good : What authority surfeits on, would relieve us; If they would yield us but the superfluity, while it were wholesome, we might guess, they relieved us humanely ; but they think, we are too dear; the leanness that afflicts us, the object of our misery, is an inventory to particularize their abundance; our sufferance is a gain to them.—Let us revenge this with our pikes, ere we become rakes : *for the gods know I speak this in hunger for bread, not in thirst for revenge.*

2 CIT. Would you proceed especially against Caius Marcius ?

CIT. Against him first ; he's a very dog to the commonality.

2 CIT. Consider you what services he has done for his country?

1 CIT. Very well ; and could be content to give him good report for't, but that he pays himself with being proud.

2 CIT. Nay, but speak not maliciously.

1 CIT. I say unto you, what he hath done famously, he did it to that end ; though soft conscienced men can be content to say, it was for his country, he did it to please his mother, and to be partly proud ; which he is, even to the altitude of his virtue.

2 CIT. What he cannot help in his nature, you account a vice in him : You must in no way say, he is covetous.

1 CIT. If I must not, I need not be barren of accusations ; he hath faults, with surplus, to tire in repetition. [*Shouts within.*] What shouts are these? The other side o' the city is risen: Why stay we prating here? to the Capitol.

CIT. Come, come.   ·

1 CIT. Soft; who comes here?

Enter MENENIUS AGRIPPA [*a Patrician and the close friend of* CORIOLANUS, *or* CAIUS MARCIUS, *as he is yet called*].

2 CIT. Worthy Menenius Agrippa; one that hath always loved the people

1 Cit. He's one honest enough; 'Would all the rest were so!

Men. What work's, my countrymen, in hand? Where go you,
    With bats and clubs? The matter? Speak, I pray you.

1 Cit. Our business is not unknown to the senate; they have had inkling this fortnight, what we intend to do, which now we'll show 'em in deeds. *They say poor suitors have strong breaths; they shall know we have strong arms, too.*

Men. Why, masters, my good friends, mine honest neighbours,
    Will you undo yourselves?

1 Cit. We cannot, sir, we are undone already.

Men. I tell you, friends, most charitable care
    Have the patricians of you. For your wants,
    Your suffering in this dearth, you may as well
    Strike at the heaven with your staves, as lift them
    Against the Roman state; whose course will on
    The way it takes, cracking ten thousand curbs
    Of more strong link asunder, than can ever
    Appear in your impediment: For the dearth,
    The gods, not the patricians, make it; and
    Your knees to them, not arms, must help. Alack,
    You are transported by calamity
    Thither where more attends you; and you slander
    The helms o' the state, who care for you like fathers,
    When you curse them as enemies.

1 Cit. Care for us!—True, indeed!—They ne'er cared for us yet. Suffer us to famish, and their storehouses crammed with grain; make edicts for usury, to support usurers; repeal daily any wholesome act established against the rich; and provide more piercing statutes daily, to chain up and restrain the poor. If the wars eat us not up, they will; and there's all the love they bear us.

* * *

Enter Coriolanus [*who has just come from quelling a bread riot in another part of the city*].

Cor. Thanks.—*What's the matter, you dissentious rogues,
    That rubbing the poor itch of your opinion,
    Make yourselves scabs?*

1 Cit. We have ever your good word.

Cor. He that will give good words to thee, will flatter
    Beneath abhorring.—*What would you have, you curs,
    That like not peace, nor war? The one affrights you,
    The other makes you proud. He that trusts you,
    Where he should find you lions, finds you hares;
    Where foxes, geese:* You are no surer, no,
    Than is the coal of fire upon the ice,
    Or hailstone in the sun. Your virtue is,
    To make him worthy, whose offence subdues him,
    And curse that justice did it. Who deserves greatness

Deserves your hate: and your affections are
A sick man's appetite, who desires most that
Which would increase his evil. He that depends
Upon your favours, swims with fins of lead,
And hews down oaks with rushes. Hang ye! Trust ye?
With every minute you do change a mind;
And call him noble, that was now your hate,
Him vile, that was your garland. *What's the matter,*
That in these several places of the city
You cry against the noble senate, who,
Under the gods, keep you in awe, which else
Would feed on one another?—What's their seeking?

MEN.　For corn at their own rates; whereof, they say,
　　　 The city is well stored.

COR.　　　　　　　　　　　Hang 'em! *They* say!
They'll sit by the fire,[4] *and presume to know*
What's done in the Capitol: who's like to rise,
Who thrives, and who declines: side factions, and give out
Conjectural marriages; making parties strong,
And feebling such as stand not in their liking,
Below their cobbled shoes. They say, there's grain enough?
Would the nobility lay aside their ruth,
And let me use my sword, I'd make a quarry
With thousands of these quarter'd slaves, as high
As I could pick my lance.

MEN.　Nay, these are almost thoroughly persuaded;
　　　 For though abundantly they lack discretion,
　　　 Yet are they passing cowardly. But, I beseech you,
　　　 What says the other troop?

COR.　　　　　　　　　　They are dissolved: hang 'em!
They said, they were an-hungry; sigh'd forth proverbs;—
That, hunger broke stone walls; that, dogs must eat;
That, meat was made for mouths: that, the gods sent not
Corn for the rich men only:—With these shreds
They vented their complainings; which being answer'd,
And a petition granted them, a strange one
(To break the heart of generosity,
And make bold power look pale), they threw their caps
As they would hang them on the horns o' the moon,
Shouting their exultation.

MEN.　　　　　　　　　What is granted them?

---

[4] The poor have no fireplaces in Rome, and no stoves, except for cooking purposes, and these are supplied only with charcoal. The climate does not require it. Could Bacon, who had travelled in Italy, make such a mistake as this?

Cor. Five tribunes to defend their vulgar wisdoms,
  Of their own choice: One's Junius Brutus,
  Sicinius Velutus, and I know not—'*Sdeath !*
  The rabble should have first unroof'd the city,
  Ere so prevail'd with me; it will in time
  Win upon power, and throw forth greater themes
  For insurrection's arguing.

Men.   This is strange.

Cor. Go, get you home, you fragments!
     Enter a Messenger.

Mess. Where's Caius Marcius?

Cor.   Here. What's the matter?

Mess. The news is, sir, the Volsces are in arms.

Cor. I am glad on't; then, we shall have means to vent
  Our musty superfluity. *   *

1 Senator (*to the citizens*). Hence! To your homes! begone!

Cor.   Nay, let them follow.
  The Volsces have much corn: *take these rats thither*
  To gnaw their garners.—Worshipful mutineers,
  Your valour puts well forth : *pray,* follow.

Exeunt Senators, Coriolanus *and followers. The citizens steal away.*

The scene now changes to Corioli, the chief city of the
Volsci, where Tullus Aufidius, the great rival of Coriolanus,
harangues the Volscian Senate in favour of war against Rome.
This scene is followed by a long colloquy between Volumnia, the
arrogant mother of Coriolanus, and Virgilia, his shrinking,
gentle wife, about his personal merits and the prospects of the
pending strife. The audience being thus prepared, the scene
opens before Corioli, where Coriolanus, with his forces, stand
drawn up for battle, in advance of his camp. The Volsces
issue from the city and make the assault, and after some fighting, the Romans, though having gained some temporary
advances, are finally beaten back to their trenches.

Cor. All the contagion of the south light on you,
  You shames of Rome!—you herd of—Boils and plagues
  Plaster you o'er; that you may be abhorred
  Further than seen, and one infect another
  Against the wind a mile! You souls of geese,
  That bear the shapes of men, how have you run
  From slaves that apes would beat? Pluto and hell!
  All hurt behind; backs red, and faces pale
  With flight and agued fear! Mend, and charge home,
  Or, by the fires of heaven, I'll leave the foe,

And make my wars on you: look to't: Come on;
If you'll stand fast, we'll beat them to their wives, .
As they us to our trenches followed.

Another alarum. The Volsces and Romans re-enter, and the fight is
renewed. The Volsces retire into Corioli, and MARCIUS follows them to
the gates.

So, now the gates are ope:—Now prove good seconds:
'Tis for the followers fortune widens them,
Not for the fliers: mark me, and do the like.

[He enters the gates, and is shut in.

This daring example inspires the Romans to fresh efforts, and
they force the gates, overcome the Volsces, and capture their
city. This is followed by a scene among the Roman soldiers,
after having sacked the town, which is so perfectly in keeping
with one described by Russell, of the capture of Sebastopol, and
by several American army correspondents who followed the line
of Sherman's march, that it seems to indicate that Shakespeare,
who never attended a campaign, had an instinctive insight into
everything. In sketching the Roman soldier, he really described
the common soldier of every country, and of all time.

Scene 5.—*Within the Town.   A Street.*
Enter certain Romans with spoils.

1 ROM. This will I carry to Rome.
2 ROM. And I this.
3 ROM. A murrain on't! I took this for silver.

[Alarum continues still afar off.
Enter CORIOLANUS and TITUS LARTIUS with a trumpet.

COR. See here these movers, that do prize their hours,
At a crack'd drachm! Cushions, leaden spoons,
Irons of a doit, doublets that hangmen would
Bury with those that wore them, these base slaves,
Ere yet the fight be done, pack up:—Down with them.

Scene 6.—*Near the Roman Camp of* COMINIUS.
Enter CORIOLANUS, *bloody.*

COR. Come I too late?
COM. Ay, if you come not in the blood of others,
But mantled in your own.

＊   ＊   ＊

Where is that slave,
Which told me they had beat you to your trenches?
Where is he? Call him hither.
COR.   Let him alone,
He did inform the truth; *but for our gentlemen,*

The common file,—(A plague ! *Tribunes for them ?*)
The mouse ne'er shunn'd the cat, as they did budge
From rascals worse than they.

In the second act Caius Marcius is invested with the hono-
rary title of "Coriolanus" (which, for convenience, I have already
used), and is brought forward by the Senate and patricians as
their candidate for Consul. The process of running for that
office required the candidate to appear publicly in the market-
place, clad in "a garment of humility" made of coarse stuff,
and to meekly solicit, under the auspices of the Tribunes, the
suffrages of The People. The Tribunes of The People, consequently, though necessarily plebeians, were men of great power
and prestige, for they could wield the masses so as to either
secure or defeat an aristocrat's election ; while The People themselves, who so abjectly cringed under innumerable strokes of
degradation, still insisted upon having their candidates come
humbly to the market-place, and wear the livery of application.
The masses, however, were always easily controlled by the
Tribunes. As an evidence of the power of the Tribunal office, it
is only necessary to refer to the fact that, in Julius Cæsar's time,
Clodius (the violator of the sacred mysteries of the Bona Dea),
one of the most noble of the old patrician families, and who, at
the same time, was possessed of vast wealth as well as family
influence, chose, by way of revenging himself on Cicero, to re-
pudiate his own aristocratic birth and honours, and to resign his
power and prestige as a Senator, in order to be elected a Tribune
of The People. By dint of incessant efforts, and by distributing
his immense means with an unsparing hand, he accomplished his
object, and having enticed the plebeians under his profitable and
tumultuous banner, succeeded in driving the influential and incomparable orator into exile.[5]

As to the dress worn by the applicants for the consulship, we
get a clear and satisfactory idea from Plutarch, who says,—

" It was the custom for those who were candidates for such a
high office to solicit and caress the people in the *forum*, and, at
those times, to be clad in a loose gown without the *tunic ;*
whether that humble dress was thought more suitable for suppli-
ants, or whether it was for the convenience of showing their wounds,
as so many tokens of valour. For it was not from any suspicion

[5] "Life of Marcus Julius Cicero," by William Forsyth (London : John
Murray, 1869), pp. 155, 175, 176.

the citizens then had of bribery, that they required the candidates to appear before them ungirt, and without any close garment, when they came to beg their votes; since it was much later than this, and indeed many ages after, that buying and selling stole in, and money came to be the means of gaining an election. Then, corruption reaching also the *tribunals* and the camps, arms were subdued by money, and the commonwealth was changed into a monarchy." [6]

This, though written of a period four hundred and eighty-eight years before the Christian era, furnishes a suggestive lesson to Americans to-day.

In the first scene of the second act, we find what is regarded as the best recommendation of Coriolanus for his civic candidature :—

MENENIUS. Marcius is coming home—Where is he wounded ?

VOLUMNIA [*the mother of* CORIOLANUS]. I' the shoulder, and i' the left arm: There will be large cicatrices to show the people, when he shall stand for his place. He received in the repulse of Tarquin, seven hurts i' the body.

MEN. One in the neck, and two in the thigh,—there's nine that I know.

VOL. He had, before this last expedition, twenty-five wounds upon him.

MEN. Now it's twenty-seven; every gash was an enemy's grave. [*A shout and flourish.*] Hark ! the trumpets.

VOL. These are the ushers of Marcius : before him
    He carries noise, and behind him he leaves tears ;
    Death, that dark spirit, in 's nervy arm doth lie ;
    Which being advanced, declines : and then men die.

Coriolanus at this point enters, receives his triumph, and then, exhibiting some impatience at the popular acclaim, remarks restively that

The good patricians must be visited,

and passes on, amid the sound of trumpets and the acclamations of the multitude, to the capitol. Thereupon Brutus (not the Brutus of Cæsar's time), and Sicinius, the Tribunes of The People, deliver themselves as follows :—

BRU. All tongues speak of him, and the bleared sights
    Are spectacled to see him ; your prattling nurse
    Into a rupture lets her baby cry,
    While she chats him ; the kitchen malkin pins
    Her richest lockram 'bout her reechy neck,

---

[6] Langhorne's " Plutarch " (Harper and Brothers, 1874), p. 169.

Clambering the walls to eye him : Stalls, bulks, windows,
Are smother'd up, leads fill'd, and ridges horsed
With variable complexions; all agreeing
In earnestness to see him : seld-shown flamens
Do press among the popular throngs, and puff
To win a vulgar station : our veil'd dames
Commit the war of white and damask, in
Their nicely-gauded cheeks, to the wanton spoil
Of Phœbus' burning kisses : such a pother,
As if that whatsoever god, who leads him,
Were slily crept into his human powers,
And gave him graceful posture.

SIC. On the sudden,
I warrant him consul.

BRU. Then our office may,
During his power go sleep.

*   *   *

I heard him swear,
Were he to stand for consul, never would he
Appear i' the market-place, nor on him put
The napless vesture of humility;
Nor, showing (as the manner is) his wounds
To the people, beg their stinking breaths.

*   *   *

SIC. I wish no better,
Than to have him hold that purpose, and to put it
In execution.

Enter a Messenger.

BRU. What's the matter?

MESS. You are sent for to the Capitol. 'Tis thought
That Marcius shall be consul : I have seen
The dumb men throng to see him, and the blind
To hear him speak : The matrons flung their gloves,
Ladies and maids their scarfs and handkerchiefs,
Upon him as he pass'd; the nobles bended,
As to Jove's statue; and the commons made
A shower, and thunder, with their caps, and shouts :
I never saw the like.

BRU. Let's to the Capitol,
And carry with us ears and eyes for the time,
But hearts for the event.

Scene 2.—*The Capitol.*
Enter two Officers, to lay cushions.

1 OFFICER. Come, come, they are almost here : How many stand for consulships?

2 OFF. Three, they say : but 'tis thought of every one, Coriolanus will carry it.

1 OFF. That's a brave fellow; but he's vengeance proud, and loves not the common people.   .   .   .   If he did not care whether he had their love, or no, he waved indifferently 'twixt doing them neither good, nor harm; but he seeks their hate with greater devotion than they can render it him; and leaves nothing undone, that may fully discover him their opposite. Now, to seem to affect the malice and displeasure of the people, is as bad as that which he dislikes, to flatter them for their love.

Coriolanus then comes in, but the flattery which is lavished upon him displeases his disdainful nature to such an extent that he retires, under the apparent pressure of a wounded modesty :—

COR. I had rather have one scratch my head i' the sun,
    When the alarum were struck, than idly sit
    To hear my nothings monstered.   [*Exit.*
MEN.   Masters of the people,
    Your multiplying spawn how can he flatter
    (That's thousand to one good one), when you now see,
    He had rather venture all his limbs for honour,
    Than one on 's ears to hear it?—Proceed, Cominius.
COM. I shall lack voice: the deeds of Coriolanus
    Should not be utter'd feebly.—It is held,
    That valour is the chiefest virtue, and
    Most dignifies the haver: if it be,
    The man I speak of cannot in the world
    Be singly counterpoised.
              *   *   *

    Before and in Corioli, let me say,
    I cannot speak him home: he stopp'd the fliers;
    And by his rare example made the coward
    Turn terror into sport. As weeds before
    A vessel under sail; so men obey'd,
    And fell below his stem. His sword, death's stamp,
    Where it did mark, it took. From face to foot
    He was a thing of blood, whose every motion
    Was tuned with dying cries. Alone he enter'd
    The mortal gate of the city, which he painted
    With shunless destiny, aidless came off,
    And with a sudden reinforcement struck
    Corioli like a planet.
              *   *   *

COM.   Our spoils he kick'd at
    And look'd upon things precious, as they were
    The common muck o' the world; he covets less
    Than misery itself would give; rewards
    His deeds with doing them; and is content
    To spend the time to end it.
              *   *   *

Re-enter CORIOLANUS.

MEN. The *Senate*, Coriolanus, are well pleased
  To make thee consul.

COR.   I do owe them still
  My life, and services.

MEN.   It then remains,
  That you do speak *to the people*.

COR.   I do beseech you,
  Let me o'erleap that custom; for I cannot
  Put on the gown, stand naked, and entreat them,
  For my wounds' sake, to give their suffrage. Please you,
  That I may pass this doing.

SIC.   Sir, the people
  Must have their voices; neither will they bate
  One jot of ceremony.

COR.   It is a part
  That I shall blush in acting, *and might well*
  Be taken from the people.

BRU.   Mark you that?   [*To* SICINIUS.

COR. To brag unto them—thus I did, and thus—
  Show them th' unaching scars which I should hide,
  As if I had received them for the hire
  Of their breath only.

    ✱   ✱   ✱

BRU. You see how he intends to use the people.

SIC. May they perceive 's intent! He will require them,
  As if he did contemn what he requested
  Should be in them to give.

BRU.   Come; we'll inform them
  Of our proceedings here: on the market-place.   [*Exeunt.*

Act II. Scene 3.—*The Market-place. Citizens assembled.*

Enter CORIOLANUS *and* MENENIUS.

3 CITIZEN. Here he comes, and in the gown of humility; mark his behaviour. We are not to stay all together, but to come by him where he stands,
by ones, by twos, and by threes. He's to make his requests by particulars:
wherein every one of us has a single honour, in giving him our own voices
with our own tongues; therefore follow me, and I'll direct you how you shall
go by him.

ALL. Content, content.   [*Exeunt.*

MEN. O sir, you are not right: have you not known
  The worthiest men have done't?

COR.   What must I say?
  I pray sir,—Plague upon't! I cannot bring
  My tongue to such a pace.

    ✱   ✱   ✱

MEN.   You'll mar all;
  I'll leave you: Pray you, speak to them, I pray you
  In wholesale manner.
COR.   Bid them wash their faces,
  And keep their teeth clean.

The haughty candidate then, under the pressure of Menenius, makes a satirical application to the people for their suffrages, which is so evidently insincere—nay, so contemptuous—that the citizens detect its tone. Nevertheless, under the awe of his presence, they give him their voices; whereupon, stripping himself rapidly and impatiently of his suppliant robes, he passes to the Senate-house to receive the more congenial aristocratic honours.

Upon further reflection, however, the citizens perceive he has only deceived and mocked them; so at the instigation of the tribunes, who suggest he has not yet been confirmed, they resolve he shall reappear in the market-place, and be obliged to undergo an honest ordeal.

The third act opens under this state of things; but " Coriolanus," having got along more easily with the Senate, appears as Consul, and, in that capacity, receives the news that the Volsces have again broken out in war. In the midst of this discussion, the tribunes Sicinius and Brutus enter, fresh from the discontented people.

COR. Behold! these are the tribunes of the people.
  The tongues o' the common mouth. I do despise them ;
  For they do prank them in authority,
  Against *all noble* sufferance.

The tribunes, nevertheless, insist he shall again go to the market-place and apologize to The People.

COR.   *Are these your herd ?*
  Must these have voices, that can yield them now,
  And straight disclaim their tongues? What are your offices?
  You being their mouths, why rule you not their teeth?
  Have you not set them on ?
MEN.   Be calm, be calm.
COR. It is a purposed thing, and grows by plot,
  To curb the will of the nobility :
  Suffer it, and live with such as cannot rule,
  Nor ever will be ruled.
BRU.   Call't not a plot:
  The people cry, you mock'd them ; and, of late,

> When corn was given them gratis, you repined;
> Scandal'd the suppliants for the people; call'd them
> Time-pleasers, flatterers, foes to nobleness.

        *   *   *

COR.   My nobler friends,
> I crave their pardons:
> *For the mutable, rank-scented many,* let them
> Regard me as I do not flatter, and
> Therein behold themselves: I say again,
> In soothing them, we nourish 'gainst our Senate
> The cockle of rebellion, insolence, sedition,
> Which we ourselves have plough'd for, sow'd and scatter'd,
> By mingling them with us, the honour'd number;
> Who lack not virtue, no, nor power, but that
> *Which they have given to beggars.*

        *   * ,   *

BRU.   *You speak o' the people*
> *As if you were a god to punish, not*
> *A man of their infirmity.*

SIC.   'Twere well,
> We let the people know't.

MEN.   What, what! his choler!

COR. Choler!
> Were I as patient as the midnight sleep,
> By Jove, 'twould be my mind.

SIC.   It is a mind,
> That shall remain a poison where it is,
> Not poison any further.

COR.   *Shall* remain!—
> Hear you this Triton of the minnows? mark you
> His absolute *shall?*

        *   *   *

BRU.   He has said enough.

SIC. He has spoken like a traitor, and shall answer
> As traitors do.

COR. Thou wretch! despite o'erwhelm thee!—
> What should the people do with these bald tribunes?
> On whom depending, their obedience fails
> To the greater bench: In a rebellion,
> Then what's not meet, but what *must be,* was law,
> Then were they chosen; in a better hour,
> Let what *is* meet, be said, *it must* be meet,
> And throw their power i' the dust.

BRU. Manifest treason.

SIC.   This a consul? no.

BRU. The Ædiles, ho!—Let him be apprehended.

SIC. Go, call the people; [*Exit* BRUTUS] in whose name, myself

Attach thee, as a traitorous innovator,
A foe to the public weal: Obey, I charge thee,
And follow to thine answer.

Coriolanus draws his sword; a tumult follows, in which the people are driven in.

COMINIUS (*to* CORIOLANUS).   Will you hence,
Before the tag return? whose rage doth rend
Like interrupted waters, and o'erbear
What they are used to bear.

MEN.   Pray you, be gone:
I'll try whether my old wit be in request
With those that have but little; this must be patch'd
With cloth of any colour.

COM.   Nay, come away.
　　　　　　　[*Exeunt* CORIOLANUS, COMINIUS, *and others.*

1 PAT.   This man has marr'd his fortune.

　　　　　*　　　　　　　*　　　　　　*

　　　　Re-enter BRUTUS *and* SICINIUS, *with the rabble.*

SIC.   Where is this viper,
That would depopulate the city,
Be every man himself?

MEN.   You worthy tribunes,—
SIC.   He shall be thrown down the Tarpeian rock
With rigorous hands; he hath resisted law,
And therefore law shall scorn him further trial
Than the severity of the public power,
Which he so sets at nought.

　　　　　*　　　　　・*　　　　　　*

BRU.   We'll hear no more:—
Pursue him to his house, and pluck him thence;
Lest his infection, being of catching nature,
Spread further.

　　　　Scene 2.—*A Room in* CORIOLANUS' *House.*
　　　　　　Enter CORIOLANUS *and Patricians.*

COR.   Let them pull all about mine ears; present me
Death on the wheel, or at wild horses' heels;
Or pile ten hills on the Tarpeian rock,
That the precipitation might down stretch
Below the beam of sight, yet will I still
Be thus to them.
　　　　　　　Enter VOLUMNIA.
1 PAT.   You do the nobler.
COR.   I muse, my mother
Does not approve me further, who was wont
To call *them woollen vassals*, things created

To buy and sell with groats; to show bare heads
In congregations, to yawn, be still, and wonder,
When one but of my ordinance stood up
To speak of peace, or war.   I talk of you;   [*To* VOLUM.
Why did you wish me milder? Would you have me
False to my nature? Rather say, I play
The man I am.

VOL.   O, sir, sir, sir,
I would have had you put your power well on,
Before you had worn it out.

COR.   Let go.
VOL.   You might have been enough the man you are,
With striving less to be so: lesser had been
The thwartings of your dispositions, if
You had not show'd them how you were disposed,
Ere they lack'd power to cross you.
    *   *   You are too absolute;
Though therein you can never be too noble,
But when extremities speak. I have heard you say,
Honour and policy, like unsever'd friends,
I' the war do grow together: grant that, and tell me,
In peace what each of them by th' other lose,
That they combine not there?
    *   *   I pr'ythee now, my son,
Go to them, with this bonnet in thy hand;
And thus far having stretch'd it (here be with them,)
Thy knee bussing the stones (for in such business
Action is eloquence, and the eyes of the ignorant,
More learned than their ears), waving thy head,
Which often, thus, correcting thy stout heart,
That humble, as the ripest mulberry,
Now will not hold the handling: Or, say to them,
Thou art their soldier, and being bred in broils,
Hast not the soft way, which, thou dost confess,
Were fit for thee to use, as they to claim,
In asking their good loves; *but thou wilt frame
Thyself, forsooth, hereafter theirs, so far
As thou hast power, and person.*

Here is a repetition of the same royal principle of perfidy
practised by Prince John of Lancaster (with the approbation of
our author), against the army of the Archbishop of York, Mowbray, and Hastings, in the Second Part of " King Henry IV.;"
the Prince putting the forces of these leaders mercilessly to the
sword, after having persuaded them to lay down their arms upon
terms, and a full pardon, secured by his princely honour :—a like
perfidy to that perpetrated against the forces of Wat Tyler and

Jack Cade (also with the approbation of the poet) after they had been induced to disband, on the most solemn promises of amnesty from the King.

The haughty office-seeker, Coriolanus, at length pursues his mother's perfidious advice, but his arrogant, unbridled nature giving way under it, he again rails at the people, who, unable to endure his insolence any longer, mercifully banish him. He then thus curses and takes leave of them :—

> Cor. You common cry of curs! whose breath I hate
> As reek o' the rotten fens, whose loves I prize
> As the dead carcases of unburied men
> That do corrupt my air, I banish *you*.

Thereupon, he at once goes over to the Volscians, betrays to them the secrets of his country, and, out of mere personal spite and revenge, leads the armies of the enemy against Rome, in which estimable attitude he is always vociferously applauded by American audiences.

His arms are successful, and he is only dissuaded from putting his native city to the sword, by the intercession of his mother, wife, and child.

For thus disappointing the Volscians of their expected spoil, however, he is conspired against by their leaders, and slain. The worst feature of the play is, so far as Shakespeare is concerned, that the patriotic Roman citizens who had justly banished him for his treasons to The People, are made to tremble with cowardice at finding him return as an invader ; and in that state of wretched fear, to confess that they did him wrong, in resenting his encroachments on their liberties.

Act IV. Scene 6.

> Men. (*to the Tribunes*).   You have made good work,
> *You, and your apron men ;* you that stood so much
> Upon the voice of occupation, and
> The breath of garlic-eaters !
> Com.   He will shake
> Your Rome about your ears.
>
> *Enter a Troop of Citizens.*
>
> Men.   *Here comes the clusters—*
> And is Aufidius with him !—You are they
> That made the air unwholesome, when you cast
> Your stinking, greasy caps, in hooting at
> Coriolanus' exile. Now, he's coming ;

21

> And not a hair upon a soldier's head,
> Which will not prove a whip; as many coxcombs,
> As you threw caps up, will he tumble down,
> And pay you for your voices. 'Tis no matter;
> If he could burn us all into one coal,
> We have deserved it.
>
> Cit. 'Faith, we hear fearful news.
>
> 1 Cit. For mine own part,
> When I said, banish him, I said, 'twas pity.
>
> 2 Cit. And so did I.
>
> 3 Cit. And so did I; and, to say the truth, so did very many of us: That we did, we did for the best; and that though we willingly consented to his banishment, yet it was against our will.
>
> Com. *You are goodly things, you voices!*
>
> Men. *You* have made good work, *you and your cry!*

It may be urged, in partial relief of the hard and revengeful nature of Coriolanus, that he finally spared Rome at the appeal of his mother; but it will be seen that he was moved rather by a selfish dread of everlasting infamy, than by her appeals, or any better motive.

> Volumnia. Thou know'st, great son,
> The end of war's uncertain; but this certain,
> That, if thou conquer Rome, the benefit
> Which thou shalt thereby reap is such a name,
> Whose repetition will be dogg'd with curses:
> Whose chronicle thus writ,—*The man was noble,*
> *But with his last attempt he wiped it out;*
> *Destroy'd his country; and his name remains*
> *To the ensuing time, abhorr'd.*

Just previous to this we had heard him say to Aufidius, the Volscian General:—

> For I will fight
> Against my canker'd country with the spleen
> Of all the under fiends.

And, right afterward, again to the Volscian commander:—

> I'll not to Rome, I'll back with you; and pray you,
> Stand me in this cause. [*Pointing to his mother and his wife.*]

There certainly could have been no better destiny in reserve for this bad man, than to be hacked to death, as he was, by the swords of those for whom he had betrayed his country.

There may be some to ask mercy for his memory, because of his bravery in battle; but that was a mere gladiatorial instinct; and others may palliate his brutal nature by reference to the savage teachings of his dam, who more than matched his vulgar curse of—

> Con. The fires of the lowest hell fold in the people!

with—

> Vol. Now, the red pestilence strike all the *trades* in Rome!

This sort of teaching, it is true, accounts for much of his perverted disposition, but it does not make bad deeds good, nor justify his enthroning in his heart the selfish passion of personal revenge above all the natural impulses, all the obligations of patriotism, all the duties of friendship, and even the ties of nature. Nor does it warrant—

> CORIOLANUS. Do not bid me
> Dismiss my soldiers, or capitulate
> Again with *Rome's mechanics!*

In this play, and in its encouragement of the aristocratic characteristics of Coriolanus, presenting them always, as the author does, for the auditor's applause, the Baconians may find a plausible argument towards their theory; for I must once more repeat, it seems incredible that William Shakespeare, who was born among the working classes—his father having been a dealer in wool, and, for a time, a trader in butchers' meat—should speak with such invariable and bitter scorn of mechanics, labourers, and tradesmen, especially in deriding the latter with his favourite epithet of "woolen slaves"[7] as the token of his most extreme contempt. From Sir Francis Bacon, such scorn of trade and labour would not have been noticeably strange; but, even from him, we find it puzzling that such contempt for the producing classes—who, certainly, are the source of all the luxuries of the rich—should have reached the point of loathing. But, whether the author of these plays was Sir Francis Bacon or William Shakespeare, we always find him treating the working man, whether of England, France, Italy, Bohemia, or Fairy

---

[7] This epithet, and Shakespeare's frequent allusions to the "greasy caps" and "woolen caps" of the multitude, doubtless had reference to the habit of dress imposed upon the lower classes in England, by Act of Parliament, in the fifteenth century, to wear woolen caps of a specified pattern, so that they might not be able to confound themselves, under any circumstances, with the gentry. Rosalind, in "Love's Labour's Lost," alludes to this practice in the satirical line, "Well, better wits have worn *plain statute caps.*" The Roman mechanics and lower classes also wore caps. The patricians and higher classes went with the head uncovered.—G. W.

Land, with unvarying detestation. If Lord Bacon was the author of the Shakespeare plays, the least we can say of him in this connexion is, that he was a hard, arrogant, proud-hearted, ungenerous, and brutal noble; if William Shakespeare, the wool-dealer's son, then he was a base, cringing parasite, devoid of all the estimable sympathies of parentage and class, and the veriest pander of all poets, to the really inferior conditions of wealth and worldly station. He has taken the god which was born in his bosom for noble purposes, subjugated it to his animal supremacy, and thrust its celestial head under the mire. He cannot be excused on the score of the habits and prejudices of his period. Mortals of all times, who have been commissioned with poetic fire, have held it in noble trust, for the elevation of the people, but Shakespeare seems to have employed his genius mainly to tread upon the unfortunate of the human race.

LEGAL ACQUIREMENTS OF SHAKESPEARE.

" In this drama, in which," says Lord Campbell, " we should not expect to find any allusion to English juridical proceedings, Shakespeare shows that he must have been present before some tiresome, testy, choleric judges at Stratford, Warwick, or West-minster—whom he evidently intends to depict and satirize—like my distinguished friend Charles Dickens, in his famous report of the trial Bardel *v.* Pickwick, before Mr. Justice Starey, for breach of promise of marriage. Menenius (Act II. Scene 1), in reproaching the two tribunes, Sicinius and Brutus, with their own offences, which they forget while they inveigh against Coriolanus, says,—

You wear out a good wholesome forenoon in hearing a cause between an orange-wife and a posset-seller, and then re-journ the controversy of three pence to a second day of audience. When you are hearing a matter *between party and party*, if you chance to be pinched with the colic, you make faces like mummers, set up the bloody flag against all patience, and in roaring for a —— pot dismiss the controversy pleading more entangled by your hearing : all the peace you make in their cause is, calling both the parties knaves.

" Shakespeare here mistakes the duties of the *Tribune* for those of the *Prætor;* but in truth he was recollecting with disgust what he had himself witnessed in his own country. Now-a-days all English judges are exemplary for despatch, patience, and good temper ! ! !"

CHAPTER XXXI.

"TITUS ANDRONICUS."

THE tragedies of "Titus Andronicus" and of "Pericles" are usually compiled among the last of the Shakespearian dramas, not that they are esteemed the most matured and worthy, but because it has been seriously doubted whether they are entitled to be classed among the works of the mind which produced "Hamlet," "Othello," "Macbeth," and "Lear." Their position in the series, therefore, instead of being originally one of honour, was rather one of suspicion, which shrewdly allotted to them the last place in the early compilations, in order that they might be handily "switched off" in case the public voice should decide against them. The general judgment, however—stimulated, no doubt, to some extent, by the desire to cling to everything which *might* have come from Shakespeare—has left them in the list of his collected works. Instead, therefore, of being ranked among the last of our poet's productions, it is pretty generally agreed they ought to appear among his first. Moreover, it is largely believed among critics that "Titus Andronicus" was his very first play; and that both that and Pericles were only his work in part. My idea is that, when Shakespeare, emerging from his position as a hanger-on at the play-houses, began to work as a producer for the stage, he tried his hand first at dramatic *adaptation*, and finding some crude and unaccepted plays within his reach, he chose two or three which he deemed the best, and built upon them.

"Titus Andronicus" and "Pericles" may, therefore, be regarded as two youthful and inexperienced productions, partaking of all the errors of the school in which they had been formed, and which school our author's prestige and practice were not yet great enough to overturn. Flashes of power and strains of melody relieve, with frequency, the deformities of the original productions, and as the striving poet breasted these vexed tides, guided alone by his reliant genius, he learned his masterful and all-commanding stroke.

The trial table of Furnival declares "Titus Andronicus" to have been an old play, and fixes its date at 1588. This makes it the immediate successor of the poem of "Venus and Adonis." Sir Francis Bacon, however, was nearly four years older than Shakespeare, and what might have been forgiven to our bard at the age of twenty-four, would hardly have been excusable in Bacon at twenty-eight; or, indeed, to Shakespeare either, at the period of life when he wrote "Romeo and Juliet." Moreover, Bacon must be credited with having achieved a greater *literary* maturity at the age of twenty-eight, than could have been acquired by Shakespeare at the same age, either from the latter's opportunities for study, or against the distracting obstacles rising from the seething ocean of London lower life.

"Titus Andronicus" is an improbable and voluntary horror, conceived originally by some coarse and cruel mind, which took a perverted pleasure in laving itself in blood, and in familiarizing its auditors with a yearning for atrocity and murder. Titus, a Roman general, who combines the qualities of both Brutus and Virginius, returns to Rome after a brilliant series of battles, conveying with him, in the train of his captives, Tamora, the Queen of the Goths, and her three sons, Alarbus, Chiron, and Demetrius. Titus has been the father of twenty-five sons himself, twenty-one of whom have fallen in battle, and he brings, on this occasion, the dead body of the last of these. The four remaining sons accompany him in this triumph, and are by his side. One of these, Lucius, demands that "the proudest prisoner of the Goths" shall be hewed to pieces, as a sacrifice *ad manes fratrum* to his unburied brother, according to the Roman custom of the time; whereupon Titus yields to them Tamora's eldest son, Alarbus, for that purpose. During this campaign, the Emperor of Rome had died, and the People, in gratitude for the services of Titus, desire to invest him with the vacant purple. The aged warrior, however, with a patriotic forbearance, rejects the temptation and decides in favour of the emperor's eldest son, Saturninus, and, at the same time, gives him the hand of Lavinia, his only daughter in marriage. Saturninus accepts both the empire and the girl, whereupon Bassianus, the emperor's

second son, claims Lavinia as his betrothed, and, drawing his
sword, bears her off from the scene, supported by three of the
sons of Titus. Mutius, the fourth son, also takes part with
Bassianus, and attempts to bar the way of Titus from Lavinia's
rescue. Upon this, the father, in a fit of ungovernable rage,
kills Mutius on the spot, and then demands of his other sons
the immediate restoration of Lavinia to the young emperor.
Saturninus, however, having been suddenly smitten with the
burning beauty of Tamora, rejects Lavinia, and takes the Gothic
queen as substitute,—a choice which old Titus, still governed by
his loyalty, sorrowfully consents to. In the second act, Titus
gives a grand hunt to the new emperor and his court, during
which revelry the two remaining sons of Tamora, at the instigation of Aaron, a Moor, who is the paramour of their mother,
murder Bassianus, and seize upon the person of Lavinia for
themselves. Tamora, coming in, seconds this vile advice, and in
her presence, and at her stimulation, the youths stab Bassianus,
and cast him into a pit, which had been artfully prepared by
Aaron for this purpose. Tamora then seeks to perform in like
manner, with her dagger, upon Lavinia; but her sons interfere,
in order to carry out the more agreeable purpose previously
suggested to them by Aaron. Tamora, after a moment's
thought, yields to the congenial wickedness of this suggestion,
and despatches her offspring to the brutal task with—

> But when ye have the honey you desire,
> Let not this wasp outlive us both to sting.

The sons follow this unnatural counsel, and then, by way of
preventing Lavinia from becoming a witness against them, cut
out her tongue that she may not expose them by speech, and
next cut off her hands, that she may not betray them by
writing.

I think Shakespeare may be acquitted of the barbarity of this
device, but he cannot be excused the error of adopting it; and,
to my mind, an author who takes advantage of the trust reposed
in him by his audience, to wound their best feelings with
unnecessary horrors, is nearly as bad as the characters who
perpetrate them. A writer should reach his climax by tolerable
steps, and he is not justified in exercising his art so as to cause
us to love a beautiful ideal, merely that he may torture it in

our presence, any more than a boy has a right to expect us to
honour him for his dexterity in driving pins through flies. We
can bear to see the beautiful Fantine cut off her golden tresses
to feed the famishing Cosette, but, when she is made to part
with the laughing glory of her mouth, by selling to the
travelling dentist her two upper front teeth to obtain medicines
for the suffering child, we can scarcely refrain from execrating
Victor Hugo as a monster, for such a wanton outrage on our
sentiments,—a monstrosity which is rendered all the greater
by the vast resources of his genius, and because he is enabled to
perpetrate the horror only through a violation of our confidence.
There is no good end to be attained by making human nature
look worse than it is, and, in my opinion, the author who
conjures up impossible crimes to torture the heart of his confiding listeners, is as bad as the real perpetrator of such cruelties
himself.

But the horrors of the second act of "Andronicus" do not finish
with the rape and mutilation of Lavinia. The villain Aaron,
who had suggested her violation to Chiron and Demetrius, decoys
two of the three remaining sons of Titus, Quintus and Martius,
to the pit where Bassianus lies slain, with the view of searching
it for game. The mouth of the pit being masked with boughs,
Martius falls in, and Quintus having given his hand to extricate
his brother, is pulled down into the hole along with him.
Having them thus snared and fast (for the pit had been pre-
arranged), Aaron brings in the emperor and train, and charges
the two live brothers in the pit, with the murder of Bassianus,
who lies dead at the bottom. Titus pleads in vain to be accepted
as the surety for his sons until their trial can come on ; but the
emperor refuses, and they are hurried off to prison.

The monster Aaron next appears to old Titus, who is now half
bereft of reason, pretending to bring a message from the emperor,
to the effect, that if he, or his brother Marcus, or his last son
Lucius, will, either of them, chop off a hand, Quintus and
Martius shall be pardoned. There is a struggle, at once, between
the two old men, and also between Lucius and the father, who
shall make the sacrifice; but Titus succeeds in first getting his
left hand to the sword of Aaron, who eagerly strikes it off, and
carries it away. In a few minutes after, and before the scene is
closed, a messenger enters, bearing the heads of Quintus and

Martius, which had been so bloodily redeemed, and Titus' own still smoking hand.

MESSENGER. Worthy Andronicus, ill art thou repaid
For that good hand thou sent'st the emperor,
Here are the heads of thy two noble sons;
And here's thy hand, in scorn to thee sent back.

Lucius, the last of Titus' sons, upon this concludes that it is time for him to fly, and he escapes from Rome for the purpose of gathering an army among the Goths, to depose the emperor and redress his father's wrongs.

In the next act, the perpetrators of the outrages upon Lavinia are revealed by the device of giving her a long staff, one end of which she puts into her mouth, and guiding the other end with her stumps, writes the names of Chiron and Demetrius in the sand; thus showing that the author had unnecessarily cut out her tongue and chopped off her hands. Titus, upon this, becomes altogether mad, and in this state affronts the emperor with sardonic messages, for which he would have been put to death, but for the timely news that the raging Lucius is approaching Rome with a great army. This danger induces the emperor to temporize with Titus, and Tamora finally succeeds in persuading the distraught old man to entreat Lucius to come into the city, to agree upon a treaty and to share a feast. Titus, however, has sanity enough left to divine their purpose, and though he consents to the proposal, succeeds in securing the persons of Chiron and Demetrius in advance, and slays them in his own house, by cutting their throats over a bowl, which Lavinia holds between her stumps. Their bodies are then made into a pasty, upon which their mother is ignorantly made to feed during the repast that follows. After Tamora has surfeited herself upon the horrid dish, Titus informs her that she has been munching and digesting the bodies of her own sons.

During the progress of the banquet (which is held in a pavilion open to the observation of the People and the troops), and just before this horrible revelation is made to Tamora, Titus mercifully stabs Lavinia, in the Virginius fashion. He next kills Tamora; the emperor then kills him; whereupon Lucius revenges his father by killing the emperor. This holocaust of murder finally winds up by the execution of the demon Aaron; after which, Lucius takes tranquil possession of the throne. The

following is the full scene of these closing horrors as taken from
the text :—

Act V. Scene 3.

Enter TITUS, *dressed like a cook.* LAVINIA *veiled, young* LUCIUS *and
others.* TITUS *places the dishes on the table.*

TIT.   Welcome, my gracious lord; welcome dread queen;
      Welcome, ye warlike Goths; welcome Lucius;
      And welcome, all: although the cheer be poor,
      'Twill fill your stomachs; please you eat of it.

SAT.   Why art thou thus attired, Andronicus?

TIT.   Because I would be sure to have all well,
      To entertain your highness, and your empress.

TAM.   We are beholden to you, good Andronicus.

TIT.   And if your highness knew my heart, you were.
      My lord the emperor, resolve me this;
      Was it well done of rash Virginius,
      To slay his daughter with his own right hand,
      Because she was enforced, stain'd, and deflow'r'd?

SAT.   It was, Andronicus.

TIT.   Your reason, mighty lord!

SAT.   Because the girl should not survive her shame,
      And by her presence still renew his sorrows.

TIT.   A reason mighty, strong, and effectual:
      A pattern, precedent, and lively warrant,
      For me, most wretched to perform the like;—
      Die, die, Lavinia, and thy shame with thee; [*He kills* LAVINIA.
      And, with thy shame, thy father's sorrow die!

SAT.   What hast thou done, unnatural and unkind?

TIT.   Kill'd her, for whom my tears have made me blind.
      I was as woeful as Virginius was:
      And have a thousand times more cause than he
      To do this outrage;—and it is now done.

SAT.   What, was she ravish'd? tell, who did the deed.

TIT.   Will't please you eat? will't please your highness feed?

TAM.   Why hast thou slain thine only daughter thus?

TIT.   Not I; 'twas Chiron, and Demetrius:
      They ravish'd her, and cut away her tongue,
      And they, 'twas they, that did her all this wrong.

SAT.   Go, fetch them hither to us presently.

TIT.   Why, there they are both, baked in that pie;
      Whereof their mother daintily hath fed,
      Eating the flesh that she herself hath bred.
      'Tis true, 'tis true; witness my knife's sharp point.
                         [*Killing* TAMORA.

SAT.   Die, frantic wretch, for this accursed deed. [*Killing* TITUS.

Luc. Can the son's eye behold his father bleed ?
　　　There's meed for meed, death for a deadly deed.
[*Kills* SATURNINUS. *A great tumult. The people in confusion disperse.*
MARCUS, LUCIUS, *and their partisans ascend the steps before* TITUS'
house.]

The mind of Shakespeare is manifest in the above language,
though with a less full, and evidently much less practised
strength, than in any other of his dramatic works.

Knight and Collier unhesitatingly ascribe the authorship of
" Titus Andronicus" to Shakespeare; Coleridge disputes the presence of Shakespeare, except in certain passages, and Gervinius
doubts its Shakespearian authenticity altogether, keenly observing that, whatever may be the truth, amongst all this variety
of opinion, " there are a few, who value Shakespeare, who
would not wish to have it proved that this piece did not proceed from our poet's pen." Further on, the same acute reasoner
observes,—

" The whole, indeed, sounds less like the early work of a great
genius than the production of a mediocre mind, which in a certain
self-satisfied security felt itself already at its apex. But that
which, in our opinion, decides against its Shakespearian authorship is the coarseness of the characterization, the lack of the most
ordinary probability in the actions, and the unnatural motives
assigned to them. The *style* of a young writer may be perverted,
and his *taste* almost necessarily at first goes astray; but that
which lies deeper than all this exterior and ornament of art—
namely, the estimate of man, the deduction of motives of action,
and the general contemplation of human nature—this is the
power of an innate talent, which, under the guidance of sound
instinct, is usually developed at an early stage of life. Whatever
piece of Shakespeare's we regard as his first, everywhere, even in
his narratives, the characters are delineated with a firm hand—
the lines may be weak and faint, but nowhere are they drawn, as
here, with a harsh and distorted touch. And besides, Shakespeare
ever knew how to devise the most natural motives for the
strangest actions in the traditions which he undertook to dramatize, and this even in his earliest plays; but nowhere has he
grounded, as in this piece, the story of his play upon the most
apparent improbability. . . . . He who compares the most
wicked of all the characters which Shakespeare depicted with this

Aaron, who cursed 'the day in which he did not some notorious ill,' will feel that in the one some remnant of humanity is ever preserved, while in the other a 'ravenous tiger' commits unnatural deeds and speaks unnatural language." [1]

[1] Act V. Scene 1.

AARON. An if it please thee? why, assure thee, Lucius,
   'Twill vex thy soul to hear what I shall speak;
   For I must talk of murders, rapes, and massacres,
   Acts of black night, abominable deeds,
   Complots of mischief, treason; villanies
   Ruthful to hear, yet piteously perform'd;

       *   *   *

       This was but a deed of charity,
   To that which thou shalt hear of me anon.
   'Twas her two sons, that murder'd Bassianus;
   They cut thy sister's tongue, and ravish'd her,
   And cut her hands; and trimm'd her as thou saw'st.

     *   *   *

   Well, let my deeds be witness of my worth.
   I train'd thy brethren to that guileful hole,
   Where the dead corpse of Bassianus lay:
   I wrote the letter that thy father found.
   And hid the gold within the letter mention'd,
   Confederate with the queen, and her two sons;
   And what not done, that thou hast cause to rue,
   Wherein I had no stroke of mischief in it?
   I play'd the cheater for thy father's hand;
   And, when I had it, drew myself apart,
   And almost broke my heart with extreme laughter.
   I pry'd me through the crevice of a wall,
   When, for his hand, he had his two sons' heads;
   Beheld his tears, and laugh'd so heartily,
   That both mine eyes were rainy like to his.

     *   *   *

LUC. Art thou not sorry for these heinous deeds?
AAR. Ay, that I had not done a thousand more.
   Even now I curse the day (and yet, I think,
   Few come within the compass of my curse),
   Wherein I did not some notorious ill:
   As kill a man, or else devise his death;
   Ravish a maid, or plot the way to do it;
   Accuse some innocent, and forswear myself:
   Set deadly enmity between two friends;
   Make poor men's cattle break their necks;
   Set fire on barns and hay-stacks in the night,
   And bid the owners quench them with their tears.

The point which we derive from this steaming vat of blood, horror, incongruity, and incredible consequence, is, that such a treatise could not have been conjured as a picture of possible human events from the cool, philosophic, exact, and rational mind of Sir Francis Bacon. He was a man of method, of reason, of logic, and of tranquil development, and he could no more have thought out, or have countenanced such absurd monstrosities, than Newton could have conceived Barbarossa, or Des Cartes have written Bombastes Furioso. Shakespeare undoubtedly was the man who adapted and produced this play, and in this connexion, I have only to add the remark of Doctor Johnson, while discussing the authenticity of another disputed performance of our author, to wit, that if the lines attributed to him in " Titus Andronicus " be not his, what other man of his time could possibly have written them?

There are but one or two other points in the text which I desire to call attention to, as bearing upon the Baconian theory, and as touching (though but slightly) the question of Shakespeare's unremitting contempt for the masses of the People. As I have been extreme in my declarations upon this point, I desire to submit to the reader every line I find, which seems, even in the remotest degree, to support argument on the other side. If there are any not noticed in these chapters, it is because they have escaped my observation.

<blockquote>
Oft have I digg'd up dead men from their graves,
And set them upright at their dear friends' doors,
Even when their sorrows almost were forgot ;
And on their skins, as on the bark of trees,
Have with my knife carved in Roman letters,
Let not your sorrows die, though I am dead.
Tut, I have done a thousand dreadful things.
As willingly as one would kill a fly ;
And nothing grieves me heartily, indeed,
But that I cannot do ten thousand more.
</blockquote>

Luc.   Bring down the devil; for he must not die
      So sweet a death, as hanging presently.

Aar.   If there be devils, 'would I were a devil,
      To live and burn in everlasting fire ;
      So I might have your company in hell,
      But to torment you with my bitter tongue !

Luc.   Sirs, stop his mouth, and let him speak no more.

The first illustration in the premises occurs in Act V. Scene 3, immediately after the wholesale killing of Lavinia, Tamora, Titus, and Saturninus has taken place.

A great tumult is the immediate result. The crowd, consisting of people of all ranks of society, separate in great confusion, or, to use the explanatory language at the head of the scene, " the people disperse in terror." To the numbers which remain, and which consist mostly of patricians, senators, and men of rank, Marcus, the brother of Titus Andronicus, thus speaks in the interest of Lucius' elevation to the throne :—

> MARCUS. You sad-faced men, people, and sons of Rome,
> By uproar sever'd like a flight of fowl,
> Scatter'd by winds and high tempestuous gusts,
> O! let me teach you how to knit again
> This scatter'd corn into one mutual sheaf,
> These broken limbs again into one body.

His speech is favourably responded to by a Roman lord, whereupon Lucius, after a little more aristocratic pressure, modestly accepts :—

> LUCIUS. Thanks, gentle Romans: may I govern so,
> To heal Rome's harms and wipe away her woe!
> But, *gentle people*, give me aim awhile.

It will be observed, however, that these speeches to " the People " and " sons of Rome " are addressed to them by politicians, who are beseeching their common suffrages for a kingly crown.

I place no importance upon the above extracts as a diversion of the argument, but I give them rather as a curiosity, in that, they are the very first instances, in the twenty-nine plays I have thus far reviewed, in which Shakespeare has allowed himself to allude to the People without some voluntary term of disrespect.

" PERICLES, PRINCE OF TYRE."

This play contributes little, if anything, to our special inquiries; and only demands a mere mention as we pass along. It is classed with " Titus Andronicus " by the commentators, as being of very doubtful authenticity, all of them rating it as one of our poet's

earliest performances, Dryden placing it as his very first.
Knight says, that the first edition of "Pericles" appeared in
1609, under the title of "The late and much-admired play called
Pericles, Prince of Tyre, with the true relation of the whole
historic adventures and fortunes of the said prince, and also the
no less strange and worthy accidents in the birth and life of his
daughter, Marina; as it hath been divers and sundry times acted
by his Majestie's servants at the Globe, on the Bank side.   By
William Shakespeare."

The story was of very great antiquity, having appeared in the
Gesta Romanorum five hundred years ago, and was first done into
English by an author named Gower, in 1554.   From Gower's
poem the play was probably constructed, the author of it, whoever he was, welding together its incongruities of time and
scene, by using old Gower as a Chorus, after the Shakespearian
fashion.   Gower is, in this way, introduced at the commencement
of every act and even in the course of an act, with some of the
weakest doggerel rhymes that can be conceived of, hardly one of
which can be reasonably attributed to Shakespeare; unless,
indeed, he was imitating that mode of the familiar narrative
rhyme of the time.   Nearly all the critics are against the authenticity of "Pericles;" but I find expressions in it—nay, whole
scenes, which cannot, in my judgment, be attributed to any
other hand than that of our poet.   I should decide the following
two lines to be Shakespeare's:—

> Kings are earth's gods: in vice their law's their will;
> And if Jove stray, who dare say Jove doth ill.—*Act I. Scene* 1.

Also, the lines of Pericles to Marina:—

> Yet dost thou look
> Like Patience gazing on king's graves, and smiling
> Extremity out of act.

Which reminds us of his previous expression in "The Twelfth
Night:"—

> She sat like Patience on a monument
> Smiling at grief.

I should also adopt, as genuine, the scene between Pericles
and the fishermen, in the second act; also the scene between
Boult and the bawd in the fourth Act, and, certainly, the
following from the third act:—

Act III. Scene 1.

Enter PERICLES, *on a ship at sea.*

PER. Thou God of this great vast, rebuke these surges,
    Which wash both heaven and hell; and thou, that hast
    Upon the winds command, bind them in brass,
    Having call'd them from the deep! O, still thy deaf'ning,
    Thy dreadful thunders; gently quench thy nimble,
    Sulphurous flashes!—O how, Lychorida,
    How does my queen?—Thou storm, thou! venomously
    Wilt thou spit all thyself?—The seaman's whistle
    Is as a whisper in the ears of death,
    Unheard.—Lychorida!—Lucina, O
    Divinest patroness, and midwife, gentle
    To those that cry by night, convey thy deity
    Aboard our dancing boat; make swift the pangs
    Of my queen's travails!—Now, Lychorida——

Enter LYCHORIDA, *with an infant.*

LYC. Here is a thing
    Too young for such a place, who, if it had
    Conceit, would die as I am like to do.
    Take in your arms this piece of your dead queen.

PER. How! how, Lychorida!

LYC. Patience, good sir; do not *assist the storm,*[2]
    Here's all that is left living of your queen,—
    A little daughter; for the sake of it,
    Be manly, and take comfort,

             *   *   *

PER.   Now, mild may be thy life!
    For a more blust'rous birth had never babe:
    Quiet and gentle thy conditions!
    For thou'rt the rudeliest welcomed to this world,
    That e'er was prince's child. Happy what follows!
    Thou hast as chiding a nativity,
    As fire, air, water, earth, and heaven can make,
    To herald thee from the womb: even at the first,
    Thy loss is more than can thy portage quit,
    With all thou canst find here. Now the good gods
    Throw their best eyes upon it!

Enter two Sailors.

1 SAIL. What courage, sir? God save you.

PER. Courage enough: I do not fear the flaw;
    It hath done to me the worst. Yet, for the love
    Of this poor infant, this fresh-new sea-farer,
    I would it would be quiet.

---

[2] You do assist the storm.—"Tempest," Act I. Scene 1.

1 SAIL. Slack the bolins there; thou wilt not, wilt thou? Blow and split thyself.[3]

2 SAIL. But sea-room, an' the brine and cloudy billow kiss the moon, I care not.

1 SAIL. Sir, your queen must overboard; the sea works high, the wind is loud, and will not lie till the ship be cleared of the dead.

PER. That's your superstition.

1 SAIL. Pardon us, sir; with us at sea it still hath been observed; and we are (running) strong astern. Therefore briefly yield her; for she must overboard straight.

    PER. Be it as you think meet. Most wretched queen!

    LYC. Here she lies, sir.

    PER. A terrible child-bed hast thou had, my dear;
        No light, no fire: the unfriendly elements
        Forgot thee utterly; nor have I time
        To give thee hallow'd to thy grave, but straight
        Must cast thee, scarcely coffin'd, in the ooze;
        Where, for a monument upon thy bones,
        And aye-remaining lamps, the belching whale
        And humming water must o'erwhelm thy corpse,
        Lying with simple shells.

In my judgment, only Shakespeare could have written these last nine lines.

Gervinius, in commenting upon this play, says, "We should therefore, prefer to assume that Shakespeare appropriated the piece soon after its origin, about 1590. At the time that the play was printed with Shakespeare's name, in 1602, it may, perhaps, have been re-prepared for Burbage's acting, and through this it may have acquired its new fame. That at that time it excited fresh sensation is evident from the fact that the performance of the piece gave rise to a novel, composed in 1608, by George Wilkens, entitled 'The true history of the play of Pericles, as it was lately represented by the worthy and ancient poet, John Gower.' In this publication we read the Iambic verses and passages of the piece transposed into prose, but in a manner which allows us to infer that the play, at that time was reprinted in a more perfect form than that in which we now read it. Shakespeare's pen—so easily is it to be distinguished—is recognized in this prose version in expressions, which are not to be found in the drama, but which must have been used upon the

---

[3] Blow till thou burst thy wind, if room enough.—"Tempest," Act I. Scene 1.

stage. When Pericles (Act III. Scene 1) receives the child born in the tempest, he says to it,—

> Thou'rt the rudeliest welcomed to this world
> That e'er was prince's child.

To this the novel adds the epithet,—

> Poor inch of nature.

Merely four words, in which every reader must recognize our poet. We, therefore, probably read this drama now, in a form which it neither bore when Shakespeare put his hand to it for the first, nor for the last time."[4]

With this recognition of Shakespeare, in the above four lines, I heartily agree, for no such flower could have blossomed from any other stock.

[4] "Shakespeare's Commentaries," by Gervinius, pp. 111, 112. Scribner's Edition, N. Y.

CHAPTER XXXII.

" MACBETH."

IT requires from a reviewer the exercise of great self-restraint, when passing through the intellectual splendours of such a composition as "Macbeth," to withstand the temptation to dwell upon its glories, while travelling along the comparatively narrow line of an allotted path; nevertheless there is but one true way to perform a duty, and that is to adhere strictly to the boundaries set for ourselves at the beginning, and not be drawn aside by allurements which may be yielded to only by the general critic. It need not surprise the reader, therefore, if this great production of our poet, which is suggestive of such commanding thoughts, should contribute so little to the scope of our review.

Mr. Thomas Kenny, who has written most ably on the subject of "Macbeth,"[1] characterizes it as "a drama of gigantic crime and terror, relieved by the most magnificent imaginative expression," yet marked with great simplicity of general design. The date of the production of the piece is set by Furnival at 1605-6; and "we may take it for granted," says Kenny, "that it was written in the time of James I., who ascended the throne March, 1603, as it contains an evident allusion to that monarch in Act IV. Scene 1, and also a complimentary reference to him in another part. The material for the play was found by Shakespeare in Holinshed's ' History of Scotland,' where the story of Macbeth is told, at page 168." There, Macbeth and Duncan are represented to have been cousins; the first a valiant gentleman, but of a cruel disposition, and the latter "so soft and gentle in his nature that the people wished the inclinations and manners of the two to have been so tempered and interchangeably shared

---

[1] "The Life and Genius of Shakespeare," by Thomas Kenny. Longman and Co., London, 1864.

betwixt them, that where the one had too much of clemency, and the other of cruelty, the main virtue betwixt these two extremities might have reigned by indifferent partition in them both." Some light is afforded as to the date in which this tragedy is laid, by James Logan's magnificently illustrated folio on the "Clans of the Scottish Highlands," in which it is stated that Macduff overcame Macbeth in 1056. See vol. i. (published by Willis and Sothern, 136, Strand, London). The play all along keeps close to the line of Holinshed, varying from it in scarcely any main particular, except in the non-appearance, in the banquet-scene, of the murdered Banquo's ghost. In treating of the second act, Kenny says, "There is in the literature of all ages no scene of pure natural terror so true, so vivid, so startling, as the murder of Duncan, with all its wonderful accompaniments. Through the magic art of the poet we lose our detestation of the guilty authors of the deed, in the absorbing sympathy with which we share their breathless disquietude."

The first illustration I find in the text exhibiting the tendency of Shakespeare's mind for almost religious homage to the sacred person of a king, occurs in Act II. Scene 3, on the discovery of Duncan's murder :—

> Mac. Confusion now hath made his masterpiece !
> Most sacriligious murder hath broke ope
> *The Lord's anointed temple*, and stolen thence
> The life o' the building.

The next illustration comes in the incantation scene in the fourth act, and it may be taken as an evidence of the Catholic bitterness of our poet against the crucifiers of the Saviour. Among the most fell ingredients of the cauldron which the Third Witch contributes to the hell-broth is—

> Liver of blaspheming Jew.

Next to this comes the following ascription of supernatural and almost godlike powers to a kingly ancestor of James II., in being able, by a mere touch of his anointed hand, to cure the terrible disease known as the king's evil. In this homage, however, it must be admitted that our poet shared his superstition with the public ; but a mind like Shakespeare's might well have been superior to such blind belief.

Act IV. Scene 3.

*England.—A Room in the English King's Palace. Present—*MALCOLM *and* MACDUFF.

Enter a Doctor.

MAL. (*to Doctor*). Comes the king forth, I pray you?

DOCT. Ay, sir, there are a crew of wretched souls,
 That stay his cure: their malady convinces
 The great assay of art; but, at his touch,
 Such sanctity hath heaven given his hand,
 They presently amend.

MAL. I thank you, doctor.   [*Exit* DOCTOR.

MACD. What's the disease he means?

MAL.   'Tis call'd the evil:
 A most miraculous work in this good king:
 Which often, since my here-remain in England,
 I have seen him do. How he solicits heaven,
 Himself best knows: but strangely-visited people,
 All swoln and ulcerous, pitiful to the eye,
 The mere despair of surgery, he cures;
 Hanging a golden stamp about their necks,[2]
 Put on with holy prayers: and 'tis spoken,
 To the succeeding royalty he leaves
 The healing benediction. With this strange virtue,
 He hath a heavenly gift of prophecy;
 And sundry blessings hang about his throne,
 That speak him full of grace.[3]

It is said by Davenant that, in recognition of this fulsome compliment, King James sent Shakespeare a letter of acknow-

[2] The image was, doubtless, suggested to the poet's mind by the little customary Catholic medal, which he, in common with all true believers, doubtless wore about his neck.

[3] The superstition of touching for king's evil continued down to the time of George III., and Dr. Johnson tells us that he himself was touched for the evil by Queen Anne. He was quite a child at the time, but remembered her Majesty as being a solemn-looking lady wearing a black silk gown and diamonds. His mother, who carried him to London to be touched, had acted on the advice of the celebrated Sir John Floyn, a physician of Lichfield.— Boswell's "Life of Johnson," vol. i. p. 25.

In the *London Gazette*, No. 2180, appears this advertisement:—"White-hall, Oct. 8, 1683. His Majesty has graciously appointed to heal for the evil upon Frydays, and has commanded his physicians and chirugeans to attend at the office approved by the prayers in the Meuse, upon Thursdays, in the afternoon and to give out tickets." On March 30, 1712, Queen Anne touched 200 persons for evil. Dean Swift firmly believed in royalty's curing the evil by the imposition of hands.

ledgment in his own handwriting. Kenny closes his remarks upon "Macbeth" by saying that "some critics claim for it the distinction of being the poet's greatest work. We believe that judgments of this description can only be adopted with many qualifications. 'Macbeth' wants the subtle life which distinguishes some of the other dramatic conceptions of Shakespeare. Its action is plain, rapid, downright; and its larger form of expression seems now and then somewhat constrained and artificial. But it was evidently written in the very plenitude of the poet's powers, and in its wonderful scenic grandeur it must for ever occupy a foremost place among the creations of his majestic imagination."

The Baconians find in this tragedy some passages which, they think, are similar to those previously expressed by Sir Francis in his philosophical works, thus indicating a unity of authorship for both. The following is one of these assumed parallels, the first extract of which is taken from Bacon's " Essay on Building :"—

" He that builds a fair house upon an ill *seat* committeth himself to prison; nor do I reckon that an ill *seat* only, where the air is unwholesome, but likewise where it is unequal."

Now comes the assumed parallel in " Macbeth," Act I. Scene 6.

> His castle hath a pleasant *seat*—the air
> Nimbly and sweetly recommends itself
> Unto our gentle senses.

I cheerfully leave the force of this proof to the judgment of the reader, and also, with equal willingness, refer to the same judgment the following remarks of Lord Chief Justice Campbell upon the evidences to be found in " Macbeth" of

THE LEGAL ACQUIREMENTS OF SHAKESPEARE.

" In perusing this unrivalled tragedy," says his lordship, " I am so carried away by the intense interest which it excites that I fear I may have passed over legal phrases and allusions which I ought to have noticed; but the only passage I find with the *juridical* mark upon it in 'Macbeth' is in Act IV. Scene 1, where, the hero exulting in the assurance from the Weird Sisters that he can receive harm from ' none of woman born,' he, rather in a lawyer-like manner, resolves to provide an indemnity, if the worst should come to the worst,—

> But yet I'll make assurance double sure,
> And *take a bond of fate;*

—without much considering what should be the penalty of the bond, or how he was to enforce the remedy, if the condition should be broken.

He, immediately after, goes on in the same legal jargon to say,—

> Our high-placed Macbeth
> Shall live *the lease* of nature.

But, unluckily for Macbeth, the lease contained no covenants *for title* or *quiet enjoyment :*—there were likewise *forfeitures* to be incurred by the tenant— with a *clause of re-entry*—and consequently he was speedily *ousted.*" So much for Lord Campbell's observations on " Macbeth."

" CYMBELINE."

" This exquisite and romantic drama," says the Rev. William Harness, " was probably written in 1609; and the plot was taken in a great degree from the Decameron of Boccacio." According to Holinshed, whose English history is the source of much of Shakespeare's work, Cymbeline began his reign in the nineteenth year of that of Augustus Cæsar, and the play opens in the twenty-fourth year of that reign. Holinshed reports him to have reigned thirty-five years in all, leaving at his death two sons, Guiderius and Arviragus, upon whose fortunes a portion of the action turns. These sons were stolen from the king in their infancy, by an old knight named Belarius, in revenge for having been banished by the king on an unjust suspicion of his complicity with the Roman enemy. Belarius carried the boys to Wales, where, when they had grown strong enough, he lived with them in a cave, and trained them to hunting and other manly exercises. This deprivation left the king with an only daughter, Imogen, who then became heiress of his crown, it being believed that the stolen boys were dead. The king, after a long period of decorous sorrow, married a widow (a feeble copy of Lady Macbeth) who brought with her an only son, named Cloten, a coarse, drunken, vicious, depraved creature, inheriting nearly all possible vices from his scheming and unprincipled mother. The new queen aimed, naturally enough, at the hand of the crown princess for her son, but when she had obtained the king's consent to the match it was suddenly discovered that Imogen had been secretly married to a gentleman named Leonatus Posthumus. This leads to the banishment of Posthumus, and to the subsequent elopement of Imogen from the court to find him. This sketch of the story is sufficient to enable the reader to appreciate our illustrations. The first of these presents itself in Act III. Scene 3, where we find Belarius seated with Guiderius and Arviragus, now grown to men's estate, in front of a cave in a mountainous country in Wales. The old man has, to this moment, kept the young princes ignorant of their noble birth, having re-named them respectively Polydore and Cadwal; and he is now discoursing with them upon the incidents of the day's hunt, preliminary to despatching them again to the mountains to renew the chase. When they are gone, our poet embraces the opportunity for Belarius to inculcate upon the British mind the innate and instinctive royalty of kings:—

How hard it is, to hide the sparks of nature !
These boys know little, they are sons to the king ;
Nor Cymbeline dreams that they are alive.
They think they are mine : *and, though train'd up thus meanly*
I' the cave, wherein they bow, their thoughts do hit
The roofs of palaces ; and nature prompts them,
In simple and low things, to prince it, much
Beyond the trick of others. This Polydore—
The heir of Cymbeline and Britain, whom
The king his father called Guiderius,—Jove !
When on my three-foot stool I sit, and tell
The warlike feats I have done, his spirits fly out
Into my story : say,—Thus mine enemy fell ;
And thus I set my foot on his neck ; even then
The princely blood flows in his cheek, he sweats,
Strains his young nerves, and puts himself in posture
That acts my words. The younger brother, Cadwal,
(Once Arviragus), in as like a figure,
Strikes life into my speech, and shows much more
His own conceiving. Hark ! the game is roused !—
O Cymbeline ! heaven, and my conscience, knows,
Thou didst unjustly banish me : whereon,
At three, and two years old, I stole these babes ;
Thinking to bar thee of succession, as

Thou reft'st me of my lands.   Euriphile,
Thou wast their nurse; they took thee for their mother,
And every day do honour to her grave.   [*Exit.*

Act III. Scene 3.

Imogen next appears before the empty cave, disguised in boy's
clothes, travelling in search of the port of Milford Haven, where
the letter of Leonatus has informed her she will find him.

Perceiving the cave, she enters it; but no sooner has she
done so than Belarius and the two brothers return, and she is
discovered. A beautiful scene of spontaneous and instinctive
affection between Imogen and her brothers (though all unconscious of their kinship) then ensues, and she consents, for the
while, to remain under their protection, reporting herself to be a
page, and giving her name as Fidele.

She is pursued sharply by the ruffian Cloten, who traces her
to the neighbourhood. Unluckily for himself, however, Cloten
falls in with Guiderius, and, being insolent, a quarrel ensues, in
which Cloten is slain.

Enter GUIDERIUS *with* CLOTEN's *head.*

GUI.   This Cloten was a fool; an empty purse,
There was no money in't: not Hercules
Could have knock'd out his brains, for he had none:
Yet I not doing this, the fool had borne
My head, as I do his.

BEL.   What hast thou done?

GUI.   I am perfect, what: cut off one Cloten's head,
Son to the queen, after his own report;
Who call'd me traitor, mountaineer; and swore,
With his own single hand he'd take us in,
Displace our heads, where (thank the gods!) they grow,
And set them on Lud's town.

BEL.   We are all undone.

GUI.   Why, worthy father, what have we to lose,
But, that he swore to take our lives?   The law
Protects not us: Then why should we be tender,
To let an arrogant piece of flesh threat us;
Play judge, and executioner, all himself.

Act IV. Scene 2.

The young men then retire, whereupon Belarius again solilo-
quizes :—

BEL.   O thou goddess,
Thou divine Nature, how thyself thou blazon'st,

In these two princely boys! They are as gentle
As zephyrs, blowing below the violet,
Not wagging his sweet head: and yet as rough,
Their royal blood enchafed, as the rud'st wind,
That by the top doth take the mountain pine,
And make him stoop to the vale. 'Tis wonderful,
That an invisible instinct should frame them
To royalty unlearn'd; honour untaught;
Civility not seen from other: valour,
That wildly grows in them, but yields a crop
As if it had been sow'd! Yet still it's strange,
What Cloten's being here to us portends;
Or what his death will bring us.

Re-enter GUIDERIUS.

GUI.   Where's my brother?
I have sent Cloten's clotpol down the stream,
In embassy to his mother: his body's hostage
For its return.

While this has been going on, Imogen, being weary at heart,
has drank a potion perfidiously given to her by the queen, but
which, though meant by the latter to be a poison, turns out
to be only a powerful narcotic. Its real faculty was to produce
a trance, which simulated death, as in the case of Juliet. It
had this effect upon Imogen, who is found, a little while afterwards, by Arviragus, lying apparently dead upon the sward.

Re-enter ARVIRAGUS, bearing IMOGEN as dead.

BEL.   Look, here he comes,
And brings the dire occasion in his arms,
Of what we blame him for!

ARV.   The bird is dead,
That we have made so much on. I had rather
Have skipp'd from sixteen years of age to sixty,
To have turn'd my leaping time into a crutch,
Than have seen this.

GUI.   O sweetest, fairest lily!
My brother wears thee not one-half so well,
As when thou grew'st thyself.

*   *   *

ARV.   With fairest flowers,
Whilst summer lasts, and I live here, Fidele,
I'll sweeten thy sad grave: Thou shalt not lack
The flower, that's like thy face, pale primrose; nor
The azured hare-bell, like thy veins; no, nor
The leaf of Eglantine, whom not to slander,
Out-sweeten'd not thy breath: the ruddock would

> With charitable bill (O bill, sore-shaming
> Those rich-left heirs that let their fathers lie
> Without a monument !) bring thee all this ;
> Yea, and furr'd moss besides, when bowers are none,
> To winter-ground thy corse.

GUI. Pr'ythee have done :
> And do not play in wench-like words with that
> Which is so serious. Let us bury him,
> And not protract with admiration what
> Is now due debt. To the grave.

ARV. Say, where shall's lay him ?

GUI. *By good Euriphile, our mother.*

ARV. Be it so :
> And let us, Polydore, though now our voices
> Have got the mannish crack, sing him to the ground,
> As once our mother ; *use like note, and words,*
> *Save that Euriphile must be Fidele.*

GUI. Cadwal,
> I cannot sing : I'll weep, and word it with thee :
> For notes of sorrow, out of tune, are worse
> Than priests and fanes that lie.

Belarius, hereupon, seeing that the boys are about to bury Imogen on terms of equality with the beheaded prince, interposes, and volunteers honours to the dead man's rank, in the following servile manner :—

BEL. Great griefs, I see, medicine the less : for Cloten
> Is quite forgot. *He was a queen's son, boys :*
> And, though he came our enemy, remember,
> He was paid for that : *Though mean and mighty, rotting*
> *Together, have one dust ; yet reverence,*
> *(That angél of the world), doth make distinction*
> *Of place 'tween high and low. Our foe was princely ;*
> *And though you took his life, as being our foe,*
> *Yet bury him as a prince.*

These expressions of grovelling homage to mere rank, in the mouth of a worthy character like Belarius, invested, as that rank was, in the body of an utter beast and ruffian, as the speaker knew Cloten to be, show an extent of base cringing and moral abasement to mere worldly station, as contrasted with the respect due that "pale primrose and azured hare-bell, pure Fidele," which is absolutely painful. It is the very worst and lowest specimen of the abjectness of royal worship that has yet appeared to us in Shakespeare ; and so shocks our better sentiments, that we can hardly refrain from hoping, in excuse, that the poet was well paid for it.

Indeed, Guiderius protests against the old man's sentiments, by saying to his brother, as he points to the hulk of Cloten :—

> Pray you, fetch him hither.
> Thersites' body is as good as Ajax,
> When neither is alive.
>
> ARV.   If you'll go fetch him,
> We'll say our song the whilst—Brother, begin.
>   [*Exit* BELARIUS.
> GUI. Nay, Cadwal, we must lay his head to the east ;
> My father hath a reason for't.
> ARV.   'Tis true.
> GUI. Come on then, and remove him.

This discrimination in favour of the headless trunk of Cloten is all the more offensive, because the boys had thought Fidele to be good enough to lay beside their (supposed) mother, Euriphile.

The illustrations which follow bear likewise upon Shakespeare's favourite discrimination against a common person for a lord. The first of these occurs in a field of battle in Britain, where Leonatus, having come in with the Roman forces from Italy, changes his clothes in order to fight for his country :—

> Therefore, good heavens,
> Hear patiently my purpose ; I'll disrobe me
> Of these Italian weeds, and suit myself
> As does a Briton peasant: so I'll fight
> Against the part I come with ; so I'll die
> For thee, O Imogen, even for whom my life
> Is, every breath, a death : and thus, unknown,
> Pitied nor hated, to the face of peril
> Myself I'll dedicate. *Let me make men know*
> *More valour in me than my habits show.*
> Gods, put the strength o' the Leonati in me !
> To shame the guise o' the world, I will begin
> The fashion, less without, and more within.
>   *Act V. Scene* 1.

In the following scene he fights in the thick of the battle with Iachimo, an Italian knight, who has slandered Imogen. He disarms and leaves him, whereupon Iachimo says,—

> The heaviness and guilt within my bosom
> Takes off my manhood: I have belied a lady,
> The princess of this country, and the air on't

> Revengingly enfeebles me : *Or, could this carl,*
> *A very drudge of nature's, have subdued me,*
> *In my profession ?* Knighthoods and honours, borne
> As I wear mine, are titles but of scorn.
> If that thy gentry, Britain, go before
> This lout, as he exceeds our lord, the odds
> Is that we scarce are men, and you are gods.

Belarius, afterward, in relating the exploit of Leonatus before the court, thus extols the strange courage of the supposed peasant :—

> BEL.   I never saw
> Such noble fury in *so poor thing*,
> Such precious deeds in one that promised nought
> But beggary and poor looks.

The two following illustrations, though not of much force, are entitled to our notice. The first illustrates the religious point, and evinces a Catholic doctrinal abhorrence of suicide; the second bears, though vaguely, upon the question of relative social estimation :—

> IMO.   Against self-slaughter
> There is a prohibition so divine
> That cravens my weak hand.
>
>   *Act III. Scene 4.*

> *   *   *

> IMO.   Two beggars told me
> I could not miss my way : Will poor folks lie
> That have afflictions on them; knowing 't is
> A punishment or trial ? Yes; no wonder,
> When rich ones scarce tell true : To lapse in fulness
> Is sorer than to lie for need : and falsehood
> Is worse in kings than beggars.

Dr. Johnson, in speaking of this play, remarks that " it has many just sentiments, some natural dialogues, and some pleasing scenes;" but adds, " they are obtained at the expense of much incongruity. To remark the folly of the fiction, the absurdity of the conduct, the confusion of the names and manners of different times, and the impossibility of the events in any system of life, were to waste criticism upon unresisting imbecility, upon faults too evident for detection, and too gross for aggravation."

Dr. Drake protests against the enormous injustice of the above paragraph by the egotistical leviathan, declaring very correctly that "nearly every page of 'Cymbeline' will, to a reader of any taste or discrimination, bring the most decisive evidence." In connexion with this vindication, however, Drake is forced to admit "that 'Cymbeline' possesses many of the too common inattentions of Shakespeare; that it exhibits a frequent violation as to costume, and a singular confusion of nomenclature, cannot be denied; but these," says he, "are trifles light as air when contrasted with merits which are of the very essence of dramatic worth, rich and full in all that breathes of vigour, animation, and intellect."

These observations by both Johnson and Drake of the incongruities of the piece as to time, manners, and costumes, and, moreover, the fact mentioned by Harness, that the poet has peopled his Rome with *modern* Italians, must all be considered as decisive against the presumed authorship by Bacon, for Sir Francis had travelled in Italy, and knew better; while, on the other hand, they are just such errors as might easily have been fallen into by William Shakespeare, the untravelled London manager.

"ROMEO AND JULIET."

Knight, in presenting this tragedy, in his last edition of the plays of our poet, states that it was first printed in the year 1597. The second edition was printed in 1599, and the title to that edition declared it to be "newly corrected, augmented, and amended." "There can be no doubt whatever," he says, "that the corrections, augmentations, and emendations were those of the author." And he adds, that "we know nothing in literary history more curious or more instructive than the example of minute attention, as well as consummate skill, exhibited by Shakespeare in correcting, augmenting, and amending the first copy of this play." This view of Knight's is, however, in opposition to the general opinion that Shakespeare rarely and never carefully prepared any of his plays for print.

"The story of it," says Hunter, "appears in a history of Verona, comparatively modern, and certainly not written until after the tale had appeared in the romance writers. They now show at Verona a cistus which they call the tomb of Juliet." To this testimony of Hunter I can add, on my own part, that during a visit to Verona in 1870, I was shown the house in which tradition reported Juliet had lived, and the garden wall over which it was said Romeo had leaped. This pleasant illusion is a never-failing resource with the local guides for the shillings and sixpences of English and American travellers.

"No play of Shakespeare's," continues Hunter, "has been, from the first, more popular than this—perhaps none so popular. The interest of the story, the variety of the characters, the appeals to the hearts of all beholders, the abundance of what may be called episodical passages of singular beauty, such as Queen Mab, the Friar's husbandry, the starved Apothecary, and the gems of the purest poetry, which are scattered in rich abundance—these all concur to make it the delight of the many, as it is also a favourite study for the few. But so tragical a story ministers to a depraved appetite in the many. The mass of Englishmen love scenes of horror, whether in reality or in the mimic representations on the stage. Shakespeare seems to have understood this, and, both here and in Hamlet, he leaves scarcely any one alive. Even the insignificant Benvolio is not permitted to live out the story. It would be profanation, however, to believe that this has been a principal cause of the extreme popularity of ' Romeo and Juliet,' which began in the author's own time, and is continued in ours."

The evidences in this play which will most interest us are those bearing upon the fact that Shakespeare's mind was thoroughly imbued with the Roman Catholic faith. We find several indications of this in the great reverence with which he always speaks of Friar Laurence, and of the *holy* or mother church, through the mouths of Romeo, Paris, Juliet, and Lady Capulet. Also through the auxiliary facts which paint the friar, unlucky as he was, as the most elevated and estimable of the *dramatis personæ*.

The first evidence we get of this religious tendency is in the lines where Romeo decides to ask the friar to marry him to Juliet :—

> Hence will I to my ghostly friar's close cell,
> His help to crave and my dear hope to tell.

The friar, however, who knows Romeo to have been a desperate young rake, rebukes him with a reference to Rosaline, a nymph with whom he had been giddily enamoured :—

> Be plain, good son, and homely in thy drift,
> Riddling confession finds but riddling shrift.

Every indication in this and subsequent conversations of the various characters who come in contact with Friar Laurence, show that Shakespeare was fully impressed with the Roman Catholic idea that marriage was a sacrament, and not a mere civil contract. Romeo says to the Nurse in the second act,—

> Bid her devise some means to come to shrift
> This afternoon ;
> And there shall she at Friar Laurence' cell
> *Be shrived and married.*

In Scene 6 of the same act, when the marriage takes place, the friar says,—

> So smile the heavens upon *this holy act,*
> That after hours with sorrow chide us not.

To which Romeo answers,—

> Amen, amen !
> Do thou but *close our hands with holy words.*
> FRI.　Come, come with me, and we will make short work ;
> For, by your leaves, you shall not stay alone,
> Till *holy church* incorporate two in one.

In the next act the friar rebukes Romeo for his intention of committing suicide, by reminding him of the Catholic canon against self-slaughter :—

> I thought thy disposition better temper'd
> Hast thou slain Tybalt ? wilt thou slay thyself ?
> And slay the lady that in thy life lives,
> By doing *damned* hate upon thyself.

The friar, being relieved by the nuptial ceremony from his concern about leaving the imprudent young couple together, now seems rather to urge the *legal* consummation of the marriage :—

> Go, get thee to thy love, as was decreed,
> *Ascend her chamber hence, and comfort her.*

But the expression which has given rise to more controversy than any other on the subject of Shakespeare's religious faith occurs in Act IV. Scene 1, where Juliet, under the coercion of her mother, and after her secret marriage with Romeo, accompanics Paris to the friar's cell, as a preliminary to her new nuptials with that gentleman. The expression is,—

> JUL. Are you at leisure, holy father, now;
> Or shall I come to you at *evening mass?*
> FRI. My leisure serves me, pensive daughter, now:
> My lord, we must entreat the time alone.

Now, it is claimed, as we have already seen, that the use of the term " evening mass" shows Shakespeare to have been ignorant of the Catholic religion, and in support of this idea the German critic, H. Von Friesen, plausibly remarks " that no Catholic writer could have spoken of *evening mass*, inasmuch as mass is essentially a morning rite." Staunton had previously noticed the same difficulty,[4] but the word *mass* in this passage is explained by Clarke as meaning generally—service, office, or prayer. Grant White, adopting in full the English Protestant view, observes, " If Shakespeare became a member of the Church of Rome, it must have been after he wrote ' Romeo and Juliet,' in which he speaks of *evening mass ;* for the humblest member of that Church knows that there is no mass at vespers."

My conclusions run the other way, and are in favour of our poet's correctness in his use of the disputed phrase. But for the full discussion of this apparent incongruity I will refer the reader back to pages 43, 46, 47, 48, and 49, in the first division of this work, as a proper portion of this chapter. For further and authoritative information going to show that Shakespeare was correct in his use of the term " evening mass," I would advise the reader to consult Duras's " Universal History of the Church," at pp. 96, 104, 197, 277, 280, 540, and 627 of vol. i., and pp. 74, 271, and 283 of vol. ii. Also to see the " History of the Franciscans, and Lives of the Saints," published at Albany by Baxter and Co.; also " Lives of the English Martyrs," published by the Catholic Publication Society of New York; and Father O'Reilly's article on Mass in " Appleton's Encyclopedia."

The character of the Nurse in " Romeo and Juliet" is also essentially Catholic. Who but a Catholic, or, at the least, one accustomed to live amongst Catholics, could have drawn this extraordinary creation, which bears so much resemblance to the old

---

[4] See note in Dowden's " Shakespeare's Mind and Art," at page 39.

23

Irish nurses and servants of our own time, with their " God rest
her soul," " God give her peace," &c.   In the first act the
Nurse says, when describing the childhood of Juliet to her mother,
Lady Capulet,—

> Even and odd, of all days in the year,
> Come Lammas eve at night, shall she be fourteen;
> Susan and she—*God rest all Christian souls!*
> Were of an age.—Well, Susan is with God.
> She was too good for me.

How very Catholic all this is!   I cannot help believing that the
original of this character must have been some old Catholic
woman of Stratford, perhaps an aunt of the poet, or some
venerable crone who held to the old faith, and was the friend of
his youth.

A little further on the Nurse says,—

> And then my husband—God be with his soul!

exactly as our Bridgets and Norahs would speak of their dead
spouses to-day.

The ball-room scene contains many very Catholic allusions,
amongst the most striking of which are the following :—

> Rom.   If I profane with my unworthy hand
>   This holy shrine, the gentle fine is this,—
>   My lips, two blushing pilgrims ready stand
>   To smooth that rough touch with a tender kiss.
> Jul.   Good pilgrim, you do wrong your hand too much
>   Which mannerly devotion shows in this,
>   For saints have hands that pilgrims hands do touch[5]
>   And palm to palm is holy palmer's kiss.
> Rom.   Have not saints lips and holy palmers too?
> Jul.   Ay! pilgrim, *lips that they* must use in prayer.
> Rom.   O, then, dear saint, let lips do what hands do;
>   They pray, grant thou, lest faith turn to despair.
> Jul.   *Saints do not move, though grant for prayer's sake.*
> Rom.   Then move not, while my prayer's effect I take.
>   Thus from my lips, by yours, my sin is purged. [*He kisses her.*
> Jul.   Then have my lips the sin that they have took.

---

[5] An evident allusion to the sacred relics and to the wax figures covering the bones of saints, which are still kissed by the Catholic pilgrims,
who are now flocking by hundreds of thousands to Lourdes, to Paray-le-
Monial, and to other like religious places.

The last few lines are singularly Catholic, for all impurity of thoughts or looks even, are rigorously condemned by father confessors, on the principle that the mere desire of love, is as bad as the actual sin, unless it be consecrated in wedlock. Juliet's declaration in the balcony scene, is in full religious agreement with the rest :—

> Three words, dear Romeo, and good night, indeed.
> If that thy bent of love be honourable,
> Thy purpose marriage, send me word to-morrow,
> By one I will procure to come to thee,
> Where and what time thou wilt perform the rite.

Juliet evidently considers that despair and death are preferable to dishonour, and her subsequent noble speeches concerning her duties as " a true wife to her true lord," are singularly Catholic in tone, for, whatever may be the faults of the Romish Church, it must be cheerfully admitted that it has always upheld the sanctity of matrimony in the most uncompromising manner.

Romeo also is a thorough Catholic, and his evident confidence in his father confessor is expressed in the lines already quoted :—

> Hence will I to my ghostly father's cell,
> His help to crave, and my dear hap to tell.

Mark, also, that Father Laurence is well aware of the previous attachment which existed between Romeo and Rosaline, a fact from which we may conclude that young Romeo had been a very regular attendant at the worthy monk's confessional. But I might quote evidences of Shakespeare's intimacy with Catholic ideas, rites, ceremonies, and customs, from almost every scene in this play, which, as I have before said, is essentially Catholic from first to last. I will conclude this chapter with the following beautiful and noble speech of Friar Laurence, who, by the way, is the beau ideal of a Catholic priest, from the fifth scene of the fourth act :—

> Heaven and yourself
> Had part in this fair maid ; now heaven hath all,
> And all the better is it for the maid ;
> Your part in her you could not keep from death ;
> But heaven keeps his part in eternal life.
> The most you sought was—her promotion ;
> For 'twas your heaven, she should be advanced,
> And weep ye now seeing she is advanced
> Above the clouds, as high as heaven itself?

O, in this love, you love your child so ill,
That you run mad, seeing that she is well.

     *   *   *

Dry up your tears, and stick your rosemary
On this fair corse ; and, as the custom is,
In all her best array bear her to church.

SHAKESPEARE'S LEGAL ACQUIREMENTS.

The evidences which Lord Campbell finds in " Romeo and Juliet " of Shakespeare's legal acquirements, are neither numerous nor, as it seems to me, are they very weighty. His lordship, however, is evidently of a different opinion. Says his lordship,—

" The first scene of this romantic drama, may be studied by a student of the Inns of Court to acquire a knowledge of the law of ' assault and battery,' and what will amount to a *justification*. Although Samson exclaims, ' My naked weapon is out : quarrel, I will back thee ;' he adds, ' Let us take the law of our sides ; let them begin.' Then we learn that neither *frowning* nor *biting the thumb*, nor answering to a question, ' Do you bite your thumb at us, sir ?' ' I do bite my thumb, sir,' would be enough to support the plea of *se defendendo*.

" The scene ends with old Montagu and old Capulet being bound over, in the English fashion, *to keep the peace*,—in the same manner as two Warwickshire clowns, who had been fighting, might have been dealt with at Charlecote before Sir Thomas Lucy.

" The only other scene in this play I have marked to be noticed for the use of law terms, is that between Mercutio and Benvolio, in which they keenly dispute which of the two is the more quarrelsome ;—at last Benvolio—not denying that he had quarrelled with a man for coughing in the street, whereby he wakened Benvolio's dog, that lay asleep in the sun—or that he had quarrelled with another for tying his new shoes with an old riband, —contents himself with this *tu quoque* answer to Mercutio :—

An I were so apt to quarrel as thou art, any man should buy the *feesimple of my life* for an hour and a quarter.—*Act III. Scene 1.*

" Talking of the *fee-simple of a man's life*, and calculating how many hours' purchase it was worth, is certainly what might not unnaturally be expected from the clerk of a country attorney."

CHAPTER XXXIII.

"JULIUS CÆSAR."

THE tragedy of " Julius Cæsar" presents the first challenge to that portion of my theme, which declares we cannot find in all of Shakespeare's dramas one single aspiration in favour of human liberty; for the patriotic part of Brutus, with its splendid invocation of the Roman conspirators to "Peace, Freedom, and Liberty," seems to be in direct conflict with my theory.

" Julius Cæsar" belongs to what are known as the three Roman plays, the first of which is "Coriolanus," and the last, " Antony and Cleopatra." I have transposed the order of the two first, however, for greater convenience in the presentation of our case. None of these plays appeared in print until after Shakespeare's death (folio of 1623), but they are generally supposed to have been produced in 1607, 1608, 1609, though Furnival's Table credits the production of " Julius Cæsar" to a period as early as 1601-3. The strongest probability is, therefore, that it belongs to that period of our poet's powers, which began soon after the opening of the seventeenth century, and shared the supreme honours of his mind with "Macbeth," "Troilus," " Othello," " Lear," and " Hamlet."

Shakespeare is entirely indebted for the story of " Julius Cæsar" to a translation from Plutarch, made by Sir Thomas North in 1579, and so faithfully has he followed this historical outline, that in portions of the play our poet seems almost to have copied from North's text. It is observable, however, that he has moulded his characters somewhat differently from Plutarch's models, and most notably has done so in the case of Brutus, to whom he has imparted a transcendant loftiness of sentiment, which history has not entirely accorded to him.[1] In speaking of

---

[1] North says, " Cassius was a cholericke man, and hating Cæsar privately, he incensed Brutus against him. . . . . . The friends and countrimen of

this figure of the play, a commentator, whose name I cannot give because the volume from which I quote has lost its title-page, aptly says, that "Shakespeare doubtless intended to make Brutus his hero; he has therefore exalted his character and suppressed his defects. Public duty has been assigned, both by the poet and the historian as the motive of Brutus for joining in the conspiracy; but particulars are added by the former, which give an amiableness to his character that we should vainly look for in Plutarch. The obligations of Brutus to Cæsar are but slightly noticed; it would have defeated the dramatist's purpose of raising him in our esteem." "The great honours and favour Cæsar showed unto Brutus," says North, "kept him backe, that of himself alone he did not conspire nor consent to depose him of his kingdome. For Cæsar did not only save his life after the battle of Pharsalia, when Pompey fled, and did, at his request also, save many more of his friends besides; but furthermore, he put a marvellous confidence in him." Moreover, Cæsar had some reason to believe that Brutus was his son.[2]

Now, in order to ascertain what kind of a patriot Brutus was, I will refer, as briefly as possible, to what is received, on all

---

Brutus, both by divers procurements and sundrie rumours of the citie, and by many bills also, did openly call and *procure him to do that he did.* Now when Cassius felt his friends, and did stir them up against Cæsar, they all agreed, and promised to take part with him, so Brutus were the chiefe of their conspiracie. They told him, that so high an enterprise and attempt as that, did not so much require men of manhood and courage to draw their swords, as it stood them upon to have a man of such estimation as Brutus, to make every man boldly thinke, that by his onely presence the fact were holy and just. If he tooke not this course, then that they should go to it with fainter hearts; and when they had done it, they should be more fearfull, because every man would thinke that Brutus would not have refused to have made one with them, if the cause had been good and honest. Therefore Cassius, considering this matter with himselfe, did first of all speake to Brutus."

[2] Plutarch, in his "Life of Marcus Brutus," distinctly states that Cæsar "had good reason to believe Brutus to be his son, by Servillia." Suetonius, in his "Lives of the Twelve Cæsars," confirms this statement, and adds to the Shakespearian words of the dying Cæsar, thus: "And thou, too, oh, Brutus, *my son!*" According to Dio Cassius he cried out, "You, too, Brutus, my son?" If he did use the expression, it may have meant more than a mere term of affection, for scandal declared that Brutus *was* his son, the fruit of an *amour* between his mother Servillia and Cæsar.—Forsyth's "Cicero," p. 419; London, 1869.

sides, as reliable history about Cæsar and his times; and I pray it may be understood, at the beginning, that I do not mean to dispute, or in the slightest degree to undervalue the sincerity, and even loftiness of Brutus' *patriotism*, because his sympathies were not with the so-called common people; for undoubtedly a man may love his *country* equally under a belief in monarchy or oligarchy, with one who is a patriot according to the democratic ideal. But the observation which I make, from the " American point of view," is, that the character and sentiments of Brutus do not infringe my theory, or relieve William Shakespeare from the charge of never sympathizing with the working classes, or with general political liberty. In short, the text of this play will show that Brutus was as unbending an aristocrat as Coriolanus, and that the only liberty for which he bathed his arms in the blood of his best friend was, the liberty of retaining the government, falsely named a Republic, in the hands of the Patricians or slave-owners, simply because he did not wish the importance of the Patrician class should be reduced by the supreme authority of a king. Brutus, doubtless, believed that the oligarchical and slave-holding form of government was the best form for the welfare of his country, but William Shakespeare wrote under a later and more beneficent experience, and he should have sympathized with the bondage and sufferings of the poor. The detestation of Coriolanus for Rome's " woolen slaves" and "base mechanics" was not a whit softened, however, by Shakespeare, toward Jack Cade and his brave followers, of the fifteenth century. It is very strange, therefore, that our poet, while writing under the light of the seventeenth century, and of the liberty which was dawning upon his own times, could never find one impulse in his heart to celebrate the march of Mercy.

In the period of Coriolanus, whom he honours with the entire weight of his admiration, the following is described by a historian of authority as the political and social condition of the Republic of Rome: [3]—

" The history of Rome during this period is one of great interest. The Patricians and Plebeians formed two distinct orders in the State. After the banishment of the kings, the

[3] " History of Rome," by William Smith, LL.D. Harper and Brothers, New York, 1875.

Patricians retained exclusive possession of political power. The Plebeians, it is true, could vote at the general elections, but, as they were mostly poor, they were out-voted by the Patricians and their clients. The consuls and other magistrates were taken entirely from the Patricians, who also possessed the exclusive knowledge and administration of the law. In one word, the Patricians were a ruling and the Plebeians a subject class. But this was not all. The Patricians formed not only a separate *class*, but a separate *caste*, not marrying with the Plebeians, and worshiping the gods with different religious rites. If a Patrician man married a Plebeian wife, or a Patrician woman a Plebeian husband, the State refused to recognize the marriage, and the offspring was treated as illegitimate.

" The Plebeians had to complain not only of political, but also of private wrongs. The law of debtor and creditor was very severe at Rome. If the borrower did not pay the money by the time agreed upon, his person was seized by the creditor, and he was obliged to work as a slave. Nay, in certain cases he might even be put to death by the creditor; and if there were more than one, his body might be cut in pieces and divided among them. The whole weight of this oppressive law fell upon the Plebeians; and what rendered the case still harder was, that they were frequently compelled, through no fault of their own, to become borrowers. They were small landholders, living by cultivating the soil with their own hands; but as they had to serve in the army without pay, they had no means of engaging labourers in their absence. Hence, on their return home, they were left without the means of subsistence or of purchasing seed for the next crop, and consequently borrowing was their only resource.

" Another circumstance still farther aggravated the hardships of the Plebeians. The State possessed a large quantity of land called Ager Publicus, or the 'Public Land.' This land originally belonged to the kings, being set apart for their support; and it was constantly increased by conquest, as it was the practice, on the subjugation of a people, to deprive them of a certain portion of their land. This public land was let by the State subject to a rent; but as the Patricians possessed the political power, they divided the public land among themselves, and paid for it only a nominal rent. Thus the Plebeians, by whose blood and unpaid toil much of this land had been won, were excluded from all participation in it."

Reforms were made from time to time, but they did not confer upon the Plebeians any substantial liberties, for the condition of things in Rome, even three hundred years later than the time of Coriolanus, is thus described by the same author :—

" Among many other important consequences of these foreign wars, two exercised an especial influence upon the future fate of the Republic. The nobles became enormously rich, and the peasant proprietors almost entirely disappeared. The wealthy nobles now combined together to keep in their own families the public offices of the State, which afforded the means of making such enormous fortunes. Thus a new nobility was formed, resting on wealth, and composed alike of plebeian and patrician families. Every one whose ancestry had not held any of the curule magistracies was called a New Man, and was branded as an upstart. It became more and more difficult for a New Man to rise to office, and the nobles were thus almost an hereditary aristocracy in the exclusive possession of the government. The wealth they had acquired in foreign commands enabled them not only to incur a prodigious expense in the celebration of the public games in their ædileship, with the view of gaining the votes of the people at future elections, but also to spend large sums of money in the actual purchase of votes. The first law against bribery was passed in 181 before Christ, a sure proof of the growth of the practice."

Now, this was the condition of things which Brutus and Cassius and their co-conspirators combined together to sustain. They never once dreamt of enfranchising their bondsmen, or of enlarging the liberties of the People. Their rebellion against Cæsar was just such a selfish and aristocratic revolt as that which, in later days, took place among the English Barons against King John, which had not one patriotic motive in it. It resulted, long afterward, in advantages to the People, it is true, but it did not contemplate any, at the time.

Cæsar, with his large and liberal nature, his mighty courage, which disdained the mean calculations of conservativism, and his notoriously kind heart, which had been shown in his pardon and promotion of Brutus after the battle of Pharsalia, was really more disposed to popular reforms than any of his Patrician contemporaries. His broad hand had been stretched out frequently toward the poor; not only in largesses of corn, but in the extension of their privileges; and he kept continually making inroads upon the power of the Patricians, by way of bringing the People and himself nearer to each other. One of his measures to this end, was the frequent increasing of the number of Patrician families from the general mass of citizens; another was the selection of the two powerful officers, entitled Ædiles Cereales, which he instituted from the Plebeian class alone;[4] and a third was the introduction of an agrarian law for a division among citizens of the rich Campanian lands. It was this latter law which, more than any other measure, alarmed the Patrician party. The bitterest opposition was instituted against it. Nevertheless, both Pompey and Crassus, on the other hand, spoke in its favour, and twenty thousand citizens, including a large number of Pompey's veterans, were benefited and politically *"enabled"* by it. In addition to this, Cæsar instituted laws, during the periods of his several dictatorships, to relieve the hardships of debtors. In the same spirit he restored all exiles, and, next, conferred full citizenship upon the Transpadani, who had previously held qualified citizenship only, under the Latin franchise.[5] This man was so large, that smaller men, like Brutus and Cassius, and Cinna, and Casca, could not help being afraid of him; and their revolt, so far as the most of them were concerned, proceeded either from motives of personal hatred or political jealousy. Certainly, it was not inspired by apprehension of his personal tyranny, for Cæsar forgave in turn almost every man who had been his enemy. *He* feared nothing. As for Brutus, though a man of high courage and lofty principle, with a profound love of country, he was a sort of patriotic Don Quixote, whom the more crafty spirits in the plot against Cæsar's life, tricked and cajoled to the support of their less worthy purpose. With this analysis of the character of the "Freedom, Liberty, and Enfranchisement," which the conspirators invoked when they struck the foremost man of all the world, we will now proceed to examine extracts from the Shakespeare text. The play opens with a characteristic illustration of the author's estimation of mechanics, citizens, and tradesmen :—

[4] Niebuhr, page 626. James Walton, London, 1870.
[5] Wm. Smith's Smaller History, p. 243.

Act I. Scene 1.—*Rome. A Street.*

Enter FLAVIUS, MARULLUS, *and a rabble of Citizens.*

FLAV. Hence; home, you idle creatures, get you home;
 Is this a holiday? What! know you not,
 Being mechanical, you ought not walk,
 Upon a labouring day, *without the sign*
 Of your profession?—Speak, what trade art thou?
1 CIT. Why, sir, a carpenter.
 MAR. Where is thy leather apron, and thy rule?
 What dost thou with thy best apparel on?—
 You, sir; what trade are you?
2 CIT. Truly, sir, in respect of a fine workman, I am but, as you would say, a cobbler.

   *   *   *

 FLAV. But wherefore art not in thy shop to-day?
 Why dost thou lead these men about the streets?
2 CIT. Truly, sir, to wear out their shoes, to get myself into more work. But, indeed, sir, we make holiday, to see Cæsar, and to rejoice in his triumph.

   *   *   *

 FLAV. Go, go, good countrymen, and, for this fault,
 Assemble all the poor men of your sort;
 Draw them to Tyber banks, and weep your tears
 Into the channel, till the lowest stream
 Do kiss the most exalted shores of all. [*Exit Citizens.*
 [*To* MARULLUS.] See, *whe'r their basest metal be not moved;*
 They vanish tongue-tied in their guiltiness.
 Go you down that way towards the Capitol;
 This way will I: Disrobe the images,
 If you do find them deck'd with ceremonies.
 MAR. May we do so?
 You know, it is the feast of Lupercal.
 FLAV. It is no matter; let no images
 Be hung with Cæsar's trophies. I'll about,
 And drive away the vulgar from the streets;
 So do you too, where you perceive them thick.
 These growing feathers pluck'd from Cæsar's wing,
 Will make him fly an ordinary pitch;
 Who else would soar above the view of men,
 And keep us all in servile fearfulness. [*Exeunt.*

At the opening of the next scene, Cæsar appears crossing the stage in grand triumphal procession towards the capital, where the experiment of playfully offering him a crown is to be performed by Antony, with a view of testing the temper of the people. After Cæsar and his train go by, Brutus and Cassius remain. The artful Cassius then begins to work upon the mind of his susceptible brother-in-law, as follows :—

CAS. Brutus, I do observe you now of late ;
I have not from your eyes that gentleness,
And show of love, as I was wont to have :
You bear too stubborn and too strange a hand
Over your friend that loves you.

BRU.   Cassius,
Be not deceived : if I have veil'd my look,
I turn the trouble of my countenance
Merely upon myself. Vexed I am
Of late with passions of some difference,
Conceptions only proper to myself,
Which give some soil, perhaps, to my behaviours ;
But let not therefore my good friends be grieved,
(Among which number, Cassius, be you one,)
Nor construe any further my neglect,
Than that poor Brutus, with himself at war
Forgets the shows of love to other men.

CAS. Then, Brutus, I have much mistook your passion ;
By means whereof, this breast of mine hath buried
Thoughts of great value, worthy cogitations.
Tell me, good Brutus, can you see your face ?

BRU. No, Cassius ; for the eye sees not itself,
But by reflection, by some other things.

CAS. 'Tis just ;
And it is very much lamented, Brutus,
That you have no such mirrors, as will turn
Your hidden worthiness into your eye,
That you might see your shadow. I have heard,
Where many of the best respect in Rome,
(Except immortal Cæsar) speaking of Brutus,
And groaning underneath this age's yoke,
Have wish'd that noble Brutus had his eyes.

BRU. Into what dangers would you lead me, Cassius,
That you would have me seek into myself
For that which is not in me ?

　　　　*　　　　　*　　　　　*

                              [*Flourish and shout.*

BRU. What means this shouting ? I do fear, the people
Choose Cæsar for their king.

CAS.   Ay, do you fear it ?
Then, must I think you would not have it so.

BRU. I would not, Cassius ; yet I love him well.
But wherefore do you hold me here so long ?
What is it that you would impart to me ?

If it be aught toward the general good,
Set honour in one eye, and death i' the other,
And I will look on both indifferently;
For, let the gods so speed me, as I love
The name of honour more than I fear death.

       *

CAS. (*speaking of Cæsar*). Ye gods, it doth amaze me,
    A man of such a feeble temper should
    So get the start of the majestic world,
    And bear the palm alone.   [*Shout. Flourish.*

BRU.   Another general shout!
    I do believe that these applauses are
    For some new honours that are heap'd on Cæsar.

CAS. Why, man, he doth bestride the narrow world,
    Like a Colossus; and we petty men
    Walk under his huge legs, and peep about
    To find ourselves dishonourable graves.
    Men at some time are masters of their fates:
    The fault, dear Brutus, is not in our stars,
    But in ourselves, that we are underlings.
    Brutus, and Cæsar! what should be in that Cæsar?
    Why should that name be sounded more than yours?
    Write them together, yours is as fair a name;
    Sound them, it doth become the mouth as well;
    Weigh them, it is as heavy; conjure with them,
    Brutus will start a spirit as soon as Cæsar.
    Now, in the names of all the gods at once,
    Upon what meat doth this our Cæsar feed,
    That he is grown so great? Age, thou art shamed:
    Rome, thou hast lost the breed of noble bloods.
    When went there by an age, since the great flood,
    But it was famed with more than with one man?
    When could they say, till now, that talk'd of Rome,
    That her wide walls encompass'd but one man?
    Now is it Rome indeed, and room enough,
    When there is in it but one only man.
    O! you and I have heard our fathers say,
    There was a Brutus once, that would have brook'd
    Th' eternal devil to keep his state in Rome,
    As easily as a king.

BRU. That you do love me, I am nothing jealous;
    What you would work me to, I have some aim;
    How I have thought of this, and of these times,
    I shall recount hereafter: for this present,
    I would not, so with love I might entreat you,
    Be any farther moved. What you have said,
    I will consider: what you have to say,

I will with patience hear, and find a time
Both meet to hear, and answer, such high things.
Till then, my noble friend, chew upon this :
Brutus had rather be a villager,
Than to repute himself a son of Rome
Under such hard conditions, as this time
Is like to lay upon us.

Cas.   I am glad, that my weak words
Have struck but thus much show of fire from Brutus.

Bru. The games are done, and Cæsar is returning.

Re-enter Cæsar, *and his Train.*

Cas. As they pass by pluck Casca by the sleeve ;
And he will, after his sour fashion, tell you
What hath proceeded worthy note to-day.

Bru. I will do so :—But, look you, Cassius,
The angry spot doth glow on Cæsar's brow,
And all the rest look like a chidden train :
Calphurnia's cheek is pale ; and Cicero
Looks with such ferret and such fiery eyes,
As we have seen him in the Capitol,
Being cross'd in conference by some senators.

Cas. Casca will tell us what the matter is.

Cæs. Antonius.

Ant. Cæsar.

Cæs. Let me have men about me that are fat ;
Sleek-headed men, and such as sleep o' nights :
Yond' Cassius has a lean and hungry look ;
He thinks too much : such men are dangerous.

Ant. Fear him not, Cæsar, he's not dangerous ;
He is a noble Roman, and well given.

Cæs. 'Would he were fatter :—But I fear him not :
Yet if my name were liable to fear,
I do not know the man I should avoid
So soon as that spare Cassius. He reads much ;
He is a great observer, and he looks
Quite through the deeds of men : he loves no plays,
As thou dost, Antony ; he hears no music :
Seldom he smiles ; and smiles in such a sort,
As if he mock'd himself, and scorn'd his spirit
That could be moved to smile at anything.
Such men as he be never at heart's ease,
Whiles they behold a greater than themselves ;
And therefore are they very dangerous.
1 rather tell thee what is to be fear'd,
Than what I fear, for always I am Cæsar.
Come on my right hand, for this ear is deaf,
And tell me truly what thou think'st of him.

Exeunt CÆSAR *and his Train.* CASCA *stays behind.*

CASCA. You pull'd me by the cloak; Would you speak with me?

BRU. Ay, Casca; tell us what hath chanced to-day,
    That Cæsar looks so sad?

CASCA. Why you were with him, were you not?

BRU. I should not then ask Casca what hath chanced.

CASCA. Why, there was a crown offered him: and being offered him, he put it by with the back of his hand, thus; and then the people fell a' shouting.

BRU. What was the second noise for?

CASCA. Why, for that too.

CAS. They shouted thrice; What was the last cry for?

CASCA. Why, for that too.

BRU. Was the crown offer'd him thrice?

CASCA. Ah, marry, was't, and he put it by thrice, every time gentler than other; and at every putting by, mine honest neighbour shouted.

CAS. Who offer'd him the crown?

CASCA. Why, Antony.

BRU. Tell us the manner of it, gentle Casca.

Casca. I can as well be hanged, as tell the manner of it: it was mere foolery. I did not mark it. I saw Mark Antony offer him a crown;—yet 'twas not a crown neither, 'twas one of these coronets;—and, as I told you, he put it by once; but, for all that, to my thinking, he would fain have had it. Then he offered it to him again; then he put it by again: but, to my thinking, he was very loath to lay his fingers off it. And then he offered it the third time; he put it the third time by: *and still as he refused it, the rabblement hooted, and clapped their chapped hands, and threw up their sweaty night-caps, and uttered such a deal of stinking breath because Cæsar refused the crown, that it had almost choaked Cæsar; for he swooned, and fell down at it: and for mine own part, I durst not laugh, for fear of opening my lips, and receiving the bad air.*

CAS. But, soft, I pray you: What? Did Cæsar swoon?

CASCA. He fell down in the market-place, and foamed at mouth, and was speechless.

BRU. 'Tis very like: he hath the falling sickness.

CAS. No, Cæsar hath it not; but you, and I,
    And honest Casca, we have the falling sickness.

CASCA. I know not what you mean by that; but, I am sure, Cæsar fell down. *If the tag-rag people did not clap him, and hiss him, according as he pleased and displeased them, as they used to do the players in the theatre, I am no true man.*

BRU. What said he, when he came unto himself?

CASCA. Marry, before he fell down, when he perceived *the common herd* was glad he refused the crown, he plucked me ope his doublet, and offered them his throat to cut.—An I had been a man of any occupation, if I would not have taken him at a word, I would I might go to hell among the rogues:—and so he fell. When he came to himself again, he said, if he had done or said anything amiss, he desired their worships to think it was his infirmity.

Three or four wenches, where I stood, cried, " Alas, good soul !"—and
forgave him with all their hearts.

BRU. And after that he came thus sad away?

CAS. Ay. [*Exit.*

        ✳   ✳   ✳

BRU. For this time I will leave you:
   To-morrow, if you please to speak with me,
   I will come home to you; or, if you will,
   Come home to me, and I will wait for you.

CAS. I will do so:—till then, think of the world.

                            [*Exit* BRUTUS.

   Well, Brutus, thou art noble; yet, I see,
   Thy honourable mettle may be wrought
   From that it is disposed: *therefore, 't is meet*
   That noble minds keep ever with their likes;
   For who so firm that cannot be seduc'd?
   Cæsar doth bear me hard, but he loves Brutus:
   If I were Brutus now, and he were Cassius,
   He should not humour me. I will this night,
   In several hands, in at his windows throw,
   As if they came from several citizens,
   Writings, all tending to the great opinion
   That Rome holds of his name; wherein obscurely
   Cæsar's ambition shall be glanced at:
   And, after this, let Cæsar seat him sure,
   For we will shake him, or worse days endure. [*Exit.*

In all of this thrilling and impassioned dialogue it will be perceived that there is not one thought of popular liberty, the only motive of the conspirators being to protect the threatened equality of Brutus, Cassius, & Co., with Cæsar, and to maintain the ascendancy of the Roman nobility, over a king. I have given the dialogue above at such length, simply because the necessities of illustration would not permit me to curtail it. Besides, the splendour of the language and the vigour of its passion excuse all the space afforded to them. It may be objected that the sour, cynical Casca is alone responsible for the above expressions of contempt towards the people, but it must be observed, that he utters these derogatory sentiments in the presence of Brutus and Cassius without rebuke or protest on their part. They must, therefore, be held answerable for participating in them.

In the scene second of the second act, when several strange portents warn Cæsar not to go forth upon the 15th of March (the Ides of March) to the Senate House, where the conspirators, fixed in their fell purpose, are awaiting him, he is entreated by his wife Calphurnia not to venture out of doors :—

> CALPHURNIA. Cæsar, I never stood on ceremonies,
>   Yet now they fright me.   There is one within,
>   Besides the things that we have heard and seen,
>   Recounts most horrid sights seen by the watch.
>   A lioness hath whelped in the streets,
>   And graves have yawn'd, and yielded up their dead:
>   Fierce fiery warriors fight upon the clouds,
>   In ranks, and squadrons, and right form of war,
>   Which drizzled blood upon the Capitol:
>   The noise of battle hurtled in the air,
>   Horses did neigh, and dying men did groan;
>   And ghosts did shriek, and squeal about the streets.
>   O Cæsar! these things are beyond all use,
>   And I do fear them.
> CÆS.   What can be avoided,
>   Whose end is purposed by the mighty gods?
>   Yet Cæsar shall go forth: for these predictions
>   Are to the world in general, as to Cæsar.
> CAL. *When beggars die, there are no comets seen,*
>   *The heavens themselves blaze forth the death of princes.*
> CÆS. Cowards die many times before their deaths;
>   The valiant never taste of death but once.
>   Of all the wonders that I yet have heard,
>   It seems to me most strange that men should fear;
>   Seeing that death, a necessary end,
>   Will come, when it will come.

Nevertheless, Cæsar, in his sublime wilfulness, goes forth, and holds his levee in the Senate House. The conspirators make their opportunity to slay him, by pleading for the repeal of banishment against the brother of Metellus Cimber, one of their number. Metellus puts the first appeal. He is followed by Brutus and Cassius, who, considering their pretensions and the dark purpose which animates their hearts, address him in a not very worthy manner :—

> BRU. I kiss thy hand, but not in flattery, Cæsar;
>   Desiring thee, that Publius Cimber may
>   Have an immediate freedom of repeal.
> CÆS. What, Brutus!
> CAS.   Pardon, Cæsar: Cæsar, pardon;
>   As low as to thy foot doth Cassius fall,
>   To beg enfranchisement for Publius Cimber.

24

Cæs.   I could be well moved, if I were as you;
       If I could pray to move, prayers would move me:
       But I am constant as the northern star,
       Of whose true-fix'd and resting quality
       There is no fellow in the firmament.
       The skies are painted with unnumber'd sparks,
       They are all fire, and every one doth shine;
       But there's but one in all doth hold his place:
       So, in the world: 'Tis furnish'd well with men,
       And men are flesh and blood, and apprehensive
       Yet, in the number, I do know but one
       That unassailable holds on his rank.
       Unshaked of motion: and, that I am he,
       Let me a little show it, even in this;
       That I was constant, Cimber should be banish'd,
       And constant do remain to keep him so.

Cin.   O Cæsar,—

Cæs.   Hence! Wilt thou lift up Olympus?

Dec.   Great Cæsar,—

Cæs.   Doth not Brutus bootless kneel?

Casca. Speak, hands, for me.

       [Casca *stabs* Cæsar *in the neck.* Cæsar *catches hold of
       his arm: He is then stabbed by several other Con-
       spirators, and at last by* Marcus Brutus.

Cæs.   *Et tu, Brute?* Then fall, Cæsar.
              [*Dies. The senators and people retire in confusion.*

Cin.   *Liberty! Freedom! Tyranny is dead!*
       Run hence, proclaim, cry it about the streets.

Cas.   Some to the common pulpits, and cry out,
       Liberty, freedom, enfranchisement!

Bru.   People, and senators! be not affrighted;
       Fly not; stand still:—ambition's debt is paid.

Then follow the wonderful appeals made by Brutus and Mark
Antony to the people, in which the masses are represented by
our author to be base, ignorant, and changeful (accordingly as they
are swayed by the accents of the respective orators), and he
makes them wind up by tearing to pieces a harmless poet who
goes by, because he happens to bear the name of one of the
conspirators. It will be perceived by the last of the above
extracts, that it is Casca, the bitter contemner of the labouring
classes, and Cinna, and not Brutus or Cassius, who utter these
misleading cries for liberty, only to inflame and mislead the People.

Another poet is introduced in the Fourth Act, at the end of
the famous quarrel between Brutus and Cassius, who, though he

forces himself upon them with the worthy purpose of reconciling the angry conflict between the two kinsmen, is most contemptuously received, and ignominiously disposed of :—

> *Enter* POET.
>
> CAS. How now? What's the matter?
> POET. For shame, you generals; What do you mean?
>   Love, and be friends, as two such men should be:
>   For I have seen more years, I am sure, than ye.
> CAS. Ha, ha; how vilely doth this cynic rhyme!
> BRU. Get you hence, sirrah; saucy fellow, hence.
> CAS. Bear with him, Brutus; 'tis his fashion.
> BRU. I'll know his humour, when he knows his time:
>   What should the wars do with these jingling fools?
>   Companion, hence.
> CAS. Away, away, be gone.   [*Exit Poet.*

It is difficult to conceive what object Shakespeare has in snubbing this innocent mediator, except it be, as in Timon of Athens, to degrade the occupation of a poet. This might be natural in Bacon, but it seems very strange in Shakespeare; therefore, as far as it goes, it scores a point, light though it be, for the Baconians.

At the end of the fourth act, Mark Antony, taking advantage of the success which he has gained through his oration to the people, makes a political combination with Octavius Cæsar, a son of Cæsar's niece, whom he had made his heir, and with Lepidus, Cæsar's Master of Horse, these three declared themselves, in triplicate, the masters of the world. In the fifth act, Brutus and Cassius (according to the play) raise an army to confront the new triumvirs. The general conflict takes place at Philippi, where Brutus and Cassius, being defeated, commit suicide by falling upon their own swords. No Catholic scruple is here interposed by Shakespeare as to "the canon 'gainst self slaughter," so it might seem that our poet, after all his preference for Brutus, intends that rebellion, even for any form of liberty, shall be punished by endless torment in a future state. Lord Campbell finds no evidences in Julius Cæsar of the legal acquirements of Shakespeare.

" ANTONY AND CLEOPATRA."

This play contributes but little to our inquiry. It was probably written in immediate connexion with " Julius Cæsar " and " Coriolanus," and it carries the fortunes of Antony to their melancholy close. It consists of one long revel of luxury and passion with Cleopatra, that " serpent of old Nile," who, having been, in turn, the mistress of Pompey and of Cæsar, died for Antony.

The first phrase we find worthy of our attention occurs in Scene 2 of Act I. :—

ANTONY.   *Our slippery people*
(Whose love is never link'd to the deserver,
Till his deserts are past) begin to throw
Pompey the Great, and all his dignities,
Upon his son.

OCTAVIUS CÆSAR.   Let us grant, it is not
Amiss to tumble on the bed of Ptolemy,
To give a kingdom for a mirth : to sit
And keep the turn of tippling with a slave ;
To reel the streets at noon, and stand the buffet
With knaves that smell of sweat : say, this becomes him.
        *   *   *
             This common body
Like to a vagabond flag upon the stream,
Goes to, and back, and lackeying the varying tide,
To rot itself with motion.
                            Act I. Scene 2.

POMPEY.   What was it,
That moved pale Cassius to conspire? And what
Made the all-honour'd, honest, Roman Brutus,
With the arm'd rest, courteous of *beauteous freedom,*
To drench the Capitol, but that they would
Have one man but a man?
                            Act II. Scene 6.

This is only the same *beauteous freedom* of which we have heard Brutus and Cassius and Casca and Cinna discourse before. It simply means freedom for nobles from a king, and is no nearer true political freedom than the howl for liberty which Caliban set up in "The Tempest" was akin to an aspiration for popular enfranchisement. The liberty which the island monster sighed for was release from *durance*, such as might have been yearned for by a galley slave. I mention this latter illustration only, because it is one of the four instances in which Shakespeare permits the words " liberty " and " freedom " to slip from his pen. In Act IV. Scene 4, an officer in Antony's palace remarks to Antony :—

> *The morn is fair.*—Good morrow, General.

My remark upon this is, that the morn is always fair in Egypt. I am assured by Egyptians that it never rains above Cairo,[6] on the Nile, and so seldom at Alexandria—say six or seven times a year—that a fair sky is not a matter for remark. Bacon would not have fallen into this mistake.

> ENOBARBUS (*a follower of Antony, who has deserted him*).
> Let the world rank me in register
> A *master-leaver*, and a fugitive.
>
> *Act IV. Scene* 9.

*   *   *

> ANTONY (*to* CLEOPATRA).   Ah, thou spell ! Avaunt !
> CLEO.   Why is my lord enraged against his love ?
> ANT.   Vanish, or I shall give thee thy deserving,
> And blemish Cæsar's triumph. Let him take thee,
> *And hoist thee up to the shouting plebeians :*
> Follow his chariot, like the greatest spot
> Of all thy sex ; most monster-like, be shown
> For poor'st diminutives, for doits ; and let
> Patient Octavia plough thy visage up
> With her prepared nails.   [*Exit* CLEO.
>   'Tis well thou'rt gone.
>
> *Act IV. Scene* 10.

*   *   *

> CLEOPATRA.   Now, Iras, what think'st thou ?
> Thou, an Egyptian puppet, shall be shown
> In Rome, as well as I : *mechanic slaves*
> *With greasy aprons, rules, and hammers shall*
> *Uplift us to the view ; in their thick breaths*
> *Rank with gross diet, shall we be enclouded*
> *And forced to drink their vapour.*
>
> *Act V. Scene* 2.

And here falls the veil upon this astounding drama, leaving Cleopatra to be added to Cressida, as the only two completed female portraitures that Shakespeare ever drew. They were not portraitures from the cold and studied pen of Bacon, but such

---

[6] Old residents of Egypt will tell us that it never rains *at* Cairo, and so they told me when I was there, in the winter of 1870; but, unfortunately for the exactness of the statement, I was caught in a smart shower in Cairo, in March of that year, and was pretty well wet through. It lasted but a few minutes, it is true, but I was generally assured afterwards that such a thing had not happened for years before—the usual assurance in all countries of the " oldest inhabitant."

only as could have sprung from the singular experience of a man of Shakespeare's life and nature.

LEGAL EVIDENCES.

In searching this play for evidences of the legal acquirements of Shakespeare, Lord Campbell remarks :—

"In Julius Cæsar I could not find a single instance of a Roman being made to talk like an English lawyer; but in Antony and Cleopatra (Act I. Scene 4) Lepidus, in trying to palliate the bad qualities and misdeeds of Antony, uses the language of a conveyancer's chambers in Lincoln's Inn :—

> His faults, in him, seem as the spots of heaven,
> More fiery by night's blackness; *hereditary*
> Rather than *purchased.*

That is to say, they are taken by *descent*, not by *purchase.*"

Lay gents (viz., all except lawyers) understand by "purchase," buying for a sum of money, called the price; but lawyers consider that "purchase is opposed to *descent*—that all things come to the owner either by *descent* or *purchase*, and that whatever does not come through operation of law by *descent* is *purchased*, although it may be the free gift of a donor. Thus, if land be devised by will to A. in fee, he takes by *purchase*, or to B. for life, remainder to A. and his heirs, B., being a stranger to A., A. takes by *purchase*; but upon the death of A., his eldest son would take by *descent*.

English lawyers sometimes use these terms metaphorically, like Lepidus. Thus a law lord, who has suffered much from hereditary gout, although very temperate in his habits, says, "I take it by *descent*, not by *purchase*." Again, Lord Chancellor Eldon, a very bad shot, having insisted on going out quite alone to shoot, and boasted of the heavy bag of game which he had brought home, Lord Stowell, insinuating that he had filled it with game bought from a poacher, used to say, "My brother takes his game—not by *descent*, but by—*purchase* ;"—this being a pendant to another joke Lord Stowell was fond of: "My brother, the Chancellor, in vacation goes out with his gun to kill—time."

CHAPTER XXXIV.

"OTHELLO."

THE period of the authorship of this mighty production of our poet's genius, is set down with tolerable certainty at 1604— in close connexion with "Hamlet," "Julius Cæsar," "Macbeth," and "Lear." "Around the year 1600," says Dowden, "are grouped some of the most mirthful comedies that Shakespeare ever wrote. Then a little later, as soon as 'Hamlet' is completed, all changes. From 1604 to 1610 a show of tragic figures, like the kings who passed before Macbeth, filled the vision of Shakespeare. * * * Having created 'Othello,' surely the eye of the poet's mind would demand quietude, passive acceptance of some calm beauty, a period of restoration. But 'Othello' is pursued by 'Lear,' 'Lear' by 'Macbeth,' 'Macbeth' by 'Antony and Cleopatra,' and that by 'Coriolanus.' It is evident that now the *artist* was completely aroused."

The story of "Othello" was taken from the Italian of Giraldo Cinthio, but Shakespeare cannot be said to be indebted to its original author for more than a thin line of narrative, which any one of an hundred of the writers of his time, might easily have conceived without much effort. He created all the characters, infused all the passion, supplied all the imagery, and, to use the language of M. Guizot, imparted to the dramatis personæ "that creative breath, which breathing over the past, calls it again into being, and fills it with a present and imperishable life; this was the power which Shakespeare alone possessed, and by which, out of a forgotten novel, he has made 'Othello.'"

Though our poet names Othello as a Moor, he has not indicated the particular country of his birth; but he seems, by a casual allusion in the fourth act, to assign him to Mauritania, in Northern Africa :—

RODERIGO. Why then Othello and Desdemona return again to Venice?

IAGO. O, no; he goes into Mauritania, and taketh away with him the fair Desdemona; unless his abode be lingered here by some accident.

In that torrid region the fiery warrior acquired his boiling temperament and his fervid imagination; and, in its wars and the personal successes of those wars, he gradually acquired that barbaric ease of bearing and consciousness of power, which makes his character, in a dramatic view, so exceedingly alluring.

His military merits must have become familiar to the surrounding States, and having, probably, been greatly honoured by Venice for some victories, when possibly he had been acting as her ally, he seems to have taken the fancy to transplant his fortunes to Italy and become a Christian. This led to his appointment as a general in the Venetian army, and to the subsequent responsibility of the defence of Cyprus, against a threatened descent upon it by an armada of the Turks. Previous to receiving this command, Othello had been living in Venice; and, to judge from more than one allusion in the play, must have been, when the scene opens, well advanced in years—certainly twice, the most likely thrice, the age of the susceptible and gentle Desdemona.

This fact, along with his barbaric origin and dingy colour, lead up to the terrible catastrophe and bloody moral which the story levels against ill-assorted marriages. Such was Othello. Desdemona, on the other hand, was a scion of one of the highest, wealthiest, and most choicely-derived patrician families of Venice. Her father, Brabantio, was the most conspicuous of the Venetian senators, close in the counsel of the Duke, and, it would appear, from Roderigo's case, that he held Desdemona very jealously aloof from even the most eligible young nobles of·the time, so there should be no likelihood of her making a *mésalliance*, or of forming any attachment without his scrunity and patronage. This exceeding carefulness by Brabantio, against the young gallants of Venice, does not seem, however, to have taken the least alarm at the visits of the old, scarred, dusky Moorish general, who, according to the language of his own incomparable defence before the Senate, seems to have had the unrestricted run of Brabantio's house. This state of things resulted in one of those amorous episodes which fill the history of human passion, and which, though they come about naturally enough, and are often, as in this case, entirely honest, are but too apt to take an oblique turn from the latent wilfulness of the fresher nature, and to run to a troubled termination. I should judge, from what Othello twice says of himself, that he was somewhere in the neighbourhood of fifty-five, perhaps sixty years of age ; and it must be noted that Shakespeare, when he produced this play was himself forty, and Bacon forty-four. Men at these periods of life do not usually make themselves older than they really are, or regard fifty, or fifty-five, as " the vale of years." It may be said, moreover, so far as Othello is concerned, that he could not have been very handsome in his features, from the term " thick lips " which is applied to him by Roderigo in the first scene of the first act ; and, also, from the fact that Iago, in the latter part of the same scene, terms him " an *old* black ram."

> OTHELLO.   Haply, for I am *black*,
> And have not those soft parts of conversation
> That chamberers have : Or, for I am declined
> *Into the vale of years.*

As to Desdemona's age, it is reasonable to suppose from what we know of the customs of the Italians of the fifteenth century, that she was probably about fifteen. Juliet, it will be recollected, was married to Romeo and affianced to Paris, when not fourteen.

Here we have these contrasted yet agreeing natures of Othello and Desdemona, enjoying too much opportunity in Brabantio's house. He, barbaresque, tropical, phosphoric, and of grand masculinity of form ; she soft, imaginative, childlike, and susceptible —the opportunity came on some languid afternoon, and their expanding souls, guided by no guile and steered by no purpose, had magnetic contact, and blending suddenly, became the victims of each other. Desdemona, it is true, was a pattern of purity and she died innocent ; but it is doubtful if she could long have remained so ; for, under the incongruities of her case, and with such an unscrupulous tutoress as Emilia at her elbow,[1] her fate would probably have been a mere question of time. The love between her and Othello was merely an animal fascination, after all.

Iago, with his clear penetrating knowledge of the world, understood this state of things, and he also thoroughly knew the

---

[1] See the dialogue between Desdemona and Emilia at the end of the fourth act.

respective natures of Desdemona and Othello. In fact, no man of common penetration could fail to understand the amorous wilfulness of Desdemona, if only from her bold statement before the full gaze of the Senate, when she threw off the authority of her father, for that of her clandestinely-acquired dusky husband.

> Des. That I did love the Moor to live with him,
> My downright violence and scorn of fortunes
> May trumpet in the world: my heart's subdued
> Even to the very quality of my lord:
> I saw Othello's visage in his mind:
> And to his honours, and his valiant parts,
> Did I my soul and fortunes consecrate.

So that in view of this girlish wilfulness, Iago felt himself warranted in advising Roderigo (whose proposals for the hand of Desdemona had been rejected by Brabantio) to still pursue her, for her *love*, notwithstanding she had become a wife :—

> Iago (*to* Roderigo). It cannot be, that Desdemona should long continue her love to the Moor,—put money in thy purse ;—nor he his to her : it was a violent commencement, and thou shalt see an answerable sequestration ;—put but money in thy purse.—These Moors are changeable in their wills ;—fill thy purse with money ; the food that to him now is as luscious as locusts, shall be to him shortly as bitter as coloquintida. She must change for youth : when she is sated with his body, she will find the error of her choice.—She must have change, she must :—Therefore put money in thy purse.—If thou wilt needs damn thyself, do it a more delicate way than drowning. Make all the money thou canst : If sanctimony and a frail vow, betwixt an erring Barbarian and a supersubtle Venetian, be not too hard for my wits, and all the tribe of hell, thou shalt enjoy her; therefore, make money. Seek thou rather to be hanged in compassing thy joy, than to be drowned and go without her.

And again, in the same vein of philosophy, Iago says to Roderigo,—

> Iago. Lay thy finger—thus, and let thy soul be instructed. Mark me with what violence she first loved the Moor, but for bragging, and telling her fantastical lies : And will she love him still for prating? let not thy discreet heart think it. Her eye must be fed; and what delight shall she have to look on the devil? When the blood is made dull with the act of sport, there should be,—again to inflame it, and to give satiety a fresh appetite,—loveliness in favour; sympathy in years, manners and beauties ; all which the Moor is defective in : Now, for want of these required conveniences, her delicate tenderness will find itself abused, begin to heave the gorge, disrelish and abhor the Moor; very nature will instruct her in it, and compel her to some second choice.

* *

Rod. I cannot believe that in her; she is full of most blessed condition.

Iago. Blessed fig's end! the wine she drinks is made of grapes; if she had been blessed, she would never have loved the Moor.

It is quite true that the whole of this argument of Iago is intended to deceive and plunder Roderigo; but it is entirely consistent with the language of the ancient's soliloquies. Iago is the character most subtly and artistically drawn of any in the piece; though to Othello is imparted more imagination and loftiness of tone. Both, however, act in the main from the same impulse—jealousy. The difference, in the morale of their motive is, that one proceeds to his revenge from an honest and irresistable sense of wrong, which never contemplates extending its punishment beyond the wronger; while, the plots of the other are mixed with calculations of self-interest, and he conspires equally against the innocent and the guilty, whenever the destruction of the former is necessary to his plans.

In the first place, Iago, who is a soldier of intellect, much service, and recognized military capacity, has been defeated in his application for chief of staff under Othello, by " one Michael Cassio," a mere book soldier, who, to use Iago's own language—

> Never set squadron in the tented field,
> Nor the division of a battle knew
> More than a spinster.

We have thus, for Iago's first motive against Othello, a sense of injustice, and a consequent jealousy of Cassio. In his soliloquy at the end of the first act, we see his second motive to be sexual jealousy, pure and simple, against both Cassio and Othello :—

> I hate the Moor;
> And it is thought abroad, *that 'twixt my sheets*
> *He has done my office.* I know not if 't be true;
> But I, for mere suspicion in that kind,
> Will do, as if for surety.

And again, in Scene 1 of Act II. :—

> Iago. That Cassio loves her, I do well believe it;
> That she loves him, 'tis apt, and of great credit:
> The Moor—howbeit that I endure him not,—
> Is of a constant, loving, noble nature;
> And, I dare think, he'll prove to Desdemona

A most dear husband.　Now I do love her too:
Not out of absolute lust, (though, peradventure
I stand accountant for as great a sin,)
But partly led to diet my revenge
For that I do suspect the lusty Moor
Hath leap'd into my seat; the thought whereof
Doth, like a poisonous mineral, knaw my inwards;
And nothing can or shall content my soul,
Till I am even with him, wife for wife;
Or, failing so, yet that I put the Moor
At least into a jealousy so strong
That judgment cannot cure.　Which thing to do,—
If this poor trash of Venice, whom I thrash
For his quick hunting, stand the putting on,
I'll have our Michael Cassio on the hip;
Abuse him to the Moor in the rank garb,—
For I fear Cassio with my night-cap too.

Here we find an equal depth and intensity of motive on the part of Iago against Othello and also against Cassio, as Othello has, on his part, against Cassio and Desdemona.

It is not my province, under the limited task I have assumed, to trace the Moor's jealousy through all of its feverish passages, nor to compare it with the cooler, more stoical, but no less profound, jealousy of Iago; but I may notice here, that we have evidence, in Shakespeare's Sonnets, that our bard had reason to be versed in all the variations of that passion, under the capricious vagaries of a certain black-eyed Messalina, who toyed with the mighty Etna of his soul, without having any true comprehension of its fires, or of her own ignorant audacity, in dealing with them.[2]　I may be allowed to remark, moreover, that my opinion differs with those of all others I have seen, as to the real and immediate motive of Othello's murder of Desdemona. Coleridge has made the observation (which Dowden thinks so true, that he says all the critics have been obliged to repeat it),

---

[2] Except to his succumbing to the fascinations of a dark-eyed and dark-haired woman who excelled in music, and (as Mrs. Jameson delicately puts it) "was one of a class of females who do not always lose all their claim to the admiration of the sex who wronged them . . . . . one who was false, fickle, and *known to him to be a traitress*, even to the guilty love he entertained for her and she had feigned for him; one for whom he endured the pangs of agony, the pain of shame, the grief of self-reproach, and the terrible emotions of jealousy."—"Shakespeare's Character and Early Career," *British Quarterly Review* for July, 1875.

that " the passion of the Moor is not altogether jealousy, but rather the agony of being compelled to hate that which he supremely loved." This I admit to be very near the truth—indeed, quite true, as far as it goes; but it does not go quite far enough. The main misery of the Moor was, that his proud, sensitive, and selfish nature felt, not only that he had been wronged by Desdemona, but that his wrong *had become known to others*, and that he had been made—

> The fixed figure for the hand of Scorn
> To point his slow and moving finger at.

Had no one known of her offence, so that he could, in his mad love and furious tenderness have seized her in his arms, and, bidding a wild farewell to the observing world, have borne her away to some jungle in Mauritania, he might there have sobbed and throbbed away his still doting life, in cursing and pitying her crime. But Iago knew it, and Cassio (as he thought) also knew it, and the high-strung soul which, under the mediating influences of love, might still have been capable of compromise, but which knew nothing of stoicism or philosophy, slaughtered the wronger, for the wound which had been inflicted on his pride.

Without arguing this point further, I submit the following as arguing it for me :—

Act III. Scene 3.

IAGO (*alone*). The Moor already changes with my poison :—
>	Dangerous conceits are, in their natures, poisons,
>	Which, at the first, are scarce found to distaste;
>	But, with a little act upon the blood,
>	Burn like the mines of sulphur.—
>					*Enter* OTHELLO.
>	Look, where he comes! Not poppy, nor mandragora,
>	Nor all the drowsy syrups of the world,
>	Shall ever medicine thee to that sweet sleep
>	Which thou ow'dst yesterday.

OTH.					Ha! ha! false to me?
>	*To me?*

IAGO. Why, how now, general? no more of that.

OTH. Avaunt! be gone! thou hast set me on the rack :—
>	*I swear, 't is better to be much abused,*
>	*Than but to know 't a little.*

IAGO.					How now, my lord?

OTH. What sense had I of her stolen hours of lust?
    I saw it not, thought it not, it harm'd not me:
    I slept the next night well, was free and merry;
    I found not Cassio's kisses on her lips;
    He that is robb'd, not wanting what is stolen,
    Let him not know it, and he's not robb'd at all.

IAGO. I am sorry to hear this.

OTH. I had been happy, if the general camp,
    Pioneers and all, had tasted her sweet body,
    So I had nothing known: O now, for ever,
    Farewell the tranquil mind! farewell content!
    Farewell the plumed troop, and the big wars,
    That make ambition virtue! O, farewell!
    Farewell the neighing steed, and the shrill trump,
    The spirit-stirring drum, the ear-piercing fife,
    The royal banner; and all quality,
    Pride, pomp, and circumstance of glorious war!
    And O you mortal engines, whose rude throats
    The immortal Jove's dread clamours counterfeit,
    Farewell! Othello's occupation's gone!

Again, in Act IV. Scene 1 :—

IAGO. So they do nothing, 'tis a venial slip:
    But if I give my wife a handkerchief.—

OTH. What then?

IAGO. Why, then 'tis hers, my lord; and, being hers,
    She may, I think, bestow't on any man.

OTH. She is protectress of her honour too;
    May she give that?

IAGO. Her honour is an essence that's not seen;
    They have it very oft, that have it not:
    But, for the handkerchief,——

OTH. By heaven, *I would most gladly have forgot it :—*
    Thou said'st,—O, it comes o'er my memory,
    As doth the raven o'er the infected house,
    Boding to all : he had my handkerchief.

Again, in the same Act :—

OTH. I would have him nine years a killing :—
    A fine woman! a fair woman! a sweet woman!

IAGO. Nay, you must forget that.

OTH. Ay, let her rot, and perish, and be damned to-night; for she shall not live: No, my heart is turned to stone; I strike it, and it hurts my hand. O, the world hath not a sweeter creature: *she might lie by an emperor's side, and command him tasks.*

IAGO. Nay, that's not your way.

OTH. Hang her! I do but say what she is :—So delicate with her needle!

—An admirable musician! O, she will sing the savageness out of a bear!—
Of so high and plenteous wit and invention!

IAGO. She's the worse for all this.

OTH. O, a thousand, a thousand times:—*And then, of so gentle a condition!*

IAGO. Ay, too gentle.

OTH. Nay, that's certain: *But yet the pity of it, Iago!—O, Iago, the pity of it, Iago!*

IAGO. If you are so fond over her iniquity, give her patent to offend; for if it touch not you, it comes near nobody.

OTH. I will chop her into messes.—Cuckold *me!*

IAGO. O! 'tis foul in her.

OTH. *With mine officer!*

IAGO. That's fouler.

OTH. Get me some poison, Iago; this night:—I'll not expostulate with her, lest her body and beauty unprovide my mind again. This night, Iago.

IAGO. Do it not with poison, strangle her in her bed, even the bed she hath contaminated.

OTH. Good, good; the justice of it pleases; very good.

IAGO. And for Cassio, let me be his undertaker. You shall hear more by midnight.

The next thing which commands our attention in the tragedy of "Othello," is the Roman Catholic tone involuntarily emitted by our poet, in various portions of the text. The first of these instances occurs in a soliloquy by Iago, near the end of the second act:—

> And then for her
> To win the Moor—*were't to renounce his baptism,*
> *All seals and symbols of redeemed sin—*
> His soul is so enfetter'd to her love,
> That she may make, unmake, do what she list,
> Even as her appetite shall play the god
> With his weak function.

This is a declaration that, though the Moor had embraced Christianity, he would renounce his baptism and all the other sacraments, seals, and symbols of his faith, such as the cross, rosary, &c., if Desdemona should command him.

Baptism forgives original sin, according to Roman Catholic doctrine, and when administered to adults it is a seal of absolute redemption. Othello could not have been married to Desdemona in Venice without having been made a Christian and a Catholic. But for his having been *fast* married, Brabantio would have easily recovered his daughter; for the text shows that no consummation of the marriage had taken place at the time of Othello's arraignment before the Senate.

Again, in the third act (Scene 4), Othello in the simmering prologue of his jealousy, takes Desdemona's hand, and studying its palm, makes use of the following purely Catholic expressions:—

> This hand of yours requires
> *A sequester from liberty, fasting, and prayer,*
> *Much castigation, exercise devout;*
> For here's a young and sweating devil here,
> That commonly rebels.

Again,—

> That handkerchief——
> The worms were *hallowed* that did breed the silk.

In the last scene, the bidding of Desdemona to prepare for death by prayer and by confession, is very Catholic. Also the exclamation of Othello to Emilia:—

> You, mistress,
> That have the office opposite to St. Peter,
> And keep the gate of hell.

Othello's last speech is full of Catholic ideas, such, for instance, as the reference to Judas in the lines alluding to Christ:—

> Like the base Judean, threw a pearl away,
> Richer than all his tribe.

To conclude, it is not certain but that Shakespeare intended Othello should be a negro. In the sixteenth century, all the dark-skinned races were called Moors in England, which term was made more expressive by being familiarized into blackamoor. Curiously enough, the historical Othello was not a Moor at all. He was a white man who held the position of a Venetian general, and was named Mora, which Giraldo Cinthio, probably, for better effect, made into Moro, which in time became Moor or blackamoor.[a] The white Othello murdered his wife under much the same circumstances as Shakespeare's Othello killed Desdemona; but, in the first case, the floor of the murdered woman's room was made to sink away, and a beam to

---

[a] "The Stage in Italy," by R. Davey, in *Lippincott's Magazine* for January, 1875.

fall across her body, and then, for a still further concealment of
the crime, the house was set on fire.   It was Giraldo Cinthio,
who, finding this story to his hand, turned the white hero of this
terrific drama into a Moor; and Shakespeare, making a step
further into the morass with which the infatuated Desdemona
had complicated her unhappy fortunes, terms him, in portions of
his text, a black.   Hunter, however, interprets Shakespeare's
use of this descriptive word to mean no more than *very dark*,
and this only as in comparison with the fair European.   " The
word Moor," adds Hunter, " was used by English writers very
extensively, and all the dark races seem by some writers to be
comprehended under it,—Sir Thomas Elyot calling even the
Ethiopians, Moors.   A distinction was made, however, between
black Moors and white Moors." [4]

One thing is certain, that Shakespeare made his attractive
hero black enough to be a shocking and repulsive contrast to the
fair, confiding, and unsophisticated girl whom he unworthily
tempted from her filial duty and her Caucasian compatibilities.
The paternal confidence which he violated to obtain possession
of her is shown by the rage of his patron Brabantio, when he
exclaims,—

> O, thou foul thief, where hast thou stow'd my daughter?

While the full extent of the incongruity of the alliance, and of
Othello's breach of confidence, may be seen by the fact that
Brabantio charges, and cannot help believing, that the ruin of
his daughter must have been brought about by drugs, charms, or
sorcery.   Finally, when Desdemona confesses her infatuation, as
a thing of her own deliberate will, the unhappy father dies of a
broken heart,—not, however, without uttering the warning :—

> Look to her, Moor, if thou hast eyes to see:
> She has deceived her father, and may thee.

In every point of view this match of the lovely Desdemona
with the old black man, has been revolting to modern audiences,
and there is no sense in which it is more repulsive than the
violence which it inflicts upon the wholesome laws of breeding.
These laws are more strictly observed in England, perhaps, than

---

[4] Hunter's "Illustrations of the Life, Studies, and Writings of Shakespeare," vol. iv. pp. 280, 281.

anywhere else; but Shakespeare, in his abounding and unceasing love for royalty, probably thought he made ample atonement and offset to the prejudice against colour, by representing his black man as descending from a line of kings :—

> 'Tis yet to know,
> (Which when I know that boasting is an honour
> I shall promulgate), I fetch my life and being
> From men of royal siege; and my demerits
> May speak, unbonneted, to as proud a fortune
> As this that I have reached.

SHAKESPEARE'S LEGAL ACQUIREMENTS.

Lord Campbell finds the tragedy of "Othello" full of evidences that Shakespeare might either have been a lawyer, or have served as an attorney's clerk.

"In the very first scene of this play," says his lordship, "is a striking instance of Shakespeare's proneness to legal phraseology; where Iago, giving an explanation to Roderigo of the manner in which he had been disappointed in not obtaining the place of Othello's lieutenant, notwithstanding the solicitations in his favour of 'three great ones of the city,' says,—

> But he, as loving his own pride and purposes,
> Evades them with a bombast circumstance
> Horribly stuff'd with epithets of war,
> And, in conclusion,
> *Nonsuits* my mediators.

"*Nonsuiting* is known to the learned to be the most disreputable and mortifying mode of being beaten : it indicates that the action is wholly unfounded on the plaintiff's own showing, or that there is a fatal defect in the manner in which his case has been got up.

"In the next scene Shakespeare gives us very distinct proof that he was acquainted with Admiralty law, as well as with the procedure of Westminster Hall. Describing the feat of the Moor in carrying off Desdemona against her father's consent, which might either make or mar his fortune, according as the act might be sanctioned or nullified, Iago observes,—

> Faith, he to-night hath boarded a land carack :
> If it prove *lawful prize*, he's made for ever;

the trope indicating that there would be a suit in the High Court of Admiralty to determine the validity of the capture.

" Then follows, in Act I. Scene 3, the trial of Othello before the Senate, as if he had been indicted on Stat. 33 Henry VII., c. 8, for practising ' conjuration, witchcraft, enchantment, and sorcery, to provoke to unlawful love.' Brabantio, the prosecutor, says,— .

> She is abused, stol'n from me, and corrupted
> By spells and medicines bought of mountebanks;
> For nature so preposterously to err . . . . .
> Sans witchcraft could not.

" The presiding judge at first seems alarmingly to favour the prosecutor, saying,—

> DUKE. Whoe'er he be that in this foul proceeding
> Hath thus beguiled your daughter of herself,
> And you of her, the bloody book of law
> You shall yourself read, in the bitter letter,
> After your own sense.

" The Moor, although acting as his own counsel, makes a noble and skilful defence, directly meeting the statutable misdemeanour with which he is charged, and referring pointedly to the very words of the indictment and the Act or Parliament :—

> I will a round unvarnish'd tale deliver
> Of my whole course of love ; *what drugs, what charms,*
> *What conjuration, and what mighty magic*
> (For such proceedings I am charged withal)
> I won his daughter with.

" Having fully opened his case, showing that he had used no forbidden arts, and having explained the course which he had lawfully pursued, he says, in conclusion,—

> This only is the *witchcraft* I have used :
> Here comes the lady—let her witness it.

" He then examines the witness, and is honourably acquitted.

" Again, the application to Othello to forgive Cassio is made to assume the shape of a juridical proceeding. Thus Desdemona concludes her address to Cassio, assuring him of her zeal as his *solicitor*,—

> I'll intermingle everything he does
> With Cassio's *suit :* Therefore be merry, Cassio ;

> For thy *solicitor* shall rather die
> *Than give thy cause away.*   Act III. Scene 3.

"The subsequent part of the same scene shows that Shakespeare was well acquainted with all courts, low as well as high; where Iago asks,—

> Who has a breast so pure
> But some uncleanly apprehensions
> *Keep leets and law-days,* and in *session sit*
> With meditations lawful?"

Here terminates the evidences of Shakespeare's legal acquirements as detected by his lordship in "Othello." I do not hold them to be of any force in the sense his lordship indicates, but, while he was busied in his search, he might as well have added the following speech by Desdemona, in Act III. Scene 4:—

> Beshrew me much, Emilia,
> I was (unhandsome warrior as I am),
> *Arraigning* his unkindness with my soul;
> But now I find *I had suborn'd the witness,*
> *And he's indicted falsely.*

This was probably overlooked by his lordship.

CHAPTER XXXV.

" KING LEAR."

THERE is no play of Shakespeare's which has elicited more comment from the critics than the tragedy of " Lear," and among the Germans it is largely regarded as our poet's masterpiece. No one disputes that it is to be classed with the mightiest efforts of his brain, and to be ranked on an equal plane with Hamlet, Othello, Troilus, and Macbeth.

" The myth of King Lear and his three daughters," says Gervinius, " is related by Geoffrey of Monmouth, who places the death of this prince 800 years before Christ." From him it was copied by Holinshed, and a play on the subject appeared upon the English stage as early as 1594. The " Lear " of Shakespeare, however, could not have been written before 1603, because " in that year, there appeared a book in London, entitled ' Discovery of Popish Imposters,' out of which Shakespeare evidently borrowed the names of the different devils which Edgar mentions in his simulated madness." Several circumstances point to the probability that it was written in 1605-6, as it was produced at the Globe Theatre on December 26 of the latter year. Three quarto editions of it appeared soon afterward (1608), which is satisfactory evidence that it was highly popular.

A previous drama of " King Lier and his Three Daughters," had appeared about ten years before, but it was a very rude production, and furnished no aid to Shakespeare, beyond what he had obtained from Holinshed.[1]

[1] The story of Lear and his three daughters, as given by Holinshed, is narrated thus :—" Leir, the sonne of Baldud, was admitted ruler ouer the Britaines, in the yeare of the world 3105, at what time Ioas reigned in Iuda. This Leir was a prince of right noble demeanor, gouerning his land and subjects in great wealth. He made the towne of Cærleir, now called Leicester, which standeth vpon the riuer of Sore. It is written that he had by his wife three daughters without other issue, whose names were Gonorilla, Regan, and

The names of the three daughters of Lear, as given in Holinshed, were changed by Shakespeare into Goneril, Regan, and
Cordelia, and the sub-plot of Gloster, Edmund, and Edgar was
added by him, in order to intensify the original horror. In this
Shakespeare succeeds to an extent which out-Herods the bloody
and unnecessary mutilation of poor Lavinia, whose hands were
cut off and whose tongue cut out, by the sons of Tamora, merely,
as it would seem, because our poet had the power of inflicting
that capricious outrage.

In this play of "King Lear," Shakespeare takes the same advantage of the confidence of his audience, by perpetrating the
shocking barbarity of plucking out the good old Gloster's eyes,
as Victor Hugo does in his wanton and irreparable destruction of the mouth of his beautiful heroine. Some of the commentators complain of this outrage by Shakespeare, likewise of the
hanging of Cordelia at the end of the play, and ascribe both to the
still clinging barbarism of the Elizabethan period, from which the

Cordeilla, which daughters he greatly loued, especially Cordeilla the yoongest
farre aboue the two elder. When this Leir, therefore, was come to great
yeres and began to waxe vnwieldie through age, he thought to vnderstand the
affections of his daughters towards him, and preferre hir whome he best
loued, to the succession ouer the kingdome. Wherevpon he first asked Gonorilla the eldest, how well she loued him : who, calling hir gods to record, protested that she loued him more than hir owne life, which by right and
reason should be most deere vnto hir. With which answer the father being
well pleased, turned to the second, and demanded of hir how well she loued
him ; who answered (confirming her saiengs with great othes) that she loued
him more than toong expresse, and farre aboue all other creatures of the
world.

"Then called he is yoongest daughter Cordeilla before him and asked of
hir what account she made of him, vnto whome she made this answer as fol-
loweth : 'Knowing the great loue and fatherlie zeale that you haue alwaies
borne towards me (for the which I maie not answere you otherwise than I
thinke, and as my conscience leadeth me), I protest vnto you, that I haue
loued you euer, and will continuallie (while I liue) loue you as my naturall
father. And if you would more vnderstand of the loue that I beare you,
ascertaine your selfe, that so much as you haue so much you are woorth, and
so much I loue you, and no more.' The father being nothing content with
this answer, married his two eldest daughters, the one vnto Henninus, the
duke of Cornewall, and the other vnto Maglanus, the duke of Albania,
betwixt whome he willed and ordeined that his land should be diuided after
his death, and the one half thereof immediatlie should be assigned to them in
hand ; but for the third daughter Cordeilla he reserued nothing."

nature of Shakespeare does not appear, says one of them, to have been entirely free. Gervinius thinks, however, we should be wrong in calling that age barbarous in which the individual could attain to such perfection of culture as we admire in Shakespeare. I do not quite see the force of this argument, but the German professor remarks with more effect when, in speaking of earlier rude periods, he says,—

"Transported into such times, we delight in the historical record of these heroic forms, of this haughty colossal manhood, of these striving natures, of these demi-gods and Titans; we find the wanton growth of impulse and passion natural to these races; we are less shocked at the abundance of cruelty, because we feel ourselves involuntarily attracted by the greater strength which was able in those days to endure heavier burdens and sufferings. Nor are we even repelled and misled by the idea that this species of manhood was in itself a myth and a fable, too far from the human nature familiar to us ever to have had reality; we know, from the well-authenticated history of the Burgundian and Merovingian houses, that such times and such men *did exist;* that family horrors, as we read them in Lear, have abounded for centuries even among Christian races, and that the crimes of Tantalus in the old tragedy are not necessarily, and from their very nature, myths and fables." [2]

Nevertheless, let me repeat, it is not justifiable for an author to minister to a perverted public taste for the horrible, or to perpetrate, through his characters, terrible crimes in our presence, for the mere purpose of witnessing, as it were, the effects of their revolting force, upon our sentiments. I am disposed to forgive almost anything to Shakespeare; or, to speak more reasonably, to accept the boundless riches he has conferred upon mankind, as a thousand times outweighing the faults he has committed, but we can never entirely pardon that heartless exercise of his power, shown in cutting out Lavinia's tongue, in the plucking out of Gloster's eyes, and in the abhorrent *hanging* of the sweet and low-voiced Cordelia, that filial saint, who breathed out her life like a crushed lily, upon her volcanic father's bosom; simply because the author can hold us at his mercy, while transfixing us with horror. These are mere abuses of God-given strength. There

[2] Gervinius, p. 617, edition of New York, 1875.

was no need, in order to reach the susceptibilities of his audience, to hang that angel of gratitude and goodness, Cordelia. He might have allowed her, in accordance with the merciful sweetness of an old ballad which was built upon the play, to have perished upon the battle-field; or, better still (according to Tate and Coleman's revised edition of the tragedy), to have soothed the previous shocks of nature with a gleam of peaceful and consoling moral moonlight by the nuptials of Edgar and Cordelia. Nothing stood in the way of this denouement, for no stern history barred the road against it, while of horrors there had already been too many. Indeed, previous to Cordelia's death, we had "supp'd full of them."

The same charge of unnecessary cruelty and unnatural depth of wickedness is, I think, to be made against the secondary plot of Gloster, Edmund, and Edgar. Edmund, the illegitimate son, is made too wicked to be human, and this may be remarked of all of Shakespeare's representative villains; such, for instance, as Richard III., Iago, Aaron in "Titus Andronicus," and Edmund of the play before us. Men in a sound state of health, and in good case with the world, as all of the above men were, do not perpetrate deeds of cruelty through a mere relish for the deeds themselves; and they do not roll their most horrid acts over like sweet morsels for soliloquy, as a cow pleasurably and reflectively turns over her cud. There were political reasons for Cornwall to dispose of Gloster, and there were strong reasons, also, why Edmund should not possess a very high consideration for the father who had put the reproach of bastardy upon him, and who coarsely and carelessly stings him with that shame. But while these reasons might, in the first case, warrant Cornwall in passing sentence of death against Gloster, and in the second, induce Edmund to conspire toward it for the sake of Gloster's honours and estates, these merely material objects do not warrant the indifference of Edmund to the horrible manner in which it is proposed to torture his father, as a preliminary to his destruction :—

REGAN. Hang him instantly.

GONERIL. Pluck out his eyes.

CORNWALL. Leave him to my displeasure.—Edmund, keep our own sister company; the revenges we are bound to take upon your traitorous father are not fit for your beholding. *Act III. Scene 7.*

Human nature is not so wicked as this represents it to be, nor so bad as it is pictured by the bloody boastfulness of Aaron. Left to its impulses, unprompted by motives of revenge or profit, human nature is good, and always inclines to good, and it is a great libel upon humanity to represent it otherwise. It is always the impulse of a crowd to rescue a man whom accident has subjected to a sudden danger; nay, let a dramatist put villainy upon the stage, so that its aspect is plain to the spectator, there will never be found a person in the entire audience who will not execrate it, and sympathize with the innocent object of its malevolence. There is always some remnant of mercy left lingering in every human heart, and Edmund, with the great influence he possessed over the three heads of the government, Goneril, Regan, and Cornwall, would not have passed quietly out, in view of the terrific intimation given him by Cornwall, without asking that the father who had reared him, and who had recently adopted him in his heart in place of the slandered Edgar, might, at least, be spared his eyes. There is no good purpose served, as I have said before, by making any description of humanity too black.

We find in this play a very curious piece of evidence bearing upon the question of Shakespeare's religious faith. In fixing the date of the authorship of " King Lear," I stated that it could not have been written before 1603, because, in that year, there appeared a book in London by Dr. Harsnet, entitled " Discovery of Popish Impostors," out of which Shakespeare evidently borrowed the names of the different devils which Edgar mentions in his simulated madness. This shows that Shakespeare, like a thrifty playwright who had a good notion of business, did not scruple to avail himself of any current circumstances of great note or popularity to attract the attention of his audiences; and by thus turning local excitements into the text of his pieces, he made them talked about and increased their popularity. We find several instances of this among his plays, and the fact that he did not hesitate to engraft one of these accidental local excitements upon such a majestic production of his genius as " King Lear," will afford a strong notion how business-like he was.

The incident I allude to is treated at length by Hunter, and it doubtless exercised as great a spell upon the attention of the good people of London in 1603 as the Tichborne case did throughout the British Isles in 1873; or as the Beecher scandal did in the United

States in 1875. The case was one of alleged witchcraft, which took place in Lancashire in 1599, in the family of a gentleman of good name and means named Nicholas Starkey, or Starchy, residing at Cleworth, in Leigh. He had a son and a daughter, who, in 1595, being then respectively of the ages of nine and ten, were seized with fits of a novel and alarming character. The family physician could not master them, so Mr. Starchy had recourse to one Edmund Hartley, a reputed conjuror, who, by the use, as it was alleged, " of certain Popish charms and herbs," succeeded in making the fits disappear for about a year and a half. The fits having then returned, Mr. Starchy consulted Dr. John Dee, a regular physician, but who was as strong a Puritan as Hartley was a Catholic. A conflict of judgment was, of course, the result, and the worthy Dr. Dee advised Mr. Starchy to call in some godly Puritan preachers, with whom they might consult as to the advisability of purifying the atmosphere by a public or private fast. Preachers on both sides soon became recruits, but the fits, despite of these pious influences, having extended themselves to three young girls, wards of Mr. Starchy, also to the servants and even to Hartley himself, who had become an inmate of the house, the excitement of the neighbourhood and of the clergy of the whole country, became intense. A religious war of this description could not terminate, in that vigorous age, to any public profit without bloodshed; so, in due course of accusation and testification, Hartley, being convicted of witchcraft (though it seems he did not have the conscience to confess it), was honourably hung. This act of justice, with some refreshing barbarities attached to it, which the writers only allude to and decline to name, took place in 1597.

There being no newspapers at that time, the enjoyment of the circumstances was confined mostly to the clergy and to a very limited circle of the town and country people, who may be characterized as the neighbours of the Starchys. In 1603, however, Dr. Samuel Harsnet, who was successively Bishop of Chichester and Norwich, and Archbishop of York, having occasion to attack the Papists, issued a book bearing the following title :—

" *A declaration of egregious Popish Impostures to withdraw the hearts of His Majesty's subjects from their allegiance, and from the truth of the Christian Religion, under the pretence of casting out devils; practised by Edmunds, alias Weston, and divers Roman*

priests, his wicked associates. Whereunto are annexed the copies
of the confessions and examinations of the parties themselves, which
were pretended to be possessed and dispossessed; taken upon oath
before His Majesty's Commissioners for Causes Ecclesiastical."

The excitement which preceded the publication of this book,
by Harsnet, had reached London, however, a year or two before
(1601), and had been ventilated in the taverns, which, in the
absence of newspapers, were mediums for the spread of all information of a general or exciting character. The whole affair was,
doubtless, discussed at "The Mermaid," the celebrated inn to
which Ben Jonson, Shakespeare, Rowley, Ford, Massinger, Cotton, Webster, and Beaumont and Fletcher used to resort; and
to its discussion there, and to Shakespeare's familiarity with the
circumstances, may be attributed his ridicule of the Puritans in
the play of "Twelfth Night;" which latter play is supposed to
have been produced in 1601-2, when this excitement about the
Starchy witchcraft was rife. To this also may be attributed our
poet's artifice of charging the Puritan steward, Malvolio, with
being possessed by devils, in order to get him locked up. Likewise to this may be assigned his subsequent mockery of the whole
of Harsnet's statements through the introduction of the absurd
names of some of his devils, such as Smolken, Flibbertigibbet,
Moduc, and Mahu, in Edgar's no less Bedlamite ravings in
"King Lear." Thus we have another singular piece of proof
that Shakespeare invariably attacks, sneers at, derides, and dis-
counts Protestants and Puritans, and never fails to treat Catholics
and the Roman Catholic religion with absolute respect and
reverence.

There is another curious circumstance brought out by Hunter
in his investigation of this Starchy witchcraft, so far as Shakespeare's impressions of it have operated upon the scenes and the
text of "Twelfth Night." The line in Act II. Scene 5, which
utterly baffled all the commentators in their endeavours to convert it into sense,—

The lady of the *Strachy* married the yeoman of the wardrobe,—

comes out under this light clearly as a misprint of the word
Starchy, and the phrase doubtless refers to some incident then
thoroughly well understood, but which has now, like the incoherent local rant of Nym, become meaningless from the mists of

time. There is another expression in "Twelfth Night" which, under the light that Hunter throws upon the motive of Shakespeare's attack upon the Puritans through the medium of the Starchy witchcraft delusion, is well worthy of observation.

Hunter thus describes what took place in the Starchy family :—

"At the beginning of 1597 the affair became more serious, for not only did the fits return to the two children of Mr. Starchy, but three other young girls, wards of Mr. Starchy, and living in the family with him, the eldest of whom was fourteen, were seized in like manner; also Margaret Byron, of Salford, a poor kinswoman of Mr. Starchy, who had come to Cleworth to make merry, was seized in like manner; also Jane Ashton, a servant of the family ; and even Hartley himself did not escape the infection. Then follows a very remarkable account of the symptoms, unlike, I conceive, to anything with which medical practice is familiar, *shouting, dancing, singing, laughing, in a most violent and inordinate manner, throwing themselves into various postures, talking incoherent and ridiculous nonsense; all of which was attributed to Satanic agency.* At length it began to be suspected that Hartley had bewitched them ; the magistracy interfered, information against Hartley for the use of magical arts was laid before a neighbouring justice of the peace. He, in fact, who had been called in to relieve them was now suspected of being himself the person by whose means it was that they had suffered so much. The young girls, when brought before the magistrate, were speechless, and afterwards said that Hartley would not let them speak against him. This was considered sufficient evidence against Hartley, and, under the pressure of the Protestant clergy, he was, as we have seen, convicted and hung." A few days after his execution, some of the girls who had been "possessed" appeared before a convocation of *ministers*, when, to resume the language of Hunter, "several of them began to blaspheme, and, when the Bible was introduced, they shouted out in a scoffing manner, 'Bible-bable, Bible-bable,' continuing this cry for some time. This was accompanied by strange and supernatural whooping, so loud that the house and the ground shook again."[3]

This explains, and makes clear, the singular expression of the

---

[1] Hunter's "Life, Studies, and Writings of Shakespeare," vol. i. pp. 384—388. London, J. B. Nichols and Son.

Clown, in "Twelfth Night," to Malvolio, when the latter is in durance, under the suspicion of being possessed with evil spirits :—

> CLOWN. Advise you what you say; the *minister* is here. Malvolio, Malvolio, thy wits the heavens restore! Endeavour thyself to sleep, and leave thy vain *bibble-babble.*

Shakespeare was here evidently treating his audience with reference to the current excitement on the subject of the Strachy witchcraft, which then possessed the public mind; and the whole of which, under the lights of three subsequent centuries of experience, it is not difficult to understand. We can readily perceive that under the tremendous revolution of sentiment which had changed the religious belief of a whole nation, the youthful minds of the two Strachy children (probably under the lead of the more susceptible imagination of the girl) had been converted into a sort of religious ecstasy, which, according to the foregoing description of Hunter, would seem to have led them into such crazy transports or religious hysteria as animate the modern ranting Methodists, or as inspire the howling dervishes of India, at the present day. I have myself seen specimens of the latter religious frenzy in the East, while of the ranters every one has observed enough of instances both in England and America.

The Strachy girl was probably the first specimen of the Puritan cataleptic Pythoness ever known to English history; and the other females of the Strachy family, doubtless, fell into her hysteric raptures from magnetic sympathy. The bewildered father, not knowing what to make of these howlings, and having failed to control the vixenish exhibition, called in, as a dernier resort, a mild, quiet, obscure Catholic clergyman, of humble degree, who probably consented to be regarded as a conjuror, rather than be prosecuted as a nonconformist. He doubtless controlled the children by soothing advice and the decorous lessons of his faith, and thus secured a truce to the girl's devilment for eighteen months. Then, probably, through some unmanageable crisis of her nature, the wilfulness broke forth again, and the result of the relapse was, that the whole party were taken before a magistrate. Sectarian jealousy was thus aroused, and the poor, hard-working, well-intentioned priest was hanged. The other women, who were drawn into these cataleptic spasms, were purely the victims of magnetic sympathy, and all of them, doubtless, could have been cured in a moment by a bucket of cold water; or, like the frenzied performers of our modern camp meetings, been restored to their tranquillity by the quiet walking away of the audiences. The Starchy girl was the first ranter we have any knowledge of; and it is a pity that poor, inoffensive Mr. Hartley should have been hung for her disease. The report that he had himself been infected by it is clearly a sectarian fabrication.

So powerfully was the public mind agitated with the Starchy witchcraft that Harsnet published a second edition of his book in 1605, while Shakespeare was at work upon "King Lear;" and, in this latter edition, the Doctor added several new illustrations. "In one of these cases," says Hunter, "six persons were supposed to be possessed," one of whom Harsnet mentions as Mr. *Edmund* Peckham. "There were not fewer than twelve priests engaged, besides *Edmunds* the Jesuit;" "and not the least curious part of the transaction," continues Hunter, "is that the possessed had given names to the devils who infested them." The list is very remarkable, as compared with the names used in "King Lear" by Edgar in his personation of Poor Tom: *Smolken, Maho, Modu, Fratéretto, Flibertigibbet, Hoberdidance, Hoberdicut,* being adopted by Shakespeare from Harsnet's vocabulary of the fiends. By putting these names into the mouth of Edgar, when he was acting in the assumed character of a Bedlamite, "it was the intention of Shakespeare," adds Hunter, "to cast ridicule upon the entire affair of the Starchy family, and to teach the people who frequented his theatre, to view the whole with contempt. The means were nearly the same as those which he had employed in 'Twelfth Night' to produce a similar result." Hunter further remarks, "that it is worthy of attention that the name of *Edmund,* which originates in a different language and at a different period of time from those of Lear, Regan, Goneril, and Cordelia, is given by Shakespeare to one of his leading characters, apparently from Harsnet's publication. The following similitude, however, is still more striking. Harsnet says, in his relation about one of the "possessed" parties, "Master Maynie had a spice of the *Hysterica Passio,* as seems from his youth: he himself terms it *The Mother,* as you may see in his confession."[4]

And thus, Shakespeare, in Act II. Scene 4:—

[4] "Hunter," vol. xi. p. 270.

> LEAR. O, how this *mother* swells up toward my heart!
> *Hysterica Passio!* down thou climbing sorrow,
> Thy element's below.

Shakespeare seems to have been in a strong vein of plagiarism, or rather of self-plagiarism, throughout this play. We find him repeating himself in several paragraphs from King John, Othello, Julius Cæsar, and Macbeth. The first instance of this occurs in Act I. Scene 2, where Edmund, breathing the very soul of Faulconbridge, makes a remarkable duplication of that character, by a fresh reference to the very period of time, which Susanna, our poet's eldest daughter, occupied for her irregular début in the Shakespeare family, subsequent to the parent's nuptial knot. Shakespeare was married to Ann Hathaway in December, 1582, and Susanna came May 23, 1583, so, his first-born appeared just about fourteen weeks before its time. Robert Faulconbridge says, in "King John," when arguing against his bastard brother's right to his father's estate,—

> And I have heard my father speak himself
> When this same lusty gentleman was got.
> Upon his death-bed he by will bequeath'd
> His land to me; and took it on his oath
> That this, my *mother's son*, was none of his:
> And if he were, *he came into the world*
> *Full fourteen weeks before the course of time.*
>
> *Act I. Scene* 1.

Now, in "Lear," Edmund, the bastard son of Gloster, puts *his* case as follows:—

> *Enter* EDMUND, *with a letter.*
>
> EDM. Thou, nature, art my goddess; to *thy* law
> My services are bound: Wherefore should I
> Stand in the plague of custom; and permit
> The curiosity of nations to deprive me,
> *For that I am some twelve or fourteen moonshines*
> *Lag of a brother?* Why bastard? wherefore base?
> When my dimensions are as well compact,
> My mind as generous, and my shape as true,
> As honest madam's issue? Why brand they us
> With base? with baseness? bastardy? base, base?
> Who, in the lusty stealth of nature, take
> More composition and fierce quality,
> Than doth, within a dull, stale, tired bed,

> Go to the creating a whole tribe of fops,
> Got 'tween asleep and awake?—Well then,
> Legitimate Edgar, I must have your land:
> Our father's love is to the bastard Edmund,
> As to the legitimate: Fine word,—legitimate!
> Well, my legitimate, if this letter speed,
> And my invention thrive, Edmund the base
> Shall top the legitimate.   *Act I. Scene 2.*

Another plagiarism upon the Faulconbridge of "King John" appears in Act II. Scene 2, where Kent says to Cornwall,—

> Yes, sir; but anger hath a privilege.

It will be seen that this is a conspicuous imitation of Pembroke's reply to the Bastard, as they stand quarreling over the dead body of Arthur:—

> PEM. Sir, sir, impatience hath his privilege.
> BAST. 'Tis true; to hurt his master, no man else.

We next find Edmund repeating the trick which Cassius played on Brutus, by showing to Gloster a letter he had forged to the disparagement of Edgar, but which he represents had been "thrown in at the casement" of his chamber, as Cassius had contrived to have done to Brutus. In the same scene Edmund devises an interview between himself and Edgar, for the incredulous Gloster to overhear, in the course of which, by the artful discussion of a different topic, we have repeated to us the singular scene between Iago, Cassio, Bianca, and Othello.

Another instance occurs in Act III. Scene 7, where Gloster, in imitation of an expression by Macbeth, says,—

> I am tied to the stake, and I must stand the course.

The expression of Macbeth is,—

> They have tied me to a stake: I cannot fly,
> But, bear-like, I must fight the course.

Let me here mention, as it is an isolated case, in support of my views as to the probable high rank of Timon's steward, that in this play of "Lear," we find a steward writing letters under Goneril's dictation (but using his own form of expression); thus showing that, in acting in this way for one of the three heads of the then British Government, he, though a steward, was exercising the function of a privy counsellor.

The course of the play now brings me to the actual plucking out of Gloster's eyes, and as it presents an instance of true worthiness in a mere serving-man, it thus, to some extent, seems to run against the theory that Shakespeare never makes a hero of an humble person, or graces him with voluntary virtue. I will give the matter at sufficient length, to enable the situation to be well understood.

The scene is in the castle of Gloster, who is entertaining Regan and her husband the Duke of Cornwall, as his guests. During their stay, Edmund has taken the opportunity thus afforded to him, to betray to the Duke the fact that his father had received a letter from the invading forces, and had furnished to King Lear the means to escape to Dover, and put himself under their protection. Upon this, the following terrific scene ensues :—

Act III. Scene 7.—*A Room in Gloster's Castle.*
Enter the DUKE OF CORNWALL, REGAN, GONERIL, EDMUND, *and Servants.*

CORN. Post speedily to my lord your husband; show him this letter—the army of France is landed.—Seek out the villain Gloster.

REG. Hang him instantly.   [*Exeunt some of the Servants.*
GON. Pluck out his eyes.

CORN. Leave him to my displeasure.—Edmund, keep you our sister company; the revenges we are bound to take upon your traitorous father, are not fit for your beholding. . . . . .
Enter Steward.
How now? Where's the king?

STEW. My lord of Gloster hath convey'd him hence:
Some five or six and thirty of his knights,
Hot questrists after him, met him at gate;
Who, with some other of the lord's dependants,
Are gone with him towards Dover; where they boast
To have well-arm'd friends.

CORN.   Get horses for your mistress.
GON. Farewell, sweet lord, and sister.
                .   [*Exeunt* GONERIL *and* EDMUND.
CORN. Edmund, farewell.—(*To the Servants*) Go, seek the traitor Gloster,
Pinion him like a thief, bring him before us :
                [*Exeunt other Servants.*
Though well we may not pass upon his life
Without the form of justice; yet our power
Shall do a courtesy to our wrath, which men
May blame, but not control. Who's there? The traitor?
Re-enter Servants, with GLOSTER.
26

REG. Ingrateful fox! 'tis he.

CORN. Bind fast his corky arms.

GLO. What means your graces?—Good my friends, consider
You are my guests: do me no foul play, friends.

CORN. Bind him, I say.   *[Servants bind him.*

REG. Hard, hard:—O filthy traitor!

GLO. Unmerciful lady as you are, I am none.

CORN. To this chair bind him :—Villain, thou shalt find—
                  · *[REGAN plucks his beard.*

GLO. By the kind gods, 'tis most ignobly done,
To pluck me by the beard.

REG. So white, and such a traitor!

GLO.   Naughty lady,
These hairs, which thou dost ravish from my chin,
Will quicken, and accuse thee : I am your host ;
With robbers' hands, my hospitable favours
You should not ruffle thus.   What will you do?

CORN. Come, sir, what letters had you late from France?

REG. Be simple-answer'd, for we know the truth.

CORN. And what confederacy have you with the traitors
Late footed in the kingdom?

REG. To whose hands have you sent the lunatic king?   Speak.

GLO. I have a letter guessingly set down,
Which came from one that's of a neutral heart,
And not from one opposed.

CORN.   Cunning.

REG.   And false.

CORN. Where hast thou sent the king?

GLO.   To Dover.

REG.   Wherefore
To Dover? Wast thou not charged at thy peril—

CORN. Wherefore to Dover? Let him first answer that.

GLO. I am tied to the stake, and I must stand the course.

REG. Wherefore to Dover?

GLO. Because I would not see thy cruel nails
Pluck out his poor old eyes ; nor thy fierce sister
In his anointed flesh stick boarish fangs.
The sea, with such a storm as his bare head
In hell-black night endured, would have buoy'd up
And quench'd the stelled fires : yet, poor old heart,
He help the heavens to reign.
If wolves had at thy gate howl'd that stern time,
Thou should'st have said, Good porter, turn the key ;
All cruels else subscribed :—But I shall see
The winged vengeance overtake such children.

CORN. *See* it shalt thou never :—Fellows, hold the chair :—
Upon these eyes of thine I'll set my foot.

> [GLOSTER *is held down in his chair, while* CORNWALL
> *plucks out one of his eyes, and sets his foot on it.*

GLO.   He that will think to live till he be old,
      Give me some help :—O cruel! O ye gods!

REG.   One side will mock another ; the other too.

CORN. If you see vengeance,—

SERV.   *Hold your hand, my lord ;*
      I have served you ever since I was a child ;
      But better service have I never done you
      Than now to bid you hold.

REG.   How now, you dog ?

SERV. *If you did wear a beard upon your chin,*
      I'd shake it on this quarrel : What do you mean ?

CORN. My villain !   [*Draws, and runs at him.*

SERV. Nay, then come on, and take the chance of anger.

> [*Draws. They fight.* CORNWALL *is wounded.*

REG.   Give me *thy* sword.—   [*To another Servant.*
      A peasant stand up thus !

> [*Snatches a sword, comes behind, and stabs him.*

SERV. O, I am slain !—My lord, you have one eye left
      To see some mischief on him :—O !   [*Dies.*

CORN. Lest it see more, prevent it : Out, vile jelly !
      Where is thy lustre now ?

> [*Tears out* GLOSTER'S *other eye, and throws it on the ground.*

GLO.   All dark and comfortless.—Where's my Son, Edmund ?
      Edmund, enkindle all the sparks of nature,
      To quit this horrid act.

REG.   Out, treacherous villain !
      Thou call'st on him that hates thee : *it was he*
      That made the overture of thy treasons to us ;
      Who is too good to pity thee.

GLO.   O my follies !
      Then Edgar was abused.—
      Kind gods, forgive me that, and prosper him !

REG.   Go, thrust him out at gates, and let him smell
      His way to Dover.—How'st, my lord ? How look you ?

CORN. I have received a hurt :—Follow me, lady.
      Turn out that eyeless villain ;—*throw this slave*
      Upon the dunghill.—Regan, I bleed apace :
      Untimely comes this hurt : Give me your arm.

> [*Exit* CORNWALL, *led by* REGAN. *Servants unbind*
> GLOSTER, *and lead him out.*

1 SERV. *I'll never care what wickedness I do,*
      If this man come to good.

2 SERV.   If she live long,
      And, in the end, meet the old course of death,
      Women will all turn monsters.

> 1 SERV. Let's follow the old earl, and get the Bedlam
>   To lead him where he would; his roguish madness
>   Allows itself to anything.
> 2 SERV. *Go thou; I'll fetch some flax, and whites of eggs,*
>   *To apply to his bleeding face. Now, Heaven help him!*
>   *[Exeunt severally.*

Here is courage and worthy purpose, for the first time, accorded by our poet to a common man. I give it fully and for all that it is worth; but it must be observed that the incident is one of meagre bounds and momentary passion, and it is not amiss to notice, that the servant who rebels against his master in the interest of humanity, meets the immediate reward of death. It may also be observed that the humanity and kindness of the two other servants was the irrepressible instinct of retainers, who had been brought up and nurtured in the family of the injured Gloster. Moreover, their rude pity was necessary as a foil and setting to the wolfish cruelty of the main actors. So far as Shakespeare is concerned, therefore, it was the dramatic artist, not the man, who spoke through the protesting serfs.

There is but little left in this play which, at present, requires our attention; but, as Catholic symptoms of the religious complexion of our poet's mind are next in order, I wish to direct attention to the following expressions:—in Act III. Scene 2, the Fool says to Lear, while the latter is invoking the full fury of the tempest on the heath,—

O nuncle, *court holy-water* in a dry house is better than this rain-water out o' door.

Again, the Fool says, during the same storm,—

No *heretics* burn'd but wench's suitors.

A most substantial instance occurs, however, bearing upon this portion of our theme, in the lines describing how Cordelia received the news of the sufferings of the poor old king, her father:—

> There she shook
> The *holy water from her heavenly eyes*
> And clamour moisten'd, then away she started
> To deal with grief alone.

In connexion with this scene, let me not pass the expression of the gentleman, who, looking with agony and commiseration upon the sufferings of Lear, exclaims,—

A sight most pitiful in the meanest wretch ;
Past speaking of in a king !

Here we recognize, once more, the worshipful leaning of our poet for a king.

SHAKESPEARE'S LEGAL ACQUIREMENTS.

I have but one further task of observation left to my scope of duty, in connexion with this play, and that is to present the evidence which Lord Chief Justice Campbell finds to support the idea that our poet had either been a practising lawyer like Bacon or an attorney's clerk.

" In Act I. Scene 4, the Fool," says his lordship, " makes a lengthy rhyming speech, containing a great many trite but useful moral maxims, such as,—

Have more than thou showest,
Speak less than thou knowest, &c.

which the testy old king found rather flat and tiresome.

LEAR. This is nothing, fool.
FOOL. Then, 'tis *like the breath of an un-feed lawyer :* you gave me nothing for it.

" This seems to show that Shakespeare had frequently been present at trials in courts of justice, and now speaks from his own recollection. There is no trace of such a proverbial saying as ' like the breath of an unfeed lawyer,' while all the world knows the proverb, ' Whosoever is his own counsel has a fool for his client. . . . .'

" I confess that there is some foundation for the saying, that ' a lawyer's opinion which costs nothing is worth nothing;' but this can only apply to opinions given off-hand, in the course of common conversation,—where there is no time for deliberation, where there is a desire to say what will be agreeable, and where no responsibility is incurred.

" In Act II. Scene 1, there is a remarkable example of Shakespeare's use of technical legal phraseology. Edmund, the wicked illegitimate son of the Earl of Gloster, having succeeded in deluding his father into the belief that Edgar, the legitimate son, had attempted to commit parricide, and had been prevented from accomplishing the crime by Edmund's tender solicitude for the Earl's safety, the Earl is thus made to express a determination that he would disinherit Edgar (who was supposed to have fled from justice), and that he would leave all his possessions to Edmund :—

> Glo.   Strong and fasten'd villain !
>
> *   *   *
>
> All ports I'll bar ; the villain shall not 'scape.
>
> *   *   *
>
> Besides, his picture
> I will send far and near, that all the kingdom
> May have due note of him ;[*] and of my land,
> Loyal and natural boy, I'll work the means
> *To make thee capable.*

" In forensic discussions respecting legitimacy, the question is put, whether the individual whose *status* is to be determined is 'capable,' *i. e.*, capable of inheriting; but it is only a lawyer who would express the idea of legitimizing a natural son by simply saying,—

> I'll work the means to make him capable.

" Again, in Act III. Scene 5, we find Edmund trying to incense the Duke of Cornwall against his father for having taken part with Lear when so cruelly treated by Goneril and Regan. The two daughters had become the reigning sovereigns, to whom Edmund professed to owe allegiance. Cornwall, having created Edmund Earl of Gloster, says to him,—

> Seek out where thy father is, that he may be ready for our apprehension.

On which Edmund observes aside,—

> If I find him *comforting* the king, it will stuff his suspicion more fully.

" Upon this Dr. Johnson has the following note :—' He uses the word [comforting] in the juridical sense, for supporting, helping.'

" The indictment against an accessory after the fact, for treason, charges that the accessory ' comforted ' the principal traitor after knowledge of the treason.

" In Act III. Scene 6, the imaginary trial of the two unnatural

---

[*] One would suppose that photography, by which this mode of catching criminals is now practised, had been invented in the reign of " King Lear."

daughters is conducted in a manner showing a perfect familiarity with criminal procedure.

"Lear places the two Judges on the bench, viz., Mad Tom and the Fool. He properly addresses the former as 'the robed man of justice;' but, although both were 'of the commission,' I do not quite understand why the latter is called his 'yokefellow of equity,' unless this might be supposed to be a special commission, like that which sat on Mary, Queen of Scots, including Lord Chancellor Audley.

"Lear causes Goneril to be arraigned first, and then proceeds as a witness to give evidence against her, to prove an overt act of high treason :—

I here take my oath before this honourable assembly, she kicked the poor king, her father.

"But the trial could not be carried on with perfect regularity on account of Lear's madness, and, without waiting for a verdict, he himself sentences Regan to be anatomized.

Then, let them anatomize Regan; see what breeds about her heart."

All I have to remark in regard to the foregoing is, that, notwithstanding the great diligence which these extracts exhibit on the part of Lord Campbell in examining the text, his lordship has singularly enough overlooked, or, perhaps, I should rather say, intentionally left out, two of the most striking evidences of Shakespeare's knowledge of the administration of the law, as it then seemed to be practised in Great Britain, which his works afford. Both of these instances occur in the famous scene in Act IV. Scene 6, where the mad old king, fantastically dressed in flowers, holds a sort of court upon the heath :—

LEAR (*to Gloster*). Look with thine ears. See how yon' justice rails upon yon' simple thief. Hark, in thine ear. Change places; and, handy-dandy, which is the justice, which is the thief?

Again :—

Through tatter'd clothes small vices do appear;
Robes and furr'd gowns hide all. Plate sin with gold
And the strong lance of justice hurtless breaks;
Arm it in rags, a pigmy's straw will pierce it.
None does offend, none, I say none; I'll able 'em.
　　　　　　　　　　　　　　　　[*Offers money.*

Take *that* of me, my friend, *who have the power*
To seal the accuser's lips.

Surely Lord Campbell, who accepted his first legal instance in this play from the mouth of a fool, as to an "un-feed lawyer," might have given some attention to the above powerful lines, from the lips of a madman.

The illustration, however, does not reflect much credit upon the administration of justice, of which Lord Campbell had been such "a shining pillar," while it would be perfectly destructive to Lord Bacon, who had been degraded from the bench and sent to prison for taking bribes. Perhaps the former idea is the reason of his lordship's silence. Of one thing we may be certain, Bacon would never have written these latter allusions to judicial corruption; or, if he had done so in 1605, when "Lear" was composed, he would have expunged them in 1623, when the Shakespearian folio was revised and published.

CHAPTER XXXVI.

" HAMLET."

THE basis of the story of " Hamlet " is found in the Latin of the Danish historian, Saxo Grammaticus, who died about 1204, from whence it found its way, with some alterations, into Belleforest's collection of novels, which was begun in 1564, the year of our poet's birth.   From this receptacle Shakespeare doubtless took the narrative, and gave it the fashion it at present wears.

" ' Hamlet ' " was most probably written," says Kenny, " towards the end of 1601, or the commencement of 1602, and first acted in the spring or early summer of the latter year."   The first edition of the play was issued in the year 1603, under the following title :—

" The Tragical History of Hamlet, Prince of Denmark, by William Shakespeare, as it hath been divers times acted by His Highness' Servants in the City of London, also, in the two Universities of Cambridge and Oxford, and elsewhere.   At London, printed for N. L. and John Trundell, 1603."

" There is an entry of this play for publication," says Hunter, " on the books of the Stationers' Company, under date of July 26th, 1602."   From the title-page, as above, it seems to have been several times acted, and the testimony of Harvey, cited by Steevens, seems to be decisive of the existence of a play called " Hamlet," in 1598, and to the fact of that play having been written by the same hand which produced " Venus and Adonis," and the " Rape of Lucrece."

" During the first ten years of Shakespeare's dramatic career," says Dowden, " he wrote quickly, producing, if we suppose he commenced authorship at the age of twenty-six (1590), some eight or nine comedies, and the whole of the great series of English historical dramas, which, when Henry V. was written, Shakespeare probably looked upon as complete.   In this decade only a single tragedy appears, ' Romeo and Juliet.'   This play

is believed to have occupied our poet's attention for several
years, but dissatisfied, probably, with the first form which it assumed, he worked upon it again, rewriting and enlarging it.
But it is not unlikely that, even then, he considered his powers
to be insufficiently matured for the great dealing, as an artist,
with the human life and passion which *tragedy* demands. Then,
after an interval of about five years, a second tragedy, 'Hamlet,'
was produced. Over 'Hamlet,' as over 'Romeo and Juliet,'
it is supposed that Shakespeare laboured long and carefully.
Thus it came about that Shakespeare, at nearly forty years of
age, was the author of but two tragedies." [1]

"The exact mode of the preparation of this tragedy," says
Hunter, "will probably never be fully ascertained. Shakespeare
seems to have worked upon it in a manner different from his
usual practice. We discover not only that large additions were
made to the play after it had been presented at the theatres, but
that very material changes were made in the distribution of the
scenes and the order of events. This seems to show that there
was no period when the poet sat down to his work, having a
settled project in his mind, and meaning to work out the design
continuously from the opening to the catastrophe; and this may
be, after all, the true reason of the difficulty which has always
been felt, of determining what the character really is, in which
the poet meant to invest the hero of the piece. It may account
also for the introduction of the scenes which appear to have been
written for the sake of themselves alone; beautiful in themselves,
but neither necessary for the maintenance of a general harmony
in the whole, nor for the carrying on the business of the story.
To this want of continuity in the composition of the piece, is also
to be attributed the great falling off in the latter portions, and
the lame and impotent manner in which what ought to be the
grand catastrophe, is brought about. . . . Had the poet
proceeded continuously, according to what (from this opening)
may be concluded to have been his first design, and shown us the
young prince made acquainted with his father's death by the
supernatural visitation, and, at the same time, engaged to avenge
it on his uncle,—this, with such an underplot as is here wrought
in of his attachment to Ophelia, the effect of his *assumed* mad-

[1] Dowden's "Shakespeare's Mind and Art," pp. 95—98. King and Co.,
London, 1875.

ness upon her, the impediments arising out of this attachment, to the execution of the main purpose, would have formed the plot of as magnificent a tragedy as hath ever been conceived from the days when first the more awful passions were represented on the stage." [1]

The question whether Hamlet's madness was real or assumed, has elicited a greater amount of dispute among the commentators than any other problem in our poet's works, and upon this point the transcendental German Shakspearians have hung more illusory theories than upon all other disputed points of our poet's philosophy combined. Indeed, could the spirit of the Sweet Swan of Avon revisit the glimpses of our moon, and be asked to review and pass its judgment upon the multitudinous meanings of which the critics have accused his obscurer paragraphs, it would probably be glad to vanish back and submit with comparative satisfaction to a few weeks of fresh fires in supplementary purgation, rather than follow the toilsome task to its perplexing end.

Kenny in treating of the madness question, shrewdly says, " that the dramatist has sometimes run closely and even inextricably together the *feigned* madness and the *real mental perturbation* of Hamlet. We should have had no difficulty," he continues, " in accepting this representation of the character, if it were only consistently maintained. It would even, under the circumstances, have been perfectly natural; but we find that, in his real mood, Hamlet retains throughout the drama, as throughout the story, the perfect possession of his faculties; his only confidant, Horatio, must feel quite assured upon that point, and we are compelled, in spite of a few equivocal passages, entirely to share his conviction." This view of Kenny's is, in my opinion, the correct one, for had Shakespeare intended to represent Hamlet as being actually mad, the fact could not have been concealed from Horatio, who possessed his entire confidence, and on whom he depended till the last. There are several other reasons supporting this conclusion, but they have been so often given it is not necessary I should repeat them.

The truth is, as Dowden states it, that " Shakespeare created Hamlet a mystery, and, therefore, it is for ever suggestive and

[1] " Hunter," vol. ii. p. 206.

never wholly explicable." I should rather put it that Shakespeare conceived his idea of the character of Hamlet in a mystified and confused sort of mood; that he worked upon it for a long while without re-shaping his initial errors, and that, while enriching it with casual beauties, he kept on loading it with new errors and fresh contradictions. Every writer accustomed to much composition, knows that if one does not start with a clear and definite conception, it is almost impossible to become clear afterward, even by the most laborious efforts of subsequent pruning or development. "Now, it is a remarkable circumstance," says Dowden, "that, while the length of the play, in the second quarto, considerably exceeds its length in the earlier form of 1603, and thus materials for the interpretation of Shakespeare's purpose in the play are offered in greater abundance, the obscurity does not diminish, but, on the contrary, deepens, and, if some questions appear to be solved, other questions in greater number spring into existence." It is not likely, therefore, that this mystery, contradiction, and uncertainty in Hamlet's character could have proceeded from the mind of Sir Francis Bacon, who was always clear, congruous, explicit and unmistakeable in his meaning, as the prince of logicians and demonstrators was sure to be.

But it is this dreamy confusion, this romantic uncertainty of mood, which gives to the German critics their vast opportunities for speculation and display. Some of them have told us that they cannot account for the wonderful charm of this play above all the others of our author, but it seems to me that the secret of the great interest which the kind-hearted general public take in the character of Hamlet, lies in the wrongs which he suffered, and the filial gentleness and religious subordination he exhibits in receiving the command and exhortations of his father's ghost. He is the disinherited prince of the fairy tale, whom we love because he has been betrayed, and in whom our interest increases as misfortune falls upon him. There is no witchcraft and no wonder in all this, as human nature when unbiassed by self-interest is inherently and invariably good. The preference which the German *critics* show for Hamlet is probably due to the mystery which our poet has allowed to dwell with the character, after all his endeavours to lift himself out of the contradictions of his first sketch. But, as the Germans claim, and, as Mezieres and other French critics admit, Hamlet represents the German national mind, and Elze declares that Freiligrath, one of the German commentators, was right in exclaiming, " Germany is Hamlet ! "[3]

The German commentators, as a rule, do not favour, or, I might rather say, will not tolerate the idea of Shakespeare being a Roman Catholic, and even honest and straightforward Gervinius is willing to contribute a gentle little artifice to mislead us on this point. In analyzing the character of the melancholy prince, he remarks, " He is essentially a man of letters; he carries memorandum books with him ; allusions to his reading are ready to him ; in advanced years he was still at the university, and longs to return there; not like Laertes, to Paris, *but at Wittenberg, a name honoured by the Protestant hearts of England.*" [4]

The obvious object of this latter expression is to suggest that Wittenberg, during Hamlet's period, was a Protestant seat of learning, and that he consequently was a Protestant. But this pleasant little artifice cannot prevail, as the Danish historian, who first wrote the story of Hamlet, died in 1204. The theory of the inuendo also meets with an equally potent difficulty in the fact that, if the Prince had been educated in a Protestant academy, its religious formula vanished with a singular rapidity, while his mind, at the same time, became imbued with the Catholic ritual with a suddenness akin to magic.

The whole of the first act is filled with Roman Catholic doctrine, imagery, and reference. The theory of purgatory and exorcism are conspicuously declared upon the entrance into the first scene of the unsettled Ghost, by the exclamation of Marcellus :—

Thou art a *scholar*, speak to it, Horatio !

But the Ghost will not be spoken to, and vanishes with all the dignity of, sepulchral reserve. It soon re-enters, apparently in search of Hamlet, but it again refuses to reply to the question of Horatio, and disappears at the crowing of the cock. Thereupon Horatio and Marcellus give the following exposition of the Catholic theory of purgatory :—

" Elze," page 246. London, McMillan and Co., 1874.
[4] Gervinius on "Shakespeare," p. 567. Scribner and Co., New York.

MAR.   'Tis gone!
We do it wrong, being so majestical,
To offer it the show of violence;
For it is, as the air, invulnerable,
And our vain blows malicious mockery.

BER.   It was about to speak, when the cock crew.

HOR.   And then it started like a guilty thing
Upon a fearful summons. I have heard
The cock, that is the trumpet to the morn,
Doth with his lofty and shrill-sounding throat
Awake the god of day; and, at his warning,
Whether in sea or fire, in earth or air,
The extravagant and erring spirit hies
To his confine: and of the truth herein
This present object made probation.

MAR.   It faded on the crowing of the cock.
Some say, that ever 'gainst that season comes
Wherein our Saviour's birth is celebrated,
The bird of dawning singeth all night long:
And then, they say, no spirit can walk abroad;
The nights are wholesome; then no planets strike,
No fairy takes, nor witch hath power to charm,
So hallow'd and so gracious is the time.

HOR.   So have I heard, and do in part believe it.
But, look, the morn, in russet mantle clad,
Walks o'er the dew of yon high eastern hill:
Break we our watch up; and, by my advice,
Let us impart what we have seen to-night
Unto young Hamlet: for, upon my life,
This spirit, dumb to us, will speak to him.

The above scene is intricately Catholic, from first to last. In the second scene of the same Act, Hamlet says,—

O, that this too, too solid flesh would melt,
Thaw, and resolve itself into a dew!
Or that the Everlasting had not fix'd
His canon 'gainst self-slaughter!

Catholics, as we have said before, do not extend the funeral rites of the church to suicides, nor permit them to be buried in consecrated ground. Protestants, on the other hand, do not trouble themselves much about the matter. At the end of this soliloquy Hamlet expresses another Catholic dogma, in the imputation of incest for marriage with a deceased brother's wife:—

> Within a month;
> Ere yet the salt of most unrighteous tears
> Had left the flushing of her galled eyes,
> She married. O most wicked speed to pos
> With such dexterity *to incestuous sheets;*
> It is not, nor it cannot come to, good.

Again, we find this thoroughly Catholic doctrine enunciated repeatedly in the scenes between Hamlet and the Ghost.

Enter GHOST.

HOR.   Look my lord, it comes !

HAM.   *Angels and ministers of grace defend us !*[5]
Be thou a spirit of health or goblin damn'd,
Bring with thee airs from heaven or blasts from hell,
Be thy intents wicked or charitable,
Thou com'st in such a questionable shape,
That I will speak to thee; I'll call thee Hamlet,
King, father, royal Dane: O, answer me:
Let me not burst in ignorance ! but tell,
Why thy canonized bones, hearsed in death,
Have burst their cerements? why the sepulchre
Wherein we saw thee quietly in-urn'd,
Hath oped his ponderous and marble jaws,
To cast thee up again ! What may this mean,
That thou, dead corse, again, in complete steel,
Revisit'st thus the glimpses of the moon,
Making night hideous; and we fools of nature,
So horribly to shake our disposition,
With thoughts beyond the reaches of our souls?
Say, why is this? wherefore? what should we do?

HOR.   It beckons you to go away with it,
As if it some impartment did desire
To you alone.

MAR.   Look, with what courteous action
It waves you to a more removed ground:
But do not go with it.

HOR.   No, by no means.

---

[5] "It is quite fair to ask whether such an exclamation would come more easily into a Catholic poet's head or into that of a Protestant poet? A Protestant thinks, and probably always did think, that the right thing to do is always to go directly to God for help: indeed, one does not see what he wants a mediator for at all. But a Catholic's natural resource in danger, is to angels and other ministers of grace."—London *Catholic Progress* of April, 1875.

Ham.	It will not speak; then I will follow it.
Hor.	Do not, my lord.
Ham.	Why, what should be the fear?
	I do not set my life at a pin's fee;
	And for my soul, what can it do to that,
	Being a thing immortal as itself?
	It waves me forth again;—I'll follow it. [*Exit.*

Scene 5.—*Another Part of the Platform.*

Enter Ghost *and* Hamlet.

Ham.	Whither wilt thou lead me? speak, I'll go no farther.
Ghost.	Mark me.
Ham.	I will.
Ghost.	My hour is almost come,
	When I to sulphurous and tormenting flames
	Must render up myself.
Ham.	Alas, poor ghost.
Ghost.	Pity me not; but lend thy serious hearing
	To what I shall unfold.
Ham.	Speak; I am bound to hear.
Ghost.	So art thou to revenge, when thou shalt hear.
Ham.	What?
Ghost.	*I am thy father's spirit:*
	Doom'd for a certain time to walk the night,
	And for the day confined to lasting fires,
	Till the foul crimes, done in my days of nature,
	Are burnt and purged away. But that I am forbid
	To tell the secrets of my prison house,
	I could a tale unfold, whose lightest word
	Would harrow up thy soul, freeze thy young blood,
	Make thy two eyes like stars start from their spheres,
	Thy knotted and combined locks to part,
	And each particular hair to stand an-end,
	Like quills upon the fretful porcupine:
	But this eternal blazon must not be
	To ears of flesh and blood.—List, list, O list!—
	If thou didst ever thy dear father love,—
Ham.	O God!
Ghost.	Revenge his foul and most unnatural murder.
Ham.	Murder?
Ghost.	Murder most foul, as in the best it is;
	But this most foul, strange, and unnatural.
Ham.	Haste me to know 't, that I, with wings as swift
	As meditation, or the thoughts of love,
	May sweep to my revenge.
Ghost.	I find thee apt;
	And duller shouldst thou be, than the fat weed

That rots itself in ease on Lethe's wharf,
Wouldst thou not stir in this: now, Hamlet, hear.
'Tis given out, that sleeping in mine orchard,
A serpent stung me: so the whole ear of Denmark
Is by a forged process of my death
Rankly abused; but know, thou noble youth,
The serpent that did sting thy father's life
Now wears his crown.

HAM. O, my prophetic soul! my uncle?

GHOST. Ay, that *incestuous*, that adulterate beast,

    *   *   *

Thus was I, sleeping, by a brother's hand,
Of life, of crown, of queen, at once despoiled;
Cut off even in the blossom of my sin,
Unhousel'd, disappointed, unaneled: [6]
No reckoning made, but sent to my account
With all my imperfections on my head:
O, horrible! O, horrible! most horrible! [7]
If thou hast nature in thee, bear it not;
Let not the royal bed of Denmark be
A couch for luxury *and damned incest.*
But, howsoever thou pursuest this act,
Taint not thy mind, nor let thy soul contrive
Against thy mother aught: leave her to heaven,
And to those thorns that in her bosom lodge,
To prick and sting her. Fare thee well at once.
The glow-worm shows the matin to be near,
And 'gins to pale his uneffectual fire:
Adieu! adieu! Hamlet, remember me.   [*Exit.*

HAM. *O, all you host of heaven!* O earth! What else?

In Act II. Scene 2, Polonius, while endeavouring to explain
the character of Hamlet's madness to the Queen, uses the following language:—

        And now remains,
That we find out the cause of this effect;
Or, rather say, the cause of this d*efect;*
For this *e*ffect *d*efective, comes by cause:

"These lines," says the *Catholic Progress* (London), for April,
1875, "look very like a reference by the author to St. Augustine,
not unlikely to have been culled from some Catholic book of

---

[6] According to Hunter, this means without the viaticum and last sacrament of extreme unction; though he is inclined to change the word " disappointed" into " unassoiled," or " unabsolved."

[7] This is pure Catholic agony at the idea of the pains of purgatory.

27

devotion." And to this I may suggest that Shakespeare's devout mother, Mary Arden, must have had constantly some such book of religious discipline always within the boy's reach, about the house. "St. Augustine says that, to look for causes of *de*flection from good, seeing that they are *de*ficient and not *ef*ficient, is much the same as wishing to see darkness, or to hear silence."

In the opening of the third act, we have the singular scene of feigned madness and real distraction, which takes place between Hamlet and Ophelia; in which scene, perceiving that the weak, docile girl is playing the spy upon him, at the direction of her father, and has told him a falsehood in the interest of those against him, he harshly orders her off *to a nunnery,*—the inevitable refuge for our poet's distressful heroines,—in a tone which, I cannot but think, was largely justified by her petty perfidy. I have already remarked, when treating of "Love's Labour's Lost," "Much Ado about Nothing," "Measure for Measure," "Merchant of Venice," "Comedy of Errors," and other plays, Shakespeare's habit of sending all of his disappointed ladies to nunneries. That course could hardly be attributed to Lord Bacon, or regarded as a Protestant proclivity.

We have further evidences of the Catholic tone and colour of our author's mind, in the memorable scene between Hamlet and his mother in this same act. The Ghost appears, but she does not see it, and upon its disappearance, she charges the vision to her agitated son's distraught condition :—

> HAMLET.   Mother, for love of grace,
> Lay not that flattering unction to your soul,
> That not your trespass, but my madness speaks :
> It will but skin and film the ulcerous place ;
> Whiles rank corruption mining all within,
> Infects unseen. *Confess yourself to heaven ;*
> *Repent what's past : avoid what is to come :*
> And do not spread the compost on the weeds,
> To make them ranker.

Let me not pass over, at this point, the first exclamation of Hamlet, at the opening of the above scene, when, seeing the Ghost enter, he exclaims,—

> A king of shreds and patches :

> *Save me and hover o'er me with your wings,*
> *You heavenly guard!*

This, again, exhibits the Catholic tendency toward the *inter-mediation* of the saints.

We come now, in the progress of this act, to Shakespeare's adoration for royalty, and contemptuous estimation of the " common people."

> The cease of majesty
> Dies not alone ; but, like a gulf, doth draw
> What's near it, with it : it is a massy wheel,
> Fix'd on the summit of the highest mount,
> To whose huge spokes ten thousand lesser things
> Are mortised and adjoin'd ; which, when it falls,
> Each small annexment, petty consequence,
> Attends the boist'rous ruin. *Never alone*
> *Did the king sigh, but with a general groan.*
>
> Act III. Scene 3.

Act IV. Scene 3.

Enter KING attended.

KING. I have sent to seek him, and to find the body.
How dangerous is it, that this man goes loose !
Yet must not we put the strong law on him :
He's loved of the distracted multitude,
Who like not in their judgment, but their eyes ;
And where 'tis so, the offender's scourge is weigh'd,
But never the offence.

Scene 5.

> The people *muddied,*
> *Thick and unwholesome in their thoughts and whispers,*
> For good Polonius' death :—
>
> *   *

GENTLEMAN (*to the King*). Save yourself, my lord ;
The ocean over-peering of his list,
Eats not the flats with more impetuous haste,
Than young Laertes, in a riotous head,
O'erbears your officers ; *The rabble call him lord ;*
And as the world were now but to begin,
Antiquity forgot, custom not known,
The ratifiers and props of every word,
They cry, *Choose we ; Laertes shall be king !*
Caps,[s] hands, and tongues, applaud it to the clouds,
Laertes shall be king, Laertes king !

---

[s] Caps are always the symbol with Shakespeare of the labouring classes, from the fact that an Act of Parliament was passed towards the close of the

QUEEN. How cheerfully on the false trail they cry!
    O, this is counter, *you false Danish dogs.*

Enter LAERTES, armed, Danes following.

KING. What is the cause, Laertes,
    That thy rebellion looks so giant-like?—
    Let him go, Gertrude ; do not fear our person ;
    There's such divinity doth hedge a king,
    That treason can but peep to what it would,
    Acts little of his will..—Tell me, Laertes,
    Why thou art thus incensed;—Let him go, Gertrude.

The opening of the fifth act brings us to what is regarded,
by Lord Chief Justice Campbell, as the most complete piece of
evidence of the legal acquirements of Shakespeare, to be found in
all his works.   I allude to the law in regard to *felo de se*, which
is developed so curiously, and yet so correctly, by the two grave-
diggers in their humorous discussion in the churchyard, over the
question whether the drowned Ophelia is entitled to Christian
burial.   The pathetic description of her death, by the unhappy
queen, who assuredly was not all bad, comes properly in at this
point :—

QUEEN. There is a willow grows aslant the brook,
    That shows his hoar leaves in the glassy stream ;
    There with fantastic garlands did she make
    Of crow-flowers, nettles, daisies, and long purples,
    That liberal shepherds give a grosser name,
    But our cold maids do dead men's fingers call them ;
    There on the pendant boughs her coronet weeds
    Clambering to hang, an envious sliver broke ;
    When down her weedy trophies, and herself,
    Fell in the weeping brook.   Her clothes spread wide ;
    And, mermaid-like, a while they bore her up :
    Which time, she chanted snatches of old tunes ;
    As one incapable of her own distress,
    Or like a creature native and indued
    Unto that element: but long it could not be,
    Till that her garments, heavy with their drink,

---

fifteenth century, requiring all mechanics and labouring men to wear caps.
Hence, the line of Rosalind, in *As You Like It :*—

" Well, better wits have worn *plain statute caps ;*"

And hence, also, the Liberty cap of the old French Revolution, which meant
liberty for the masses.

> Pull'd the poor wretch from her melodious lay
> To muddy death.   *Act IV. Scene 7.*

The doubt which this throws upon the poor girl's intention, narrowly admits her to the jealous rights of Catholic burial, and saves her body from being condemned by the English law, (for Shakespeare's law is always English,) from being buried in a cross-road, with a stake driven through it. We find this doctrine, both of the Church and of the statute, exhibited in the following scene at the grave, in which Laertes protests, to the officiating priest, against the religious meagreness of the ceremony which is grudgingly allowed to his dead sister :—

LAER. What ceremony else
PRIEST. Her obsequies have been so far enlarged
     As we have warranty : Her death was doubtful ;
     And, but that great command o'er-sways the order,
     She should in ground unsanctified have lodged
     Till the last trumpet ; for charitable prayers,
     Shards, flints, and pebbles, should be thrown on her.
     Yet here she is allow'd her virgin rites,
     Her maiden strewments, and the bringing home
     Of bell and burial.
LAER. Must there no more be done ?
PRIEST.   No more be done !
     We should profane the service of the dead,
     To sing a *requiem*, and such rest to her,
     As to peace-parted souls.
LAER.   Lay her i' the earth ;—
     And from her fair and unpolluted flesh
     May violets spring !—I tell thee, churlish priest,
     A minist'ring angel shall my sister be,
     When thou liest howling.   *Act V. Scene 1.*

The scene between the two grave-diggers in comic discussion of the law, both of the Church and of the statute, concerning *felo de se*, presents itself properly at this point :—

Enter TWO CLOWNS, *with spades, &c.*

1 CLO. Is she to be buried in Christian burial, that wilfully seeks her own salvation ?

2 CLO. I tell thee, she is ; therefore make her grave straight : the crowner hath set on her, and finds it Christian burial.

1 CLO. How can that be, unless she drowned herself in her own defence ?

2 CLO. Why, 'tis found so.

1 CLO. It must be *se offendendo* ; it cannot be else. For here lies the

point: If I drown myself wittingly, it argues an act : and an act has three branches ; it is, to act, to do, and to perform : Argal, she drowned herself wittingly.

2 CLO. Nay, but hear you, goodman delver.

1 CLO. Give me leave. Here lies the water ; good : here stands the man ; good : If the man go to this water, and drown himself, it is, will he, nill he, he goes ; mark you that : but if the water come to him, and drown him, he drowns not himself : Argal, he that is not guilty of his own death, shortens not his own life.

2 CLO. But is this law ?

1 CLO. Ay, marry is 't ; crowner's-quest law.

2 CLO. Will you ha' the truth on't ? If this had not been a gentle-woman, she would have been buried out of Christian burial.

1 CLO. Why, there thou say'st : And the more pity ; that great folks shall have countenance in this world to drown or hang themselves, more than their even Christian.—*Act V. Scene* 1.

This singular scene, and the amount of law contained in it, notwithstanding its excessive comicality, could not, of course, escape the scrutiny of Lord Chief Justice Campbell, and he alludes to it as " the mine," which of all others in our author " produces the richest legal ore." He declares that the discussion proves " that Shakespeare had read and studied Plowden's report of the celebrated case of Hales *v.* Petit,* tried in the reign of Philip and Mary, and that he intended to ridicule the counsel who argued, and the judges who decided it."

His lordship describes this case at considerable length, but as I find it put more clearly by Judge Holmes, in his work on the " Authorship of Shakespeare," I will adopt that version of the case in preference to the version of his lordship. Judge Holmes says,—

" Sir James Hales, a Judge of the Common Pleas, having been imprisoned for being concerned in the plot to place Lady Jane Grey upon the throne, and afterwards pardoned, was so affected in mind as to commit suicide by drowning himself in a river. The coroner's inquest found a verdict of *felo de se*, under which his body was to be buried at a cross-road, with a stake thrust through it, and his goods and estates were forfeited to the crown. A knotty question arose upon the suit of his widow for an estate by survivorship in joint-tenancy, whether the forfeiture could be considered as having taken place in the lifetime of Sir

---

⁰ Plowden's Report, p. 256-9.

James Hales; for, if it did not, she took the estate by survivorship.

"Serjeant Southcote argued for the lady, that, as long as Sir
James was alive, he had not killed himself, and the moment that
he died, the estate vested in the plaintiff. 'The felony of the
husband shall not take away her title by survivorship, for in this
manner of felony two things are to be considered: First, the
cause of the death; secondly, the death ensuing the cause; and
these two make the felony, and without both of them the felony
is not consummate, and the cause of the death is the act done in
the party's lifetime, which makes the death to follow, and the
act which brought on the death here was the throwing himself
voluntarily into the water, for this was the cause of his death;
and, if a man kills himself by a wound which he gives himself
with a knife, *or, if he hangs himself, as the wound or the hanging*,
which is the act done in the party's lifetime, is the cause of his
death, so is the throwing himself into the water here. For, as
much as he cannot be attainted of his own death, because he is
dead before there is any time to attaint him, the finding of his
death by the coroner is, by necessity of law, equivalent to an
attainder, in fact, coming after his death. He cannot be *felo de
se* till the death is fully consummate, and the death precedes the
felony and the forfeiture.'

"Serjeant Walsh, on the other side, argued that the forfeiture
had relation to *the act done* in the party's lifetime which was the
cause of his death. '*Upon this, the parts of the act are to be
considered; and the act consists of three parts*. The *first* is the
imagination, which is a reflection or meditation of the mind,
whether or no it is convenient for him to destroy himself, and
what way it can be done. The *second* is the resolution, which is
a determination of the mind to destroy himself, and to do it in
this or that particular way. The *third* is the perfection, which
is the execution of what the mind has resolved to do. And this
perfection consists of two parts, viz., the beginning and the end.
The beginning is the doing of the act which causes the death;
and the end is the death, which is only a sequel to the act. *And
of all the parts, the doing of the act* is the greatest in the judgment of our law, and it is, in effect, the whole. *The doing of the
act is the only point* which the law regards: for, until the act is
done, it cannot be an offence to the world, and when the act is

done, it is punishable. Inasmuch as the person who did the act is dead, his person cannot be punished, and, therefore, *there is no way else* to punish him but by the forfeiture of those things which were his own at the time of his death.'

"Bendloe cited a case in which 'a heretic wounded himself mortally with a knife, and afterwards became of sound mind, and had *the rights of Holy Church*, and after died of the said wound, and his chattels were not forfeited;' and Carus cited another, 'where it appears that. one who had taken sanctuary in a church was out in the night, and the town pursued him, and *the felon defended himself with clubs and stones*, and would not render himself to the king's peace, and we struck off his head; and the goods of the person killed were forfeited, for he could not be arraigned, because *he was killed by his own fault*, for which reason, *upon the truth of the matter found*, his goods were forfeited. Here the inquiry before the coroner *super visum corporis* . . . is equivalent to a judgment given against him in his lifetime, and the forfeiture has relation to the act which was the cause of his death, viz., the throwing himself into the water."

"Dyer, C. J., giving the opinion of the Court, said, 'The forfeiture shall have relation to the act done by Sir James Hales in his lifetime, which was the cause of his death, viz., the throwing himself into the water.' He made five points—'First, the quality of the offence; secondly, by whom the offence was committed; thirdly, what he shall forfeit; fourthly, from what time; and fifthly, if the term here shall be taken from the wife.' . . . . *As to the second point*, it is an offence against nature, against God, and against the king. Against nature, *for every living thing does, by instinct of nature, defend itself from destruction;* and, then, to destroy one's self is contrary to nature, and a thing most horrible. Against God, in that it is a breach of his commandment, *Thou shalt not kill;* and to kill himself, by which he kills, in presumption, his own soul, is a greater offence than to kill another. Against the king, in that hereby he has lost a subject, and (as Brown termed it) he being the head, has lost one of his mystical members.' . . . . It was agreed by all the judges, 'that he shall forfeit all his goods; for Brown said the reason why the king shall have the goods and chattels of a *felo de se* . . . . is not because he is *out of Holy Church*, so that,

for that reason, the bishop will not meddle with them ; . . . .
but for the loss of his subject, and for the breach of his peace,
and for the evil example given to his people, and not in respect
that Holy Church will not meddle with them, *for he is adjudged
none of the members of Holy Church.'*

" *As to the fourth point,* viz. to what time the forfeiture shall
have relation ; the forfeiture here shall have relation to the time
of the original offence committed, which was the cause of the
death, and that was the throwing himself into the water, which
was done in his lifetime, and this act was felony. . . . . So that
the felony is attributed to the act, which is always done by a
living man, and in his lifetime ; for Sir James Hales was dead,
and how came he to his death ? By drowning. And who
drowned him ? Sir James Hales. And when did he drown
him ? In his lifetime. So that Sir James Hales, being alive,
caused Sir James Hales to die ; and the act of the living man
was the death of the dead man. But how can he be said to be
punished alive, when the punishment comes after his death ?
Sir, this can be done no other way than by divesting out of him
his title and property, from the time of the act done which was
the cause of his death, viz. the throwing himself into the water."

Lord Campbell, of course, argues from this case that Shakespeare had a very considerable knowledge of the law ; and Judge
Holmes, who is the chief expounder of the Baconian theory,
says,—

" A careful comparison of these passages may satisfy the
critical reader that the author of the play had certainly read this
report of Plowden. They are not adduced here as amounting to
proof that the author was any other than William Shakespeare,
but rather as a circumstance bearing upon the antecedent probabilities of the case ; for there is not the slightest ground for a
belief, on the facts which we know, that Shakespeare ever looked
into Plowden's Reports ; while it is quite certain that Francis
Bacon, who commenced his legal studies at Gray's Inn in the
very next year after the date of Plowden's preface, did have
occasion to make himself familiar with that work, some years
before the appearance of " Hamlet." And the mode of reasoning
and the manner of the Report, bordering so nearly upon the
ludicrous, would be sure to impress the memory of Bacon, whose
nature, as we know, was singularly capable of wit and humour."

It thus appears, according to Lord Campbell and Judge Holmes, that the author of "Hamlet," whoever he was, must have read this Report of Plowden, which his lordship, who is the most emphatic of the two, declares he not only must have read, but *studied*. Now, I am not so positive about this point, though I think it not unlikely that both of them are right. It would have been very natural for a man of Shakespeare's keen sense of the ridiculous, on hearing this case of Hales *v.* Petit discussed by the wits, poets, and lawyers, who spent their hours of relaxation in the bar-room of the hospitable "Maiden," to have asked one of his legal friends to lend him Plowden for his more complete enjoyment of the case; but it is quite as likely that he acquired a full knowledge of the whole of it, by the repeated discussions and heated disputes which such an exceptional proceeding would be sure to have given rise to in a first-class London tavern. Doubtless, it was re-acted there, after the fashion of the comic trial-scene between Prince Hal and Falstaff at the "Boar's Head" in Eastcheap, and the parts of Serjeants Southcote and Wright, Chief Justice Dyer, and, possibly, the dead Sir James and 'Dame Margaret his widow, distributed among the tipplers and roysterers of the occasion. Certainly there could have been no rarer fun to such a mind as Shakespeare's; and in this way, perhaps, its comicality became transposed into one of the most peculiar productions of his comic genius, through the inimitable and immortal dialogue of the grave-diggers. On the other hand, while Shakespeare would have been sure to view the case of Hales *v.* Petit in its most ludicrous aspect, and to have embodied it accordingly, I think it may be received as equally certain, that the mind of Bacon would have entertained the argument only with the gravity of a lawyer, and have incarnated it, had he touched it at all, not as a piece of fun, but as a precedent and serious authority.

It must be observed also, that in the time of Shakespeare there were no newspapers for the circulation of current information among the people. The art of printing had only been devised by Caxton in 1467, barely a hundred years before, and, though an octavo printed single news-sheet made its appearance in the latter part of the sixteenth century, it contained scarcely anything beyond a few advertisements and the movements of the court. London taverns, in the time of Shakespeare, therefore, were the resorts of lawyers, scholars, attorneys' clerks, and, sometimes, of judges and personages of very high degree. The " Mermaid," in Bread Street, which seems to have been the favourite resort of our poet, was frequented by a club founded by Sir Walter Raleigh ; and here Raleigh himself, Ben Jonson, Beaumont, Fletcher, Shelden, Cotton, Carew, Martin, Donne, and others, their chosen companions, met for social and convivial enjoyment—I dare not add, for the more modern solace of pipes and tobacco, because

> The fat weed
> That rots itself in ease on Lethe's wharf,

though then recently brought home by Raleigh, had not yet fallen into common use.[1]

"There (says Fuller) all the students of the literature and manners of those days have reasonably agreed in placing the scene of the wit-combats between Shakespeare and Jonson," the fame of which had reached Fuller's time, and caused him to imagine the encounter of the two, like that between a Spanish great galleon and an English man-of-war; Jonson, like the former, built far higher in learning, and solid, but slow in his performances; Shakespeare, like the latter, less in bulk, but lighter in movement, turning and tacking nimbly, and taking every advantage by the quickness of his wit and invention.[2]

---

[1] It has been said that Shakespeare never gave any evidence of his knowledge of tobacco ; but I think that " The fat weed which rots itself in ease on Lethe's wharf," is a distinct reference to it.

[2]
> What things have we seen
> Done at the " Mermaid "! heard words that have been
> So nimble, and so full of subtle flame,
> As if that every one from whom they came
> Had meant to put his whole wit in a jest,
> And had resolved to live a fool the rest
> Of his dull life ; then when there hath been thrown
> Wit able enough to justify the town
> For three days past, wit that might warrant bo
> For the whole city to talk foolishly
> Till that were cancell'd, and, when that was gone,
> We left an air behind us which alone
> Was able to make the two next companies
> Right witty, though but downright fools, more wise.
>   *Letter to Ben Jonson.*

But to return to the question as to the extent of Shakespeare's legal acquirements, I think that Lord Campbell makes a much stronger point for the affirmative, than in the grave-diggers' scene, when he says,—

"Hamlet's own speech, on taking in his hand what he supposed might be the skull of a lawyer, abounds with lawyer-like thoughts and words :"—

Where be his quiddits now, his quillets, his cases, his tenures, and his tricks? Why does he suffer this rude knave now to knock him about the sconce with a dirty shovel, and will not tell him of his action of battery? Humph! This fellow might be in's time a great buyer of land, with his statutes, his recognizances, his fines, his double vouchers, his recoveries : is this the fine of his fines, and the recovery of his recoveries, to have his fine pate full of fine dirt? will his vouchers vouch him no more of his purchases, and double ones too, than the length and breadth of a pair of indentures.

"These terms of art," adds his lordship, "are all used seemingly with a full knowledge of their import; and it would puzzle some practising barristers with whom I am acquainted to go over the whole *seriatim,* and to define each of them satisfactorily."

His lordship also finds in the following allusion to the disputed territory, which was the cause of war between Norway and Poland, a substratum of law in Shakespeare's mind :—

> We go to gain a little patch of ground,
> That hath in it no profit but the name,
> To pay five ducats, five, I would not farm it,
> Nor will it yield to Norway or the pole
> A ranker rate, should it be *sold in fee.*

How Shakespeare, or any intelligent tradesman of his time, could have known less law than is indicated by the term *fee simple,* I cannot well conceive.

"Earlier in the play," continues his lordship, "Marcellus inquires what was the cause of the warlike preparations in Denmark,—

> And why such daily cast of brazen cannon,
> And foreign mart for implements of war?
> *Why such impress of shipwrights, whose sore task*
> *Does not divide the Sunday from the week?*

Such confidence, in England, has there always been in Shakespeare's general accuracy, that this passage has been quoted, both by text-writers and by judges on the bench, as an authority upon the legality of the *press-gang*, and upon the debated question whether *shipwrights*, as well as *common seamen*, are liable to be pressed into the service of the royal navy."

Finally, says his lordship,—

" Hamlet, when mortally wounded in Act V. Scene 2, represents that death comes to him in the shape of a sheriff's officer, as it were, to take him into custody under a *capias ad satis-faciendum :—*

> Had I but time (as this fell serjeant, Death,
> Is strict in his arrest), Oh ! I could tell you, &c."

I cheerfully leave this to the reader without argument; but I regret that, in concluding my review of the plays of Shakespeare, in this analysis of the tragedy of " Hamlet," I am obliged to point out what certainly looks like a wilful neglect of duty on the part of my Lord Chief Justice Campbell. At the request of Mr. J. Payne Collier, a distinguished commentator, his lordship, being esteemed the most fit man in England, undertook the task of investigating the text of the Shakespeare writings for evidences of the legal acquirements of the author. Having accepted this responsibility and the honours which pertained to it, he was bound to perform the task, not only diligently and fully, but also impartially, to any and every interest which might arise or be comprehended in the premises. I concede, that, in the main, his lordship has done so (though I have not been always able to agree with him), and I admit moreover, that the observation of his lordship has been so vigilant, and his scrutiny so minute, that he has found proofs of our poet's legal erudition even in his casual but correct use of such terms as "purchase," "several," "fee," and "fee-farm." Nay, he has even gone to the extent, in the play we had last in hand ("Lear"), of conceding to him a comprehensive legal insight, through the clown's declaration, that "the breath of an un-feed lawyer" was worth nothing, because it cost nothing. His lordship's estimation of the weight of these legal expressions, I cheerfully confess ought to be a great deal better than mine (though I must assume my privilege of disagreeing with him), but I think I have a right to complain, along with the rest of the world whom his lordship agreed to serve in this matter, for his wilfully concealing a portion of the evidence when he found it rasped his own profession, or, I should rather say, when it touched the reputation of the lofty class of legal dignitaries, to which his lordship's learning and ability had justly raised him.

I observed, in my review of " Lear," that, notwithstanding the great diligence which Lord Campbell had shown in analyzing the Shakespearian text, he had, singularly enough, overlooked, or, perhaps, intentionally left unnoticed, two of the most striking evidences of Shakespeare's knowledge of the administration of the law, as it then seemed to be administered in Great Britain. Both of these instances occur in the famous scene in Act IV. Scene 6, where the mad old king, fantastically dressed in flowers, holds a sort of court upon the heath :—

LEAR (*to the blinded Gloster*). Look with thine *ears.* See how yon' justice rails upon yon' simple thief. Hark, in thine ear. Change places; and, handy-dandy, which is the justice, which is the thief?

Again,—

Through tatter'd clothes small vices do appear;
Robes and furr'd gowns hide all. Plate sin with gold
And the strong lance of justice hurtless breaks;
Arm it in rags, a pigmy's straw will pierce it.
None does offend, none, I say none ; I'll able 'em.   [*Offers money.*
Take *that* of me, my friend, *who have the power*
To seal the accuser's lips.

My remark upon the above was, "Surely Lord Campbell, who accepted his first legal instance in this play of ' Lear ' as to an ' un-feed lawyer,' from the mouth of a fool, might have given some attention to the above powerful lines, though from the lips of a madman." All this was suppositively put against Lord Campbell as a case of possible oversight; but the following evidence of his lordship's tampering with the testimony, or rather concealment, of the facts, for the protection of the reputation of the English bench, disposes of that theory. Like the above instances from " Lear," the suppressed extract affords one of the most conspicuous evidences of Shakespeare's intimate knowledge of the corruption of the English judiciary that could possibly be presented. It occurs in the language of the King, in the third scene of Act III. of " Hamlet," where, stung by

remorse, his majesty is about asking Heaven's forgiveness for
his crimes. He says,—

> *In the corrupted currents of the world,*
> *Offence's gilded hand may shove by justice ;*
> *And oft 'tis seen, the wicked prize itself*
> *Buys out the law :* But 'tis not so above :
> *There* is no shuffling, *there* the action lies
> In his true nature ; and we ourselves compell'd,
> Even to the teeth and forehead of our faults,
> To give in evidence.

This terrible accusation against the integrity of the English
judiciary Lord Campbell *would not* give ; so, without reflecting
injuriously upon his lordship, I am forced, by the necessities of
criticism, to repeat the remark I made at the close of my review
of the tragedy of " Lear ;" that " of one thing we may be
certain, Sir Francis Bacon, who, when Lord Chancellor, was
sent to the Tower for selling his decisions *for money* while
presiding on the bench, would never have written these allusions
to judicial corruption had he been the author of the Shakespeare plays ; or, had he done so in 1605, when 'Lear' was
composed, he would have expunged these condemnations of his
own crime when the Shakespearian folio was revised and published in 1623."

Part III

THE MUSICAL OR EUPHONIC TEST.

SHAKESPEARE AND BACON'S RESPECTIVE SENSE OF MELODY, OR EAR FOR MUSIC.

28

CHAPTER XXXVII.

THE EUPHONIC TEST.

HAVING finished my scrutiny of the Shakespearian dramas, with the view of exhibiting the writer's aristocratic inclinations, his contempt for the labouring classes, his religious predilections, and his defective knowledge of the law, in order to mark the width of distance, in the way of personality, between him and Bacon, I come now to the final test, whether the essays of the latter and the plays of our poet could have been the productions of one and the same mind. This question I take to be susceptible of absolute demonstration, according to the laws of elocution and of musical sound. A writer's musical sense, or *ear for music*, governs the euphony and tread of his expression. This *ear* for sound, following the instincts of taste, and falling always toward one cadence and accord, insensibly forms what writers call a *style*. This style, when thoroughly fixed, enables us to distinguish the productions of one author from another, and is usually more reliable as a test of authorship even than handwriting, inasmuch as the latter may be counterfeited, while a style of thought, united with a form of expression consonant to that tone of thought being a gift, cannot be imitated as handwriting can. A fixed style, like that either of Bacon or of Shakespeare, is, therefore, undoubtedly, susceptible of analysis and measurement by the laws both of music and of elocution. Having been satisfied, from the first, that this test would prove decisive, summoning, as it almost does, the august shades of the two dead giants into court, I reserved it for the last. Being unwilling, however, in a matter of so much importance, to depend solely upon myself, I addressed a letter to Professor J. W. Taverner, a very high authority in elocution and *belles lettres* in the United States, requesting an analysis and comparison of the Plays and Essays from his standpoint in art, and asking a decision, as far as that critical examination would enable him to give one, of the problem involved. The following is the essay of the Professor on the text above given :—

The respective Styles of Shakespeare and Bacon,[1] *judged by the Laws of Elocutionary Analysis and "Melody of Speech."*

BY PROFESSOR J. W. TAVERNER.

DEAR SIR,—I will now set forth, as plainly as I can, the theory of Shakespearian versification, to which you refer. As for the Baconian theory of the authorship of Shakespeare's plays, which I remember to have been first started by Miss Bacon, at New-haven—I prejudged it. It appeared to me, by the force of a single reflection, to be as unworthy of examination, as to seriously consider if two bodies could occupy the same place at the same time.

The reflection to which I refer is this : That when we regard the works of great men—the sculpture and paintings of Michael Angelo, the architecture of Inigo Jones, the dramatic works of Shakespeare, and, I am obliged to mention for my arguments, the works of Lord Bacon—we see the rounded thought of "a life," as it grew and spread—like one of those giant trees of California, with its roots in the earth just where it started. The life-work of each had its roots in an idea, a soil, a *genius* (not an industry), from which all sprang. Each such work is, as I said, the expression of "a life," and of a life commenced and continued under

---

[1] Bacon's style was clear and strong, well-balanced and rhythmical, but not sweet. Meares in the "Wit's Treasury," published in 1598, speaks of Shakespeare as *the mellifluous and honey-tongued Shakespeare*, in whom "the *sweet* and witty soul of Ovid lies," as witness his Venus and Adonis, his Lucrece, and his *sugred sonnets* among his private friends. Chettle, in 1603, thus alludes to him while reproaching him for his silence on the death of Queen Elizabeth :—

  Nor doth the *silver-tongued* Melicert
  Drop from his *honied* muse one sable tear.

Ben Jonson, in his eulogy on "The memory of Shakespeare," says,—

    Even so the race
  Of Shakespeare's mind and manners brightly shines
  In *his well-turn'd and truly filed lines.*   G. W.

certain auspices. He, therefore, that wrought the one, could not have performed the work incident to the other, without entirely new conditions from the start. How much less possible is it that one could have accomplished the joint works of any *two*.

Not the least among these, but, perhaps, the greatest wonder of them all is Shakespeare. The world has been accustomed to regard the author of these marvellous plays, as the wonder of the world and the king of men. It is certain, whoever he was, that from childhood he was growing to the work, cultivating his imagination, accumulating his materials, his mind left to its bent, but little interfered with from without; even too severe and strict an education, would have dwarfed his imagination, and stopped this mighty mind in its career. Its education must greatly have been an education of choice.

And now we are asked to concede that these plays, and all that they contain, needed no such one-sided devotion and mental proclivity, and was not so much of a work after all, for Lord Bacon, whose chief and earnest devotion of his mind and time was not surrendered to this work, (but is well understood and fully admitted by his biography to have been exerted in a different direction,) yet supplemented these dramatic works as a mere pastime, in hours of relaxation from severe and absolute duties and labours.

It is not so unreasonable, I am willing to admit, apart from historical proof to the contrary, to dispute the authorship of Shakespeare's plays, but utterly unreasonable to think to find the author in one, who was at the same period filling the world otherwise with a light, an effulgence of brightness of only a somewhat lesser magnitude. So Lord Bacon is ruled out, by a sort of an intellectual alibi, for he was somewhere else busily engrossed with something else. To have done the one work, precludes the possibility of having done the other, as it would for both an oak and a pine-tree to grow from the same seed. Understand me, that if they were both works of mere literary labour, like those of Schlegel (for so I judge Schlegel), this would not apply, but being both works of genius, and one at least (the plays) of both genius and of art, this does apply.

As the handwriting of any one man among thousands can be determined by experts, so no lengthy examples of the style—the expression and language of any two authors of note, can fail to indicate the individual mind to which the one or the other belongs. The handwriting is so determinate, because dependant on such an infinite combination of circumstances—the whole conformation and structure of the hand ; the relation of the thumb and fingers that hold the pen, the angle by which they are inclined, the length of the lever from the point where the hand rests ; but still further by those more delicate indications through the action of the nerves and the characteristics of the mind of the chirographer.

But how much more extensive are the combinations that constitute the style, the language, the adornments, the illustrations, the figurative expression, the place of the emphasis, the form of the phrases, the source of the metaphors, the character of the similes ; but our enumeration would become too long ; then, finally, that emanation of the rhythm of the breathing, and of the pulse, and the endowments of the ear, that marshals all those forms and phrases in a certain order with reference to melody and cadence.

To make up the characteristics of some of these, what a combination of antecedents ! Every day that the author lived, every trouble, happiness, and accident that he experienced, every book that he chanced to read, every study that he earnestly prosecuted, every virtue and every vice that grew in his character, every trait and bias and inclination in science, in theology, in philosophy, and music, contributed to produce and form the united result.

We shall therefore proceed to judge, by these signs, whether it is not impossible that the works of Shakespeare could have been written by Lord Bacon, and equally so that those of Bacon could have been written by Shakespeare.

We can readily detect, as a peculiarity appertaining to different writers, certain *repeated forms*, showing that every writer exhibits a fashion, or uses some geometrical or metrical arrangement in which the words instinctively place themselves. I presume, that with some authors, and most certainly with Shakespeare, it might require a tedious examination to find out what prevails, but, with Bacon, we are so far fortunate, it is scarcely possible to read a page without detecting more than one such prevalent habit.

I shall present examples, sufficient in number, and those taken solely from the "Essays," and, when they are brought together, I think that it will seem quite unnecessary to *state* that the same repetitions (I mean in form only), cannot be produced from the pages of Shakespeare.

Upon examination of the limited poetry which we have from the pen of Bacon ["The translation of certain Psalms into English verse"], I find nothing to criticize. Like unto Shakespeare, he takes good note of any deficiency of syllabic pulsation, and imparts the value but of one syllable to the dissyllables "heaven," "wearest," "many," "even," "goeth;"—and to "glittering," and "chariot," but the value of two, precisely as Shakespeare would. But we have no means of ascertaining if he would have pronounced "ambitious" as four syllables, as Shakespeare invariably does, and as the reader may find if he will consult Mark Antony's oration.

On the one side of this investigation, therefore, we are confined to what may be revealed in prose composition.

The outcome of the life-long process to which we have referred, by which the style of a writer is formed—*that* feature of it to which our treatment of this subject, for the present, relates—is the most subtle; for we have to investigate that of which the writer himself was, possibly, the most unconscious—that which, like his gait or some other habit, has perhaps received no *positive* attention whatever. Yet, it may be held that nothing becomes more rigid and fixed than the mould and matrix in which his thoughts are ultimately fashioned and expressed. The modes of thinking would, in some instances, have to be identical, to produce identical melodies of speech.

In Shakespeare's prose we shall find that all this is marvellously free and varied, and that his blank verse conforms strictly to a certain set of chimes. In Bacon, besides Latin forms we shall not lack examples of a certain sort of duplicates and triplicates, antithetic parallelisms, and harmonic or alternate phrases (and, to use a strong Baconianism), *and the like.*

A distinguished reviewer says that "Bacon, like Sydney, was the warbler of poetic prose." And this is true, not solely in the sense of using poetic illustration, an illustration identified with the development of thought, the close combination of the intellectual and the imaginative, but in his adherence to a frequent repetition of prose melodies. But they have not the rhythm of the beat of the ocean on the sea-shore like those of Shakespeare. They resemble rather, in some instances, the formula of the Rule of Three; and others, showing the mathematical mind of the author, are constructed precisely in form, as that, 1 a equals 2 b; 2 a equals 4 b. And others are like three times three are nine, three times four are twelve, and three times five are fifteen.

Let us give some illustrations of these:—

. " A man cannot speak to his son but as a father, to his wife but as a husband, to his enemy but upon terms."

" Crafty men contemn studies, simple men admire them, and wise men use them."

" Where some ants carry corn, and some their young, and some go empty." " Studies serve for delight, for ornament, and for ability." " The chief use for delight is in, etc., for ornament is, etc., and for ability in, etc." " Reading maketh a full man, conference a ready man, and writing an exact man." " For they cloud the mind, they lose friends, they check with business." " They dispose kings to tyranny, husbands to jealousy, wise men to irresolution."

But in all this there is an obvious rhythm, every member is equally balanced. For compare the above with the following, where each member is drawn out longer:—

" The advantage ground to do good, the approach to kings and principal persons, and the raising of a man's own fortunes."

There is no end to Bacon's repetition of these triple clauses always equally balanced:—

" Some of prey, some of game, some of quarrel." " Desires of profit, of lust, of revenge." " Give ear to precept, to laws, to religion," " of books, of sermons, of harangues." " He tosseth his thoughts more easily, he marshaleth them more orderly, he seeth how they look when they are turned into words."

For the abundance of forms such as these has it been said, that no author was ever so concise as Bacon. Yet the question may be asked, if Shakespeare had to put the same thoughts as the following, would he express them in the same way? " Some books are to be tasted, others to be swallowed, and some few to be chewed and digested."

Distinguished Shakespearian commentators, who will reject, as being unsafe to adopt, many critical arguments founded upon the merit or demerit of certain passages, or even of an entire play, will attach the greatest importance to any similarity or dissimilarity in the versification. Nothing is regarded as a surer indication of authenticity than such external signs. Bacon, himself, gives testimony to the weight and value of such evidence, for he himself relates that Queen Elizabeth, being incensed with a certain book dedicated to my Lord of Essex, expressed an opinion that there was treason in it, and would not be persuaded that it was his writing whose name was to it; but that it had some more mischievous author, and said, with great indignation, that she would have him racked, to produce his author. "I replied," says Bacon, "Nay, Madam, he is a doctor; never rack his person, but rack his style; let him have pen, ink, and paper, and help of books, and be enjoined to continue the story where it breaketh off, and I will undertake, by collating the styles, to judge whether he were the author or no."

Of this part of the style, which is simply addressed to the ear, and not unto the mind, or limited to some faculty of it that might be regarded as the counterpart of the eye, has possessed such an attraction for some persons that they have become thereby attached to certain authors, and have made them their constant companions, chiefly for this æsthetic kind of gratification.

It is said that Lord Byron made Disraeli's "Literary Characters" his inseparable companion, though I may infer it was for the sake of the endless variety of intellectual experiences, with which Byron would doubtless have felt so much active sympathy.

What but this music of language produced the great fascination of Ossian's poems? I doubt if it were not this which constituted the chief effect of Sterne, and made him for a time a household work.

It is certainly the great and unique charm of Edgar Allan Poe.

It has a marvellous attraction for the young, upon whom will be often produced an indelible impression, thus derived through example and admiration. So, from a life association, springs up the various habitual intonations of the Scotch, the Irish, the English, and the American, that you may know them, meet them in whatever part of the world you may.

No writer, however intellectually great or independent he may afterwards become, but in his day had his bias, and has been influenced by the fascination of another. And two men, who are contemporaries, though they may be attracted alike and come under the same influence, yet in its blending with their individual natures, and modified more or less by that receptivity derived from previous preparation to submit them to the impression; and, as the nature of the one would be to absorb less or to reflect more, the result would be invariably different.

There is nothing so characteristic as the acquired and natural endowments of the mind of an author, that shows the true metal of the mine from which they are taken, as the similes which he employs. All such anologies are just such as most readily occur to the mind of the writer. How different will they be with different men. In Shakespeare, those of his that are *sui generis* are drawn from the forces of nature; he goes at once to the fountain head—he does not borrow them at second hand, nor look into the accidents of life for an illustration. Those of Bacon, on the other hand, are such as are suggested by the habit of a close observation of life and manners, of the observances of the court, of the dictates of prudence, of the experience and moral allowance of the lawyer—they may be drawn from nature, but it is nature as exhibited in the life of the animal, its sagacity and cunning, and qualities that help to self-preservation: as in that one of his wherein he says, " As among beasts, those which are weakest in the course, are yet nimblest in the turn, as it is betwixt the greyhound and the hare." Very shrewd indeed, but therein it has the mental stamp of Lord Bacon. He has put his mark upon it: *shrewdness*, the quickest and most responsive faculty of the individual character.

The simile is as a spark that is to be elicited from an electrically-charged substance; the moment for the spark has come, it can't deliberate how it shall deport itself, there is so much of it, or so little, according to circumstances. Thus nothing is so sure an indication of the man. When he projects the simile, he looks in upon himself. He is confined to nothing. There is the storehouse—a glance only, and he picks up the brightest gem that suits his purpose. Be he rich or poor, parsimonious or prodigal, he must wear the robes suited to his state and station.

Similes as mental products, are very distinct from all other forms of figurative language. A simile is unique. Metaphor and such like may belong to only a *part* of a phrase, there may be but a few words with a figurative meaning introduced within a sentence; but a simile is complete. It has its own beginning and ending. Bacon has to accompany some of his with an explanation. Here is one with a double explanation :—

"Like choler, which is the humour that maketh men active, earnest, and full of alacrity, and stirring if it be not stopped; but if it be stopped, and cannot have its way, it becometh as dark, and thereby malign and venomous; so, &c."

Where could you find in Shakespeare a simile constructed like this?

To determine more positively the impress of *individuality* which this form, above all others, supplies, I shall place alongside of Shakespeare and Bacon, those also of Shelley and of the Bible.

The unification of the simile, both in structure and execution, is a peculiarity attaching generally to all those of the Bible, of Shakespeare, and of Shelley, and is so essential an attribute for the consideration of the elocutionist, because, through the least failure, either in conception or execution, in this regard, vague, false, or ridiculous meanings have sometimes been conveyed, both on the stage and in the sacred desk. This necessary compliance in elocution is but the conforming of the delivery to the psychological conditions under which the simile had its parturition in the mind of the author. To take example from stage utterances :—

> *And Pity, like a naked, new-born babe,*
> *Striding the blast,*

has been so pronounced as if "the naked new-born babe" was striding the blast,

> *Or heaven's cherubim, horsed*
> *Upon the sightless coursers of the air;*

as if "the cherubim" was intended as horsed upon the sightless coursers of the air.

It is Pity, the bold figure and personification which Macbeth has suddenly introduced, which thus conveys its pitiful tale of assassination and murder, and starts the tears in every eye.

Then, again, in the first part of the same speech :—

> *Besides, this Duncan*
> *Hath borne his faculties so meek, hath been*
> *So clear in his great office, that his virtues*

Will plead like angels trumpet tongued, against
The deep damnation of his taking off.

I am almost afraid to say what distinguished elocutionists—if tragedians, whose elocution has invariably been mere blind experiment, may be called such—have spoken these lines, as if the thought were "angels trumpet-tongued," instead of its appearing that Duncan's *virtues* would plead trumpet-tongued. The punctuation which should not be suffered to mislead, is the cause of some of these errors.

This essential attribute of the simile I shall show hereafter as peculiarly attaching to those of Shelley, and, however lengthy any simile might be, that his mind embraced it like a single ray of light emanating therefrom.

In the following example from the Bible either the presence of the commas, or ignorance of that elocutionary feature in the simile, which is to render it in its entirety, has led to similar faults (Psalm i. 3) :—

And he shall be like a tree, planted by the rivers of water, which bringeth forth his fruit in his season.

This, when rendered disjunctively, "*and he shall be like a tree,*" we cannot see wherein he is like a tree. Nor can we perceive how he can be "like a tree planted by the rivers of water;" for that is to be carried away by the flood: "*that bringeth forth his fruit*" is now too late. The light is thus broken and scattered. But presented as a unit, having one continuous flow of the voice, the sense is plain.

Again, in Psalm xix. 6, with the reading of which everybody is so familiar, and which has been heard so often, thus :—

Which is as a bridegroom . . . . coming out of his chamber,
And rejoiceth as a strong man . . . . to run a race.

Now, by this disjunctive reading, we would not know whether "coming out of his chamber" was predicated of the sun, or of the bridegroom, nor whether "to run a race" referred to the bridegroom, the sun, or the strong man. But the simile, preserved in its entirety, and given to the ear in a compact form, is full of energy and meaning :—

Which is . . . . "*as a bridegroom coming out of his chamber,*"
And rejoiceth . . . . "*as a strong man to run a race.*"

How little of this character can be imparted to any simile, so conceived as to carry an explanation afterwards like this one from Bacon :—

Like bats amongst birds, they fly by twilight.

I introduce this, at this point, to show that there may be a radical difference in the manner a simile may spring up in the mind. This latter form is indicative of a mental habit entirely distinct from the above examples, and if we shall find hereafter that no such mental habit attaches to the author of Shakespeare's plays, and yet is almost the invariable method with Bacon, it will be all-sufficient of itself, without the argument of the enormous difference in the similes themselves, and the sources from which they are derived.

Shelley abounds in similes, more so than any other poet. In the "Skylark" we have a string of them, if I may use the phrase, each simile being as a bead, distinct in character and colour, that is to be separately threaded. The elocution demands that the mind shall not be taken up with the parts, but embrace the whole: it must not be allowed to rest on "the glow-worm," but on all that is said about it :—

> Like a poet hidden
> In the light of thought
> Singing hymns unbidden
> Till the world is wrought
> To sympathy, with hopes, and fears it heeded not.

> Like a high-born maiden
> In a palace tower,
> Soothing her love-laden
> Soul in secret hour
> With music sweet as love that overflows her bower.

> Like a glow-worm golden
> In a dell of dew
> Scattering unbeholden
> Its aeriel hue
> Amidst the flowers, and grass that screen it from the view.

> Like a rose embower'd
> In its own green leaves
> By warm winds deflower'd

Till the scent it gives
Makes faint with too much sweet,
These heavy-winged thieves.

Sound of vernal showers
On the twinkling grass.
Rain-awaken'd flowers,
All that ever was
Joyous and clear and fresh thy music doth surpass.

Further examples: "Like a wolf, that had smelt a dead child
out," [the Spring] "Like the spirit of love felt everywhere,"
[panted] "Like a doe in the noon-tide."

No one can mistake in perceiving the individual character of
the mind, if not its peculiarity, that produced the whole of these.
They are very beautiful; but there is a peculiar sentiment about
all of them that they would be at once pronounced as Shelley's,
and not one of them could possibly be assigned to Shakespeare.

SIMILES FROM SHAKESPEARE.
From Othello.

Like to the Pontic Sea
Whose icy current and compulsive course
Ne'er knows retiring ebb; but keeps due on,
To the Propontic and the Hellespont.

From Henry V.

Let it pry [the eye] through " the portage of the head
Like the brass cannon."

Let the brow o'erwhelm it,
As fearfully " as doth a galled rock
O'erhang and jutty his confounded base,
Swill'd with the wild and wasteful ocean."

I see you stand " like greyhounds in the slips
Straining upon the start."

From Macbeth.

And " overcome us like a summer's cloud "
Without our special wonder.

i.e., No more than as a summer's cloud.

No one can fail to recognize the mental stamp of Shelley in

the similes quoted from *him ;* and as manifestly is there present the individual impress, the boldness and daring of the one and the same hand in those taken from Shakespeare.

What a corruscation of poetic force and beauty appertains to each! I speak of those of Shakespeare and of Shelley, and yet the peculiar brilliance of each is so distinct, that, like two gems of fabulous value in the hands of a judge, the one could not be mistaken for the other. But it is not needful to judge these two minds one with the other, but in the light of them, to view the handiwork of Lord Bacon, in the same direction, to examine *his* similes; and not with the intention to discover a dull stone against a brilliant, but to prove it, however solid, and true, and genuine, certainly not one of the same class.

" Glorious gifts and foundations, are ' like sacrifices without salt.' "

" Like the market, where many times if you can stay a little, the price will fall."

" Like common distilled waters, flashy things."

" Like precious odours, most fragrant when they are incensed or crushed."

" Like an ill mower, that mows on still, but never whets his scythe."

" Virtue is like a rich stone, best plain set."

These are good for every-day wear. Not one of them has, or admits of that characteristic which makes the simile so attractive to an accomplished elocutionist. But they all have the feature which I before mentioned, of an explanatory appendage. How practical the character of the invention that calls them forth! and how completely stamped, like the others, with the individuality of the author, and indicative of a handiwork utterly incapable of claiming the signet furnished by the examples above.

It would be as easy to suppose by these evidences, Bacon and Shelley to have been one and the same author, as that these several specimens of Shakespeare and of Bacon could proceed from one and the same mind.

But so unlike is Bacon psychologically in his avowed works to Shakespeare, that he affords almost no opportunity to institute comparisons. Where we would advance the characteristic embodiments of human passion and emotion emanating from Shakespeare, we turn to Bacon to find nothing but a negative. No examples whatever with which to compare those individual flashes of fire and soul, by which Shakespeare appears as the master of the human heart. To speak in elocutionary terms, where can we find in Bacon passages admitting of guttural vibration embodying the sentiments of scorn, pride, spleen, and aversion, such as may be found in " Coriolanus," and in " Timon of Athens "? Where any such opportunities of abrupt utterance bearing like lightning flashes the vocal symbol of anger such as Shakespeare presents frequently enough, but more particularly in " Richard II.," in the character of Margaret of Anjou, in " Richard III." and in " King Lear"? Where the possibilities of the aspirate, in its several features of heartfelt earnestness growing out of a variety of emotions? Where the expression of sarcasm and irony, as it attaches to Constance, in the midst of her maternal grief? To Faulconbridge with his humorous sallies? To Margaret of Anjou in her panther-like rage? We might as reasonably demand the same throughout nearly the whole scale of the passions. Indeed, within the whole of *this* range of mental forces we can turn all the angles of reflection to view, and exhibit the many colours of this psychological polygon, as of Shakespearean identity; but against all these in Bacon we find nothing but a plain surface. And (supposing him capable of the Shakespearean dramas) the evidence that when Bacon wrote as Bacon, he was certainly able to send all these mighty energies to sleep, and to float somewhat as a flat-bottomed boat over a smooth lake; although according to the upholders of the theory which we are called upon to refute, when he undertook to write the tasks of Shakespeare he became a new man, all his scholarly decorum he dashed aside, his usual mathematical sentences (1 *a* and 2 *b*, 2 *a* and 4 *b*) were never allowed to occur. No longer spake he as if he said, " I am Sir Oracle." And getting completely out of his flat boat, his rugged way is now on the highest crests, and in the deepest valleys of the angry ocean.

CHAPTER XXXVIII.

THE EUPHONIC TEST (CONTINUED).

In this chapter will be found the conclusion of the analysis by Professor Taverner, accompanied by the opinions to which the examination brings him. His views are of great force, and there is one point in particular, in which the Professor is exceedingly strong, and which it will be perceived also is entirely new. He calls attention to the fact that, while the text of Shakespeare is so full of trite legal expressions, as to induce even an English Lord Chief Justice to make an argument that he had been bred a lawyer, or was, at least, an articled attorney's clerk, Lord Bacon, who, it is known, was thoroughly a lawyer, very rarely allows himself to be betrayed into a legal phrase. The only one instance of any importance (says the Professor) which appears in Bacon's voluminous text, in his use of the word *caveat*—a word which does not appear in Shakespeare at all. And this omission the Professor infers, will be all the more surprising if the author of the writings of Bacon and Shakespeare were one and the same man, since the word *caveat*, meaning simply a warning, would have come naturally to the writer's mind in many of the exigencies of his dramatic scenes. I will add also that the word *caveat* is so full of musical balance and tone, that Shakespeare would have been likely to have used it often, had he been as legally familiar with it as was Bacon. But I think that Professor Taverner, though quite correct in saying Shakespeare never used the word *caveat* in any of his recognized productions, has overlooked the fact that our poet has presented it, in the slightly-altered form of *caveto*, in the mouth of ancient Pistol.

In Henry V., Act II. Scene 3, when that worthy person is about going off with Nym and Bardolph to the wars in France, he conjures Dame Quickly, whom he has made his wife to

29

beware how she allows irresponsible persons to run up tavern scores :—

> PISTOL.   My love, give me thy lips.
>   Look to my chattels and my moveables ;
>   Let senses rule : the word is " Pitch and Pay, Trust none ; "
>   For oaths are straws, men's faiths are wafer cakes,
>   And hold-fast is the only dog, my duck ;
>   Therefore *caveto* be thy counsellor.

There can hardly be a doubt that this term *caveto* is Pistol's bombastic version of the plain word *caveat*, or caution.

That portion of the Professor's treatise which is surmounted with the inter-heading of "Mental Differences of the Two Men mathematically demonstrated," is also specially worthy of consideration. The parallelisms between Shakespeare and Lyly, in this connexion, are likewise very curious. The Professor resumes his task as follows :—

RETROGRESSION.

Much that is submitted in this chapter it was intended should have appeared in the earlier part of my last communication ; it follows that some portion of that also was intended as a sequence to this. Under these circumstances, the reader may chance discover some appearance of repetition, as well as the unavoidable retrogression in the argument. This, it is hoped will be overlooked. I was certainly compelled to wait until the passages which I had selected from Bacon for special interrogation were kind enough to reveal to me something of their idiosyncrasies, and the time that has been afforded me for further scrutiny has elicited some features of importance, which I was unable to perceive before

THE LAW OF RHYTHM.

This investigation has been fraught with difficulty, in consequence of its being necessary to seek for manifestation of laws of rhythm in prose composition, where it has been very truly said that " its range is so wide that we can never anticipate its flow." For what is rhythm ? It is but that law of succession which is the regulating principle of every whole, that is made up of proportional parts ; it is present in the dance, when we consider it as applied to things of motion; its intervals are to be detected in sculpture and architecture, in our furniture and ornaments, where we see it extended to things of matter; but, when we consider it in its relation to sound, it is potent in the highest degree in music and in poetry, and the manipulation of it by Shakespeare in his blank verse is definite in the extreme, and the laws of rhythm there maintained are so perfect and reliable as to become from time to time an index to his meaning where our keenest discriminations are liable to be misled, and would otherwise fail. For all verse may be defined as a succession of articulate sounds, " regulated by a rhythm so definite, that we can readily foresee the results which follow." That is, that the recurrence of the accents at such points have that degree of regularity, that we anticipate the return of the accent, but in prose we are not able so to anticipate its recurrence, while the pleasure we derive from verse is founded on this very anticipation. It may be seen, then, the difficulty that has been here encountered, and what immense difference and advantage it would have been, had we had instead, to judge of blank verse on both sides.

DIVERSE MUSICAL EAR OF SHAKESPEARE AND BACON.

Shakespeare and Bacon looked upon the same events, read the same authors, their minds were brought very much under the same popular influence, yet their writings do not indicate any such resemblance as even these considerations would justify, much less any approach to that identity in thought, word, phrase, melody, and psychological bias which would be more than possible, if the Baconian theory were true. But on the contrary, as we shall see, these writings contain most unquestionable marks of being derived from natures totally diverse, dictated by a very opposite life purpose, and moulded and expressed by a distinct musical sense or ear. Moreover, it could be shown, if so extensive and nice an investigation were desirable, and I were not restricted in the direction of my thoughts, that among the words employed by Bacon, not merely technical, but literary words, are many that do not appear in Shakespeare, and that innumerable Shakespearian words Bacon fails to use. A single yet noteworthy instance occurs on the first page of Bacon's Works. Among the arguments used on the side of the Bacon theory, that Shakespeare had legal training and culture, one is that he so often illustrates a thought by an appropriate legal term. How is it then that Bacon, being a lawyer, so very seldom himself uses a legal phrase by way of illustration?

A PECULIAR PROOF OF LEGAL DIFFERENCE.

And in this one rare instance that I remember, which occurs on his first page, he uses the term a *" caveat,"* and it is somewhat to the point to say that that term, so ready to spring from the mind of Bacon, is not found in Shakespeare. And, moreover, what is its definition? a caution, a warning—pretty wide scope for its use. How many hundreds of times in all the cross purposes of the drama would opportunity and need for this expression arise, but never by any chance is it mentioned by Shakespeare as a *" caveat."* Surely, to judge Shakespeare as learned in the law, because of his use of ordinary legal phrases, might have the shadow of a reason if the doctor and the lawyer had not, in all times, furnished society with an apt quotation to be employed with zest by everybody except themselves. Let me repeat, then, that as far as this article is concerned, it is intended chiefly to prove that the Shakespeare dramas cannot be said to exhibit any of the peculiar analogies, the phrase constructions, the prose melodies, and other external features, which remain to be set forth as *Baconianisms;* nor, on the other hand can Bacon's works show any reproduction of the style and form of metaphor and simile common to Shakespeare, nor any repetition of those more subtle forms of melody and cadence, which proceed from the dictates of the musical sense, and are characteristic of the prose passages of the plays.

MENTAL DIFFERENCE MATHEMATICALLY DEMONSTRATED.

Besides thus comparing these authors with themselves, it will be somewhat parallel, and a step further in confirmation of their non-identity to compare each of them with another, where one is found to agree and the other to disagree. This is to follow a good axiom in mathematics, that where one is like, and the other unlike to a third, they must be unlike to each other. I refer to the writings of Lyly. Whether it is to be considered that Shakespeare so often imitated these writings because of his admiration and appreciation of their merits; or whether it was

as some have held, in sarcastic derision of some false conceit or
pompous expression; or because of his readiness to take advantage of any popular excitement, which has been pointed out,
for this reason he gave to the public on every new occasion
scraps from writings so popular with distinguished patrons of
the drama, as is recorded to be in the mouth of every lady
at court;—it matters not, the fact remains that these resem-
blances or parodies extensively exist, and are to be found in
so many of the plays, both tragedies and comedies; whilst
the writings of Bacon are not in any way affected from the
same source.[1] The collated passages, highly interesting of
themselves, from which I shall quote but a few examples, are
taken from an admirable and most concise publication by Wm.
Lowes Rushton. ["Shakespeare's Euphuisms," Longman,
Green, and Co., London, 1871.]

"The Euphues of Lyly was published before Shakespeare
began to write for the stage. It is said that 'all the ladies of
the time were Lyly's scholars, she who spoke not euphuism
being as little regarded at court as if she could not speak French,'
and that 'his invention was so curiously strung that Elizabeth's
court held his notes in admiration.'"

PARALLELISMS OF SHAKESPEARE AND LYLY.

Shakespeare and Lyly use often the same phrases, the same
thoughts, and play upon the same words.

It is evident that Shakespeare was very familiar with this
book, wherein I see the origin of many of the famous passages in
his works. No line of Shakespeare's has been so much questioned and curiously regarded as this one in "As You Like It :"

> Which, like the toad, ugly and venomous,
> Wears yet a precious jewel in his head.

---

[1] John Lyly, or Lilly, born 1553, died 1600, M.A. of Oxford, a court wit
and poet. "His elaborate, fanciful, and dainty style became the model of
court conversation;" it is parodied in Sir Pierce Shafton's speeches in "The
Monastery," and in "Love's Labour's Lost" in "Don Armado." He wrote
plays and songs: was parodied in Marston's "What You Will," and Jonson's
"Cynthia's Revels." He founded a new English style, marked by fantastic
similes and illustrations, formed by attributing fanciful and fabulous properties to animals, vegetables, and minerals.—*Encyclopedia.*

The passage bearing a similiar reference, in Lyly, reads thus :—

" That the fayrer the stone is in the Toade's head, the more pestilent the poyson is in her bowelles ; that talk the more it is seasoned with fine phrases, the lesse it savoreth of true mean-ing."

> Far from her nest the lapwing cries away,

says Shakespeare (*Comedy of Errors, Act IV. Scene 2*).

" Lapwing . . flyeth with a false cry farre from their nests, making those that look for them seek where they are not," were the words of Lyly.

> Two may keep counsaile if one be away,

is the smooth and almost bird-like utterances of Lyly's prose, from which Shakespeare makes a blank verse line, with scarce an alteration :—

> Two may keep counsel, putting one away.

But the saying is true, " The empty vessel makes the greatest sound."

> *Henry V., Act IV. Scene 4.*

Where did Shakespeare find the saying ?—

> The empty vessell giveth a greater sound than the full barrell.

BENE. Why, i' faith, methinks she's too low for a high praise, too brown for a fair praise, and too little for a great praise : only this commendation I can afford her, that were she other than she is, she were unhandsome ; and being no other but as she is, I do not like her.—*Much Ado about Nothing, Act I. Scene 1.*

I know not how I should commend your beauty, because it is somewhat too brown ; nor your stature, being somewhat too low, etc.

The advice of Euphues to Philautus is probably the origin of the advice of Polonius to Laertes.

> And these few precepts in thy memory see thou character.

And to thee, Philautus, ... if these few precepts I give thee be observed.

Some parts only of the following passages are placed close together, so the resemblance between *these few precepts* may be more easily seen :—

POLONIUS. Give thy thoughts no tongue.
EUPHUES. Be not lavish of thy tongue.

POLONIUS. Do not dull thy palm with entertainment of each new-hatch'd unfledged comrade.

EUPHUES. Every one that shaketh thee by the hand is not joined to thee in heart.

POLONIUS. Beware of entrance to a quarrel.

EUPHUES. Be not quarrellous for every light occasion. Beware, etc.

POLONIUS. Give every man thine ear, but few thy voice.

EUPHUES. It shall be there better to hear what they say, than to speak what thou thinkest.

There is much further resemblance to the advice of Polonius in other parts of Euphues :—

POLONIUS. Costly thy habit as thy purse can buy, but not expressed in fancy.

EUPHUES. Let your attire be comely, but not costly.

If Bacon had had to write Polonius' advice to his son, we may learn of what character it would be by consulting Bacon's three essays " Of Travel," " Of Cunning," and " Of Negotiating." These three essays of themselves, carefully studied, would fully convince that their author could never have produced Polonius' advice to his son. I do not, however, intend to pursue that line of argument, but to peer at once, if I can, into the rhythm of Bacon's sentences, and advance to something that can be measured and counted. In his essay, " Of Travel," he has this passage :—

" The things to be seen and observed are : the courts of princes, especially when they give audience to ambassadors ; the courts of justice while they sit and hear causes : and so of consistories ecclesiastic ; the churches and monasteries, with the monuments which are therein extant ; the walls and fortifications of cities and towns, and so the havens and harbours ; antiquities and ruins ; libraries, colleges, disputations, and lectures where any are ; shipping and navies ; houses and gardens of state and pleasure, near great cities ; armouries, arsenals, magazines, exchanges, burses, warehouses, exercises of horsemanship, fencing, training of soldiers, *and the like.*"

SHAKESPEARE'S SUPERIOR MUSICAL EXPRESSION.

Bacon's arena here, as elsewhere in all similar instances, embraces merely the municipality, or, at most, the nation ; Shakespeare's is invariably the world. With Bacon it is society

—not mankind—but the influential classes, and the things which they create of wealth and power; with Shakespeare it is nature, and all those things of life and energy that spring from her teeming breast. With regard to the above extract, the musical ear of Shakespeare and Bacon may be therein shown to differ in two particulars: Firstly, that when Shakespeare has occasion to present any such series of particulars, he will not be found to continue a succession of couplets thus: "churches and monasteries," "walls and fortifications," of "cities and towns," and so the "havens and harbours," "antiquities and ruins," "shipping and navies;" nor, secondly, will he ever, except sometimes for a comic effect, bring up suddenly at the close of any such series with a jerk, like unto the above passage from Bacon ending with "*and the like.*" But such terminations are by no means of rare occurrence with Bacon. They are innumerable. And among those ending with the same phrase we meet with :—

"—dreams, divinations, and the like." "—orators, painful divines, and the like." "—sometimes upon colleagues, associates, and the like." "—lions, bears, camels, and the like." "—vain opinions, flattering hopes, false valuations, imaginations as one would, and the like."

"Sometimes purging ill-humours, sometimes opening the obstructions, sometimes helping the digestions, sometimes increasing appetite, sometimes healing wounds, ulcerations thereof, and the like."

So, also, in further illustration of this "chippy" ending, take the following passage :—

"For, as the astronomers do well observe, that when three of the superior lights do meet in conjunction, it bringeth forth some admirable effects." Really! It bringeth forth admirable effects!

Obvious as it appears to me, it would perhaps amount to little in argument, to urge that it would be impossible for Shakespeare to have written the above passage. But we will proceed to examine how the musical faculty of Shakespeare is governed in bringing to a close any similar succession of particulars. His invariable method is so to construct the terminational words—and the same would be true in the event of any climax—as to afford the opportunity of what is known in elocution as harmonic or climateric couplets, which imparts something of a triumphant flourish at the end. So uniform is this, that it matters not where in Shakespeare we take our illustration. Whether it be Brutus' speech to the Romans, or Marc Antony's oration, or any of Henry the Fifth's speeches to his soldiers, or his address to Lord Scroop, the result would be, in all instances, the same. We will choose an illustration of no more elevated a style than Biondello's descriptions of Petruchio and Grumio. In the first description, that of Petruchio, the last item, is *" a woman's crupper of velure,"* which has this sort of pendant for a finish :—

Which hath *two letters* for her name, fairly set down in *studs*, and here and there pieced with pack-thread.

Now this is the flourish of which I spoke, but for comic effect, as I was indicating it is permitted to end as a sort of *failure*, with the objectionable jerk on *pack-thread*, which brings in the laugh, as every one will readily understand, who are any way conversant with the tricks of low comedians. In the other instance, the description of Grumio is finished off for a like effect, with this addendum :—

A *monster*, a very MONSTER in apparel, and *not* like a Christian footboy or gentleman's lackey.

In this he, the actor, is allowed to come off with the appearance of more triumphant success :—

BION. Why Petruchio is coming, in a new hat, and an old jerkin ; a pair of old breeches, thrice turned ; a pair of boots that have been candle-cases, one buckled, another laced ; an old rusty sword ta'en out of the town armoury, with a broken hilt, and chapeless ; with two broken points : his horse heaped with an old mothy saddle, and stirrups of no kindred : besides, possessed with the glanders, and like to mose in the chine ; troubled with the lampass, in-fected with the fashions, full of wind-galls, sped with spavins, rayed with the yellows, past cure of the fives, stark spoiled with the staggers, begnawn with the bots ; swayed in the back, and shoulder-shotten ; ne'er-legged before, and with a half-checked bit, and a head-stall of sheep's-leather ; which, being restrained to keep him from stumbling, hath been often burst, and now repaired with knots ; one girth six times pierced, and a woman's crupper of velure, which hath two letters for her name fairly set down in studs, and here and there pieced with pack-thread.

BAP. Who comes with him ?

BION. O, sir! his lackey, for all the world caparisoned like the horse ;

with a linen stock on one leg, and a kersey boot-hose on the other, gartered with a red and blue list; an old hat, and 'the amours or forty fancies' pricked in't for a feather: a monster, a very monster in apparel, and not like a Christian foot-boy, or a gentleman's lackey.

Bacon's ear does not lead him to seek any such free, independent, and exultant expression of enthusiasm of which this is somewhat indicative.

When the subject is of a more serious and elevated character this form of delivery centres in the cadence with force, grace, and dignity combined, producing the noblest effects known to the stage.

The following, from Shakespeare, include nothing more than the cadences attending the climaxes and endings of the speeches from which they are taken. The effect, I think, will be felt by most people, especially those who have been attendants at the theatre. Nothing can be farther from Shakespeare than such terminations with which these culminating passages are contrasted:—

> Do break the clouds ‖ as did the wives of Jewry
> At Herod's bloody hunting slaughter-men. *Henry V.*

> Cry—God for Harry, England, and Saint George! *Henry V.*

> If that same demon, that hath gull'd thee thus,
> Should, with his lion gait, walk the whole world,
> He might return to vasty Tartar back
> And tell the legions ‖—I can never win
> A soul so easy as that Englishman's. *Henry V.*

> Arrest them to the answer of the law;—
> And God acquit them of their practices. *Henry V.*

> Look you here,
> Here is himself, marr'd as you see, with traitors.
> *Julius Cæsar.*

> And put a tongue
> In every wound of Cæsar, that should move
> The stones of Rome | to rise and mutiny. *Julius Cæsar.*

> Shall in these confines, with a monarch's voice,
> Cry *Havoc* | and let loose the dogs of war;
> That this foul deed shall smell above the earth
> With carrion men groaning for burial. *Julius Cæsar.*

> I'd make a quarry
> With thousands of these quarter'd slaves, as high ‖
> As I could pick my lance. *Coriolanus.*

This grace and glow of termination is sometimes by Shakespeare aided by a rhyme :—

> Then brook abridgment; and your eyes advance
> After your thought, straight back again to France.   *Henry V.*
>
> And grant as Timon grows, | his *hate* may grow
> To the whole *race* || of mankind, high and low.   *Timon of Athens.*
>
> We'll then to Calais; and to England then; |
> Where ne'er from France arrived more happy men.   *Henry V.*
>
> Then shall I swear to Kate, and you to me; |
> And may our oaths well kept and prosperous be.   *Henry V.*

You have now only to glance at the close of all or some of Bacon's essays, and of his other works, and the endings of his long paragraphs to be satisfied that he never, from any sense of melody, seeks at any time to produce any such cadences whatever. And the absence of this mode of termination in Bacon's writings indicates in him a very different musical sense or feeling from that of Shakespeare. As further confirmation of Bacon's habitual omission in this respect when any such opportunity would occur, I shall trespass on the patience of your readers to give one or two very short extracts; and I shall then endeavour to present other positive peculiarities of Bacon.

Thus, in his fine essay on Superstition he says,—

" The causes of superstition are, pleasing and sensual rites and ceremonies; excess of outward and pharisaical holiness; over great reverence of traditions, which cannot but load the church; the stratagems of prelates for their own ambition and lucre; the favouring too much of good intentions, which openeth the gate to conceits and novelties; the taking an aim at divine matters by human, which cannot but breed mixture of imaginations; and, lastly, barbarous times, especially joined with calamities and disasters."

Again, in his remarkable essay on Travel, he remarks,—

" As for triumphs, masks, feasts, weddings, funerals, capital executions, and such shows, men need not to be put in mind of them; yet are they not to be neglected. If you will have a young man to put his travel into a little room and in short time to gather much, this you must do : first, as was said, he must have some entrance into the language before he goeth; then he must have such a servant, or tutor as knoweth the country, as was likewise said; let him carry with him also some card, or book, describing the country when he travelleth, which will be a good key to his inquiry; let him keep his diary; let him not stay long in one city or town, more or less as the place deserveth, but not long; nay, when he stayeth in one city or town, let him change his lodgings from one end and part of the town to another, which is a great adamant of acquaintance; let him sequester himself from the company of his countrymen, and diet in such places where there is good company of the nation where he travelleth; let him, upon his removes from one place to another, procure recommendation to some person of quality residing in the place whither he removeth, that he may use his favour in those things he desireth to see or know; thus he may abridge his travel with much profits."

I shall now proceed to furnish positive examples, to prove that the musical guidance of the ear of Bacon tends, whenever he speaks sententiously, and the language admits of it, to equally balance his sentences, and the clauses which they contain, one against the other, either regularly, or alternately, by giving to them the same number of syllables, and also by some other expedients. When the first member of a sentence, composed of four clauses, is short, and the following long, the corresponding clauses which follow, receive the same adjustment. For example :—

" Read not to contradict and confute, | Nor, to believe and take for granted; | Nor, to find talk and discourse, | But to weigh and consider."

The first two clauses are each of nine syllables; the latter two clauses are each of seven.

" These men mark when they hit, | but never when they miss."

In each of these clauses there are the same number of syllables.

" He that hath the best of these intentions | is an honest man; | and that prince that can discern of these intentions, | is a very wise prince."

Here the clauses are ten syllables and five: twelve syllables and six.

" He that seeketh to be eminent good, amongst able men, hath a great task, | but that is ever good for the public; | but he that plotteth to be the only figure amongst cyphers, | is the decay of the whole age."

Here the syllables are twenty to ten, and sixteen to eight.

" They do best who if they cannot but admit love, | yet make it keep quarter; | and sever it wholly from their serious affairs, | and actions of life."

This passage presents an alteration, i. e. twelve syllables and six; and then again, twelve syllables and six. The word " action " being pronounced as three syllables, as it was then.

Is not this definite of the kind of melody of speech that belongs to Bacon? How exact the ear! It counts its seconds like the pendulum of a clock.

"The virtue of prosperity is temperance, | the virtue of adversity is fortitude."

" Prosperity is the brains | of the Old Testament, | adversity is the brains | of the New."

This gives the repetition of seven syllables, and the proportion of six and three.

" It is better to have no opinion of God at all, | than such an opinion as is unworthy of Him; | for the one is unbelief, the other is contumely."

Here we have an example of three groups, each of fourteen syllables.

Like unto like, more than similarity, is the guiding law of Bacon's ear; when therefore we can reflect a likeness in the sentences in some other way, he is equally gratified. Thus, if I use the terms " light " and " shadow " for expressions viewed with, or growing out of a favourable or unfavourable senti- ment in the mind (psychological bias), I can diagram the logical arrangement of the thought to which I allude, and this balancing of *ideas* instead of *syllables*, somewhat after the following manner :—

First Form :—*Light,—Shadow ; contrasted shadow, contrasted light ;* or,

Second Form :—*Light,—Shadow; parallel light, parallel shadow ;* or,

Third Form :—*Amelioration of shadow : augmentation of shadow ;* arranged in the same order.

These mental melodies, if I might so call them, are very extensive in Bacon. An example or two from the Essay " Of Parents and Children " will suggest my meaning :—

" Children sweeten labours | but they make misfortunes more bitter. | They increase the care of life, | but they mitigate the remembrance of death."

" The *joys* of parents are secret, | and so are their *griefs* and *fears* ; | they cannot utter the one, | nor they will not utter the other."

These are sufficient, perhaps, to suggest this additional Baconianism, and to enable the reader to recognize, in Bacon's works, the numerous occurrences of this class. Many such illustrations would be tedious. All the sentences of Bacon, that we have been scanning thus far, were composed of either two clauses, or of four, but the most remarkable peculiarity in Bacon, in this feature of the rhythmical adjustment of clauses, attaches to those sentences of his which are composed of triple clauses of equal dimensions, and which possess such regularity, which he never seeks to disturb, but rather aims to accomplish, as to bring a return unto the ear, much like unto the repetition of the multiplication table in a village school. Let me give some illustrations of these, and I am sure you will admit that they are just as regular as " three times three are nine, three times four are twelve, and three times five are fifteen."

" A man cannot speak to his son but as a *father*, to his wife but as a *husband*, to his enemy but upon *terms*."

" Some books are to be *tasted*, others are to be *swallowed*, and some few to be chewed and *digested*."

" Crafty men *contemn* studies, simple men *admire* them, and wise men *use* them."

" Reading maketh a *full* man, confidence a *ready* man, and writing an *exact* man."

" Judges ought to be more *learned* than witty, more *reverend* than plausible, and more *advised* than confident."

" The *advantage* ground to do good, the *approach* to kings and principal persons, and the *raising* of a man's own fortunes."

But the equality of these triple clauses is not the only rhythmical characteristic. Bacon's ear can stand a great deal more than that in the way of rigid and unbended rhythm. He avails himself, accordingly, of the place of the emphasis, and adheres to it with persistency. Therefore we find the emphasis regularly on the *last* word in the first and second examples, on the last but one in the third and fourth examples, on the last but two in the fifth example, and near the beginning (on the second word) in the sixth.

It behoves us, now, to ascertain and show how Shakespeare acts when he is on the verge of making sentences like unto these. When he has advanced so far that you may say he has either to perform the like, or to avoid it. We know, beforehand, because we are too familiar with his rhythm to expect to find his text to more resemble the prim regularity of a French garden than the free, wild nature of a tangled forest.

Shakespeare does not appear to object to four or more clauses of somewhat equal character and duration, but he does to three. We find that, in avoiding this jingle of triple clauses, which we saw attached to those which we have produced from Bacon, he either adds others, or he so enlarges and amplifies the third clause, that the effect is the same; e.g.:—

MARG. Nay, by'r lady, I am not such a fool to think what I list; nor I list not to think what I can; nor,——
> *Much Ado about Nothing, Act III. Scene 4.*

Now, will not Shakespeare finish this sentence like unto Bacon? Add but a few words, and the thing would be done; but, no, indeed, this next clause is destined to break the regularity:—

——Nay, by'r lady, I am not such a fool to think what I list; nor I list not to think what I can; nor, indeed, I cannot think, if I would think my heart out of thinking, that you are in love, or that you will be in love, or that you can be in love.

The next example is from a speech of Benedick, "Much Ado about Nothing" (Act I. Scene 1):—

That a woman conceived me, I thank her; that she brought me up, I likewise give her most humble thanks; but that I will have an escheat winded in my forehead, or hang my bugle in an invisible baldrick, all women shall pardon me.

Cannot every one see the greater perfection of this over the other regularity? But that matters not, we argue only for the distinction.

Not to go beyond "Much ado About Nothing," to hunt for examples, take the following passage (Act IV. Scene 1) :—

> FRIAR.   I have mark'd
> A thousand blushing apparitions start
> Into her face; a thousand innocent shames
> In angel whiteness bear away those blushes ;
> And in her eye there hath appear'd a fire,
> To burn the errors, that these princes hold
> Against her maiden truth.

How evident it is that another hand is here at work, and one that scrupulously avoids the characteristics of the Baconian sentences! But a few lines further on, in the same scene, we find a passage suited to our purpose. In the following fiery speech of Leonato, the father of the slandered "Hero," observe the animated and stirring effect of Shakespeare's varied rhythm, produced in a way directly contrary to Bacon by a sudden *change* in the place of the emphasis :—

> LEON.   If they speak but truth of her,
> These hands shall tear her; if they wrong her honour,
> The proudest of them shall well hear of it :
> Time hath not yet so dried this blood of mine,
> Nor age so eat up my invention,
> Nor fortune made such havoc of my means,
> Nor my bad life reft me so much of friends,
> But they shall find, awaked in such a kind,
> Both strength of limb, and policy of mind,
> Ability in means, and choice of friends,
> To quit me of them throughly.

Not another line need be presented to establish the distinction between the music and melody of such passages as we have reviewed in Bacon and this which reigns in Shakespeare.

Although I am supposed to be confined to narrower and more technical limits, to which I have sought to keep, it may not be considered improper of me, in closing these remarks, to advert, in the briefest manner, to a single feature of individuality which we think paramount in our poet.

SUPERIOR BREADTH OF HIS NATURE.

What, then, of that wide and wonderful sympathy with human nature, which he must have had, and by which alone he could so have depicted the wide tide of passions, and the innermost emotions of both man and woman, all of which he must have been able so keenly to feel? And where, in Bacon, do we find the evidence of the possessions of such sympathy? To listen to these secret throbs of human emotion in any great degree, we should need to travel over his whole continent. But as here, the comparison on our side is as "all the world to nothing," I may well rest content by simply helping the reader, out of his own abundance of recollections, to recall one or two as they come to my own mind. Go with me, then, to look upon Lear, "as mad as the vexed sea," and, in the midst of thunders and lightnings, addressing first these awful forces of nature, and then, from them, the equally awful iniquities of the world :—

> Blow, wind, and crack your cheeks! rage! blow!
> You cataracts, and hurricanes, spout.
> You sulphurous and thought-executing fires,
> Vaunt couriers to oak-cleaving thunderbolts.
>   And thou all shaking thunder
> Strike flat the thick rotundity o' the world!
>   Let the great gods
> That keep this dreadful pother o'er our heads
> Find out their enemies now.
>   Tremble, thou wretch,
> That hast within thee undivulged crimes,
> Unwhipp'd of justice.
>   Hide thee, thou bloody hand;
> Thou perjured, and thou simular man of virtue
> That art incestuous: Caitiff, to pieces shake,
> That under cover and convenient seeming
> Hast practised on man's life! Close pent-up guilts,
> Rive your concealing continents and cry,
> These dreadful summoners grace.

Look upon Coriolanus like a mad and wounded lion, and with his heart "made too great for what contains it,"—

> Cut me to pieces, Volsces; men and lads,
> Stain all your edges on me.—Boy! False hound!

30

> If you have writ your annals true, 'tis these,
> That, like an eagle in a dove-cote, I
> Flutter'd your Volscians in Corioli.

Step stealthily, lighted by the moon, to the presence of Juliet's body in the tomb, place yourself in the darkness, and there hear Romeo with a broken heart murmur to himself,—

>   O, here
> Will I set up my everlasting rest;
> And shake the yoke of inauspicious stars
> From this world-wearied flesh.

And, after an ominous silence, as with one swoop, he seeks the silent shore with his desperate and life-destroying agent :—

> Thou desperate pilot, now at once run on
> The dashing rocks thy sea-sick, weary bark!

Recall, in like manner, the other tragic characters of this poet in the hours of their greatest anguish, and tell me if these are not individual experiences of which Bacon gives no possible indication. But this is superfluous, because, as I have said, there is nothing in the Baconian treasury with which to compare these crises of emotion; they belong to the one structure of all others in the world, but one so conspicuous, that it stands high above all that genius has raised on the face of the earth, so towering and wide that the pyramids of Egypt cannot hide it; more complex, and infinitely richer in its art contents than that of St. Peter's at Rome—stands this treasure-house, over whose gates is nscribed the *one* name,

SHAKESPEARE.

CHAPTER XXXIX.

RECAPITULATION AND CONCLUSION.

WITH the euphonic or rhetorical test, as applied respectively to the verbal music and rhythmical modes of expression of Shakespeare and Sir Francis Bacon, terminates the inquiry upon the question of dramatic authorship as between them; and I think it will be conceded by every reader that I was fortunate in being able to entrust the elocutionary portion of the problem to Professor Taverner. Indeed, he has been so masterly in his analysis, and has brought to the treatment of the question confided to him, such an amount of philosophic insight and consideration, that no reinforcement of his argument is required at my hands. We perceive that the contrasts of literary style are, under the direction of the ear, as distinct and various as the inflections of the human voice, and through his examples it becomes apparent to any one who has crossed even the threshold of the euphonic mysteries, that it is as impossible for the comparatively cold ear of Lord Bacon to have been the author of the melodious plays of Shakespeare, as it would have been for Dante to have produced the verse of Petrarch, or for Carlyle to have written the sonnets of Tom Moore. Indisputably our poet was the great master of that school of prose melodists of which Gibbon, Addison, Doctor Johnson, Junius, Macaulay, and Newman are subordinate examples, while Bacon, on the other hand, may be said to lead the colder school, of which our readiest example is Carlyle.

I have but to add, in closing this portion of my undertaking, that the euphonic or musical test was no part of my original purpose. But though it presented itself, incidentally, during the course of the Baconian analysis, I find no reason to regret the space it has required. To the multitude, its proofs may appear less potent than some others I have advanced, but with scholars and rhetorical experts the euphonic test will probably be more fatal to the Baconian theory than any other.

The religious test also sprang incidentally from the dispute of authorship, for it must be evident that a theological inquiry could have no importance in an examination which proceeded from an American point of view. It will be perceived, therefore, that I had no sectarian aim to serve, as some have charged while the foregoing chapters were in course of serial publication. The sectarian inquiry grew from the numerous evidences of a devotional Romanistic spirit in the Shakespearian text, and as these all ran one way, and breathed one sectarian tone, and, what was still more significant, as the writer of the plays frequently contrasted these Catholic solemnities with a vehement contempt for the reformed faith and for Protestants of every degree, it was impossible to leave the religious inquiry out of the discussion. I am not responsible for the proofs I have adduced, but I am free to say that I can conceive of no reason why Lord Bacon should have secretly slandered his much exhibited belief, nor how such a peculiarly practical nature as his, could have enjoyed such a pointless perfidy, under the cowardly mask of an alias.

It has been said, by way of explaining the Romanism of Shakespeare's writings, and of his custom of arraying his most estimable characters in the vestments of the Latin Church, that the plots of his plays are placed before his time, and that his persons must necessarily be of the Catholic faith; but this does not explain our poet's minute familiarity with the formula and doctrines of the Roman faith; since it is well known that no Catholic Services were permitted by law to be performed in England during Shakespeare's period; nor does this suggestion quite account for the predilection exhibited by the writer of the plays to burlesque and scandalize Protestants and the Protestant faith. In the discussion of the Baconian theory, therefore, the religious point must be regarded as the domineering test; for unless it can be shown that Bacon was secretly a Catholic, the Shakespearian plays cannot possibly be attributed to him.

The question as to the legal attainments of our poet, which has attracted great attention through the opinions of Lord Chief Justice Campbell, is only second in importance, on the point of authorship, to the sectarian inquiry. In dealing with this unexpected difficulty, I found myself involved with the dangerous responsibility of often not agreeing with such high authority as

Lord Campbell, and even of expressing, now and then, very different views from those which the text had suggested to his lordship. And, in a general way, it seemed to me that his lordship, in replying to Mr. Payne Collyer's inquiry, as to the extent of Shakespeare's legal attainments, with the view of testing the Baconian theory, took too narrow a gauge—when attempting to show that Shakespeare might have been an attorney, or an attorney's clerk—to measure the legal stature of Lord Bacon.

We know that Bacon was not only master of the profoundest lore of his profession, but we always find him handling his facts in the broadest and most philosophical spirit; while, on the other hand, the writer of the plays constantly violates all the congruities and philosophy of law, and exhibits such a legal deficiency in his moral adjustments of rewards and punishments, and, particularly, evinces such indifference to the instinctive logic of retaliation, that it is utterly unreasonable to attribute the authorship of these productions to a lawyer of any degree, much less to such a lawyer as Lord Bacon.

The plays most conspicuous for these legal errors and deficiencies are,—The " Two Gentlemen of Verona," " The Comedy of Errors," " Measure for Measure," " A Winter's Tale," and most notably " The Merchant of Venice." The examination of these productions, from the point of view I indicate, will doubtless be as destructive of the Baconian fallacy, with lawyers, as the demonstrations of the euphonic test must be with rhetoricians.

We may be told, at this stage, that such an extent of search and demonstration as I have devoted to these Baconian points is not necessary to dispose of a bubble which had never floated among the public with any amount of success; and we may be flippantly assured that the inexorable reasoning faculty of Time alone, would, of itself, dispel the fallacy; but such contemptuous treatment is not adequate to the destruction of a theory which has received the support of such minds as that of Lord Palmerston in England, and such scholars and critics as Judge Holmes and General Butler in America. Bubbles thus patronized must be entirely exploded, or they will be sure to reappear, whenever the world has a sick or idle hour, and delusions find their opportunity to strike. Moreover, nothing is lost by our inquiries, after all, beyond a little time; and I doubt not that all true admirers of our poet will agree, that one new ray of light which may thus be thrown upon the character and history of Shakespeare, will justify octavos of discussion.

It was the Baconian pretension, at any rate, which gave the deciding impulse to the undertaking of this work. My original intention had been to confine my labour to an examination of the plays, with the view solely of ascertaining the character of Shakespeare's social and political sympathies from an American point of view, but it has been seen how this motive has been involuntarily extended, and how utterly absent it has been from any special design to undervalue Shakespeare's acquirements, his morals, or his genius. It is by no means an agreeable task to expose the deformities of one's favourite author, but all mere mortals must be held responsible for their errors, in the general interest of mankind, and the duty of exhibiting these errors is all the more incumbent, according to the authority of the author who commits them. The world must move on, and Shakespeare must face the ordeal of improved ideas, with all others; and those who love him most, may solace themselves with the reflection, that there will be more renown left to him, even after his purgation, than to any other poet of the world.

It undoubtedly gives many well-intentioned persons pain to have to tear and patch a favourite ideal, but, as I have already said, the general interests of mankind are superior to personal considerations, and it is weak to resist any process that is required by reason. The blind idolaters of Dante, doubtless, protested in their time, against the frankness of the writers who showed him to be mean, crafty, and malignant; so, likewise, have admiring biographers of Bacon protested against the exposures which justified Pope in characterizing him as "The wisest, brightest, meanest of mankind;" but the just condemnation of moral defects do not prevent Dante from being worshipped to this day, as the greatest of the Italian poets, or deduct, in the least, from the renown of Bacon, as the greatest philosophical writer of any land or age.

When, therefore, we find Shakespeare, despite the clearness of his observation and of his towering capacity, deliberately falsifying history in order to check the march of liberal ideas, as in his misrepresentation of the character and purposes of Jack Cade, or as in his patronage of despotism, murder, and incest, through his attractive and popular portrait of Henry VIII.; when we hear him commending the massacre of thousands, in violation of solemn terms of truce, as in "Henry IV.," Part Second, and in the Second Part of "Henry VI.;" when we listen to his inculcations of contempt for mechanics and mechanical pursuits, and note his unbounded detestation for all the labouring classes, as in "Coriolanus," and, indeed, throughout his works,—we of this day feel bound to interpose our protest, and to question his right of respect for these opinions in either English or American modern households.

It has been pleaded that the manners and morals of the age in which Shakespeare lived, excuse not only his political illiberality, but palliate even the coarseness of his text; but this defence becomes of very little weight when we find the same age producing historians, who prided themselves on their veracity, even when it ran counter to the Court, and by writers whose chaste and decorous style commended their works to a large contemporaneous popularity. Of these latter, Lord Bacon was a bright example, while Hall and Hollinshed, the historians of the day, are a standing reproach to Shakespeare, since he followed their chronicles faithfully in all that enabled him to eulogize the nobles, but perverted them at once, whenever he had an oportunity to vilify the People. It is always a doubtful privilege for a writer to tamper with the rigours of history, even to aid a moral purpose, but nothing can palliate a deliberate untruth for the purposes of evil.

It may be thought by some that I have been too diligent in searching for evidences of Shakespeare's servility to rank, but the candid reader will do me the justice to observe that I have not offered every instance as an argument, and will also bear in mind that my engagement to give every expression tending to illustrate that point left me no discretion. I had constituted the reader as the judge, and accumulation even of trifles has a certain gravity in argument of which he had the right to weigh. Accumulations of an unvarying tendency form presumptions, and presumptions, though not conclusive, have a logical bearing on a case.

Candid readers will likewise do me the justice to observe that, earnest as I have been in some of my condemnations of the Shakespeare text, I am far behind several of the most eminent English critics in their censure of our poet's faults. Doctor

Johnson says, in his incomparable preface, that Shakespeare "has faults sufficient to obscure and overwhelm any other merit;" that he sacrifices virtue to convenience, and is so much more careful to please than to instruct, that he seems to write without any moral purpose; that he makes no just distribution of good and evil, nor is always careful to show, in the virtuous, a disapprobation of the wicked; he carries his persons indifferently through right or wrong, and at the close dismisses them without further care, and leaves their examples to operate by chance. This fault the barbarity of his age cannot extenuate, for it is always a writer's duty to make the world better, and justice is a virtue independent of time or place." In speaking of " Love's Labour's Lost," Doctor Johnson declares the play to be " filled with passages that are mean, childish, and vulgar, and some which ought not to have been exhibited, as we are told they were, before a maiden Queen."

Ben Jonson, when told that Shakespeare had never blotted out a line, wished " that he had blotted out a thousand." Bagehot says, in his " Estimates of Some Englishmen and Scotchmen," that Shakespeare had two leading political ideas,— " First, the feeling of loyalty towards the ancient polity of his country, not because it was good, but because it existed. . . . The second peculiar tenet of his political creed is a disbelief in the middle classes. We fear he had no opinion of traders. . . . You will generally find that, when a citizen is mentioned, he is made to do or to say something absurd."

Says Hazlitt,—" The whole dramatic moral of ' Coriolanus ' is, that those who have little shall have less, and that those who have much shall take all that the others have left. The People are poor, therefore they ought to be starved. They work hard, therefore they ought to be treated like beasts of burden. They are ignorant, therefore they ought not to be allowed to feel that they want food, or clothing, or rest, or that they are enslaved, oppressed, or miserable."

Gervinius, the master of the German Shakespearians, taking up this view of Hazlitt's, remarks that " Shakespeare had a leaning to the aristocratical principle, inasmuch as he does not dwell on the truths he tells of the nobles in the same proportion as he does on those he tells of the People."

All of these censures are more than justified by the illustrations I have given from the plays. Nevertheless, I have not gone so far as Doctor Johnson, when he says that Shakespeare " has faults sufficient to obscure and overwhelm any other merit," for at the end of this inquiry I find myself still of the opinion that his merits largely outweigh his faults, and adhere to the expression of my preface, that "his works are the richest inheritance of the intellectual world." That he is, in short, the one man who, above all others, whether alive or dead, has contributed more happy hours to the civilized world, certainly to those in it who speak his language, than any other man who ever lived.

In concluding my task, I have only to add that, if I have contributed any new light to a subject which has taxed so many patient intellects so long, I am sufficiently well paid.

POSTSCRIPT.

JUST as I have brought my labours to a close, here comes to me a little volume containing some evidence on the subject of Shakespeare's personal history, which I deem worthy of being presented in connexion with Professor Taverner's Analysis. It is entitled " Bacon *versus* Shakespeare: a Plea for the Defendant. By Thomas D. King, Montreal and Rouse's Point, New York. Level Printing and Publishing Company, 1875." The entire of Mr. King's volume is ingenious, and exceedingly well written. He is a faithful believer in Shakespeare's having been the author of the plays attributed to him, and towards the close of his book presents some exceedingly curious observations respecting the evident Warwickshire origin of our poet, coinciding with our musical point.[1] Says Mr. King,—

"Johnson, himself born in a neighbouring county, first pointed out that the expression 'a mankind witch,' in 'The Winter's Tale' (Act II. Scene 3) was a phrase in the Midland Counties for a violent woman. And Malone, too, showed that the singular expression in 'The Tempest' (Act I. Scene 2), 'we cannot miss him,' was a provincialism of the same district. It is not asserted that certain phrases and expressions are to be found nowhere else but in Shakespeare and Warwickshire. But it is interesting to know that the Warwickshire girls still speak of their 'long purples' and 'love in idleness;' and that the Warwickshire boys have not forgotten their 'deadmen's fingers;' and that the 'nine men's morris' is still played on the corn-bins of the Warwickshire farm stables, and still scored upon the greensward; and that Queen Titania would not have now to complain, as she did in 'The Midsummer Night's Dream,' that it was choked up with mud; and that 'Master Slender' would find his shovel-board still marked on many a public-house table and window-sill; and that he and 'Master Fenton,' and 'good Master Brook,' would, if now alive, hear themselves still so called.

"Take now, for instance, the word 'deck,' which is so common throughout the Midland Counties, but in Warwickshire is so often restricted to the sense of a hand of cards, and which gives a far better interpretation to Gloster's speech in the Third Part of 'King Henry VI.' (Act VI. Scene 1):—

> Alas, that Warwick had no more *forecast*,
> But whiles he thought to steal the single ten,
> The king was slyly finger'd from the *deck ;*

---

[1] Bacon was born in York House, London. York House stood on the site of the old Hungerford Market, close by the Charing Cross Railway Station, and has an existing record in Inigo Jones's graceful water-gate, half-buried at the end of Northumberland Street.

as, of course, there might be more kings than one in a pack, but not necessarily so in the hand. The word 'forecast,' too, both as verb and noun, is very common throughout both Warwickshire and the neighbouring counties. This word 'forecast' is also used by Spenser, and others of Shakespeare's contemporaries; and, though obsolete, except among the peasantry of the Midland districts, is still employed by the best American authors.

"All the commentators here explain pugging-tooth as a thievish tooth, an explanation which certainly itself requires to be explained; but most Warwickshire country-people could tell them that pugging-tooth was the same as pegging or peg-tooth, that is the canine or dog-tooth. 'The child has not its pegging-teeth yet,' old women still say. And thus all the difficulty as to the meaning is at once cleared.

"But there is an expression used both by Shakespeare and his contemporaries, which must not be so quickly passed over. Wherever there has been an unusual disturbance or ado, the lower orders round Stratford-on-Avon invariably characterize it by the phrase 'there has been *old* work to-day,' which well interprets the porter's allusion in 'Macbeth,' (Act III. Scene 3), 'If a man were porter of hell-gate, he should have *old* turning the key,' which is simply explained in the notes as 'frequent,' but which means far more. So, in 'The Merchant of Venice' (Act IV. Scene 2), Portia says, 'We shall have *old* swearing;' that is, very hard swearing.

"A peculiar use of the verb 'quoth,' the Saxon preterite of to speak, is very noticeable among the lower orders in Warwickshire. Jerk, quoth the ploughshare; that is, the ploughshare went jerk.

"The expressive compound *blood-bolter'd*, in 'Macbeth' (Act IV. Scene 1), which the critics have all thought meant blood-stained; now *bolter* is peculiarly a Warwickshire word, signifying to clot, collect, or cake, as snow does in a horse's hoof, thus giving the phrase a far greater intensity of meaning. There is the word *gull* in 'Timon of Athens' (Act II. Scene 1):—

> But I do fear
> When every feather sticks in his own wing,
> Lord Timon will be left a naked *gull*,
> Which flashes now a phœnix;

which most of the critics have thought alluded to a sea-gull, whereas it means an unfledged nestling, which to this day is so called in Warwickshire. And this interpretation throws a light on a passage in the First Part of 'King Henry VI.' (Act V. Scene 1) :—

> You used me so
> As that ungentle *gull*, the cuckoo's bird,
> Useth the sparrow;

where some notes amusingly say that the word alludes to the voracity of the cuckoo. The Warwickshire farmers' wives, even now, call their young goslings *gulls*.

"*Contain* yourself is a very common Warwickshire phrase for restrain yourself; Timon says to his creditor's servant, '*contain* yourself, good friend.' ('Timon of Athens,' Act II. Scene 2).' In 'Troilus and Cressida' (Act V. Scene 2), Ulysses says,—

> O *contain* yourself,
> Your passion draws ears hither.

"In the 'Two Gentlemen of Verona' (Act IV. Scene 4) we find Launce using the still rarer phrase of '*keep* himself,' in the same sense to his dog Crab, when he says, 'O! 'tis a foul thing when a cur cannot *keep* (*i. e.* restrain) himself in all companies.'

"From 'Shakespereana Genealogica,' in the chapter headed 'Remarks on Names belonging to Warwickshire, alluded to in several plays,' the following excerpts are taken:—

"Mr. Halliwell has shown that persons of the name of Ford, Page, Horne, or Herne belonged to Stratford. In the records of the borough, published by that excellent writer, notices of receipts and payments are found as follows:—

1597, R. of Thomas Fordes wiffe vi s. viij d.

1585, Paid to Herne for iij dayes work, ij s. vj d.

"The name of the melancholy Lord Jaques belongs to Warwickshire, where it is pronounced as one syllable: 'Thomas Jakes of Wonersh' was one of the List of Gentry of the Shire, 12 Henry VI. 1433. At the surrender of the Abbey of Kenilworth, 26 Henry VIII. 1535, the Abbot was Simon Jakes, who had the large pension of £100 *per annum* granted to him. *Monasticon*, vol. vi.

"A family by the name of Sly, rendered famous by their place in the Induction of the 'Taming of the Shrew,' resided at Stratford, and elsewhere in the county, in the Poet's time; and he no doubt drew the portrait of the drunken tinker from the life. Stephen Sly was a labourer in the employ of William Combe, 13 Jac. I. 1616. (Page 330, Halliwell's "Stratford Records.")

"In the serious business of 'The Taming of the Shrew,' one of Petruchio's servants is called 'Curtis;' this was a Stratford name. Anne Curteys, widow, a knitter, was living there in 1607: and John Curteys, a carpenter, is found there in 1615. In Petruchio's household twelve or thirteen of his men-servants are named, of whom one only, the 'ancient, trusty, pleasant Grumio,' belongs to Italy, all the rest are most thoroughly English: and as Philip, Nathaniel, Nicholas, Joseph, and Gabriel, are not uncommon names, we incline to believe that Shakespeare took them from his contemporaries Philip Henslowe, Nathaniel Field, Nicholas Tooley, Joseph Taylor, and probably Gabriel Harvey, a poet, the friend of Spenser.

"Among the characters in the play of 'Henry V.' are three soldiers whose Christian names are found in the folio of 1623, and, therefore, very properly retained in this edition, although usually omitted. 'John Bates, Alexander Court, and Michael Williams,' are private soldiers in King Henry's army."

With this notice of Mr. King's views, the whole case is with the court.

INDEX.

"ALL'S WELL THAT ENDS WELL,"
151; character of Helena, 155; in-
delicacy of the scene with Parolles,
156; Coleridge, Elze, and Mrs.
Jameson on Helena, 155—157;
religious points, *ib.*; legal phrases,
159.

Ann Hathaway, Shakespeare's wife,
24.

"Antony and Cleopatra," instances
of Shakespeare's use of the words
"liberty" and "freedom," 360;
Cleopatra and Cressida, his only
two completed female portraitures,
361; legal evidences, 362.

Arden (Mary), Shakespeare's mother,
a Roman Catholic, 20.

Aristocracy and Churchmen of
England have an interest in denying that Shakespeare was a Catholic, 67.

"As You Like It," its plot, 139;
Adam, almost the only character
in humble life that escapes our
poet's contempt, 140; Catholic
evidences, 142; licentious impropriety of the language of Beatrice,
143; law evidence, 144.

Author's motives for writing this
work, 1.

B.

Bacon (Lord), his parliamentary
career, 14; may possibly have
heard some unplayed MSS. of
Shakespeare read, 15; his marriage; his mercenary character,

17; his committal to the Tower,
and his death, *ib.*

Bacon's (Delia) "Philosophy of
Shakespeare's Plays Unfolded," 1;
republished, 13.

Baconian Theory (The), first mooted
by Delia Bacon, of Boston, 1; the
theory supported by Lord Palmer-
ston and General Butler, U.S.,
4; attracts the attention of the
English Aristocracy, *ib.*; Miss
Bacon's Essay republished in
England; supported by Mr. W. H.
Smith, by a writer in *Fraser's
Magazine*, and Professor Nathaniel
Holmes of Harvard University,
Cambridge, Mass., 13. See *Holmes.*

Bagehot (Walter), 294, 460.

Blackstone (Sir William), 165.

Brutus (Marcus), Shakespeare's character of the Roman patriot in
"Julius Cæsar," 345; Brutus no
sympathiser with the so-called
common people, 347; the movement simply an aristocratic revolt,
like that of the English Barons
against King John, and not with
a view to the liberty of the masses,
ib.

Butler, Gen., U.S., a supporter of the
Baconian Theory, 1, 4, 457.

C.

Campbell's, Lord Chief Justice,
opinion on the legal acquirements
of Shakespeare, 74; first illustration, 76; subsequent illustrations
throughout his Plays adduced by

G.

Gervinius, 95, 101, 117, 325, 401, 460.
Grant White (Richard), 18, 41, 341.
Greene and Nash, their envious attacks on Shakespeare, 19.
Guizot (M.) on the play of "Othello," 363.

H.

Hamlet," date of production, 397; Opinions of Hunter, Dowden, and Kenny, 397, 398: Gervinius, Elze, and the German commentators, 401; the Catholic tone and colour of Shakespeare's mind prevail throughout this play, 401—406; his adoration of royalty, 407; the gravediggers' scene, 409; the Case of Hales *v.* Petit, extract from Judge Holmes, 410—413; Lord Campbell on the report of Plowden, 413; the "Mermaid" in Bread-street the favourite resort of the poets of that day, 415; significant suppression by Lord Campbell of an extract reflecting on the English judiciary, 418.
Halliwell (Mr.), 18, 35, 84, 464.
Harness, Rev. W., 8, 21.
Harsnet's (Dr.) book, "Discovery of Popish Impostors," and the Starkey or Starchy case, 381.
Hazlitt on "Coriolanus," 292, 460.
"Henry IV.," Part I., Falstaff introduced as a foil to Prince Henry, 196; the play a continuation of political history, *ib.;* the legal Points, 197.
——— Part II., probable date of its production, 199; the treacherous, shameful deed in the Fourth Act passed over without censure by the poet, 204; the immorality and obscenity of some scenes conclusive against the Baconian Theory, 206.
"Henry V.," its date proved by the reference to Essex in the Fifth Chorus, 207; remarks of Hunter, Schlegel, Knight, Gervinius, and Kenny, 207—209; Shakespeare's reverent mention of the Catholic religion, 210, 215; extract significant of the poet's want of sympathy with the commonalty, 119.

"Henry VI.," Part I., its doubtful authorship, 220; the total absence of any sympathy with the common people throughout these plays, 221; his ungenerous portraiture of Joan of Arc, 221.
——— Part II., Shakespeare's want of liberalism exhibited in his perversion of the history of Jack Cade, 227, 244—254; the cruel caricature of Cade by Shakespeare has prevented other poets from doing justice to a patriot's memory, 254.
——— Part III.—Shakespeare treats crime as the privilege of kings and nobles, and the inheritance of the poor, 256; the legal acquirements of Shakespeare as shown in the Histories of the Henries, 257.
"Henry VIII."—Dispute as to the date of its production, 267; Cranmer's speech possibly an interpolation, 268; Buckingham, Queen Katharine, Wolsey, and Cranmer, 269—275; Shakespeare's portrait of Henry VIII. a painful perversity of genius, 275; his reverent treatment of Queen Katharine, 276.
Holmes (Judge) supports the Baconian Theory, 13, 17, 67, 195; Case of Hales *v.* Petit as stated by Judge Holmes, 410—413.
Hunter (Joseph), 160, 178, 339, 384, 397.

I.

Identity of style in Shakespeare's Epitaph with the lines on Timon's tomb, 291.
Importance of Shakespeare's teaching to the Ruling Classes in Great Britain, 6, 7.

J.

Johnson (Dr.), on "Henry VIII., 68; note on Bertram, 155; on Shakespeare's Comedies, 175; on his being touched for the King's Evil, 329, *note;* on "Cymbeline," 337; severe criticism on our poet, 460.

RECENT NOVELS.

I.

THE SHADOW OF THE SWORD. A Romance. By ROBERT BUCHANAN. 1 vol., 8vo. Paper covers, 75 cents.

"Mr. Buchanan is a poet, and this romance may be to some extent regarded as a prose poem. The pictures with which the story abounds are bright with the fancy that finds its most natural expression in verse; the coloring is that of a poetical artist, and the weird-like imagination which throws its lurid light upon one page, and the blackness of a great cloud upon another, is that of a man who has seen visions and dreamt dreams. . . . Readers will not be disappointed, if they are willing for a season to exchange the realism of modern fiction for the poetical conceptions, the exciting incidents, the strong passions, and glowing fancy, that belong to high romance."—*London Spectator.*

"Wild, striking, and animated with much of the poetry of the rugged Breton coast, where the scene is laid."—*Illustrated London News.*

"A weird and powerful romance."—*Figaro.*

II.

RARE GOOD LUCK. By R. E. FRANCILLON, author of "Earl's Dene," "Zelda's Fortune," etc. 8vo. Paper. Price, 50 cents.

"Rare Good Luck" is a stirring romance for Christmas-times. It contains a great deal of picturesque incident, strange adventures, and graphic character-drawing, so that, between shipwreck rescues, disappearances and reappearances, struggles with tigers, warfare with men, and escapades in the name of love, it affords abundant entertainment for a winter night's reading.

III.

FALLEN FORTUNES. By JAMES PAYN, author of "Lost Sir Massingberd," "Walter's Word," etc., etc. 8vo. Paper. Price, 75 cents.

"It is a very good novel, with a well-contrived plot, and a style that is always easy and sometimes sparkling."—*London Academy.*

"The characters are very cleverly drawn, and have the merit of developing their marked peculiarities with an individual force that is very attractive to their audience. Whoever read 'Lost Sir Massingberd' will be sure to welcome Mr. Payn's latest and perhaps best work."—*Boston Gazette.*

"Mr. Payn has not mistaken his vocation. Of the several novels he has written there is not a poor one among them. He has excellent taste, and writes gracefully and with fine discrimination. His characters are portraits from Nature, and his descriptions are graphic and poetic. 'Fallen Fortunes' is very fascinating."—*Albany Journal.*

IV.

MY OWN CHILD. By FLORENCE MARRYAT. 1 vol., 8vo. Price, 75 cents.

"Florence Marryat knows how to write a story that will hold the attention of her readers to the end, and she has done this in her last tale."—*Cleveland Herald.*

"It is a capital story, well told."—*Catholic Mirror.*

"'My Own Child' is the best novel she has written for a year or two."—*Boston Globe.*

V.

THE THREE BRIDES. By C. M. YONGE, author of "The Heir of Redclyffe." 1 vol., 12mo. Cloth. Price, $1.75.

"This novel bids fair to equal the reputation which was attained by 'The Heir of Redclyffe' and 'Heartsease,' which have been read and wept over by many thousands of readers."

VI.

THE LAND OF THE SKY; or, Adventures in Mountain By-ways. By CHRISTIAN REID, author of "A Question of Honor," etc. 1 vol., paper covers, illustrated, 75 cents; cloth, $1.25.

The "Land of the Sky" is part story and part adventure; it relates the vicissitudes and experiences, humorous and otherwise, of a number of travelers in a summer jaunt amid the mountains of North Carolina. There is some good character-sketching, not a few amusing incidents, the thread of a love-story, and some capital descriptive passages.

VII.

COMIN' THRO' THE RYE. One vol., 8vo. Paper covers, 75 cents.

"A very amusing and well-written story. The history of the youth of the Adairs is extremely amusing, and told in a bright and witty manner. . . . One of the pleasantest novels of the season."—*Morning Post.*

"It is a clever novel, never dull, and the story never hangs fire."—*Standard.*

NEW YORK: D. APPLETON & COMPANY, PUBLISHERS.

JOAN:

A NOVEL.

By RHODA BROUGHTON,

AUTHOR OF "COMETH UP AS A FLOWER," "GOOD-BYE, SWEETHEART!" ETC.

1 vol., 8vo. Paper covers . . . . . 75 cents.

"Rhoda Broughton's latest novel is decidedly her best. In every respect it marks an advance on the part of this vivacious novelist."—*Cleveland Herald.*

"The plot is simple but interesting, the characters are sketched with consummate skill and are finely contrasted, the dialogue is bright and witty, the descriptive passages are graphic and picturesque, and there is a spirit and vigor about the whole book which acts like a tonic upon the mind of the *blasé* novel-reader."—*Boston Courier.*

"It is astonishing with what skill she interests her readers, not only in her marvelously-drawn characters, but in herself."—*Milwaukee Sentinel.*

"In her stories the plot is always simple, yet of adequate interest to rivet the attention; her characters are sketched with consummate skill, they are never crowded on her canvas, but always afford the necessary artistic contrast; her dialogue is bright, terse, and vivid, and there is withal great depth of pathos."—*Pittsburg Chronicle.*

"Rhoda Broughton is unmistakably the most original and potent light that is now arising in the sky of English fiction."—*Home Journal.*

"In all of Rhoda Broughton's novels there are infinite pathos, pure sentiment, and clear character-drawing."—*Kansas City Times.*

"If 'Joan' is not her best novel, it is vastly superior to the common run of current romances. The story is not original, but it is at least interesting, for 'Joan' herself is interesting, and the book is full of landscape-scenes that show a deep, constant, and often poetic feeling for Nature."—*London Correspondent of Tribune.*

BY THE SAME AUTHOR.

COMETH UP AS A FLOWER. 12mo. Cloth, $1.50. Cheap edition, 8vo, paper covers, 60 cents.

NOT WISELY, BUT TOO WELL. Library edition. 12mo, $1.50; 8vo, paper covers, 60 cents.

NANCY. 12mo. Cloth, $1.50; paper covers, 8vo, 75 cents.

GOOD-BYE, SWEETHEART! Library edition. 12mo. $1.50. Cheap edition, 8vo, paper covers, 75 cents.

RED AS A ROSE IS SHE. Library edition. 12mo. Cloth, $1.50. Cheap edition, 8vo, paper covers, 60 cents.

NEW YORK: D. APPLETON & CO., PUBLISHERS.

APPLETONS'

AMERICAN CYCLOPÆDIA.

NEW REVISED EDITION.

Entirely rewritten by the ablest writers on every subject. Printed from new type, and illustrated with Several Thousand Engravings and Maps.

The work originally published under the title of THE NEW AMERICAN CYCLOPÆDIA was completed in 1863, since which time the wide circulation which it has attained in all parts of the United States, and the signal developments which have taken place in every branch of science, literature, and art, have induced the editors and publishers to submit it to an exact and thorough revision, and to issue a new edition entitled THE AMERICAN CYCLOPÆDIA.

Within the last ten years the progress of discovery in every department of knowledge has made a new work of reference an imperative want.

The movement of political affairs has kept pace with the discoveries of science, and their fruitful application to the industrial and useful arts and the convenience and refinement of social life. Great wars and consequent revolutions have occurred, involving national changes of peculiar moment. The civil war of our own country, which was at its height when the last volume of the old work appeared, has happily been ended, and a new course of commercial and industrial activity has been commenced.

Large accessions to our geographical knowledge have been made by the indefatigable explorers of Africa.

The great political revolutions of the last decade, with the natural result of the lapse of time, have brought into public view a multitude of new men, whose names are in every one's mouth, and of whose lives every one is curious to know the particulars. Great battles have been fought, and important sieges maintained, of which the details are as yet preserved only in the newspapers, or in the transient publications of the day, but which ought now to take their place in permanent and authentic history.

In preparing the present edition for the press, it has accordingly been the aim of the editors to bring down the information to the latest possible dates, and to furnish an accurate account of the most recent discoveries in science, of every fresh production in literature, and the newest inventions in the practical arts, as well as to give a succinct and original record of the progress of political and historical events.

The work has been begun after long and careful preliminary labor, and with the most ample resources for carrying it on to a successful termination.

None of the original stereotype plates have been used, but every page has been printed on new type, forming in fact a new Cyclopædia, with the same plan and compass as its predecessor, but with a far greater pecuniary expenditure, and with such improvements in its composition as have been suggested by longer experience and enlarged knowledge.

The illustrations, which are introduced for the first time in the present edition, have been added not for the sake of pictorial effect, but to give greater lucidity and force to the explanations in the text. They embrace all branches of science and of natural history, and depict the most famous and remarkable features of scenery, architecture, and art, as well as the various processes of mechanics and manufactures. Although intended for instruction rather than embellishment, no pains have been spared to insure their artistic excellence; the cost of their execution is enormous, and it is believed that they will find a welcome reception as an admirable feature of the Cyclopædia, and worthy of its high character.

This work is sold to subscribers only, payable on delivery of each volume. It is completed in sixteen large octavo volumes, each containing about 800 pages, fully illustrated with several thousand Wood Engravings, and with numerous colored Lithographic Maps.

PRICE AND STYLE OF BINDING.

In extra cloth, per vol.	$5.00	*In half russia, extra gilt, per vol.*	$8.00
In library leather, per vol.	6.00	*In full morocco antique, gilt edges, per vol.*	10.00
In half turkey morocco, per vol.	7.00	*In full russia, per vol.*	10.00

*** Specimen pages of the AMERICAN CYCLOPÆDIA, showing type, illustrations, etc., will be sent gratis, on application.

D. APPLETON & CO., PUBLISHERS,

549 & 551 Broadway, New York.

APPLETONS' JOURNAL:

A MONTHLY MISCELLANY OF POPULAR LITERATURE.

NEW SERIES.

TWENTY-FIVE CENTS PER NUMBER. THREE DOLLARS PER ANNUM.

APPLETONS' JOURNAL is now published monthly; it is devoted to popular literature and all matters of taste and general culture—published at a price to bring it within the reach of all classes. It contains superior fiction, in the form of serials and short stories; papers graphically descriptive of picturesque places; articles upon men of note, and upon the habits of different peoples; essays upon household and social topics; articles of travel and adventure; scientific and industrial articles written in a graphic and popular style. In brief, the aim is to be comprehensive, including in its plan all branches of literature and all themes of interest to intelligent readers. Each number is illustrated.

TERMS: Three dollars per annum, postage prepaid, to all subscribers in the United States; or Twenty-five Cents per number. A Club of Four Yearly Subscriptions will entitle the sender to an extra subscription gratis; that is, five copies will be sent one year for twelve dollars. For $7.20, APPLETONS' JOURNAL and THE POPULAR SCIENCE MONTHLY (full price, eight dollars), postage prepaid.

THE POPULAR SCIENCE MONTHLY.

CONDUCTED BY E. L. YOUMANS.

This periodical was started (in 1872) to promote the diffusion of valuable scientific knowledge, in a readable and attractive form, among all classes of the community, and has thus far met a want supplied by no other magazine in the United States.

Containing instructive and interesting articles and abstracts of articles, original, selected, translated, and illustrated, from the pens of the leading scientific men of different countries; accounts of important scientific discoveries, the application of science to the practical arts, and the latest views put forth concerning natural phenomena, have been given by *savants* of the highest authority. Prominent attention has been also devoted to those various sciences which help to a better understanding of the nature of man, to the bearings of science upon the questions of society and government, to scientific education, and to the conflicts which spring from the progressive nature of scientific knowledge.

THE POPULAR SCIENCE MONTHLY is published monthly in a large octavo, handsomely printed on clear type, and, when the subjects admit, fully illustrated. Each number contains 128 pages.

TERMS: $5.00 per annum, or Fifty Cents per Number. Postage free to all Subscribers in the United States.

THE ART JOURNAL:

An International Gallery of Engravings,

BY DISTINGUISHED ARTISTS OF EUROPE AND AMERICA;

WITH ILLUSTRATED PAPERS IN THE VARIOUS BRANCHES OF ART.

THE ART JOURNAL is a quarto monthly publication, superbly illustrated and printed, and specially devoted to the world of Art—Painting, Sculpture, Architecture, Decoration, Engraving, Etching, Enameling, and Designing in all its branches—having in view the double purpose of supplying a complete illustrated record of progress in the Arts, and of affording a means for the cultivation of Art-taste among the people. Each number is richly and abundantly illustrated on both steel and wood, and no pains are spared to render this "ART JOURNAL" the most valuable publication of the kind in the world. It contains the Steel Plates and Illustrations of the LONDON ART JOURNAL, a publication of world-wide fame (the exclusive right of which, for Canada and the United States, has been purchased by the publishers); with *extensive additions devoted principally to American Art and American topics. Published monthly. Sold only by Subscription.* Price, 75 Cents per Number; $9.00 per Annum, postage prepaid.

Subscriptions received by the Publishers, or their Agents. AGENCIES: 22 Hawley St., Boston; 922 Chestnut St., Philadelphia; 22 Post-Office Avenue, Baltimore; 53 Ninth St., Pittsburg; 100 State St., Albany; 42 State St., Rochester; 103 State St., Chicago; 30 W. 4th St., Cincinnati; 305 Locust St., St. Louis; 20 St. Charles St., New Orleans; 230 Sutter St., San Francisco.

D. APPLETON & CO., Publishers, 549 & 551 *Broadway, N. Y.*